DATE DUE

~~NO 19 97~~		
MY 3'00		
~~MY 2 '00~~		

DEMCO 38-296

With Thomas Edison's invention of the phonograph, the beautiful music that was the preserve of the wealthy became a mass-produced consumer good – a sound recording – cheap enough to be available to all. In 1877 Edison dreamed that one day there would be a talking machine in every home, but even his legendary vision could not have foreseen the way that recorded sound would pervade modern life.

America on Record provides a history of sound recording, from the first thin sheet of tinfoil that was manipulated into retaining sound to the home recordings of rappers in the 1980s and the high tech digital studios of the 1990s. This volume examines the important technical development of acoustic, electric, and digital sound reproduction – including the cylinder, 78-rpm disc, 45-rpm microgroove single, LP, and CD – while outlining the cultural impact of recorded music and movies. It describes jazz, blues, swing, rock, rap, and film dialogue against the business and technological background of sound recording.

America on record

America on record
A history of recorded sound

ANDRE MILLARD

University of Alabama at Birmingham

CAMBRIDGE
UNIVERSITY PRESS

ıe University of Cambridge
, Cambridge CB2 1RP
10011-4211, USA
ırne 3166, Australia

© Cambridge University Press 1995

First published 1995

Printed in the United States of America

Library of Congress Cataloging-in-Publication Data
Millard, A. J.
America on record : a history of recorded sound / Andre Millard.
   p. cm.
Includes bibliographical references and indexes.
ISBN 0-521-47544-9 (hardback). – ISBN 0-521-47556-2 (paperback)
1. Phonograph. 2. Sound recordings – United States. 3. Music –
United States – History and criticism. I. Title.
ML1055.M47 1995
621.389'3'0973 – dc20
                                    94–41312
                                         CIP
                                         MN

A catalog record for this book is available from the British Library.

ISBN 0-521-47544-9 Hardback
ISBN 0-521-47556-2 Paperback

Contents

Preface

America on Record is an attempt to describe the technological development and cultural impact of sound recording from its inception to the early 1990s – "from Edison's phonograph to gangsta rap," as one reviewer put it. As space is limited, I have not provided a full account of the technology or its cultural effects – I leave this to the experts – but instead a concise narrative which covers the significant events and explains the relationship of these two important forces. This is an interdisciplinary book intended for students in History and American Studies, and their pressing schedules have been uppermost in my mind during the preparation of the manuscript.

The history was written during a time of rapid technological advance, and I have no doubt that more innovations in digital sound recording will have been made before the book appears in print. I ask the reader's indulgence for sections that may appear outdated and hope that the machines described in the closing chapters have not become obsolete in the short time from manuscript to published book.

Researching and writing this book was truly a pleasure. I owe a great debt to Raymond Wyman, Professor Emeritus of the University of Massachusetts at Amherst, who not only read the manuscript several times but also gave me the benefit of his years of experience with audio visual technology. Peter Copeland, recording engineer and Conservation Manager of the British Library National Sound Archive in London, also went through the manuscript and helped me understand much of the technology. My friend Ed Pershey of the Tsongas Industrial History Center was full of his usual insights and guided me along the path to a readable book.

Several important archives were made available to me. I want to thank the staff of the Edison National Historic Site, especially Doug Tarr and Jerry Fabris; Sam Brylawski of the Recorded Sound Reference Center at the Library of Congress; Dan Morgenstern of the Institute of Jazz Studies, Newark; Emmett Chisum of the American Heritage Center at the University of Wyoming, Laramie; Dick Cooper of the Alabama Music Hall of Fame; and Tina McCarthy of the Sony/CBS music archives, New York. Ruth Edge and her staff at the EMI archives in Hayes near London were most helpful, and I still have fond memories of the EMI canteen. Chris Moult of the Listening Service of the British Library patiently provided me with hours of taped oral histories. Sheldon Hochheiser of the AT&T archives in New Jersey not only guided me through that excellent collection but also reviewed the sections on the transition to sound in motion pictures and gave me some useful advice.

Many of my colleagues were kind enough to review parts of the manuscript. My friends Paul Israel, Greg Field (both of the Edison Papers), Mark Clark, David Morton, Larry Wharton, and Virginia Whatley Smith willingly gave me their time and expertise. Allen Koenigsberg looked at the early sections on the talking machine and cleared up many of the errors. Roger Thorne and Domenic Coombe spent many pleasant hours with me talking about early recordings and playing them for me. Joanne Nathan of Unique Recording Studios was very generous with her time and assistance, as were Kim Adamian of Sony Electronics and Mary Ison of the Prints and Photographs Divison at the Library of Congress.

Kevin Gustin did the computer work on the composite picture of the record catalogues (Figure 4.4), and Richard Anderson drew the diagrams. I thank them both for their fine work.

The staff of Sterne Library, University of Alabama at Birmingham, especially Gordon Dunkin, Marilyn Grush, Eddie Lusker, and Bonnie Ledbetter, gave me their usual friendly, expert assistance. A final word of thanks to Debbie Givens, center of gravity and administrator of the History Department at UAB.

Every effort has been made to locate copyright owners of the material quoted or reproduced in the text. Omissions brought to our attention will be credited in subsequent printings.

Excerpt from "A Nice Groove" from The Talk of the Town, *The New Yorker*, 26 February 1966, is printed by permission; © 1966, 1994. The New Yorker magazine, Inc.

Excerpts from "In the Hotel Splendour 1980" from the MAMBO KINGS PLAY SONGS OF LOVE by Oscar Hijuelos. Copyright © 1989 by

Oscar Hijuelos. Reprinted by permission of Farrar, Straus & Giroux, Inc.

Excerpts from the following song lyrics:

Introduction

Recorded sound is surely one of the great conveniences of modern life. We can conjure up sounds at will from a talking machine, not just the sound of our own voices but the finest music ever made, and all with the convenience of a touch of a button. In a world oppressed by the consequences of progress, the phonograph and its descendants have provided us with cheap and plentiful distraction in the comfort of our own homes. It has made living in small, windowless, air-conditioned rooms a little easier, replacing the shared Victorian pleasures of bandstand and music hall with the solitary delight of a private world of sound.

The novelty of hearing a recording of one's voice is a little over 100 years old. In November 1877 Thomas Edison invented the phonograph in his Menlo Park laboratory, a feat which earned him worldwide fame and the nickname of "The Wizard of Menlo Park." Although the term *phonograph* had been coined years before, this famous invention marked the real beginning of recorded sound technology. To the millions of Americans and Europeans who marvelled at what they thought was a great scientific achievement, Edison's phonograph perfectly represented the new machines which were changing their lives: the telephone, electric light, safety razor, street car, camera, and automobile. The phonograph provided a service which had been unimaginable to its listeners before 1877 – it was truly a modern technology.

In the late nineteenth century, it was not only inventors who looked into the future and saw a marvelous new age created by machines. In 1888 the writer and social reformer Edward Bellamy published *Looking Backward, 2000–1887*, a view of a future society "so simple and logical" in which many of the burdens of industrial America had been lifted. One of the features of this utopia was that the finest music was piped into homes by telephone wires from special studios where professional musicians played around the clock. Bellamy anticipated re-

1

corded sound when he described "An arrangement for providing everybody with music in their homes, perfect in quality, unlimited in quantity, suited to every mood, and beginning and ceasing at will."[1]

Thomas Edison was also a visionary, a man who made it his business to see into the future, and who often made reckless claims about the potential of his inventions well before he had even made them work. Flushed with the pride of inventing the phonograph, he made the most astounding claims for it, which anticipated Bellamy's prophecies. Edison thought it would become commonplace, one of life's universal pleasures. The beautiful music which was the preserve of the very rich, available to only a few lucky city dwellers, was to become a mass-produced consumer good – a sound recording – which would be cheap enough to be available to all. The talking machine would be as useful as the telephone.

From the vantage point of the late twentieth century, all these wild predictions now seem obvious: the talking machine has become an essential part of life in an industrial society. In 1877 Edison dreamed that one day in the distant future there would be a talking machine in every home. A hundred years later, the average house would contain two or three. In 1977 there was hardly a living room or den in the United States and Western Europe which did not have a home "stereo" made up of amplifier, record player, radio, and tape recorder. Most homes also had a smaller system, a portable record or tape player, in the childrens' rooms or in the kitchen.

By the 1970s the universal medium of recorded sound was the compact tape cassette. No less an engineering wonder than the microgroove long-playing disc it superseded, the cassette had the advantages of small size and easy handling. The recorded sound of a cassette tape emerges from countless transistorized machines, from the wake-up call in the bedside alarm clock to the telephone answering machine. It can be found in numerous child's toys, in the dashboard of the car in the garage, and even in a waterproofed unit in the shower. The tape cassette has replaced the revolving disc as the most widely used format for recorded sound. It can be heard all over the globe. In the developing nations of Africa and Asia, it is an eagerly adopted Western technology. In advanced industrial societies, there are more cassette players than there are households.[2]

Recorded sound has expanded well beyond the phonograph invented by Edison. It is a major source of the programs heard on the radio, for the tradition of live broadcasting declined after World War II. The same is true for television, which abandoned live programs very quickly. Most of its programs are recorded, and the video tape which saves the image also saves the sound, including the commercial messages and the "canned" laughter, which is an indispensable part of television entertainment.

It is easy to forget that recorded sound played a major role in motion pictures, another modern technology that began in Thomas Edison's fertile laboratory. He followed the invention of the phonograph with that of the motion picture camera; his idea was for recorded sound and images to go together. They still do. Sound is an integral part of the movie experience, and film sound has often been at the leading edge of recorded sound technology. The latest sound-reproducing systems are introduced to the public in film theaters. Stereophonic sound was developed for use in theaters in the 1930s. Quadrophonic sound was first experienced at the movies. The technologies developed to make movies talk have been successfully applied to the recording of popular music. Our home stereos are scaled-down versions of the mighty sound systems found in film theaters.

Recorded sound is not confined to the home or places of entertainment. The drive to work is usually not done in silence because the car radio, cassette, or compact disc player comes as standard equipment in the American automobile. Recorded sound also soothes the brow of the office worker as he or she takes the elevator to one of the numerous floors of the skyscraper – the typical work place of the twentieth century. Working in America is often done to the accompaniment of recorded music, which is very carefully chosen to ensure the productivity of the listener.

The widespread broadcast of recorded sound in the work place began in World War II, when it was discovered that music decreased the boredom associated with continuous, repetitive assembly-line work. The British government commissioned an important study on "Fatigue and Boredom in Repetitive Work," which found that the man watching the bottle-capping machine or the woman soldering connections became tired not only from physical exertion but because of boredom. Music distracted the workers from their tasks without taking their eyes off the job.

Employers who played music in factories found that instead of leaving their benches or machines, workers were more apt to be found whistling or singing while they worked. The management took special care to fit the tempo of the music to the pace of the work. Martial and "peppy" music was used to get employees ready for work, while slow, sentimental ballads were never played on rainy days. The main qualification was for music to be "easily recognized, easily sung, easily heard."[3] This was the beginning of the insidious "easy listening" music which awaits us in elevators and restaurants and fills in the time while we wait to be connected to telephone lines.

Background music came of age during World War II. By decreasing fatigue and raising morale, it made significant contributions to productivity, and some estimates found it increased output by as much as 25 percent.[4] This revelation was to have enormous impact on the history of recorded sound. In the short run it brought music into the factory and office; in the long run it completely altered the sonic environment in America, leading to the omnipresence of canned music in every aspect of life. In the past, manual labor in the United States had been eased by work songs, the chants of the slaves, field hollers, or whistling while you worked in a textile mill. In the twentieth century the anonymous sounds of the talking machine usurped this function.

In both public and private places, the tyranny of recorded sound is hard to escape. Eating, shopping, and travelling are discretely serenaded by endless loops of magnetic tape. It is difficult to think of a place that does not have a concealed loudspeaker issuing forth the soothing sounds of recorded music. Even churches have succumbed to using tape-recorded bells in place of the real thing.

Edison and the other inventors of recorded sound were so enthusiastic about their achievements because the real thing in the 1870s was restricted to the great concert halls in a few major cities and music rooms in the homes of the very rich. Although the technology of recorded sound was international in nature – it came about as the result of the transatlantic movement of men and ideas – its development occurred in the United States. What especially pleased Edison was that it democratized entertainment. It was fitting that Yankee ingenuity should provide the means to put opera into the parlors of working men (as Edison always liked to claim) and make good music an affordable consumer good.

Yet Edison could not have predicted, or even imagined, that recorded sound would be so omnipresent in twentieth-century industrial society. Recorded music is a constant in the home, the work place (whether in office or factory), and in public places. It is heard in supermarkets, malls, trains and planes. This constant background noise, often called *Muzak* after the company that pioneered recorded music in the work place, has led some unwilling listeners to question the benefits of recorded sound. It was "synthetic music," as Aldous Huxley called it in *Brave New World*, which could just as easily pacify as enlighten the masses. What had started as a machine to bring beautiful music to silent places, to bring the art of the concert hall into the living room, became corrupted into a device which saturated the senses with an unremitting bombardment of recorded sounds. And Edison, who happily retreated behind the wall of silence brought by his deafness, would probably have been one of the first to denounce it.

Business and technology

The growth of the technology of recorded sound and the business enterprise based upon it exceeded even Edison's grandiose plans for the phonograph. Putting a talking machine into every home and supplying it with records became a big business in America. One hundred years after the thin sheet of tin foil was teased and tortured into retaining sounds of speech, a vast international industry produced players and recordings by the millions.

In the United States alone, about $3 billion worth of recordings were sold in 1977 (at retail prices). These were played on an estimated 75 million record players (playback units) in American homes. In 1976 over 3 million portable and table phonographs were sold by American manufacturers, and over 2 million phonographs and 17 million tape recorders were imported into the United States.[5] As the centennial of Edison's invention approached, Americans purchased 273 million long-playing records, 190 million 45-rpm singles, and over 127 million cassette and eight-track tapes.

This book is an account of the growth of this industry, a history which by necessity reflects the technological development of recorded sound, from the tin foil wrapped around Edison's phonograph to the compact disc. This is a story primarily of change, for the industry built on the phonograph was driven forward by the constant disruption of innovation: new materials for records, new systems of recording, new kinds of machines, and new types of recorded music. In an intensely competitive business, one invention after another arrived to upset the fragile balance between the great companies and change the relationships of the old powers with the new.

The industry of recorded sound reflects the broad themes of American business history. The small, independent companies founded by the inventors evolved into big businesses at the turn of the century, when three large companies dominated the industry. These organizations became even larger during the 1920s and 1930s when dramatic advances in recording technology made it easier to establish entertainment empires. Some of the most powerful and innovative American companies were players in this drama, such as AT&T, General Electric, RCA, and Warner Bros. Their mastery of the technology of recording made it possible for them to dominate several branches of the immensely profitable business of popular entertainment.

American industrial dominance came to an end in the postwar decades, and Japanese companies proved to be fierce competitors in the consumer electronics market. Companies like Sony and Matsushita were responsible for many critical innovations. Big Business grew ever bigger in the 1970s and 1980s as a wave of mergers produced vast, integrated media empires. Multinational organizations such as Sony and Philips then dominated a global business in which recorded-sound products were but one element in the mechanization of entertainment.

The technological history of the phonograph breaks down into three parts, each reflecting a different method of recording sound. The acoustic era began in 1877 with Edison's invention of the phonograph and ended in the late 1920s when a new system of electrical recording superseded it. The electrical era of the 1930s and 1940s was represented by the 78-rpm shellac disc and the vacuum-tube phonograph or radio/phonograph combination. Its technological high point was reached in the 1950s and 1960s with microgroove vinyl discs (the 45-rpm single and the 33-rpm long player) and the record player (based on transistors instead of vacuum tubes). By the 1970s magnetic tape slowly overtook the revolving disc as the main form of recording sound. The 1977 sales year reflected the rapid growth of sales of prerecorded cassette tapes and pointed to the dominance of this format in the years that followed. The digital era began in 1982 with the commercial introduction of the compact disc (CD).

The technological history of recorded sound also covers the history of motion pictures. The electrical era began with the first sound pictures. The techniques and equipment perfected in film studios for use in the "talkies" slowly spread to recording studios. In the 1950s magnetic tape was used to save television pictures as well as sound. The first digital recording equipment of the 1970s was based on video recorders for television.

The development of recorded-sound technology was often the result of the diffusion of ideas and techniques between film makers and record companies. This is a critical factor in the rapid advance of a technology which has brought so many new products in the relatively short time period of a hundred years. In many cases the recording engineers in film studios and their counterparts involved in producing popular songs were all working for the same business organization. The integrated, multinational corporation with interests in many different areas was the ideal vehicle to develop new technology.

The history of recorded sound provides us with an ideal case study of the causes and consequences of technological change. One thing that the tumultuous story of the phonograph tells us about technological change is that it is rarely absolute and final. Threatened men live long, and so-called obsolete technologies have managed to survive in the face of clearly superior competitors for long periods. For example, years after the microgroove record replaced the shellac 78-rpm disc, companies continued to press them and make the little steel styli which were needed to play them. And over 10 years after the CD appeared, the microgroove disc showed no sign of disappearing. This endangered species of vinyl continued to be pressed, purchased, and cherished in the 1990s. It has a small but vociferous band of supporters who refuse to accept that digital technology provides a better sound:

> CDs are to records what videos are to movies: sampled, scanned, and coarse, missing huge chunks of information. . . . If you want fake, processed, artificial, lifeless, dimensionless sound . . . go spend $15 for the privilege and buy CDs.[6]

The history of recorded sound technology is not therefore a catalogue of one smashing innovation following another, a procession of new and improved machines with each one superior to the one it replaced. If there is one lesson a businessperson might learn from this history, it is that technology does not count for everything in this high-tech industry. Emphasizing the machine and putting technical considerations above artistic ones was the mistake made by Thomas Edison, and it proved fatal for his phonograph. Time and time again it was the mass appeal of the music recorded and not performance of the record or player that was critical in achieving commercial success.

Buying a stereo system is often an ordeal by high technology, a baffling initiation into a highly complex area of mysterious machines and puzzling acronyms: db, THD, S/N, kHz, and so on. No matter how many technical considerations are included in the analysis of sound reproduction, the enjoyment of recorded music is purely a subjective affair – there is no real way to prove that one machine or record sounds superior, other than listening to it, and everybody hears the music differently. Whatever the technical advances incorporated into the stereo, appreciating it is still relative.

There are still many people enjoying cylinder phonographs today. Devotees of acoustic recording can be found all over the world, playing their 2- and 4-minute records on well-oiled phonographs. Allen Koenigsberg's *Antique Phonograph Monthly* has a subscription list of over 2,000. Most enthusiasts use their machines to play back the sounds of the past, but several of them still use theirs to record music. The first recording studio established by Edison in his West Orange laboratory has been revived to record with acoustic phonographs. In a fine country house just outside of London, Brian Thorne and Dominic Combe use the same type of machines, and the same kind of techniques, in an acoustic recording studio. They would not claim that their recordings are superior to the compact discs made by Denon or Deutsche Grammophon, only that they get more enjoyment listening to the old cylinders. And surely that is the point.

Technology and history

The novelty of the phonograph was that it could preserve a part of life that had previously been a fleeting experience. Live music lasts only as long as the performance, for that short time when one hears the music, and after that it is just a memory. With proper care, a recording can last a lifetime or even longer, preserving the perform-

Figure 0.1. Victor stresses the permanence of its recordings. (Courtesy of General Electric)

ance for many years after the musician is dead. The noun *record* is therefore an appropriate term for the product of the recording industry. It is not just a consumer product but an artifact of a time gone by.

The sound recording has brought us more than the enjoyment of music, for it is as good a piece of evidence about the past as a primary source document from an archive or a faded old photograph. Americans living in the last decades of the nineteenth century found themselves in the unique position of being able to save small slices of their existence, to capture their images on photographic film and their voices on wax cylinders. Edison and the other inventors involved in making talking machines imagined that they would be able to create libraries of sounds, not just great pieces of classical music but also messages from the important men of the day and records of the great speeches of "our Washingtons, our Lincolns, our Gladstones" which would help in the preservation of language and national values.[7] They recorded poets and politicians as well as opera singers and pianists.

A sound recording is a piece of historical evidence. It has an impact that goes well beyond the written word or photographic image. Records enable us to listen in on history, to hear it again as it happened. The crash of the airship *Hindenburg* in New Jersey in 1937 is well preserved on film, but it is the spoken account of the disaster which brings the event to life and stirs the emotions. While only Lord Carnarvon was lucky enough to accompany Howard Carter when he entered the tomb of Tutankhamen, we can still hear Carter's dramatic account of the great moment against the swish and crackles of a worn 78-rpm disc. The recent discovery of some phonograph cylinders reputed to be of the poet Walt Whitman caused great excitement, for it was suddenly possible to hear the poems as the poet intended them.

Businesspeople have been using dictating machines to preserve their correspondence since the 1880s. Presidents as far back as Franklin Roosevelt placed recording machines in the White House to provide an exact record of historic decision making. In 1971 President Richard Nixon made a fateful decision to install tape recorders in the White House. The Secret Service planted voice-activated machines in the Oval Office, Lincoln Sitting Room, Cabinet Office, Nixon's private suite in the Executive Office Building, and the Presidential retreat at Camp David.

When the presence of the Nixon tapes was first made known in July 1973, at the height of the Watergate scandal, 4,000 hours of conversations had been recorded on 950 reels of tape. These tapes did more than provide undeniable evidence that the President had ordered the cover-up of the Watergate break-in; they gave a detailed and intimate picture of the Presidency with the stark honesty that other records had not been able to reveal. Although many of the expletives were deleted when transcripts of the tapes were released to the public, they did as much to damage Nixon's reputation as the recorded conversation with H. R. Haldeman on June 23, 1972, in which they decided to deceive the FBI about the Watergate affair.

Other pieces of recorded sound which bring us into close contact with the past are the speech of President Roosevelt delivering the war resolution in Congress after Pearl Harbor and the broadcasts of Edward R. Murrow from London during World War II, but none were as important in American history as the Nixon tapes, which cost him the presidency and are still at the center of a legal wrangle.[8]

Unfortunately for historians, very few of the sounds of American history have been recorded. We have only brief aural glimpses of the past. We can go back to the early twentieth century for the first politicians' voices on record, beginning with Taft and Roosevelt (the recordings of Gladstone, Lincoln, and other nineteenth-century leaders were faked for the phonograph), but what we hear are prepared speeches and not the dialogue of decision making. We have radio broadcasts from the 1920s onwards, but very few historic events. We have the sound of Lindbergh's plane taking off from Long Island as he headed across the Atlantic in 1927 and his interviews when he returned, but nothing in between. We do not have one continuous archive of recorded sound for any aspect of American life from 1877 to the present, except that of the music and humor which was recorded for entertainment purposes.

Technology and culture

When the talking machine companies were trying to create a market for their products in the early years of the twentieth century, one of the attractions of sound recording was to bring back memories of times gone by. In advertisements they reminded the public that nothing re-creates the past like the sound of a favorite song. There is a great deal of truth in this claim, for when we listen to the music of the 1960s or the 1920s those familiar tunes help us conjure up mental images of the past.

The vast number of recordings made of popular entertainment, music, radio broadcasts, and film sound tracks from the turn of the century onwards is an important archive of popular culture. Recorded sound was a technology for the masses, and these recordings were at the heart of a new mass culture of entertainment. The content of these records reflected the times in which they were produced, providing us with insights into those who listened and those who produced them.

Technology did more than preserve a record of a shared culture; it also influenced it. Recorded sound was the great educator, attracting generations of performers into musical careers and schooling them in styles of music which were often not written down. The recording proved to be the means of diffusing styles and bringing ethnic or regional music to a larger audience. The music it saved could go on to inspire countless young musicians. The music which went unrecorded faded from history without a trace.

Recorded sound played the critical part in the development of two uniquely American styles of popular music: jazz and rock'n'roll. The blues and jazz records made in the 1920s and 1930s formed a cultural archive of recorded sound that was a treasure trove for young musicians in the years after World War II, and not just those in the United States but the youth of the industrialized world.

The talking-machine industry was an international enterprise, with the free movement of ideas and machines across borders. The United States was always the base for the multinational companies in the nineteenth and early twentieth centuries because the advances in technology were normally made in American laboratories. Although Europe provided much of the music, America was the source of the machines. Around World War I, this international division of labor was altered; the United States became the source of the new sounds and images that transformed popular culture in the 1920s. Recorded sound was one of the foundations of this movement, which spread over the western world but retained a distinctly American character. The influential music and movies were made in the United States and distributed about the globe by American multinational companies.

The technology of recorded sound has played a very large part in the diffusion of American culture overseas. It figures prominently in what some scholars have called *cultural imperialism*. In popular music, in the sound tracks of motion pictures, and in the dialogue of television programs and advertisements, recorded sound has become the voice of the United States to the world. And nothing brings home the immediacy of the cultural experience like its sounds, whether it is the clipped sentences of Jimmy Cagney on screen or the blues shouting of Big Bill Broonzy on record. The industry that mass produces these sounds has effectively marketed its products all over the world, making the music and speech of North Americans a global product and facilitating the diffusion of American culture. What was heard by the many millions who have listened to the scratchy 78s of Louis Armstrong, or the fading sound track of a Warner Bros. gangsters movie, was America on Record.

PART ONE
THE ACOUSTIC ERA

1. The inventors

In the last decades of the nineteenth century, the United States was at a crossroads: a sparsely populated agricultural country, only a few hundred years away from the wilderness discovered by the colonists, was about to enter a period of unprecedented economic growth to become the world's greatest industrial nation. A large part in this economic transformation was played by inventors, a group of men who devised the new technology which was the key to rapid industrialization. Their achievements were acknowledged worldwide as the "Yankee ingenuity" that transformed the United States into an industrial giant.

Of all the inventors of the nineteenth century, Thomas Edison is the best known. Statistically he holds the most U.S. patents (a record which will probably never be beaten), and mythologically he is the world's greatest inventor – the "Wizard of Menlo Park" whose magic helped create the modern industrial society in which we live. Edison became a legend in his own time; unlike most of his fellow inventors, he died rich and famous.

The invention which gained Edison his fame was the phonograph. Although nowadays we think of this machine as a mechanical entertainer, it was in fact part of a communications revolution, a revolution which brought so many dramatic changes in American life that it far exceeds any of the so-called communications or computer revolutions of the twentieth century. By 1850 inventors had developed a system of communications in which an electric current could be used between two places to replace the letter delivered by hand or by horseback. Messages now moved at the unimaginable speed of electricity. The rapid communications afforded by the telegraph became one of the foundations of American industrial growth. By the 1860s it had spawned a great international business and a host of research laboratories: the telegraph was the high-tech field of the 1860s and 1870s.[1]

17

Edison was part of this dynamic new field of telecommunications. He was one of many ambitious young men who saw the telegraph as the most profitable field for new inventions. He worked as an itinerant telegrapher in the 1860s, moving from place to place and doing some inventing in his spare time to improve the equipment with which he worked. Another amateur inventor was Alexander Graham Bell, a teacher of the deaf in Boston, who hoped to make a better living by devising new telegraph transmitters and receivers.

The inventors came from all backgrounds and from all walks of life. Some had some experience in the mechanical arts and others (like Bell) had little but ideas and ambition. Many were recent immigrants from Europe, such as Emile Berliner, who left Germany and the threat of conscription into the Prussian army to seek his fortune in the United States in the 1870s. After a succession of jobs – working as a clerk in a store, selling glue, and painting backgrounds for photographs – he obtained employment in a chemical laboratory and started his study of physics and electricity.

Some inventors worked in laboratories of the large telegraph companies such as Western Union; others made do with makeshift apparatus in their lodgings. Those who could not afford their own work areas rented out space in machine shops, where precision tools and skilled workmen could be hired to make experimental equipment.

Invention in the late nineteenth century was not purely an intellectual affair. Men like Edison and Bell invented by doing, by turning their ideas into working models and then trying to make them work. The critical flash of insight often came in operating their apparatus.[2] Experimental transmitters and receivers had to be made up by skilled craftsmen before any new idea could be tested. Edison frequented the shop of Charles Williams in Boston, where he went to experiment after finishing work at the Western Union office. A few years later Bell had his devices made at this same shop, where he made the acquaintance of a mechanic named Thomas Watson, who was to figure large in his future.[3]

The appeal of the telegraph was twofold for the aspiring inventor. First, an improved transmitter or receiver was worth a lot of money, as was evident in the lucrative prices Edison obtained for his quadruplex telegraph patents. He used the income from various research contracts to build a laboratory in Menlo Park, New Jersey, and this set him along a path that was to lead to some of the most astonishing inventions of the nineteenth century. Edison's rise from penniless tinkerer to well-known inventor with his own laboratory was an inspiration to others who hoped to emulate his success.

The other attraction of the telegraph was that this technology was in its infancy and there were more valuable inventions to be made. The messages could not be sent very quickly or very far, and only one at a time went along the wire. Edison's quadruplex idea enabled four messages to be sent on one line and therefore increased the capacity of the network four times. He also worked on an automatic telegraph – a device that stored telegraph code on punched tape, which could then be run through the transmitter at high speeds – to quicken the pace of communication.

These innovations, and many more like them made by other inventors, brought about a more efficient use of the capital equipment of the telegraph companies and improved the service they offered to the customer. But they did not alter the fundamental basis of telegraphic communication; it was still dots and dashes created by interrupting the flow of current from transmitter to receiver. Some visionary inventors devoted their efforts to the speaking telegraph, which could transmit and receive the sound of the human voice – a task so difficult that many considered it to be impossible. Charles Bourseul of France had tried to transmit speech over wires around 1854 but had failed, as did many other inventors. The quantum leap to use electric currents to transmit the sound of the human voice was first accomplished by accident, and by a rank amateur in the business of invention.

The secret of electric speech

During the 1870s Alexander Graham Bell worked on several ideas to improve the telegraph. He was interested in the harmonic telegraph, which could send more than one message along the wire. It used tuning forks or steel reeds that were resonant at different frequencies to transmit dots and dashes as signals of these different frequencies along the same wire. At the end of the wire were several receivers, each tuned to a different frequency; each one responded selectively to the incoming messages.

Bell was experimenting with one of these devices in 1875. It consisted of a group of steel reeds each attached to an electromagnet, which acted as a transmitter by making and breaking a circuit. At the other end of the wire was a corresponding receiver arrangement of reeds and magnets. The steel reed was a thin slice of metal attached to one pole of the electromagnet with its other end just projecting over the opposite pole of the magnet. While Bell was experimenting with magnetizing the reed and creating varying currents, he accidentally discovered that plucking the reeds next to the electromagnet would produce a current which would activate the magnet at the other end, causing the reeds attached to it to vibrate and produce an audible sound.

Bell had three of these transmitters in one room of the attic of Williams' shop, with three receivers in another room attended by his assistant, Watson. As Bell activated the current in each transmitter in turn, the corresponding reed in the receiver in the next room sounded, except for the last one. The reed had probably become stuck to the pole of the electromagnet. With the current turned off, Bell shouted to Watson to free the reed, and as Watson plucked the reeds Bell saw that his own reed was vibrating. He excitedly told Watson to keep plucking the reeds and then, moving close to his transmitter, he listened to the sound of them vibrating, convinced that what he heard was the pitch and the amplitude of that sound in Watson's room. His biographer, Catherine Mackenzie, described this moment of insight: "And then, . . . by accident, and for a fraction of a second, the clue to electric speech flashed into the noise and heat of that dusty Boston attic."[4]

Although not as dramatic as Mackenzie described it, this event did persuade Bell that it might be possible to transmit the sound of speech along a wire. He told Watson that if he could find a way of making a current of electricity vary in its intensity as air varies in density as sound passes through it, "I can telegraph any sound, even the sound of speech."[5] He experimented with the transfer of the mechanical movement of sound in the air into the variation of a minute electric current produced by electromagnetism. This research eventually led him to the conclusion that the complexities of pitch and timbre in human speech could be transmitted electrically – the waves caused by sound were analogous to the variable waves of electricity. He hoped that a current of electricity could be produced that varied in intensity precisely and exactly as the sound waves varied.

Once he grasped the principle of transforming sound waves into electric currents, Bell asked Watson to build an instrument that used a thin membrane diaphragm with a metallic center instead of the reed. The pressure of the sound hitting the diaphragm was faithfully duplicated by the moving sliver of metal as it interacted with a magnetic field to produce a varying current. In reverse, an electromagnet next to the diaphragm could vibrate it – reproducing sounds by its subtle movement – as current passed through its windings. Throughout 1875 Bell and Watson worked to perfect the telephone transmitter before applying for a patent. By February 1876 they had a model in which the electric current was provided by a battery; this current was modulated by the movement of the diaphragm.

On the evening of March 10, 1876, Bell and Watson were experimenting with this device in their boarding house: Bell at the transmitter in one room and Watson with the receiver in another. This was the night when Watson heard the famous words "Watson, come here, I want you!" – the first words to be transmitted on the telephone.[6] Throughout the summer of 1876, the two men developed their ideas. They built a new form of telephone transmitter which used a diaphragm attached to the poles of an electromagnet by a metal armature. This magneto-telephone was publicly demonstrated to several groups in 1876. Bell took out a patent for his invention and began to talk with businessmen about constructing a communications system that would compete with the wires of Western Union.

Bell's experiments in Boston followed the work of many others in the realm of electricity and acoustics. His telephone was based on the scientific principles of electromagnetism developed by Hans Oersted in Denmark in 1820, and on Michael Faraday's study of the induction of electric current, which was published in England in 1831. Bell's research was not much different from that carried out by aspiring inventors all over Europe and the United States, but Bell came to the important conclusion first. As his biographer, Robert Bruce, has pointed out: "In retrospect, it seems obvious that if the magnet were brought close to a flexible metal diaphragm and a variable current passed through the coil (of the electromagnet), the magnet would cause the diaphragm to vibrate to produce sound."[7]

Bell was not alone in his experiments on the harmonic telegraph. Thomas Edison also saw great potential in this technology and took out several patents on it. In Chicago, Elisha Gray worked on harmonic (or acoustic) telegraphy as a means to send a number of messages simultaneously. An ex-carpenter with two years of college to his credit, Gray had become a professional inventor and manufacturer of telegraph instruments. Gray succeeded in transmitting sounds by the same methods that Bell used to transmit speech. By the time that Bell moved to Boston, the term *telephone* had already been applied to an acoustic telegraph invented by Philip Reis of Germany in 1861. This device used the vibrations of sound to move a diaphragm that activated a make-and-break telegraph circuit. Although Reis believed that his device could transmit the sound of the human voice, like Gray he concentrated on sending musical tones.

Bell managed to beat his many competitors in this field by being the first to apply for a patent on February 14, 1876, just a few hours before Elisha Gray arrived at the patent office to file a preliminary application for virtually the same idea. But Bell was first, and his triumph was complete.

The first public demonstrations of Bell's telephone were accompanied by incredulity and amazement. The squeaky voice emerging from the wooden box that held the assembly of wires, the metal diaphragm, and electromagnet was a bewildering herald of a new era in communications. Instead of by dots and dashes, messages could now be sent exactly the way they were spoken. The revelation that sound could be transmitted along a wire caused consternation in the board rooms of the telegraph industry and unbridled excitement among the international fraternity of inventors.

The widely dispersed group of experimenters who had been working on harmonic and speaking telegraphs were electrified by the news of Bell's telephone. The pioneering experiments of Bell, Gray, and Reis were quickly replicated in hundreds of workshops and laboratories. Bell's apparatus was far from being a commercial technology; the sound from the telephone receiver was faint, and it worked only over short distances. There was plenty of room for improvement. At the Menlo Park laboratory, Edison devised a better telephone transmitter, which sent a clearer and stronger sound to the receiver. Berliner followed the same path in his workshop in Washington.

In the years that followed Bell's invention of the telephone, there was a worldwide study of variations in electric currents that could reproduce sounds. The thin metal diaphragm and electromagnet assemblies were put together, tested, examined, and rebuilt. Many more amateur and professional inventors grew familiar with the delicate electromechanical devices that picked up sound waves and turned them into electric currents. Increased familiarity with the diaphragms and electromagnetic assemblies, which turned the faint vibrations of sound waves into undulating currents, was to bear fruit in the flood of new telephone transmitters and receivers which were submitted to the patent office.

These experiments were also to prepare the ground for the development of a technology for recording sound, and it is certainly not a coincidence that technology to save telephone messages occurred only a year after Bell transmitted those famous words to Watson.

Saving and reproducing sound

The requirement to record and reproduce sound was a direct consequence of this revolution in communications. With millions of important messages now flowing from place to place, it became desirable to capture and store them for reference. Saving incoming messages and replaying them later at a comfortable speed also made it possible to use unskilled operators to cope with the exponential increase in messages.

The automatic telegraph achieved both of these goals. Morse code was punched into a strip of paper in the form of holes. These holes made electrical contact in the transmitter which caused breaks in the circuit. The strips of paper could be run through the transmitter at very high speeds. At the receiving end, the electrical pulses were recorded onto a strip of paper either by electrochemical changes or by an electrically activated ink recorder.

Thomas Edison had plenty of experience in automatic telegraphy when he opened his Menlo Park laboratory in 1876. He wanted this first industrial research facility to produce a stream of useful innovations, practical inventions that would meet a well-defined need in commerce or industry. Consequently, he directed his experiments into the new field of electrical communications. An improved telephone was one of his priorities because Western Union wanted their own machine to help ward off the threat from Bell's telephone.

Edison had already covered a great deal of ground in his research on the telegraph and telephone. He knew how to turn sound waves into mechanical movement that could induce electric currents. He knew how to manipulate electromagnetic attraction to move switches and make circuits. He had studied the work of many other inventors

in the field, examining obscure telegraph patents in European journals. He was well versed in the theories of the German scientist Her-
mann Helmholtz on the nature of sound waves. He was also aware
of the work of Leon Scott in France, whose "phonautograph" used
a stylus attached to a membrane diaphragm to trace out the undulations of sound waves on a cylinder covered with smoked paper. The
development of the telephone transmitter familiarized Edison with the
thin discs of metal or animal membrane which acted as a diaphragm
by vibrating to produce sound waves. All these pieces of information
were to be brought together in the invention of the phonograph.

As was usual in his laboratory, Edison directed his teams of experimenters to work on several related projects in 1877. He was engaged in the job of producing an improved telephone for Western
Union. In addition to this "speaking" telegraph, Edison and his men
worked on harmonic and automatic telegraphs. During the summer
of 1877, he took some time off from the telephone to sketch out a
few ideas for recording incoming messages. As a commercial inventor
he realized the value of saving telephone messages, especially as he
correctly anticipated that businessmen would be the first to use them
to replace written communication.

The devices he drew were inspired by his earlier inventions of automatic telegraphs that employed strips of treated paper marked with
the dots and dashes of Morse code. He made one important addition.
In previous experiments he had been struck by the force of the sound
waves moving a diaphragm and wondered if a needle attached to the
center of a diaphragm could be powered by sound to make a mark.
One night in July 1877, his staff rigged up an indenting stylus connected to a diaphragm, which in turn was attached to a telephone
speaker. As Edison shouted into the speaker, a strip of paraffin-coated
paper was run underneath the stylus. An examination of the strip
showed the irregular marks made by the sound waves. When the strip
was pulled back under the stylus, the group of men crowded around
the laboratory table heard, with disbelief, the faint sounds of Edison's
shouts of a few minutes previous. His chief assistant, Charles Batchelor, remembered that the sounds were not by any means a perfect
reproduction, "but the shape of it was there, and so like the speaking
that we all let out a yell of satisfaction and a 'Golly it's there' and all
shook hands."[8]

The next day Edison made note of the experiment and wrote that

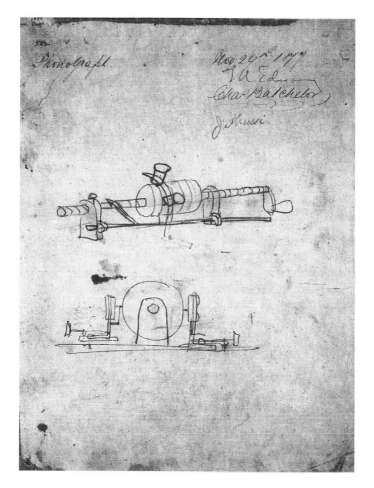

Figure 1.1 Edison's sketch of the phonograph, reputedly of November 1877. (U.S. Department of the Interior, National Park Service, Edison National Historic Site [hereafter cited as ENHS])

"the spkg vibrations are indented nicely & theres no doubt that I shall be able to store & reproduce automatically at any future time the human voice perfectly."[9]

This amazing claim was not made into reality until December 1877 when the laboratory workers made up a working phonograph. It consisted of a cylinder attached to a long feed screw turned by a hand crank. A sheet of tinfoil was carefully wrapped around the cylinder.

On one side of the cylinder was the recording assembly, a funnel-like mouthpiece (similar to the one used for the telephone) connected to a thin metal diaphragm to which a steel stylus was attached. Shouting into the funnel vibrated the diaphragm and moved the stylus, which incised the spiral analog of the sound waves onto the soft metal foil as it was turned. On the other side of the cylinder, a playback reproducer of stylus and diaphragm was run back over the indentations in the foil to vibrate the diaphragm in the same way that the recording had been made. The listener had to pay close attention to discern the faint noises coming from the vibrating diaphragm.

Demonstrated at the office of *Scientific American* on December 6, 1877, the phonograph quickly became the rage. As word got out, people flocked to the building in New York City and packed into the room to hear the machine talk. When the news appeared in the press, train loads of people, "great crowds of people" as Batchelor remembered, arrived at the laboratory to hear "with astonishment" the sounds of their own voices.[10] Even the President of the United States wanted to hear the talking machine.

The acclaim given to the phonograph has tended to obscure the fact that although this was a marvelous invention, it was more of a step forward along a well-travelled path than a great breakthrough.[11] As with many of Edison's inventions, part of its achievement was to bring together several ideas. It was an application of the work done by Leon Scott and others. The phonautograph made a tracing of the sound waves as they vibrated the diaphragm. Edison took this idea one step further and found that the impression of the sound could be used to reproduce the original. The inventors who had been working in the same areas as Edison had the idea at their fingertips but did not see it. As Bell wrote in 1878: "It is a most astonishing thing to me that I could possibly have let this invention slip through my fingers."[12]

Bell must have been astonished not only because he had been working along the same lines as Edison and not seen how sound waves could be mechanically reproduced, but also because the phonograph was such a simple idea. Edison's achievement was to establish that sounds could be recorded and re-created with just the mechanical power of the stylus vibrating as it moved up and down on the minute indentations on the paper or tinfoil. In considering the possibilities of recording sound, Edison thought that saving messages would require the same transformation of sound waves into electrical impulses that had been successfully used in the telephone. It made sense that the method used to create electric speech might be the means to save and retrieve it.

The critical experiments carried out in Menlo Park in the summer and fall of 1877 proved that the storage and recovery of sound could be done without the electrical transformation used in the telephone. There was a simpler way, and Edison had found it. When he announced that he had devised a "wonderfully simple" apparatus for recording the human voice, for once he was not exaggerating.

Although the tinfoil phonograph made an enormous impression on the public and on the fraternity of inventors, it had very little commercial potential. Edison, the most commercially minded of all inventors, had stumbled on it in the pursuit of other goals. He called it an "invention pure and simple" that he had discovered rather than methodically sought out. He saw it in terms of a device to save incoming phone calls, and as such it was the first attempt to make a telephone answering machine.[13] He also saw it as a means to increase the length of telephone transmission by situating it at the end of one line and then playing a recording of a message on another line. The phonograph acted as a telephone "repeater." But since only about a minute or two of sound could be saved by the tinfoil phonograph, it could not serve practically in either function.

Several other problems had to be solved before it could be considered a commercial machine. The tinfoil could be used only two or three times before it deformed and the message was lost. The intelligibility of the replayed sound depended on the even turning of the crank, for even a slight change in speed distorted the sound beyond recognition. This was not an easy machine to operate. Ed Pershey, the curator of the Edison National Historic Site for some years, has considerable experience coaxing a recording out of the tinfoil phonograph. He commented that "Although the process is, in essence, simple, it takes dexterity and a fair amount of luck to achieve success."[14]

The disembodied sounds and squeaks emerging from the tinfoil could be discerned by the listener, but it took practice to recognize speech. Edison had demonstrated a principle, but his phonograph could not save and reproduce sounds accurately or consistently enough to be useful to the casual listener. In the years after 1877, Bell and his associates made the telephone one of the most profitable inventions of the nineteenth century, but the phonograph remained a novelty, a scientific toy.

The talking machine takes shape

Edison could choose from several formats in his development of the talking machine. In addition to the cylinder, there was the revolving disc and the strip recording. The staff of the Menlo Park laboratory tried out several types of disc (or plate) records, in which the sound waves were incised in a spiral on the flat surface of the disc. Edison had plenty of experience in using strips of paper or foil as recording material in prior experiments in telegraphy. In his patent of December 1877, he described the strip of tinfoil which passed under the stylus and received the indentations of sound waves in the form of a continuous groove.[15]

With three possible formats to choose from, Edison concentrated on the cylinder; it was simple to build, and he was familiar with the revolving cylinder and stylus arrangement from his work on telegraphy and from the numerous lathes that were found in his laboratory. The way that the stylus scratched the revolving cylinder was exactly the manner in which the cutting tools of lathes shaved off ribbons from revolving pieces of metal. It was therefore familiarity which determined that the cylinder model would be exhibited to the world as the phonograph.

In the winter of 1877/1878, the experimenters at Menlo Park were hard at work improving the talking machine. They even built a disc model which had better sound reproduction than the original cylinder version, and Edison wrote confidently to his financial backers that "a practical marketable machine" was within his reach.[16]

Yet this did not happen for many years. Edison's attention never stayed on one subject for very long, and he was soon drawn to other experimental projects, such as improving his telephone transmitter for Western Union. In late 1878, at a critical point in recorded-sound experiments, Edison stopped work on electrical communications to concentrate on the development of a high-resistance incandescent electric light, which was an invention with a clearly defined use and a great potential market. The same could not be said for the tinfoil phonograph, and it languished in the Menlo Park laboratory while

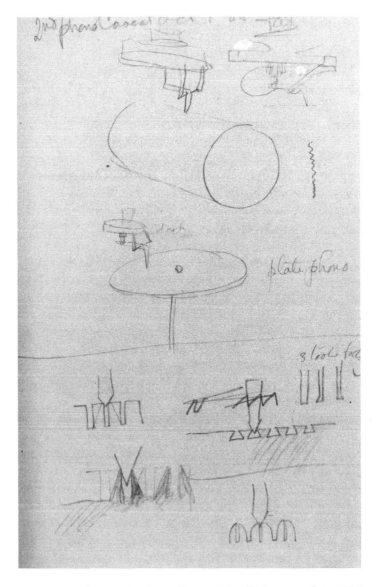

Figure 1.2. Edison's idea for a disc or "plate" phonograph in 1888. (Author)

Edison set up the first system of electricity supply from a central power station in New York City. The task of turning his phonograph invention into a practical device therefore fell to other inventors.

Alexander Graham Bell had almost stumbled on the phonograph idea in 1874, when he speculated that the phonautograph format could be used to re-create the original sound. But Edison beat him to it, as he also beat Bell to the carbon button transmitter that dramatically improved the telephone. Nevertheless, Bell saw commercial potential in sound recording and began to think about it when he set up his own laboratory in 1880 to investigate the science of sound. He was joined in his Volta laboratory by his cousin Chichester Bell, who was well versed in physics and chemistry, and Charles Tainter, a precision instrument maker who had worked in Charles Williams' shop making telegraph equipment.

Together they experimented on acoustic and electrical technologies. They even investigated the idea of recording sound photographically. Bell demonstrated in 1880 that it was possible to transmit speech over a beam of light. The "Photophone" was later developed at the Volta laboratory. In 1884 and 1885 Bell and Tainter made experiments on recording sound as spiral waves on glass discs coated with emulsion. They manipulated the sound to cause variations in a light source which they recorded on the sensitive photographic emulsion on the revolving disc.[17]

The most important project undertaken at the Volta laboratory was the development of a commercial machine based on Edison's phonograph. They substituted wax for the tinfoil on the cylinder and coated a layer around a cardboard core. While the phonograph's needle displaced the recording medium, indenting the sound wave upon it, Tainter's idea was to cut or engrave an impression on it. The end of the cutter was shaped like a chisel, and it made a cleaner cut than the indenting stylus. The result was a more intelligible sound and a little less background noise. The wax cylinder was much more durable than the tinfoil and could be taken on and off the machine without deforming the groove of the sound wave.

Bell and Tainter's machine was arranged the same way as the phonograph, except that there were two parallel axes, one for the cylinder and one for the lead screw which held the reproducer. The recording cutter and reproducing arm were moved precisely along the wax cylinder by a lead screw assembly, which ran parallel to the turning axis

of the cylinder. It worked like the feedscrew of a lathe. Tainter tried
to balance the reproducing stylus assembly so that it would float in
the groove, enabling it to react to the tracing of the sound waves
while riding out the imperfections on the wax surface.[18]

The improved talking machine developed in the Volta laboratory
was named the *graphophone*. In terms of ease of operation and fidelity of sound reproduction, it was a vast improvement on the phonograph. After many years of experiments, the three Volta associates
obtained several patents in 1886 and took their machine to Edison
with a proposition to join together and commercially exploit the new
technology. But Edison would have none of it, and smarting from the
slight of having others improve his famous invention, he returned to
his phonograph. After years of neglect he was finally going to perfect
the recording of sound.[19]

In 1887 Edison finished the construction of a large laboratory in
West Orange, New Jersey. Shortly after the facility opened at the end
of the year, he demonstrated an improved phonograph. The wax cylinder and general arrangement of this model owed a lot to the graphophone, but instead of a hand crank it was powered by an electric
motor which was placed underneath the revolving cylinder. It drove
the cylinder spindle through a system of bevelled wheels. As the cylinder turned, a lead screw moved the reproducer along the cylinder's
groove.

The recording and reproducing diaphragms were joined together in
the form of a pair of spectacles. The operator shouted into a small
horn attached to the recorder, and the vibrations of the diaphragm
moved the sharp tip of the recording stylus. After it had cut the
groove of the sound wave into the soft wax cylinder, the spectacle
frame was then turned to bring the reproducer stylus onto the groove
of the cylinder, and the user listened to the recording through an
eartube connected to the reproducer.[20]

Edison and his experimental teams at the West Orange laboratory
continued to experiment on sound recording and to improve the talking machine. After weeks of intensive work in the summer of 1888,
Edison announced that he had finally perfected the phonograph. It
now came in a rectangular box which enclosed the electric motor.
The cylinder and reproducer assemblies were fixed to a metal plate
on top of the box. The most prominent feature of the machine was
the tapered mandrel – a shaft of metal which held the cylinder – which

ran along the top plate. After sliding a cylinder on the mandrel, the user swung the diaphragm assembly onto it and started it turning.[21]

During this time Edison made frequent pronouncements from the West Orange laboratory that the talking machine was now ready for commercial introduction. But these were no more than a smoke screen to give him time to recover lost ground in the technology of recorded sound. Many of the international fraternity of inventors, who had once applied their talents to the telephone, were now fully engaged in recording sound. Edison's English patents on the phonograph had lapsed in 1885, leaving the field wide open on both sides of the Atlantic to the many newcomers who thought they could produce a better machine. Most of their efforts were variations of the basic phonograph configuration, but one design broke away from the cylinder idea.

The gramophone used a disc instead of a cylinder. It was the work of Emile Berliner, who demonstrated it in 1888. It was powered by a hand crank and had the same kind of diaphragm and stylus assembly that could be found on any talking machine. The gramophone did not employ a lead screw to move the stylus along the groove in playback; instead the spiral groove in the disc gently pushed the stylus across the face of the record. Where Edison and Tainter had employed a vertical (up and down) cut in recording sound waves onto the cylinder, Berliner employed a lateral cut in which the stylus moved from side to side.

In 1888 and 1889 the stream of talking-machine patents produced in the United States and Europe turned into a flood. At the West Orange laboratory, Edison led his teams of researchers in an intense campaign to turn a laboratory device into a dictating machine that could be used by businessmen. Bell and Tainter were doing the same thing in Washington. They faced a multitude of problems. The hand crank that turned the cylinder or disc had to be turned at constant speed or the pitch of the reproduction changed noticeably. This was asking too much of the average user and consequently another power source had to be found. The inventors experimented with electric motors, clockwork and spring motors, foot treadles, gravity feeds (in which a weight pulled down a cord attached to a spindle), and even water power.

The other major concern was the reproduction of sound. There were endless possible variations in the critical assembly of stylus and diaphragm: different materials and shapes for the diaphragm, clever mechanical connections between stylus and diaphragm, and a wide variety of shapes and sizes for the air chamber that enclosed the diaphragm. Each inventor had his own system, and each guarded his secrets.

While the majority of the inventors worked in the cylinder format, Berliner and his associate Werner Suess perfected the disc player. In 1889 they joined their diaphragm to a large horn which was counterbalanced and supported by an arm to glide across the face of the disc. The container which held the diaphragm and recording stylus was called the *soundbox*. Over the next few years, they refined this design by improving the hollow connecting elbow between the soundbox and horn. The simple hand crank of their early models evolved into a crank turning two small wheels connected by a cross-belt. Turning the crank on one of the wheels transferred the power smoothly to the turntable.[22]

Berliner's success meant that two of the three forms of talking machine described by Edison in his first patents had been successfully developed. There were plenty of cylinder or disc designs to choose from in the two decades after 1877, yet the third format – the continuous strip – had been ignored. Only one inventor saw the potential of this format and outlined an apparatus that recorded sound onto a ribbon of metal or fabric covered with particles of metal.

The mechanical engineer Oberlin Smith visited Edison's Menlo Park laboratory in 1878. Like many other inventors he saw that the weakness of the phonograph was the fragility of the grooves in the metal foil which were formed and deformed by recording. He thought of using metal strips that could be altered by the influence of sound waves without actually touching the metal. He was the first to describe a method of recording based on magnetizing strips of metal. In an article published in 1889, Smith rejected the mechanical means of recording in favor of using the electrical method of magnetizing the recording medium. Smith correctly pointed out the disadvantage of acoustic recording: the friction of stylus in the recording groove inevitably caused distortion and unwanted noise. On the other hand, a magnetic transformation of the recording medium did not involve the direct physical contact that caused surface noise.[23]

In taking the route of magnetic recording, Smith was going back to the initial point of departure of the phonograph inventors – that

Figure 1.3. Emile Berliner examining his disc record. (Library of Congress)

sound recording would have to be done in the same way as the telephone converted sound waves into electric currents. The electrical signal of these currents was the thing to be recorded, not the actual wave form of the sound. Bell and Tainter had started towards this goal in 1885 when they described a device that used an electromagnetically activated diaphragm (something like the one found in Bell's telephone) to record on a wax paper strip.[24]

The great problem was how to imprint the signal of sound waves onto such a hard material as metal, and for this reason Smith's idea was not taken up by any of the inventors. Smith did not incorporate his theories into a working model. We shall probably never know if he managed to make his revolutionary idea work. It was not until 1898 that a patent was taken out for a system of magnetic recording, and it was a measure of how far the technology of recorded sound

Figure 1.4. Poulsen's telegraphone, showing the recording wire on two spools. (Mark Clark)

had travelled that this invention was the work of the Danish engineer Valdemar Poulsen.

Like all the other inventors before him, Poulsen's approach to sound recording was heavily influenced by his work on the telephone. In much the same way that Edison came to the phonograph, Poulsen set out to develop a commercial device for saving telephone messages rather than a new system of recording sound. He found that the variable currents generated by a telephone transmitter or microphone could be used to produce local magnetization of a steel wire, causing in effect a magnetic pattern whose magnetic variation exactly matched the variations of the current. Poulsen believed that this principle would also work with strips of magnetically treated paper or metal tape, and with this idea he anticipated modern tape recording. His first wire recorder was appropriately called the *telegraphone* – a name that encompassed the relationship of telephone, telegraph, and phonograph.[25]

By 1900 inventors had established the three formats of recorded sound. Although the simplicity of the phonograph had temporarily prevented the application of telephone technology to recording sound, experiments to transform speech into electric currents provided results which were later applied to electrical recording. Edison invented a carbon button telephone transmitter in 1877 which changed resistance in a circuit in proportion to the mechanical pressure placed on it by a vibrating diaphragm. Berliner also devised a variable-pressure transmitter which paralleled Edison's carbon button idea. Both of these inventions were important precedents for the microphone.

Even the invisible forces which would someday carry the signal of recorded sound had been discovered. In 1883 Edison noticed that moving streams of electrical forces within the vacuum of a light bulb deposited a dark film on the inside of the glass. What Edison had seen was the work of electrons, a force too small to be seen and too mysterious to be identified but too important to ignore. This phenomenon was later called the *Edison Effect*, and it was the starting point of the research that was to lead to the vacuum tube. It would be 50 years before the era of acoustic recording brought into being by the phonograph was replaced by a new electrical technology based on the vacuum tube. In the meantime Edison and the other inventors built up great business empires on acoustic sound recording.

2. A phonograph in every home

Edison always said that the phonograph was his only real discovery, the only invention he stumbled upon rather than deliberately set out to find. Having invented it, he then had to find a use for it. Musical entertainment was one of the first uses he predicted for the phonograph, although it was by no means the only one. The inventors claimed that it would change education, politics, and business communication in addition to providing entertainment. Edison also thought it could be adapted for phonographic books for the blind, the teaching of elocution, and speaking clocks.

The phonograph was invented to save telephone messages, and the ability to record speech opened up several commercial uses. Chief among these was its employment as a dictating machine for businessmen. A talking machine could be used to replace the tedious exchange of letters with the recorded message of the phonograph cylinder. The inventors hoped that the cylinder could be sent through the mail with the ease of a letter. The advantage was that the recipient got an exact record of the sender's message as he dictated it, substituting a sound recording for correspondence. The paperless business office was anticipated well before the advent of personal computers and modems.

Edison hoped that this idea would transform office work. The electric light, telephone, and typewriter were slowly changing the American office, facilitating the task of managing the larger business organizations of the late nineteenth century. When used as a dictating machine, the phonograph promised to further ease the burden of business administration by mechanizing correspondence. The device that had begun as a complement to the telephone was now seen as an adjunct to the typewriter.[1]

At the same time that Edison was imagining the phonograph as the ultimate business tool, he also made a prophetic statement about its future. "This machine," he wrote in 1878, shortly after the clamor surrounding the invention had died down, "can only be built on the American principle of interchangeability of parts like a gun or a sewing machine."[2] Edison the inventor clearly demonstrated that he had also grasped the article of faith of American business in the late nineteenth century – mass production using standardized parts. The sewing machines and guns he mentioned were made in the thousands by an entirely new system of production. It involved the fabrication of a product out of identical, standardized parts made by special machine tools. The product was broken down into parts, each of which was made to a precise standard, and assembled by unskilled labor who bolted or screwed the parts together. This replaced the practice of craftsmen fashioning products out of parts that were individually made for each job.

The American system of manufacture offered a high volume of output with lower unit costs, and the higher the output the lower the cost. Edison decided that the phonograph should not be made under the craft system, which operated in the machine shops where he had his inventions made up. Instead of an expensive, precision-built machine made by skilled craftsmen, the phonograph would be mass-produced by special machines and unskilled labor. The American system would make the talking machine an inexpensive consumer good for the masses in the twentieth century.

The technology of recorded sound was introduced at a time when the United States was fast becoming one of the world's greatest industrial powers. The output of Yankee ingenuity, the stream of inventions produced in the last half of the nineteenth century, had not been left to languish among the documents of the patent office but instead had inspired new manufacturing industries. Edison was a businessman as well as an inventor. He had realized at an early stage of his career that the inventor rarely got the financial rewards of introducing a new technology; the profits went to the industrialist and the financier. Like Bell, Gray, and Berliner, he quickly set up factories to make his inventions and formed companies to market them.

Elisha Gray formed the Western Electric Company to make his telegraph equipment; this company was to play a significant role in the history of recorded sound. Bell built his Volta laboratory on the proceeds of a large cash prize for inventing the telephone and created the Bell Telephone Company on the basis of his patents. Chichester Bell and Charles Tainter formed the Volta Graphophone Company

Figure 2.1. Assembling gramophones in Berliner's Washington shop. (Library of Congress)

in 1887 and acquired the Howe sewing machine factory of Bridge-port, Connecticut. The graphophones produced here had the same wood base and foot treadle used in sewing machines. Berliner created the American Gramophone Company in 1891 and then the United States Gramophone Company in 1893.[3]

Edison was already an experienced industrialist before he built the

Menlo Park laboratory, and he lost no time in setting up companies to market the output of his "invention factory." The Edison Speaking Phonograph Company was formed in 1878; many of its members were also involved in telephone companies. Once Edison had moved from Menlo Park to West Orange in 1887, he began to construct two large factories to assemble talking machines. This industrial complex was called the Edison Phonograph Works. It was the first part of an ambitious plan to fill the Orange Valley with factories, all making the new products invented at the laboratory.

There were as many business enterprises as there were uses for recorded sound technology: talking dolls, speaking cash registers, and automatic coin-in-the-slot phonographs which could be used in amusement arcades. Some companies were established primarily to market machines made by others. The Columbia Phonograph Company was formed in Washington in 1889 to sell phonographs and graphophones as dictating machines. In the 1890s most large American cities had their own phonograph company, ranging from the Metropolitan Company of New York to the Pacific Phonograph Company of San Francisco.

The talking-machine industry was to take the same path followed by several new technologies in American business: boom and bust. The first inventions led to the formation of many small companies which energetically attempted to cash in on the new idea. They competed in local or regional markets with no clear business strategy other than survival. Numerous different types of machines were manufactured and sold, but there was no attempt at standardization and very little interchangeability of records. It was not long until a capitalist came along with the money and a plan to create order.

Jesse Lippincott set out to rationalize the talking machine business in the same way that John D. Rockefeller was to consolidate the petroleum industry and J. P. Morgan brought order to the railroads. The overriding goal of all these nineteenth-century financiers was a monopoly or oligarchy in which a few large companies fixed prices and standardized output. Monopoly power eliminated what many businessmen thought was wasteful competition, and it came naturally to the technological systems such as the telephone and electric light.

After acquiring the rights to sell the products of the American Graphophone Company (the successor of Bell and Tainter's Volta Graphophone Company), Lippincott set out to purchase rights to sell

Edison's phonographs, which he did in September 1888.[4] He now controlled the output of the two leading forces in the industry of recording sound. His company bought the output of the factories set up by Edison and Bell, and the customer could choose between the phonograph and the graphophone. Lippincott's North American Phonograph Company sold franchises to local entrepreneurs, which guaranteed exclusive sales areas. As its name suggests, the company aimed to cover the continent with a network of local franchises.

The business strategy was to produce a commercial dictating machine to be leased rather than sold to customers, a practice which followed the example of the telephone. Unfortunately it failed because the technology upon which Edison, Bell, and Lippincott pinned their hopes could not do the job. As a business machine the phonograph or graphophone was difficult to use, expensive to maintain, and almost impossible to understand. Operating one required a delicate touch and great patience. The recording needle had to be placed onto the cylinder at just the right angle and constant adjustment was required to keep it there. The battery-driven electric motors were unreliable and could not provide a steady turning motion. The surges and drops in power of the motor changed the speed of the turning cylinder and distorted reproduction.[5] The batteries had to be kept filled with noxious chemicals and were not welcomed in offices.

Although the manufacturers of talking machines were committed to the theory of the American system of mass production, they found it very difficult in practice. The smallest mistake in assembling the diaphragm and stylus assembly meant that the machines would not work properly, and in this product every imperfection could be clearly heard, if it was heard at all. Even if the machines did work at the factory, many did not survive the bumpy ride to local franchises. Too many phonographs and graphophones refused to speak when they were taken from the packing cases. All sorts of unexpected problems confounded the manufacturers. For example, it was found that a chemical in the wax cylinder tarnished the metal recording stylus and made it stick in the groove after a few days of use.[6]

In the unlikely event that the talking machine could be coaxed to work, the poor quality of sound reproduction often discouraged the customer. One called the sound of the phonograph "a parody of the human voice"; others were less kind and compared it to noises made by animals or birds.[7] The stenographers who had to type the recorded messages complained that they could not understand them. It was soon obvious that this technological revolution in the work place was doomed.

By 1890 sales of dictating machines had completely dried up and the North American Phonograph Company was on the verge of bankruptcy. In 1891 only nineteen franchisees remained out of the original thirty-three.[8] But worse was to follow. In 1893 the United States' economy suffered a serious downturn that lasted over 5 years. The great depression of the nineteenth century began with a financial panic in 1873 and spread to every quarter of the American economy by the 1890s. Not even the industries based on new technology were immune to the fall in demand for goods and services; the electrical supply industry that had been established by Thomas Edison almost went under. Giant electrical manufacturers like General Electric and Westinghouse moved perilously close to bankruptcy. Employment declined precipitously, and with it went consumer spending. Nobody was buying talking machines. The bright future anticipated for recorded sound in 1877 had grown perilously dim by 1893.

The talking machine as entertainment

Just when it appeared that the talking machine might die out, another commercial use was found for it. The entertainment value of the phonograph had first been evident when Edison demonstrated his invention to crowds of people at his Menlo Park laboratory, for there was a great novelty in hearing anything that had been recorded. Soon Edison began to market a portable outfit for use by "travelling phonograph exhibitors." This consisted of a phonograph with hearing tubes for up to fifteen customers and a collection of fifty pre-recorded cylinders containing vocal, instrumental, and miscellaneous entertainment. At this point records were sold by volume and not by subject. The customer bought a dozen mixed records instead of choosing the songs he or she preferred.

An automatic, coin-operated machine was devised for exhibitors in 1889. Dropping a nickel in the slot brought the listener one play of the cylinder record (there was no choice of recordings) and satisfied the desire to hear music. Despite the depression people still wanted to be entertained, and these machines met this need for only a nickel. The poor sound reproduction did not seem to affect the enjoyment

Figure 2.2. Listening through eartubes to the wonderful talking machine. (ENHS)

of recorded sound by the public listener, who (unlike the stenographer and typist) did not have to strain to hear every word.

This entertainment proved so popular that thousands of coin-slot phonographs were manufactured. They were grouped together in arcades in hotels, railway stations, shop fronts, and other public places. This was an extremely profitable venture; the small businessman had to tend his machine only once a day to change the record and collect his nickels. One machine was installed at the Palais Royal Saloon on Pine Street, San Francisco, in November 1889. By March 1890 it had earned over $1,000.[9]

Penny arcades brought automated entertainment to the public. After Edison successfully developed motion pictures at his West Orange laboratory in the early 1890s, they were soon on display in peephole viewers, called *kinetoscopes*. Coin-slot phonographs and kinetoscopes were installed side by side in amusement arcades, bringing to the pub-

lic the wonders of sight and sound that could be miraculously reproduced at will.

The nickel-in-the-slot phonograph kept the industry alive in the
dark days following the disastrous end of the dictating-machine venture in 1891. It provided more than income for the companies that
manufactured them; the experience of operating the coin-slot phonograph provided an important lesson in marketing recorded sound
that was to shape the future of the business.

The first amusement phonographs (as they were called) were sold
to the public to record and replay, for the object was to save the
music enjoyed in the sitting rooms of the upper classes; it was not a
music maker itself but a complement to the piano and violin. The
original intention of Edison, Tainter, and Berliner was to make the
hardware and leave recording to the customer. The unexpected popularity of the coin-slot players changed this strategy, for suddenly
there was a strong demand for pre-recorded cylinders.

Thomas Edison was one of the first to realize that the record business could be the most profitable part of the industry of recorded
sound. He found that there was money to be made in supplying pre-
recorded cylinders. In the slow year of 1891, for example, the New
York Phonograph Company spent $15,000 on "original" masters. In
1890 Edison told the North American Company that "what I want
is the manufacture of duplicates," revealing that he had grasped the
basic principle of the talking-machine business: more money could be
made by selling many records rather than the one machine that played
them.[10]

He initiated an experimental project to find a way to mass-produce
pre-recorded cylinders. There were several mechanical methods available that could transfer a cut from one cylinder to another, but this
approach was expensive and time-consuming and, worst of all, produced inferior-sounding copies. There had to be a better way, and
Edison set out to find it.

He conceived of a duplicating system in which one master recording
was used to mold many copies. The wax he was using for his cylinders
was soft enough to take an impression from a harder (and warmer)
material. The problem was to make the master harder and warmer
without defacing the minute grooves on its surface. His idea was to
produce a metal negative of the master cylinder by electroplating a
layer of metal onto the wax. This created a negative (or matrix) of

the original, which could be used to mold exact duplicates. After years of experiments he found that a vacuum deposit technique could plate a thin layer of gold on the white wax master. This microscopic layer was built up by electroplating copper or nickel on it to form a metallic matrix, a process that took several days and the utmost care. After the original cylinder was removed, the matrix was cleaned with benzene and dipped into hot wax to make an exact copy of the original master recording. Cooling the metal mold enabled the cylindrical wax duplicate to shrink and be removed from the inside of the matrix.

Many problems had to be overcome before these experiments yielded a commercial process. The heating and cooling of the wax master during the process caused expansion and shrinkage of the wax surface, which deformed the grooves and caused sound distortions. As most of the duplicating process could not be seen, the experimenters had to guess the amount of contraction and then make allowances for it during the plating and molding steps.[11] Removing the duplicate from the inside of the matrix was difficult and often caused damage to the grooves. For 10 years Edison's laboratory teams faced failure and frustration in this project, but he pushed them on knowing how important this project was to the future of his phonograph. It was not enough to find a method that worked; it had to be a cheap and reliable process which could produce millions of inexpensive copies of pre-recorded cylinders.

The wax composition of the cylinder was the critical element in these experiments; it had to be soft enough to capture the minute undulations of the sound signal, yet hard enough to survive the rigors of duplication and retain all the characteristics of the wave form in the groove. These were demanding criteria.

The inventors experimented on a wide range of waxes as a medium for recording. Many used basic beeswax as the main ingredient of their first wax cylinders, but this proved to be too soft and tended to clog up the grooves. Bell and Tainter used ozocerite wax on their cardboard cylinders. Edison started with a soft white soapy wax and then tried combinations of stearic acids (as contained in beef tallow), beeswax, and ceresin wax in his cylinder compound. He finally settled on a brown wax mixture of stearic acid and ceresin, but this also suffered from being too soft. Berliner's first discs were made of hard vulcanized rubber. He then moved to wax compounds, experimented with celluloid, and finally settled on shellac (a hard natural resin) as the material for his discs. All sorts of waxes could be found in the laboratories of the inventors: mineral waxes such as ozocerite and ceresin, montan wax extracted from lignite and also used in polishes, carnauba waxes, and spermaceti wax taken from whales.[12] The specific ingredients of the wax compound used to make up cylinders and discs were jealously guarded by each inventor.

At roughly the same time that Edison had started his experiments on duplicating, Emile Berliner also had realized that the key to making the gramophone a musical entertainer was to find a way of duplicating recordings. In a speech made in 1888, he predicted that sometime in the future all talking machines would be able to play standardized pre-recorded discs. Bearing in mind the complete chaos of technical standards of the industry at the time, this was an amazing prophecy. Berliner envisaged a process in which millions of duplicates could be made from a master recording. He also anticipated huge sales of popular recordings and expected that prominent artists would make a steady income from record sales.[13] In one remarkable speech he had accurately predicted the future of the record business. Yet this was a future based on the successful conclusion of the duplication experiments.

As he had often done in the past, Berliner embarked on a series of experiments that paralleled the work of Edison. He decided to use a metal master disc to create perfect duplicates. Rather than electroplate a wax original as Edison had done, Berliner recorded directly onto a zinc plate covered with fatty film and then applied acid to etch the groove marked in the film. These discs could be played as they were or electroplated in copper to make matrices. Then Berliner stamped the metal matrix onto a blank disc of wax or hard rubber. He perfected the process in 1893 and was soon selling 7-inch discs with his name marked on them. The disc came in a paper sleeve which had the song's lyrics printed on it in case the listener could not make out all the words. The customer could choose from a list of about fifty selections. Unfortunately the sound quality of his duplicates was not very good, and sales were low.

In the race to find a method to mass-produce duplicates of recordings, the disc experimenters were at a decided disadvantage, because their duplicates did not sound as clear and distinct as an Edison cylinder. The acid used to etch the groove in the disc masters eradicated some of the sound waves, causing indistinct or "muddy" reproduction. Disc records also suffered from a hissing surface noise, which was made by the steel stylus rubbing along the groove in the wax.

In 1896 Berliner's Gramophone Company made a contract with a machinist to manufacture a spring motor for the gramophone. This innocuous business deal was to have a profound effect on the talking-machine industry. Eldridge Johnson had a small machine shop in Camden, New Jersey, making wire stitching machines. Like Edison in the 1870s, Johnson ran his shop to make a living and support his experiments. His inventions were made up in the shop, and he had already obtained several patents before the Gramophone Company contacted him. After several unsuccessful attempts, Johnson finally produced a quiet, well-regulated spring motor based on the design of another Camden mechanic, Levi Montross.[14] This success brought him closer to Berliner's company and encouraged him to improve the sound reproduction of the gramophone. Soon he was manufacturing complete machines for the Gramophone Company based on his improvements of Berliner's original design.

Eldridge Johnson was enough of a businessman to recognize that the gramophone did not have a commercial future due to inferior sound reproduction. He therefore concentrated his experiments on recording and the duplication process. He replaced the zinc disc covered with fatty film used by Berliner with a solid wax disc. He did not spend years in the laboratory perfecting the wax compound as Edison's experimenters had done; instead he simply melted down several Edison cylinders to get his wax. After making sure that the surface of the master disc was perfectly flat, Johnson began to record on it.

Once an acceptable master recording had been made, Johnson faced the problem of making a matrix from the wax master – the same problem that Edison had confronted earlier. After more than 2 years of experiments, Johnson came up with much the same solution. His masters were first covered with a fine layer of metal dust, and then more metal was electroplated onto the primary layer to make the negative matrix. The matrix was then used to stamp the duplicate onto soft wax blanks.

The resulting duplicates had none of the surface noise that spoiled the Berliner discs and had a much louder reproduction than an Edison cylinder. The disc format could now challenge the cylinder on its own terms. Johnson had managed to transfer the technique that Edison had perfected for the cylinder to Berliner's disc. He borrowed from Edison's prior experiments and used Edison equipment in his recording. The proximity of Johnson's shop in Camden to the Edison laboratory in West Orange probably played a part in the diffusion of this technology.

In 1899, when Johnson had achieved his first success in his duplication process, the experimental team at West Orange had finally produced acceptable duplicates of pre-recorded cylinders from their matrices. They used the matrix to make up a sub-master from which many copies of the original were molded. They faced the difficult task of turning this experimental process into commercial practice and producing duplicates that met the standards of reproduction demanded by the "old man," for Edison was insistent that his records should sound just like the original performance – a totally unreasonable expectation at that time.

By 1900 both Johnson and Edison were finally ready to start commercial mass production of duplicates. While the transfer of a laboratory process to a commercial plant had caused years of delays for Edison, Johnson found it easy to set up the equipment to duplicate thousands of discs a day. The advantage of using the disc format was that stamping out duplicates was was much easier than forming them in cylindrical molds. Johnson designed all the machines used in the duplication process, and by 1902 he had established a record plant at Camden.

Edison was only 1 year behind him in introducing his "New High Speed Hard Wax" molded records duplicated from electroplated masters. These cylinders were made with a harder wax than the original white and brown compounds and could hold a deeper cut. He devised special machines to plate masters in bulk and set up a large duplicating plant at the West Orange factory.

Eldridge Johnson's conclusion that his duplicating process was "an invention that was to revolutionize the talking machine industry" was not much of an exaggeration, for cheap pre-recorded records were the prerequisite for mass marketing of recorded sound.[15] Although it was certainly not easy to build a record player, it was much harder to make exact copies of recordings. The duplicating process was a key innovation, and, as Johnson's statement indicates, all emphasis in the industry of recorded sound was on the technology. If unsuitable equipment had doomed the dictating machine, then successful innovation had saved the amusement phonograph.

The commercial value of this innovation was soon evident. As records became more plentiful, prices tumbled from $1 or $2 each to 75¢ and 50¢ as millions of them flooded the market. Once the customer had purchased a player, he or she soon began to build up a library of recordings. Edison was not disappointed in his expectations for profit from this business; the molded cylinder records that sold for 50¢ cost only 7¢ to make.[16]

The talking-machine business had finally taken off. The perfection of the duplication process coincided with the introduction of spring-motor–powered players, which were lighter, cheaper, and easier to operate. The central problem of the power source to turn cylinder or disc had been solved. Spring motors were now available which could be regulated to provide an even turning motion to the end of the record. The "first-class, plain, practical" machine that Edison had been seeking for years was powered by a spring motor.[17] They were soon being mass-produced in the thousands.

In the first years of the new century, there was a boom in sales of spring-motor machines and records. The companies could hardly make records and players fast enough to meet demand. In the 1899 sales year, Edison sold over $750,000 worth of phonograph merchandise, and the following year sales exceeded $1 million. By 1900 about 32,000 examples of the basic Johnson/Berliner spring-driven gramophone had been sold in the United States. Johnson formed the Victor Talking Machine Company in 1901 on his patents and those of Berliner. Victor's annual sales rose from 7,570 machines in 1901 to 94,557 in 1910. From 1901 to 1910 over 600,000 machines were made in Johnson's Camden works, and in 1911 alone 124,000 were sold.[18]

In 1897 only about 500,000 records had been sold in the United States. By 1899 this number had reached 2.8 million and was rising steadily. Factories that once produced less than a hundred units a day were now producing thousands as improved record presses were introduced in the first decade of the twentieth century.

The Big Three

The new prosperity of the industry of recorded sound brought important changes to its business organizations. Edison had made the most of the death of Lippincott and the demise of the North American Phonograph Company to extricate himself from his contractual obligations to Lippincott's franchisees. He established his own National Phonograph Company in 1896. The formation of the Victor Company was precipitated by the knowledge that the record-duplicating process was a success and the future was assured for the disc format.

The other leading company was Columbia of Washington, D.C., the only survivor of Lippincott's empire. Under the direction of Edward Easton, a congressional stenographer who had seen the potential of Bell and Tainter's graphophone as early as 1887, Columbia acquired the rights to manufacture graphophones (absorbing the old American Graphophone Company) and quickly introduced a spring-motor model to compete with the Edison and Johnson versions. While Edison and Johnson stayed committed to one format for their talking machines, Easton was a pragmatic businessman who positioned his company to manufacture in both cylinder and disc formats.

The Edison, Victor, and Columbia companies were known as *the Big Three*. They dominated the market with their strong patent position and extensive manufacturing plant. After many years of hard lessons and repeated failure, they had finally applied the American system of manufacture with interchangeable parts to the talking machine.

Each of the Big Three manufactured a line of models, ranging from the tiny record player that sold for around $10 to the elaborate cabinet models made to look like antique furniture, which cost $400 or $500. Their engineering departments finalized the basic design of each machine and made measured drawings of each part. They designed special machine tools to make each of these parts to the standard. Some tools had only one function, such as the drill press, which made the holes in the top plate. Engineers worked out the steps of production, and the workers assembled the parts together in a carefully arranged sequence.

The workers were trained in the operation of the machine tools and drilled in the steps of manufacture. The Italian, Greek, and Irish immigrants who toiled in Edison's West Orange factories or Johnson's Camden plant provided the inexpensive labor that was a vital element in mass production. Many of the problems in the early days of the Edison Phonograph Works were the result of inadequate training of unskilled workers.[19] It took time to turn them into an efficient and disciplined work force.

The great factories were organized into separate departments, each under the control of a hard driving foreman. The delicate diaphragm and reproducer assemblies were carefully constructed and tested in one department. Another department produced the wooden case for the machine, and another was responsible for the assembly of spring motors. Metal-working shops constructed the amplifying horns, which were attached to the diaphragm or soundbox. The metal top plate, which supported the revolving cylinder or disc and the reproducer assembly, was cast in one area of the factory, drilled and machined in another, and combined with all the other parts in the final-assembly shed. Rigid inspection was enforced at all stages of production to ensure that parts met the standard. The top works underwent two tests before being fitted into the cabinet, and a final test was carried out before the machine was crated and shipped.

The production of records for these machines took place in another industrial complex. The chemicals were made in bulk in huge heated vats. Company chemists monitored the mixing of ingredients and created new methods of quality control to ensure that the wax mixture corresponded to the secret formula.

Initial production of molded cylinders from matrices was done by hand. Young boys poured hot wax into molds which were fixed onto a large circular frame. As the frame revolved and the cylinders cooled, other boys took them out. Soon this process was automated. The molds were heated, and the exact amount of hot wax was poured into them; then the mold was spun rapidly to coat its inside with wax. The molds were carried on conveyor belts to a cooling bath to shrink the wax duplicates, and a press pushed them out of the mold. Each machine could produce thousands of molded cylinders a day.[20]

By the first decade of the twentieth century, the Edison Phonograph Works established in 1888 had been enlarged and many new concrete buildings added to it. The two great assembly halls were full of moving parts and busy workers who tended hundreds of custom-built, semi-automatic machines. The operator only had to put in the piece of metal, start the machine, and then pull out the part. Separate buildings contained the chemical plants to make wax compounds and the lines of record presses. The complex had its own railroad system and generated its own electricity, heat, and steam. At the height of production, it employed over 10,000 men.[21]

Much the same thing went on in Johnson's factories in Camden, New Jersey, and in the old Graphophone factory at Bridgeport, Connecticut. As production increased, Eldridge Johnson's small shop was slowly engulfed by the many factory buildings erected to make machines and discs, as he followed the same strategy of expansion pursued in northern New Jersey by Edison. The one-story brick building in Camden, the original Johnson machine shop, was soon dwarfed by a cement, steel, and glass complex of manufacturing plant and administrative offices, presenting a scene remarkably similar to the one at West Orange.

A tour of the Camden plant began at the cabinet factory, where 5,000 men constructed elaborate wooden cases for the talking machine. Each floor of this six-story building was devoted to one stage of production: gluing the frame together and fixing veneer to the wood base, carving the ornamentation of the cabinet, sanding, staining, and painting. In a small corner on the sixth floor, a group of skilled craftsmen gilded the ornamental detail on the most expensive models. The sawdust waste from this factory often amounted to fifteen tons a day.

In another factory building, the metal parts of the machine were cast, cut, and shaped. Separate departments produced the hinges and screws required in assembly. As an experienced machinist, Eldridge Johnson took special interest in the machine tools which produced the parts. Everywhere in the factory were special machines to do just one job: an immense stamping machine made the turntable out of a sheet of steel, another press forced the center spindle into it, and yet another machine plated it with nickel before it went to a workbench where a young woman cut out the green felt cover and glued it to the turntable. The winding crank that projected from the side of the disc player and turned the spring motor inside was made automatically. All the operator had to do was to ensure a steady supply of metal to the press and stand back.

The shop that produced the soundboxes was staffed with young women, for it was believed that they were more adept at handling the delicate mechanisms. In 1917 this assembly line was described as coming "straight out of the Ford Motor Company," for each girl on the line had only a single operation to perform before the assembly moved on to the next station.[22] Their work, and all the other work done in the plant, was subjected to the constant scrutiny of tests and inspection. One lesson that had been learned early on was that quality control was absolutely essential in manufacturing talking machines.

The Big Three were not the only companies manufacturing talking machines; there were numerous smaller concerns which competed at the low end of the market for cheaper machines and records. Their products usually looked like those of the Big Three and had familiar names – Ediphone, Vitaphone, Talkophone, Zonophone, and Keenophone – but a much smaller organization stood behind them. Most of them manufactured machines based on the new spring motors. The Chicago Talking Machine Company, for example, introduced spring-motor models based on the patents of Edward Amet. Its Echophone sold at around $10.

For every large company with a well-established patent position, there was a smaller company which copied the patented designs of others. A member of the Berliner organization, Frank Seaman, broke away from the parent company and introduced his Zonophone machine, which was a copy of the Berliner gramophone. Although litigation abounded in the phonograph business, it could not stem the deluge of talking machines nor eliminate the competition.

The Big Three dominated the industry not only because they were large enough to manufacture efficiently and support research laboratories, but also because they marketed on a large scale. They were typical of the larger business organizations of the late nineteenth century which reached beyond local markets to operate nationwide. With the aid of the railroad and improved communications, they could manage a national marketing network to distribute the output of their great factories. Without mass marketing, there was no point in mass production.

Selling an entirely new kind of consumer item, one more complex than any offered to the American public up to that time, was no easy task. The phonograph had been invented to meet a specific need in the communications industry, where technological change was a way of life and the skills to operate delicate machinery already existed. Diverting it into the home opened up a vast new market, but it also raised a whole series of marketing challenges. The first was to convince prospective customers that the talking machine could indeed talk. Then came the job of persuading them that pre-recorded music was a desirable addition to their home life.

There was certainly no lack of potential customers in the United States at the turn of the century; the population almost doubled between 1880 and 1910. Much of this increase in numbers came from

America's cities, which were growing at a furious rate. Between 1880 and 1900 the urban population of the United States moved from 28 percent to 40 percent of the total.[23] Immigrants were entering the country at a rate of around 1 million a year, and many Americans were leaving the farm for the promise of urban life. The densely packed population of the cities provided an ideal market for the phonograph and gramophone.

Americans were also enjoying more leisure time as the agricultural society evolved into an industrial economy and less time was spent working. The workday of the industrial labor force was slowly reduced, freeing up time for pleasurable diversions. Instead of being self-sufficient, the American family now purchased the things they needed, and the great department stores in the cities, the "palaces of consumption," were established to tempt them with a host of new consumer products.

The boom in sales of talking machines corresponded with a return to prosperity in the United States. With the worst of the great depression over by 1897, many Americans now had the money to purchase one, and manufacturers had a model to suit every pocket. As Edison claimed: "There is no family so poor that it cannot buy a talking machine."[24] Perhaps this was not quite the truth, but Edison and his competitors had successfully lowered their prices and brought what was once a luxury good within reach of the working classes.

The Big Three used a system of jobbers (wholesalers) and retail dealers to market their output. In the early days of the phonograph, travelling merchants had sold talking machines from the back of carts. Hardware and furniture stores often added a phonograph to their inventory of goods, where it sat next to a sewing machine or music box. In the 1890s Edison claimed that his phonograph provided the best opportunity for a small businessman, because a small down payment to the jobber and a shop front was all that was required to deal in this exciting new product.

Each of the Big Three maintained a chain of exclusive dealers who were forced to toe the company line on prices and standards of repair. The companies fought retailers and department stores who attempted to discount prices. Although the Victor disc and Edison cylinder models could often be found side by side in stores, the Big Three discouraged retailers from selling the products of the competition, and

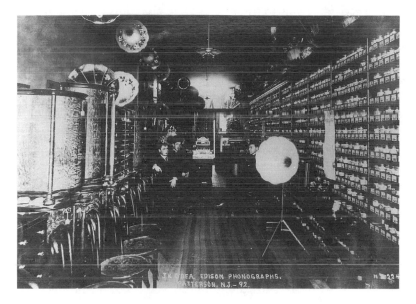

Figure 2.3. A shop selling Edison phonographs and records in 1892.
(ENHS)

the lack of standardization made it impractical for a store to carry
goods from different companies.

The difficulties of operating a talking machine ensured that the licensed dealer would be the major retail outlet. One could buy a cheap
model from the Sears Roebuck catalogue or from the local hardware
store, but if it did not sound right there was the problem of finding
someone to repair it. The technical problems of marketing the dictating machine in the 1880s had not been forgotten; consequently
entertainment phonographs were to be sold from dealerships who had
technical expertise. The dealers adjusted the machines after taking
them out of the packing cases and repaired them in the likely event
of a breakdown. They also stocked a range of attachments to improve
reproduction or enable the user to play different types of records.

An important consideration which drew customers to the fran-
chised dealer was the choice of records. Only a large store could stock
the ever-increasing selection of records and provide booths for customers to listen to them before buying – in those days the only way

to hear a recording was to listen to it being played by a friend or visit the local record shop. By 1910 the average store needed a stock of 3,000 to 5,000 records to keep pace with the output of new songs and changing public taste. The large stores in big cities carried many thousands of cylinders or discs in specially constructed libraries.

The Big Three sponsored national advertising campaigns to support their retail outlets, promote their machines, and bring public attention to their new recordings. Advertising was a growing business in the first decades of the twentieth century as newspapers and cheap magazines made their way into millions of homes across the country. The talking-machine companies were early and enthusiastic users of advertising. At first they just showed the machine and explained how it worked. The wonder of recorded sound was still a novelty, and it was enough just to describe it. Edison's phonograph was portrayed as "The Miracle of the 19th Century . . . It will Talk, Sing, Laugh, . . . pronouncing every word exactly." All companies followed Edison's strategy of stressing the technical features of the product and the experimental and manufacturing resources that stood behind it, a common practice in nineteenth-century advertising.[25]

The Edison company naturally invoked the genius of the world's greatest inventor in their advertisements. All the world knew about Edison. His name or image was on every phonograph and record sold by his company, and his trademark signature became one of the best-known company logos of that time. Not many of the listening public knew about Eldridge Johnson and his inventions.

The Victor Company did not use an inventor in its advertising, nor did it continually stress the advances made in its laboratories. It preferred to show a small dog sitting next to the machine. "His Master's Voice" was the name of a painting of a dog called Nipper listening intently to a recording of his owner coming out of the horn of a gramophone. Nipper had an appealing expression, and his image was reproduced on millions of machines, records, and advertisements. The Victor Company patented the picture in 1900 and put about $40 million into promoting it until Nipper became recognized all over the world.[26] In fact there were few places where one could not see the dog listening to the gramophone. Nipper still lives today in the advertisements of RCA, which took over Victor in 1929. He has grown older (and a bit plumper) and now has a puppy to help him pitch RCA products and carry on the line. Unfortunately the point of the advertisement is now lost. "His Master's Voice" was Victor's way of persuading the public that its system of mechanical sound reproduction sounded exactly like the original.

The millions of dollars spent on advertising was a critical part of the campaign to put a talking machine in every home. Here was something every American should have, along with a Singer sewing machine or a Kodak Brownie camera. It could educate the young, entertain adults, and bring back cherished memories for the elderly. Listening to it was a great way to spend those long winter nights, and, as everybody knew, music was the way to soothe the fevered brow and create a world of imagined pleasure wherever it was heard.

The competitive edge

As "the richest contribution science has made to the entertainment and instruction of the world," recorded-sound products leaned heavily on advances in technology, both real and imagined. Each manufacturer claimed superior reproduction. The business was founded by inventors and driven forward by constant innovation. The Big Three had to maintain programs of research and development or risk losing their position as leaders of the industry. The Victor Company could claim in 1914 that it had thousands of patents in reserve, ready to deal with any technological advance of its competitors.[27] An improvement which brought an increase in sound quality or playing time was commercially significant and quickly exploited. An important innovation – such as a new material for records – brought a dramatic improvement in the fortunes of the innovator and struck fear into the hearts of technological laggards.

The introduction of celluloid records is a case in point. As one of the first types of plastic, it could be easily molded and in its final form had a hard surface which could capture more of the frequencies in the sound spectrum than softer wax records. This was especially noticeable in the low (bass) notes, which cut a deeper groove in the record. Celluloid was hard but not brittle – an important selling point for buyers still coming to terms with the fragility of records. The first cylinders made out of celluloid were rather optimistically called "indestructible."

The inventor Thomas Lambert of Chicago patented the use of celluloid as a recording material in 1900. Columbia and the Indestructible Record Company soon began to issue them with a great fanfare of publicity. Those record manufacturers who did not have access to celluloid (because it was patented) were now on the spot; they had to defend the durability of their records in the face of Columbia's campaign to make this a major issue. This war of publicity broke up a tacit agreement among the Big Three not to criticize each other's products. In the ensuing melee the merits and disadvantages of cylinder or disc and celluloid or shellac records were hotly disputed.[28]

The unbreakable record was a real threat to Edison's cylinder business, which by 1907 was already suffering from competition with the longer-playing disc. At first all cylinders and discs played for about 2 minutes, but harder waxes and narrower grooves brought longer playing times that were appreciated by the customers. Edison's laboratories had to come up with an answer or risk losing market share. The most pressing need was to increase the playing time of the cylinder to match the larger discs. In 1908 the 4-minute Amberol cylinder was introduced, and 4 years later came the Blue Amberol cylinder of celluloid laid around a plaster of Paris core. The bright blue dye was not its only distinguishing feature, for the clarity and brilliance of its reproduction still impresses listeners today.

The Amberola phonograph, which was brought out to play the new cylinders, had an enclosed horn in a wooden cabinet that bore more than a passing resemblance to the Victor Company's extraordinarily successful Victrola model. Introduced in 1906, the Victrola combined new technical features, including an enclosed horn, and an entirely new look. Instead of the rectangular box with a horn on top of it, the Victrola had all the working parts concealed. The Edison Amberola copied this design. Edison was not the first to jump on the Victrola bandwagon, because the market was swamped with imitations, such as the Columbia Company's Grafonola and the Concertola, Humanola, Gabelola, and Vitanola of lesser companies. The legal department at Camden energetically hounded the infringers, but this hindered the sale of only the most blatant copies of Victor's popular machine.

The rampant copying of technical innovation and the claims and counterclaims of technological superiority indicate that the focus of the industry was on technology. But this was not the only factor in making the talking machine a common household item. After the most troublesome bugs had been eliminated and sound reproduction improved to the point where it was recognizable, the important selling points were cultural rather than technological. The surface, duration, and sound quality of the record was certainly important, but not as important as the music recorded. This fact was made clear in the first years of the twentieth century when the quality of one voice, and the fortuitous sympathy with which the gramophone reproduced it, achieved a commercial breakthrough for the talking machine.

The laboratories of the Big Three had made such progress in sound reproduction by this time that they believed that it would soon be possible to record the more demanding sounds of symphonic music and opera – the "good music" that had previously eluded them. The attraction of "good music" and "high-class" recordings was that it brought new prestige to a product which was often considered to be little more than a toy.

A handful of recordings of the Italian tenor Enrico Caruso in 1902 marked a creative milestone in the history of recorded sound because they raised it to the realm of "good music." These recordings proved to be of such importance to the industry that their production is shrouded in myth. An employee of the gramophone company was sent to Milan, Italy, to record a series of ballads. Fred Gaisberg heard Caruso sing at the La Scala opera house and was so impressed that he decided to ask him to record. The story told by Gaisberg was that the $400 fee demanded by Caruso was so large that the headquarters of the company refused him permission to make an agreement, but Gaisberg went ahead on his own initiative, and the rest, as they say, is history. The archives of the company tell a slightly different story, for it is clear that they were ready and willing to pay large fees for good performances. Although $400 at that time was a great deal of money, the company was prepared to pay even more for a well-known singer.[29]

In 1902 Caruso was a young man with a growing reputation, but he was far from being an international star. He was one of a new generation of opera singers who were injecting more emotion and drama into their performances.[30] Caruso's voice was perfectly suited to the talking machine; it emerged from the horn with such clarity and power that it seemed to fill the room with music. Unlike sopranos and bass voices, the full range of the tenor fell within the narrow band of sound frequencies picked up by the recording horn. The warmth of Caruso's tone and the emotion of his singing were also captured on disc and faithfully recreated through the horn of the gramophone.

Caruso recorded ten songs for his $400. There was no rehearsal and little delay as he sang one song after another into the horn. The job was done in a few hours. Yet the release of these recordings on Victor Red Seal records in the United States brought immediate acclaim and a furious pace of sales. The record generated so much interest that Caruso was offered a contract to appear at the Metropolitan opera house – probably the first time a singer received an invitation to perform solely on the basis of a recording. The impact on the record business was even greater. As his son recalled later, the sale of records made a small fortune for his father (about $5 million) and a large one for Victor.[31] Red Seal records gave the humble talking machine the status of a musical instrument. It was now sold in a better class of stores along with pianos and violins and was purchased by consumers who had the money to buy more expensive models.

Caruso went on to make many more best-selling recordings, which were sold at premium prices as music lovers everywhere scrambled to obtain copies for their collections. One of Caruso's most popular recordings, "On with the Motley" from "I Pagliacci" (1907) was the first recording to sell a million copies.[32]

Once Caruso had demonstrated that recorded sound could do justice to a great singer, the stars of the concert hall followed. Adelina Patti, Nellie Melba, and many others were soon to make their own recordings. The enormous prestige of a superstar like Melba, her international reputation, and the fact that any recording made by her was an event, gave the talking machine a new respectability. It had gone from a mere novelty that amused the masses with popular songs to a musical instrument that took the finest music available and preserved it forever. It was no longer an anonymous voice that came out of the horn of the talking machine but the "Golden Voice" of Melba or Patti.

The prestige that this gave to the talking machine was immeasurable. It opened the doors to collaboration with the world's finest composers and musicians. The agreement of the composer Umberto Giordano to work with Caruso to record some of his music was called "a testimony for the gramophone such as no talking machine has received before" by an executive of the company.[33] The publicity given to these recordings was quickly translated into dollars and cents.

Victor's Red Seal records reversed the trend in the industry towards lower prices for records. When cylinders could be bought for 25¢ or less and discs went for 50¢, the $2 Red Seal or the Columbia Grand Opera were very expensive records, but the companies soon found out that the market could bear even higher prices. The demand for recordings of the well-known singers seemed to be unaffected by price; consequently more "celebrity records" were issued at prices of up to $5 per disc. These records could be recognized by the special colors of their labels. When Francesco Tamagno agreed to record for Victor in 1903, he was paid $8,000 for twelve sides. He stipulated a distinctive colored label, and this practice was followed by other stars, including Melba (mauve), Patti (cerise pink), Battistini (orange), and Clara Butt (dark blue).[34] The discerning record buyer could choose from a hierarchy of classical recordings distinguished by the color of their labels. The records that had once been sold by the dozen had become precious artifacts, the great performances of the greatest artists in the world, not just to be enjoyed but to be revered and saved so that they could be played to succeeding generations of listeners. These were not just mere renditions of songs; they were historic performances.

The first records to bear names on them reflected the importance of the inventor: Edison's picture was on the cardboard cover of his cylinders, and Berliner's name was etched on his first discs. The name of the selection and the performer was sometimes given by a recorded announcement at the beginning of the song. By 1907 the inventor had been replaced by the opera star as the selling point of the record. The record had gone from an unmarked cylinder, with a slip of paper to identify it, to an artifact of a consumer culture.

Celebrity recordings favored the large companies, for only they had the resources to sign the great singers and arrange for special recording sessions. These assets were forcefully promoted. The importance of the star performer in marketing forced record companies to enter into exclusive contracts with the leading figures in the music world. Artist exclusivity was a powerful tool in marketing, and each company wanted to claim that a great star recorded only with them, implying that other companies' records were not good enough. Frequent and bitter squabbles broke out between them over claims of artist exclusivity.

Great singers were vital to the marketing strategies of the Big Three and were therefore in a position to negotiate lucrative contracts. Caruso was the first to get a royalty for each record sold. He also received a yearly payment of $2,000 to ensure that he would record only for Victor and the British gramophone companies. He was the first of the stars groomed by the record companies.

Looking back from the perspective of the 1990s, when celebrity is an essential part of entertainment, it seems inevitable that the star system would emerge in the record business as it did in motion pictures. Yet the pioneers of recorded sound saw it differently. Edison, for one, thought the emphasis should be on the quality of the recording rather than the reputation of the singer, maintaining that the public would prefer faithful reproduction to "a rotten scratchy record by a great singer."[35] He even resisted putting the performer's name on the recording. As an inventor he wanted all the attention to be on the machine and its performance, and as a businessman he was reluctant to pay the fees demanded by celebrities. Edison would have preferred to sell anonymous records by the dozen, but Victor and its prestigious red labels ruined this plan. The great names sold records, and records helped the careers of the great names. After 1902 the interests of Caruso and Victor were inseparable, and when Victor claimed that their record of Caruso was actually Caruso, "as truly Caruso as Caruso himself," they revealed the union of company and performer as well as performance and recording.

In the twentieth century the focus of the advertising message shifted from emphasizing the technology of the talking machine to the music it could play and the art of the performance. Mechanical reproduction of music at an affordable price was offered as a replacement for a piano and years of practice.[36] And mechanical reproduction brought music of the highest quality. Nobody could play the piano like the great performer and composer Serge Rachmaninoff, as the Victor Company pointed out, and now you could experience this music at home. "Wouldn't you like to have these Metropolitan stars as your Christmas guests?" asked the Edison company as it depicted a group of well-known singers standing next to a phonograph. Victor relentlessly promoted its Red Seal recordings as a magical alternative to attending a concert – "No need to wait for hours in the rain." Rec-

Figure 2.4. Victor claims that its Caruso record brings "not only his art, but his personality." (Courtesy of General Electric)

ords provided the means of bringing the finest music ever made into the home, as part of a permanent library of recorded sound.

Victor's brilliant success in recording and promoting "good music" was followed by all the major talking-machine companies. Recorded sound could be depicted as "the most refining influence" on modern life. It conferred "social charm" in addition to providing relaxing diversions from the stress of everyday life. Music in the home was presented to the American public as a needed antidote to the pressures of the twentieth century: an automatic relief after a hard day at the office or factory. Edison was not alone when he claimed (in his phonograph advertisements) that "music is a necessity in your home, not a luxury."[37]

3. The international industry of recorded sound

The period from 1900 to 1920 marked the high point in the fortunes of the talking machine. With a small interruption caused by the depression of 1907, each succeeding year of the twentieth century brought higher sales. A record player stood proudly in the sitting rooms of millions of Americans, and there was little to challenge its position as the leading form of home entertainment. Where once only the upper classes could enjoy fine music, usually in the form of a piano, now everybody could afford it. The phonograph had ushered in the age of mechanical entertainment in America, and it was to prepare the ground for many other high-tech entertainers in the future.

The Big Three had succeeded in the daunting task of mass-producing complex machines and pressing millions of exact duplicates of recordings. They had built massive industrial plants. Their interests ranged from stockpiles of chemicals used in their records to contracts with well-known musicians and singers. They had recorded some of the world's greatest musical figures and made a permanent record of their art.

Each of the Big Three did millions of dollars of business each year. In 1914 the U.S. census found that there were eighteen manufacturing establishments in the industry with a total value of output that exceeded $27 million. Of this total $4 million was accounted for by Edison and $16 million by Victor.[1]

Edison, Victor, and Columbia held almost every important patent for talking machines and records. The legal battles among them slowly grew less violent and disruptive in the second decade of the twentieth century, although Victor did its best to prosecute those who had infringed on its Victrola patents. The entry of Edison into the disc market in 1913 did not bring the legal battle that his lawyers had feared: the Edison Diamond Disc player was not too blatant a copy of the Victrola, and it did not threaten Victor's sales.[2]

Figure 3.1. Pressing disc records in the Edison plant around 1914. (ENHS)

The large companies lived in an atmosphere of friendly rivalry that came far short of the all-out trade war which had erupted at the turn of the century. They discussed forming a cartel to fix prices and adjudicate patent disputes but failed to bring it into being. Despite the efforts of several smaller companies and the large discount stores like Wanamaker's, the Big Three managed to maintain their prices. Profits were high enough to tolerate the numerous small competitors who made inferior machines and nondescript records.

The Big Three perfectly represented the "Age of Big Business" in America. All were committed to high-volume, low-cost production, and all managed a national network of dealers. They were all vertically integrated operations, like many of the large industrial concerns at that time. Businessmen such as Andrew Carnegie, John D. Rockefeller, and Henry Ford had assembled vast enterprises in which they controlled every aspect of manufacture from the provision of raw materials to the marketing of the final product. The advantages of this strategy were the elimination of the middleman and complete control over production. The large talking-machine companies also followed this strategy, supervising the process from recording studio to record store.

Edison, Easton, and Johnson were no different from Carnegie or Rockefeller, but the challenges confronting them were more complex than those facing makers of steel or refiners of petroleum. In the talking-machine business, the raw materials were not only metal and chemicals but also the musical talents of those who sang into the recording horns. Each of the Big Three operated recording studios and maintained long-term contractual relationships with performers. As the first large-scale entertainment business, they had to be closely connected to the world of music. They had to keep abreast of technological advance and the changing tastes of the audience for music: two disparate and volatile factors in the economic equation.

The technology and the music were part of an international movement of people and ideas. The technology had emerged from the intercourse between the United States and other developed industrial nations in Western Europe. Both Bell and Berliner, for example, were immigrants to the United States, as were several other important inventors. They brought with them their machines and tools and, most importantly, their ideas. The mature industry of recorded sound continued to draw upon this international dialogue of technology.

While the technology of sound recording was formed in the United States and then diffused to Europe, musical styles and performers moved in the opposite direction. Europe was the center of the world of music: Milan, London, and Paris were the undisputed leaders of fashion and culture, both high and low. The great opera houses, leading concert halls, and trend-setting vaudeville acts were all to be found in Europe.

For these reasons the talking-machine companies had to operate internationally. They were first established in the United States and then in Europe. Edison formed a phonograph company in London in 1878 right after he invented the phonograph to promote the tinfoil machine. After the new "perfected" phonograph was unveiled at the West Orange laboratory in 1888, it was immediately despatched to England in the care of Col. George Gouraud, Edison's English agent and the proprietor of the Edison Phonograph Company of the British Isles.[3] This company placed a large order for the new machines and set about marketing them in Europe. From the outset, the business relationship of England and the United States was critical in the international diffusion of recorded sound.

Emile Berliner followed Edison's practice of selling the rights of his inventions to foreign investors. He visited Germany in 1889 and arranged for some of his machines and records to be manufactured by a toy company. His gramophones were imported directly into England, but little was done to exploit the European market until 1897, when William Barry Owen was sent from the United States to organize a European company. The Gramophone Company of Great Britain began operations in 1897; it immediately began to compete for customers with the Edison Bell Consolidated Phonograph Company, the successor to the Edison Phonograph Company.[4] Berliner built a record-pressing factory in Hanover, Germany, to supply the requirements of several new European affiliates: the Deutsche Grammophon Company of Berlin, the Compagnie Francaise du Gramophone of Paris, and their Russian, Austrian, and Spanish subsidiaries.

The third member of the Big Three soon established itself in the European market. The Columbia Graphophone Company set up branches in Paris and London in 1899; these offices supervised its overseas operations. It did not play a large part in the international struggle between the phonograph and gramophone until Louis Sterling arrived from New York in 1909 to direct the company.

Although these businesses were largely financed by Europeans, the technology was imported from the United States. The first method of diffusion was the simple export of machines and records to overseas depots for resale in Europe. The presses for Berliner's large Hanover record plant came from New York, for example. The flow of technical information from the United States to Europe was vital. The improvements which emerged from Edison's or Johnson's laboratories were sent across the Atlantic and incorporated into talking machines in London or Berlin.

The process to duplicate recordings was one of the most important technologies transported to Europe. Edison and Berliner sent their skilled technicians across the Atlantic to set up equipment to electroplate masters and make matrices. Their chemists followed with the secret recipes for wax compounds. Laboratory workers and chemist's assistants often found themselves on a transatlantic steamer with a very important mission to establish a manufacturing plant in Europe.[5]

These men often stayed in the European factories for many years to train other technicians and supervise production.

The skills that these Americans took with them were craft skills, not the kind that can be learned in college but the kind that come with years of experience and a craftsman's feel for his materials. Diffusion of the technology of recorded sound could be achieved only with the movement of skilled men. Edison and his generation of inventors and entrepreneurs were highly mobile individuals who crisscrossed the Atlantic. Many left homes in Europe to seek their fortunes in America; others were adventurous Americans who thought nothing of the long sea voyage across the ocean in the pursuit of profit.

Fred Gaisberg was typical of this group. An American by birth, he began in the industry as a laboratory assistant at the age of 16 and went on to work in several company labs, including those of Volta, Columbia, and Berliner. He worked with Berliner in the early 1890s when the first commercial gramophones were constructed. After the Gramophone Company was established in London in 1897, he travelled there to establish the company's first recording studio. He was accompanied by Joseph Sanders, whose task was to build a pressing plant.[6] Gaisberg became the chief recorder and artistic scout for the company in Europe. It was in this capacity that he made his fateful trip to Milan in 1902.

The production of Caruso's historic recordings illustrate the international character of the industry. The records were made in Italy by an American in the pay of the English branch of the gramophone company. An executive of the Russian branch of the organization is said to have had the idea of specially marked celebrity records. Caruso's masters were delivered to the German company's pressing plant in Hanover, which provided duplicates for the European market on the HMV (His Master's Voice) label. They went to the United States to be duplicated at Victor's Camden plant. From this point they were marketed not only in the United States but in South America and the Far East.

Once the American companies had successfully established themselves in Europe, they began to extend their operations farther afield. Edison, Columbia, and Victor were soon operating in South America and the Pacific. The Japanese Victor Company (JVC) was formed to bring gramophones to the Far East. The British Gramophone Company looked to the Indian subcontinent as a vast new market for recorded sound. Australia was next to hear the music of imported talking machines. In 1907 the British and American gramophone companies refined their trading relationship in an ambitious agreement which divided the globe between them.

The outbreak of war in Europe in 1914 severely disrupted these international operations. Beginning with a conflict between France and England on one side and Germany and Austria–Hungary on the other, it spread across the world and finally engulfed the United States in 1917. Although the United States remained neutral when hostilities broke out in 1914, the interruptions in world trade had an immediate effect on the American economy. The Royal Navy began a blockade of Germany, which cut off the supplies of chemicals to the United States, especially phenol, which was an important ingredient in making records. In 1914 Edison's factories were the largest importer of phenols in the United States. The German answer to the British blockade was to send their submarines into the North Atlantic to sink ships heading for the British Isles or France. This discouraged transatlantic travel, and soon the flow of master recordings from all points of Europe to the pressing plants in West Orange and Camden dried up.

The coming of war had an immediate impact on record catalogues. The companies kept a respectable American neutrality by offering recordings of military music by both British and German bands. A customer could walk into a record store and purchase "Highlanders, Fix Bayonets" or "The Kaisermarch" depending on his or her allegiance. In 1915 many people were in a less warlike mood; "I Didn't Raise My Boy to Be a Soldier" was the most popular record that year.[7]

Two years later the United States was set to enter the conflict, and Americans had resigned themselves to war. Tin Pan Alley song publishers had naturally produced hundreds of patriotic songs to meet the musical requirements of a nation at war, ranging from the belligerent "We're Going to Whip the Kaiser" to the sentimental "We'll Meet Again." Recordings of "Over There" dominated the best-selling lists for 1917.

Although the companies had been claiming for years that the talking machine was an indispensable part of modern life, it took a world war to bring this fact home to their customers. With cabarets and music halls closed, and many entertainers enlisted, the public was now

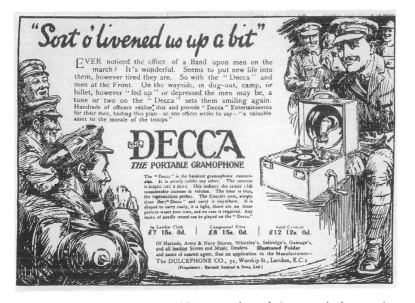

Figure 3.2. The portable gramophone brings musical entertainment to the troops at the front. (Author)

making its own music by playing the piano or by listening to the phonograph at home. The companies could now claim with some justification that "we are no longer manufacturing a specialty but a standard product of such importance in home comfort as to be a necessity."[8]

While growing ever more popular at home, the talking machine became an essential part of military life. The record companies had tried to persuade customers that music could evoke all sorts of pleasurable sensations and rekindle fond memories. The war proved that nothing could remind a soldier of home better than music. Sales of machines boomed. Every billet and army camp had one, and even in the front lines one could hear the refrain of a popular song coming from a tin horn. One visitor to the Western front reported:

> A crack in the mud plastered wall reveals a candle on a biscuit tin and two or three weirdly lit faces listening to the strains of the latest revue . . . bringing memories of happier days.[9]

Fred Gaisberg's brother William went to the front in 1918 to provide us with the one authentic sound recording of that terrible war.

His recording machine was set up near the British lines at Lille, and it captured the sounds of an artillery bombardment of gas shells on the Germans – an ironic juxtaposition of the benign and the malevolent products of twentieth-century technology.

The last thing the men in the trenches wanted to hear was the sound of guns. Both sides had their favorites, and some popular songs could be heard on both sides of No Man's Land. The war years brought the American and Western European nations closer together, for they were united in a common cause and they shared a common music. "It's a Long Way to Tipperary" was a favorite with all the troops at the front, and recordings of it were hits on both sides of the Atlantic.

Boom and bust

At war's end there was a surge of consumer spending, and sales of records and players rose encouragingly. The 1920 sales year was the best ever for the Edison organization, which sold goods amounting to $22 million. Yet Edison was not optimistic about the future and warned his executives to prepare for a harsh, competitive business environment in the coming years. His gloomy expectations were not far wrong, for after a brilliant beginning, the decade of the 1920s proved to be a nightmare for the talking-machine industry.

The basic problem was that there were too many companies competing in a market that was already showing signs of saturation. The dominance of the Big Three and the atmosphere of calm stability came to an end when many new ventures crowded into what had become a very profitable business. In 1914 there had been 18 companies in the industry of recorded sound, but by 1918 this number had increased to an astounding 166. The attraction of this business is not hard to find; the value of its products had shot up from $27 million in 1914 to $158 million in 1918, an increase of over 500 percent in 4 years.[10] The boom in sales and profits was not the only factor enticing entrepreneurs. Most of the basic patents for phonographs and gramophones had expired by 1917, which removed a serious barrier to new entrants.

The flush times attracted the attention of businessmen from all aspects of the entertainment world. Victor Emerson had been general manager of the Columbia record division for 17 years when he left to form Emerson records in 1916. The Banner Record Company was part of Plaza Music of New York, which made music rolls. Arto records was created by the Standard Music Roll Company. Several piano manufacturers created talking-machine companies: the Aeolian line of high-quality phonographs and the Vocalion record label of the well-known Aeolian Piano Company; the Gennett Record Company formed by Starr Piano of Richmond, Indiana; and the Medallion record label launched by the Baldwin Piano Company of Cincinnati.[11]

Several of the new entrants were manufacturing companies who saw phonographs as a profitable new line. The Paramount label was formed by the Wisconsin Chair Company, a furniture maker which moved from making cabinets for phonographs to making the complete machines. Once it was discovered that people would buy machines only if they could get a supply of records, the company set up a small record operation.[12] The Brunswick–Balke–Collender Company manufactured billiards and bowling equipment. It began to make talking machines in 1916 and records in 1920. Several small manufacturers who had supplied component parts of machines went into production of complete units.

The foreign market for American machines and records had provided an important outlet for excess production, but this dried up when European products were made to compete with American exports. It did not take too long until the leading European concerns began to look to the United States as a market. The Carl Lindstrom group of companies operated in Central Europe, and it owned important labels such as Odeon and Parlophone. It was represented in the United States by the OKeh Record Company, which was formed in New York in 1915 by Felix Kahn, one of Lindstrom's associates. The French Pathe Freres Company, which had established itself as a manufacturer of film equipment, began exporting its discs and players in 1914. It offered a full line of models, from $15 to $175, and a record catalogue strong in the classics.[13]

The typical new entrant was a small company whose products – machine, records, or both – were priced low. They usually depended on the recording and manufacturing facilities of other companies. Many bought masters from recording studios and paid for them to be pressed in record factories. For example, the Regal and Cameo companies had their 50¢ records pressed by a private record maker, the Scranton Button Works, and sold them through Macy's and other chain stores. Oriole's 25¢ records were pressed from masters acquired from Emerson.

The Big Three were not directly challenged by any of the new entrants, although Aeolian and Brunswick – each with a full line of machines and strong record catalogues – were considered a threat by Johnson and Edison.[14] Yet the sheer number of competitors continually forced down prices and eroded profit lines. When department and general stores added cheap records to their shelves, the trade of the Big Three's retail networks was reduced. Edison's predictions about cut-price competition turned out to be true, and by 1921 prices had slumped. The Big Three saw their sales decline precipitously: Edison went from 140,000 disc players sold in 1920 to 32,343 in 1921; Victor from 560,000 to 320,000; and Columbia went bankrupt.[15]

The normally optimistic *Talking Machine World* now had to admit that the market for machines was saturated. Over 20 years of mass-producing and marketing basically the same product – the spring-motor disc player – had put a phonograph or gramophone in every American home, but what then? The only hope for the industry was the continuing sale of records. In the period up to 1914, the focus had been on perfecting mass production and improving the technology of recorded sound, but after 1919 the emphasis was on pushing sales, especially sales of records. Companies large and small now staked their survival on a record catalogue that kept pace with the changing taste in popular music. The challenge of mass-producing complex machines had now evolved into the problem of accurately predicting the public's musical needs and recording music to suit it. The manager of Edison's Phonograph Division concluded that "the company who correctly solves these problems will dominate the trade."[16] He was absolutely right.

The small companies suffered an initial disadvantage in this struggle, because the Big Three had signed up most of the well-known classical singers and musicians and had exclusive contracts with the stars of vaudeville. It was simple necessity that pushed the independent companies into recording new types of music and exploiting new audiences for recorded sound. Although their recordings had none of the prestige of the Big Three's classical records, they did bring important new music such as blues and jazz to the American public.

In the nineteenth century, when the phonograph was still a novelty, the market for recordings was ill defined. Records were a generic product sold by quantity and not by musical type. The introduction of the high-priced celebrity record at the turn of the century created the market for "good music" and helped to focus marketing efforts onto the middle classes. But as competition in the business increased in the 1920s, companies were forced to seek customers at both ends of the social ladder.

A changing economy at the time of World War I created new audiences for recorded sound. The United States became the arsenal of democracy. Those who stayed at home enjoyed prosperity and high incomes, especially the people at the lower end of the social scale. The business strategy of "a phonograph in every home" naturally led manufacturers to exploit every segment of the market, including minorities and the working classes – even the low-paid immigrants who toiled in their factories.

In order to gain access to the minority markets in American cities, the companies began a program of recording music for narrowly defined ethnic groups – hoping that such specialized recordings would encourage these groups to purchase players and, sooner or later, regular records. "How Recognition of the Pride of Race Will Increase Record Sales" was the title of an article in *Talking Machine World*.[17]

Although every minority audience in the cities was addressed by record companies, rural dwellers had been largely ignored by them. The rise in prices of agricultural commodities during the war boosted personal incomes in the South and brought a talking machine within the budget of many more people. New industrial jobs in Southern cities and ports also made this market more attractive to the record companies, who now began to cultivate the custom of rural blacks and what they called "the cheaper white trade" in the South and West. A talking machine was a highly desirable luxury good in many of these homes. As one commentator noted, "In the delta of Mississippi it was not unusual to find a ramshackle carpetless darky shanty boasting a bright red mahogany $250 Victrola."[18]

Until World War I, African Americans were concentrated in the rural South and several Southern cities and therefore not considered to constitute much of a market by the record companies, who were all based in the Northeast. The "Great Migration" of over a million African Americans from the South changed this situation. Hundreds

Figure 3.3. A child plays with a primitive gramophone in the rural South in the 1930s. (Library of Congress)

of thousands of them moved to cities like Chicago and Detroit. At the same time the flood of European immigrants was reduced to a trickle by the war. Not only were there large concentrations of black customers in large cities but also their incomes had risen as a result of the war – the lack of white labor gave them a rare opportunity for high-paying factory work. The long lines outside record stores on Friday nights was evidence of the importance of this segment of the market.[19]

In February 1920 the recording director of the OKeh Company of New York agreed to record a young black singer called Mamie Smith. Her initial release sold well enough in Harlem music stores to bring her back to the studio to make some more masters. Her recording of "Crazy Blues" was an instant success. It sold at the unprecedented rate of about 7,500 records a week and achieved total sales in excess of 70,000.[20]

"Crazy Blues" began a musical fad in America which encompassed recordings of all sorts of female singers and all types of musical styles gathered together under the loose title of "blues," which had first been introduced as commercial music by W. C. Handy. Although the initial audience for this music was black, it soon crossed over into the white mainstream popular market, where the really high sales were. The record companies scrambled to sign up female blues artists. Records of love lost and faithless lovers poured out from their presses as fast as they could record them. The leading artists of this genre were Ma Rainey, Bessie Smith, Ida Cox, and Alberta Hunter, but there were hundreds more, and most of them are now forgotten.

The success of "Crazy Blues" even encouraged the formation of the first record company owned by African Americans – the Black Swan label formed in 1921 by Harry Pace, who was the partner of W. C. Handy in a music publishing business. Pace thought that the time was right to branch out into records, and his Black Swan discs were proudly advertised as "The Only Genuine Colored Record. Others Are Only Passing for Colored."[21]

Including those "passing for colored" were the great Victor and Columbia companies, which bolstered their sagging business with blues records. Columbia signed Bessie Smith in 1923. She began her career as a protege of Ma Rainey in a travelling group called the Rabbit Foot Minstrels. After she learned her trade in vaudeville and music halls in the South, she moved North. Her debut on record, "Downhearted Blues," sold an estimated 800,000 copies in the first 6 months of release. Her prolific output for Columbia (about 300 sides) were the most popular race recordings of the 1920s, and her total sales of around 6 million discs provided the income for Columbia to weather some severe financial crises during the 1920s.[22]

Many record companies and manufacturers of talking machines went out of business in the 1920s. Of all the new entrants of the post-war boom, only Brunswick managed to survive as an independent concern. The Aeolian Company, with its fine machines and Vocalion records, was bought out by Brunswick in 1925. Columbia took over the OKeh Company and its important holdings in blues and "jass" (as it was first known) in 1926. Those who remained in the record business had to adjust to bitter competition and the changing musical tastes of the 1920s. As the Victor recording manager had said about "jass" records back in 1917: "This dance music changes from day to day and this [jazz] might be something entirely new which we should get after at once."[23] Failure to respond quickly to new fads could result in a precipitous drop in sales.

The downfall of the Edison company proved beyond any doubt that artistic considerations now outweighed technology in the talking-machine business. It was entirely appropriate that the company founded by the great inventor should focus on the machine and not the music on the records. In 1913 Edison finally deserted the cylinder format and introduced the Edison Diamond Disc player. Announced as Edison's "greatest triumph" and his "masterpiece," it was the final culmination of years of experiments to perfect the recording of sound. The reproduction was so good, it was claimed, that it was superior to listening to live music in the imperfect acoustic environment of the opera house. The Diamond Discs themselves were marketed not as mere recordings but "re-creations" of the original sounds.

The selling point of this machine was its diamond-tipped stylus, but the real innovation was in the composition of the Edison discs, which were made of a new material based on phenol resins. It was called *condensite* and was similar to Bakelite. A hard, easily molded plastic, it provided the best recording surface to date. The first releases were plagued with an annoying surface noise, but the improved discs introduced after World War I had superior reproduction. The sound of the human voice was so well reproduced by an Edison Diamond Disc that the company sponsored a series of "tone tests" to illustrate how close a recording could come to the real thing. Although there was a great deal of showmanship involved in the "experiment," and the singers were practiced in duplicating the sound of the phono-graph, audiences did find it difficult to distinguish the sound of a machine from that of the human voice. Edison had proved his point.[24]

Although the "phonograph with a soul" marked a brilliant inno-vation, it was hampered by the limited selection of records. Edison insisted on personally approving every recording issued on a Diamond Disc. His opinionated views about music were probably more serious a handicap in this task than his partial deafness. He disliked modern dance music, and this was an enormous disadvantage in the popular music market. When his sales staff carried out customer surveys, they found that their listeners liked the sound quality of the Diamond

Discs but would not buy them because of the unappealing musical selections. This was the main reason why Edison's sales dropped throughout the 1920s.[25]

Back in the 1880s the content of the recording counted for nothing. The little experience gained in selling records indicated that the public would buy whatever they could get. By the time of World War I, the type of music recorded was an important consideration; by the 1920s it had become the main factor in the success or failure of a phonograph company.

4. The music

When the inventors grasped the commercial opportunities for pre-recorded sound, they gave little consideration to what kind of music would be recorded, unaware of the importance that it would have for their businesses. Faced with the challenge of duplicating discs or cylinders, they saw recording as another technical problem, and the limitations of acoustic recording basically determined what music could be put on record.

The wave form cut into the wax changed proportionately with the pitch of the sound during recording: high frequencies caused narrow, densely packed waves, while the low notes caused the stylus to move longer distances to create longer wave forms. Loud sounds or deep bass notes forced the stylus to the edge of the groove and sometimes beyond it, ruining the recording. Drums were therefore excluded from recording studios, and technicians always waited with nervous anticipation as singers reached for the climactic high notes. Too loud a recording made the diaphragm vibrate rapidly, causing "blasting" on the playback, which distorted the sound.

The early talking machines were unable to reproduce certain sounds, especially the sibilants or "S" sounds. The soft sounds of string instruments, such as the cello and violin, were difficult to reproduce. The stroh violin, which had a sound box and horn attached to it, was developed for acoustic recording. As bass notes were very hard for the horn to pick up, tubas were often used to provide the bass. The piano also presented difficulties. Technicians took the back off an upright piano and then lifted it up onto boxes to bring the instrument full into the horn. Pianists were instructed to play loudly, "double forte."[1] The piano sound reproduced by the phonograph was harsher and more percussive than the original. Critics of the talking machine described its thin, metallic tone as "tinny."

The first recording engineers, called *recorders*, had a limited number of choices of what to record.[2] They naturally gravitated to sounds

Figure 4.1. A recording session at the Edison studios showing stroh violins with horns attached. (ENHS)

that could be best reproduced with the technology at hand. This explains the plethora of "artistic whistling" records made in the 1880s and 1890s and the popularity of the banjo and xylophone, whose metallic sounds suited acoustic recording. The development of the phonograph as a business machine had steered recording techniques towards the sound of the voice, especially the male voice, and the phonograph did a better job of reproducing the voice than it did a musical instrument. Many of the first recordings were of speeches or recitations by famous men. This category was a fixture in recording catalogues of the nineteenth century, covering not only the great men of the age – such as William Jennings Bryan and several Presidents – but also versions of famous speeches, such as the Gettysburg Address, which were spoken by actors. Some voices sounded better on acoustic recordings than others. Given the choice, recorders chose volume over quality, because it was the strength of the voice that powered the stylus to cut the wave form into the wax.

Recording a voice with a single accompaniment was popular because of the limited sensitivity of the acoustic machine, which could pick up sounds only a few feet from the horn. Recording several instruments at once posed problems of arranging them around the horn without crowding out the softer sounds or the distant players. As the sound source moved away from the horn, there was a drop in volume, and a distance of more than a few feet produced a drastic reduction in sound. During instrumental parts of songs, vocalists moved out of the way quickly as the musicians made for the recording horn.

Short songs accompanied by a piano therefore became a staple of early recorded sound. Vocal selections were taken from well-known operatic solos, from light classical music, and from popular songs. All music played in the studio had to be specially arranged to suit the phonograph, for it was the machine which determined what could and could not be recorded. When the companies issued their first catalogues of recordings, they were organized under the type of sound reproduced: bass, baritone, and tenor solos; band and orchestra selections; and recitations.

The 1890s were the golden age of operatic singing. Stars such as Adelina Patti and Nellie Melba had international reputations and a devoted following of music lovers.[3] Yet the performers on records tended to be anonymous or little known; the great stars refused to sing into the horn of the phonograph because they knew that it could not do justice to their voices. Despite the glowing recommendations that littered the record catalogues, the first attempts to record the leading singers of the concert halls were unsatisfactory. The great range and subtle harmonics of Melba or Patti were reduced to squeaky, disembodied voices emerging from the horns of talking machines. Although unauthorized archival recordings committed these famous voices to wax, it was done for the benefit of posterity, not for art.

Shunned by opera houses and concert halls, the recorders had to look elsewhere for music. They found it on the stages of music halls and band stands. The policy of making the talking machine a fixture in every home naturally pushed them to record the entertainment of the masses rather than the culture of the elite. One recorder admitted that a few excerpts of opera sung by an Italian tenor were "our only concessions to high brow tastes." The most popular recordings of the late 1880s were novelty songs such as "Daddy Wouldn't Buy Me a Bow-Wow" and sentimental favorites like "After the Ball."[4]

In the 1890s popular music was defined by the military brass bands and vaudeville. Both were extensively recorded. The marching band of brass instruments and drums was commonplace in nineteenth-century America. During the Civil War more military music was heard because many new bands were formed. When the war was over, band music was the popular music of America. It was no longer restricted to military organizations. It could be found in streets, parks, and factory yards. It was played in concert halls, music theaters, ballrooms, and circuses. In cities such as New Orleans and Chicago, band music was an important part of everyday life, and it could be heard in schools, factories, fraternal organizations, and even in orphans' homes.

The strident sound of trumpet, tuba, and trombone was well suited to the recording horn, overcoming the lack of sensitivity of the phonograph. This made it an ideal music to record.

At the same time that the talking-machine companies were building up their record catalogues, several bands had caught the public's attention and had developed a large following by constant touring of the United States. The leading band of the 1890s was led by John Philip Sousa. This was a time of rising patriotism, and his music managed to reflect this feeling. Marches such as "The Stars and Stripes Forever" were received with enthusiasm by a large audience. It was said that Sousa "represents the energy and blatant assertiveness of America. His music is idiomatic of his race."[5] John Philip Sousa and his band was a fixture in the recording catalogues of all the early companies, despite his well-known aversion to what he called the "canned music" of the phonograph. His records were among the first to achieve large sales, a result of their adequate reproduction on the phonograph and a well-established audience for the music.

It is unlikely that the listener heard all of Sousa's band on early recordings because of the difficulty of picking up the sound of sixty musicians arranged around a recording horn. Although the companies advertised orchestral music on their records, it was a limited version. The various "orchestras" recorded in the 1890s were small affairs concentrated around brass and woodwind instruments, such as Edward Issler's Orchestra, which was a staple of the North American Company's cylinders in the 1880s and 1890s. The glorious sounds of the great symphony orchestras were not to be found on records.

On the other hand, the comic songs and sentimental ballads of the music hall were much easier to record and also appealed to a wider audience. The introduction of the talking machine occurred at a time when vaudeville dominated popular entertainment. From the large theaters in the cities to the smaller and more humble halls in provincial towns, the vaudeville or variety show was a great attraction. In the 1890s there were about 1,000 large music halls in the major cities of the United States and approximately 4,000 smaller ones. Many were organized under one management, such as the Keith and Albee empire of 400 halls.[6] The bill usually consisted of eight to ten separate acts that covered song, dance, comedy, revues, juggling, acrobats, and anything else the promotor thought would entertain his audience.

Vaudeville's mix of humor and song was well suited to the cylinder and disc: it did not tax the primitive state of phonograph technology, and it could be formed into short and easily recognized pieces of entertainment. The major limitation of the first talking machines was the very short playing time of 2 or 3 minutes. Whatever was recorded had to fit within this rigid and unalterable time limit, which was determined by the size of the cylinder and the number of grooves that could be cut into it.

The shorter duration of entertainment was the first noticeable impact of new technology on American culture. An important difference between a live performance and one provided by machine was that the latter was much shorter. The phonograph, motion picture, and player piano all delivered entertainment which had to be squeezed into short time periods. Because the playback was so brief, it had to be instantly recognized by the listener; thus record companies chose familiar entertainment. Faced with the novelty of the machine, listeners were reassured by music that they already knew. For technical as well as commercial reasons, the phonograph reflected broad public tastes.

Popular vaudeville entertainers such as Harry Lauder were able to make the transition from public performance to recording studio with ease. They were accustomed to projecting their voices in the music hall, so they approached the recording horn with more confidence and power in their voices than other singers. The comic routines and ballads of Lauder, including the popular "I Love a Lassie," were well known to many people in Europe and America. The music-hall audience knew these songs well enough to be expected to join in the

Figure 4.2. Harry Lauder recording for the Gramophone Company and obviously enjoying himself. (Courtesy of EMI Music Archives)

chorus. The phonograph offered them the opportunity to repeat the experience in their own homes by singing along with the record.

The comedy of the music hall was translated into humorous monologues, comic songs, and sketches. Ethnic humor was immensely popular with the multi-ethnic population of American cities. The adventures of Flanagan, Casey, and Cohan appealed to an audience that was very much aware of the divisions of nationality but not easily offended by ethnic or racial slurs. A cursory examination of the first record catalogues reveals that the most popular of all humorous material in the record catalogues were called *coon* songs, in which white vaudeville artists portrayed black stereotypes in comic monologues and songs.

The popularity of coon songs in the 1890s and early 1900s was the continuance of a vein in American entertainment that went back to the days of slavery. The minstrel shows, which began in the 1840s and became a popular national entertainment after the Civil War, mixed song and dance with comedy. Although minstrelsy as popular

Figure 4.3. An advertisement for *coon* songs, showing the typical minstrel-show performer. (ENHS)

entertainment peaked in the late 1890s, its songs and humor continued to be popular. Its music was now grouped under the title "Coon Songs" in record catalogues, and by 1900 most record companies maintained a separate line of "Negro" or "coon" selections that ran the gamut of comic monologues, including whistling and clogging records. The great number of coon songs in catalogues led the companies to subdivide this genre into "Negro" songs, Negro love songs and lullabies, "pickaninny" songs, "old man Negro" songs ("interspersed with pathetic sayings," as one catalogue described it), and Negro songs and dances.

Coon songs were a fixture in recording catalogues because they were already well known to the audience; they did not tax the technology of acoustic phonographs, and most of all, they were cheap to record – the first "coon" performer on the Edison cylinders doubled as a clerk.[7] One of the first best-selling cylinders was "The Laughing Song," recorded by the ex-slave George W. Johnson in 1891. The first African American to make records, Johnson was found panhandling in the streets of Washington. He recorded his distinctive laugh for a pittance and did it about 40,000 times before mass duplication of master recordings was introduced.[8]

Recorded sound and the American melting pot

"Coons" were by no means the only stereotypes diffused by recordings; there were also hackneyed depictions of Irish immigrants and country folk. There were songs about nagging wives and hen-pecked husbands – one record was described as "a graphic exposition to what matrimony can bring a man" – and suggestive songs about less than virtuous women. "Feed the Kitty," a Columbia record released around 1909, was about a married man who talks in his sleep about a certain kitty, "the same kitty helps defray her expenses in a fashionable hotel."

Nostalgia for a time gone by was a major theme of the music of vaudeville and phonograph, "the dear old songs of heart and home" as one recording catalogue put it. Sentimental ballads had proved to be a successful product of this popular culture of stage, record, and sheet music. Songs such as "After the Ball" and "Down on the Wabash" had demonstrated mass appeal before the introduction of the phonograph.

In the late nineteenth century, a musical hit was measured by its acclaim on the stage and the number of sheets of music sold. A thriving industry, centered on the mythical "Tin Pan Alley" in New York, produced the music used in all forms of entertainment. Tin Pan Alley was the home of the song writer and music plugger, and the noise of hundreds of songs being demonstrated at the same time was probably responsible for the name.[9] Its product was the sheet music used in music halls and kept on the family piano. In the same way that new technology brought down the price of cylinders and discs, improved printing methods helped lower the price of sheet music from several dollars to 25¢ per song. The manufacturers of pianos had mastered the same techniques of the American system of mass production that put a phonograph in every home. Hundreds of thousands of instruments were sold every year, and each piano supported the regular purchase of music. When recorded sound first began to make an impact on entertainment, sheet music already had a mass market.

Paul Dresser was the foremost composer of sentimental ballads, which sold millions of sheets of music in the 1890s. His "On the Banks of the Wabash" of 1898 perfectly reflected the nostalgia that dominated popular songs. Dresser was of German descent, and the German sentimental tradition was reflected in his songs. The themes were of motherhood and filial love, the mood one of loss.[10] "Write a Letter to Our Mother" and "Where Is My Wandering Boy Tonight" reflected the hurt of the move to the city or to another world. The millions of immigrants who had travelled to the United States could certainly relate to these themes.

Delivered with melodramatic effect, the Irish and German nostalgic songs struck a chord in the record-buying public. A sweet Irish tenor singing:

> But my heart is sad and weary
> How can she be Mrs. Leary
> When I'm off to Philadelphia in the morning

could be guaranteed to touch those who had left loved ones across the ocean, and the record companies were well aware of the importance of music to the immigrant.[11]

American cities brought together many different nationalities. Millions of Europeans had emigrated to the Americas by the time that Edison invented the phonograph. By 1900 one-third of the population of the United States was foreign born or of foreign parentage, and the number was much higher in the great cities. The music of the old country was the immigrants' link to home, and with 35 million of them "keenly on the alert for anything and everything which will keep alive the memories of their fatherland," the record companies were quick to oblige with Irish ballads, German waltzes, and Scandinavian folk songs.[12]

As the number and variety of immigrants grew, so too did the number of special ethnic sections of the catalogues of the record companies. Beginning with Irish, Scotch, and German music, the ethnic sections soon included songs for Spanish and French listeners. The pattern of immigration to the United States changed at the turn of the century, and this was reflected in record catalogues. The first wave of immigrants came from northwestern Europe. By the 1880s the majority of immigrants came from southern and eastern Europe. Greek, Polish, Hebrew, and Russian sections were therefore added to catalogues. By the time of World War I, record companies offered ethnic records for nearly every nationality of the American melting pot, including Oriental and far eastern selections.[13]

Popular songs were full of sentimental images of a world that had been lost, including the rural America of farms and plantations that had been left behind in the great movement to the cities. Highly romanticized depictions of the Old South were especially popular: "Carry Me Back to Old Virginny" (1878) sold millions of copies of sheet music and was a best-selling cylinder record. The incongruity of a minstrel performer singing about the good old days of slavery appears not to have disturbed American audiences at this time. The Old South of slavery and violence was not the one depicted in sheet music and records; instead it was one of unchanging tradition and family values.

These themes appealed to the audience of music halls and owners of phonographs. Newcomers to the city, these men and women had an ambivalence to the wonders of industrial society and its technology. They enjoyed the benefits of new lifestyles but looked back with nostalgia at the pre-industrial age. Listening to the wonderful talking machine was one of the new entertainments in America, but its cylinders and discs often depicted an imagined rural society that had not been touched by industrialization or the march of technology. It was a society so idealized that it had little correspondence to the hardships and poverty of farm life. The companies recorded sentimental favorites that romanticized rural life, such as "Church Scene from the Old Homestead" or "When It's Moonlight on the Prairie," and thought nothing of the basic contradiction of what they were doing – nostalgia was good for business.

The growing gulf between urban and rural life, and the clash between traditional and modern values, was reflected in recordings. It could be lamented, or it could be laughed at. A standard in the comic monologue recordings was the country bumpkin who had to come to terms with urban society. Of all these figures, "Uncle Josh" was the

Figure 4.4. A composite picture of illustrations from Edison recording catalogues, each one defining a category of music. (Author)

most popular. Played by the vaudevillian Cal Stewart, Uncle Josh
picked his way through every conceivable misfortune and misunder-
standing in the big city. Uncle Josh went to get a haircut in a fancy
emporium, rode the street car, had his photograph taken, and risked
all the other new conveniences of American life. His humorous adventures could be enjoyed on cylinder, disc, and silent film.

Although the talking machine was sold in both city and rural America, the music and humor it reproduced was predominantly that of the city. The music industry was centered in the city, New York City to be exact, and it was probably not a coincidence that Uncle Josh was usually to be found there. The music of farm and village was rarely found in the early recordings, although there was a great deal of recorded music which posed as the authentic sound of the heartland and the plantation South. The folk music of Appalachia or the American West was not committed to record, nor was the blues music being made along the Mississippi Delta in the Deep South. Spiritual music of church and meeting hall was likewise ignored by the record companies.

By the early twentieth century, record companies had begun to divide up the audience for recorded sound: comic songs for the working classes, operettas for the middle classes, ballads that appealed to immigrants, and patriotic band music that they hoped would be bought by all good Americans. Their audience was growing more knowledgeable about music and more demanding in the levels of musicianship they wanted to hear – a consequence of the impact of first-class bands, such as the one led by Sousa, and the greater frequency of performance. Sousa had made his fortune from his patriotic marches, but his concerts included the music of Wagner, Tchaikovsky, and Rossini.

The record companies played on the appeal of what they termed "high-class music." In 1898 an advertisement for the Ediphone (which was not a product of the Edison laboratory) made this distinction clear, claiming that this model should not be confused with commonplace machines "to catch the nickels of the masses, and tickle the popular ear with music of the most ordinary character." Instead the Ediphone furnished "a higher order of musical recordings" to be enjoyed "in a parlor of refined people."[14]

The policy of recording "good music" was not merely the result of the record companies' artistic aspirations; it was part of a strategy to raise the price of their products and market them to the affluent classes. Models such as the Victrola had a certain snob appeal that could be sustained only by "high-class" recordings such as Victor's premium-priced Red Seal records. These expensive records were the perfect complement to a $200 talking machine.

By the time that the Victrola was sweeping the country around

Figure 4.5. A nice middle-class family recording at home, as staged by the record company. (ENHS)

1910, the popularity of opera and its celebrities had reached a peak. New York was said to be "opera mad," and its glamorous performers received the public's adulation.[15] The professionalization of the music industry led to the "virtuoso phenomenon," and the first international stars of the entertainment world were drawn from the stages of opera houses a good 5 years before motion pictures produced a new galaxy of celebrities. In both businesses the creation of stars was inextricably linked with marketing the product. The talking-machine industry found out that the reputation of their recording artists sold their products.

It was not only refined "society people" who were impressed by the celebrity record. The marketing department of the Edison company found out that many record buyers who did not purchase Red Seal records, and had no interest in opera, believed that these prestigious recordings of high culture proved that Victor records were technically superior.[16] All record companies discovered that there was money in art.

The companies who built their advertising campaigns around the "good music" on their records helped to create the perception of a division between art forms that were high or low, and (without actually saying it) they defined what was the preserve of the ignorant masses. They were part of a movement to elevate culture, to turn the symphonic music and opera of Europe into the high art of America. Unlike other groups involved in this transformation of the ways we think about our culture, the record companies did not depreciate popular music as coming from the lowest levels of society, but they did their part in the polarization of American society by publicizing the differences between "good music" and "popular music."[17]

As one of the chief promoters of "good music," the record companies had taken it upon themselves to educate their audience. The Victor Company published *The Victor Book of the Opera,* which went through eight editions between 1912 and 1929. A cross between a primer on opera and a catalogue of recordings, this publication served the twin purposes of musical education and sales promotion. Victor and Edison also produced several books for use in schools. Their goal was to elevate the taste of their customers; it was hoped that a listener who first purchased rag and novelty records would graduate to "a better type of music," which was not only more culturally uplifting but also more costly. The talking machine could then be depicted as an important force in civilizing the masses; in "fulfilling a great mission," the companies were also selling more expensive records.[18]

Much of the "good music" heard in the United States came from Europe. The industry of recorded sound leaned heavily on European talent to provide masters for classical music, and many of the popular songs played in the United States in the 1880s were of European origin, whether it was the musical theater of Gilbert and Sullivan or the sentimental ballads of Ireland or Germany. Americans listened to "When Irish Eyes Are Smiling" recorded by Chauncey Olcott and "It's a Long Way to Tipperary" performed by the great Irish tenor John McCormack. Both these songs enjoyed great popularity on both sides of the Atlantic, but they were fundamentally European in inspiration and character. Most of the stars of popular music were based in Europe.

World War I interrupted the flow of masters from Europe to the United States. It revealed the American companies' dependence on European artists for their recordings and forced them to lean more heavily on home-grown talent. At the same time a fundamental shift in the market for recorded sound brought new popular music to recordings, a music which owed nothing to European influences and which was to reverse the flow of musical culture from Europe to the United States.

The rise of American musical theater in the years leading up to the outbreak of World War I showed that entertainment which was derived from European sources could be molded to reflect American influences. George M. Cohan was a force in this movement. He grew up in a vaudeville family and first appeared on stage at age nine. He could sing, dance, and do comedy routines. He went on to write and produce musical plays with an energy and self-confidence that perfectly mirrored the new age of twentieth-century America. His "plays with music" were full of American colloquialisms and homespun characters. "Give My Regards to Broadway" and "The Yankee Doodle Boy" came from his first big hit on Broadway, "Little Johnny Jones," and these two songs were the basis of popular records.[19] Both were recorded in 1905 by Billy Murray, a music-hall star who had made some of the first recordings on cylinder in the 1880s and achieved fame by interpreting Cohan's songs for the phonograph.[20]

Musical comedy brought together the minstrel show, comic opera, and the variety show. It provided the music for recordings from the turn of the century, when it made its mark on Broadway, through to the present, when every show has its original cast album. The first acoustic recordings of songs made popular on Broadway were not the originals but altered versions that were designed to suit the short playing time and limited fidelity of the talking machine. Billy Murray recorded several songs from Broadway musicals which became American standards: "You're a Grand Old Flag" (1906), "By the Light of the Silvery Moon" (1910), and "I Love a Piano" (1916).

These popular songs were American in character but differed little from the songs played in English music halls. In fact they were played in Europe, either live or on record, and did not strike listeners as a radically different music which could be identified with a national or cultural origin. The same could not be said for jazz and blues, which were so remarkably different from anything heard by Europeans that they immediately registered new images in the mind of the listener. They were unmistakably American – in rhythm, tempo, and content – and they put their own special mark on the popular culture of the industrialized West in the 1920s. So profound was this influence of recorded sound that the decade is often called the *Jazz Age*. This term, coined by the author F. Scott Fitzgerald, perfectly reflected the spirit of the times.

5. Recorded sound in the Jazz Age

The 1920s will always be remembered as the decade of prohibition, unrestrained hedonism, and the wild excesses of its "flaming" youth. There were radical changes in social behavior and in the way young people looked, dressed, and acted. Jazz reflected the lifestyle and aspirations of this affluent group, who had found "a native American music as traditionally wild, happy, disenchanted, and unfettered as it had become fashionable for them to think they had become."[1] Jazz expressed this reckless exuberance so well that the name given to the 1920s by F. Scott Fitzgerald has remained ever since.

Despite its image of wild abandon, jazz was a carefully crafted music that was created and promoted by the industry of recorded sound. It was another stage in the process of adapting African American music for popular consumption: a process that had begun with the coon song and was to continue through rock'n'roll to rap. The single most important cultural accomplishment of the industry of recorded sound in the twentieth century was to make the music of black Americans the popular music of the world.

At each stage of this process, the cultural identity of African Americans was systematically removed from the music, making the final recording a commercial product which could conform to the values of a white society. The coon song came from the minstrel shows that supposedly represented "genuine darky life in the South" but which were the work of white performers in grease paint or burnt cork. A small number of black touring troupes were organized and controlled by whites. Although inspired by the African American culture of the slave plantation, the minstrel shows were a travesty of slave music and dance arranged for white audiences.[2]

The same could be said for the coon songs on record. One only has to consider the titles of the most popular recordings to see this. "All Coons Look Alike to Me" was one of the first coon songs to become widely popular, and it was frequently recorded in the late

1890s and early 1900s. It was followed by an even bigger hit, "Who Dat Say 'Chicken' in Dis Crowd?" (1898), which was also recorded in many different versions.

The records of coon songs were evidence of a pattern of prejudice that was an integral part of American society and a long tradition in its entertainment. The minstrel song "Jump Jim Crow" (written by the actor Tom Rice around 1828) gave its name to the resurgence of race discrimination in the South after the Civil War. Jim Crow laws kept the races apart. The minstrel shows were segregated and played to segregated audiences. If a troupe contained both black and whites, it was only at the end of the performance that both races were ever on stage together. Although several African American song writers contributed popular coon songs (in addition to many other types of songs), most of the authors of the coon songs were white. The lyrics often contained painfully offensive renditions of African American dialect: "Keep in de Middle ob de Road" or "I's Your Nigger if You Wants Me, Liza Jane."

Coon songs and the black-faced minstrels who performed them presented a nonthreatening view of the freed slaves that was welcomed in white America. The image of the African American created for the minstrel show presented a reassuring stereotype, a childlike, uncomplicated person who accepted a fate of discrimination and poverty and lived for simple pleasures. "Its Hard to Be a Nigger" ran the refrain of one of the songs, but it was doubtful that the white performer who sang it used this lyric as social comment. Instead black Americans were depicted as happy simpletons occupied primarily with food and sex. The Columbia recording "Run, Bruder Possum, Run" was described as:

> A quaint Negro warning to the little animal which the colored race finds so peculiarly attractive as a table delicacy . . . in the real Southern dialect, with bright syncopated music.[3]

These stereotypes extended to magazine articles, cartoons, novels, jokes, and even the new entertainment of motion pictures. The first film showing African Americans starred Lucie Daly's "Pickaninnies" tumbling and dancing in 1894. Motion pictures at this time, such as "The Chicken Thieves" (1896), typically reinforced distorted images of African Americans.[4]

Record companies promoted the coon song with no reservations and little overt racism. Humorous songs like "I'd Rather Be a Nigger Than a Poor White Man" or "No Coons Can Come Too Black for Me" were listed in their catalogues along with recordings of President Taft speaking on the "Rights and Progress of the Negro." The companies did not hide the identity of their black artists, but they rarely paid them royalties.

Whether performed by African American artists or pantomimed by white vaudevillians in burnt cork, the music and dance of minstrelsy set the direction of popular entertainment. Publication (in sheet music form) of the first "rags" in 1896 started the ragtime craze. Although Scott Joplin's masterpieces were not recorded, the record companies did issue many rags by lesser artists. These records played an important part in the explosive growth of ragtime's popularity at the beginning of the twentieth century.

Ragtime was essentially written piano music, which posed a problem for the recorders because the piano did not reproduce well on cylinders and discs.[5] Ragtime records were thus confined to banjo solos, but the syncopated rhythms slowly penetrated record catalogues, and soon much popular dance music was described as "syncopated."

African American influences were also felt in dance. The Cakewalk, a syncopated dance step which couples performed in unison, was introduced by the vaudeville star Bert Williams in 1896. Its roots were in the African circle dance, but it was soon taken up with great enthusiasm by all levels of American society. The Cakewalk became a national craze, with competitions and lessons held all over the country. The record companies were quick to cash in on this with numerous cylinders such as "De Coonville Cake Walk" and with short films depicting these dances. The Cakewalk became the first of many new dances that had their origins in African American culture. They allowed closer contact of the sexes in more expressive and uninhibited dances, which were faster in tempo than traditional dances. They also brought a great many more Americans to dance as a form of entertainment and in doing so brought revenue to dance halls, dancing schools, and the record companies who provided the music.

Carried by numerous records, the syncopated rhythms of African American music flowed from minstrel songs to ragtime and then into popular song. The black face of minstrelsy extended from vaudeville to musical theater and soon made the transition to other cultural forms. "The Jazz Singer" marked its appearance in motion pictures; this film, noted for the new technology of sound, was also an important step in the wider diffusion of black-faced stereotypes.[6] Minstrel humor could be found on radio in the highly successful series "Amos 'n Andy." It was still around in the 1940s, notably in Bing Crosby's "Holiday Inn," and in the 1950s when "Amos 'n Andy" made the transition to television.

While black music and dance was powering the popular culture of twentieth-century America, African Americans as a group did not see their lot improving. The success of minstrel shows did bring about a relaxation of the segregation of entertainment, and more black performers made their way onto vaudeville stages. They slowly reclaimed the minstrel genre and took a share in its profits. The song "Who Dat Say 'Chicken' in Dis Crowd?" came from an all-black revue of 1898, "Trip to Coontown," which was the first of several successful Broadway shows written and performed by African Americans.[7] While talented performers such as Bert Williams enjoyed international acclaim and a steady income from the numerous recordings they made, numerous other black entertainers were denied a fair share of the profits generated by the commercialization of their music, dance, and humor. Sadly this was to be the pattern in American popular entertainment.

The best-known song of the ragtime craze, and the best-selling recording, was Irving Berlin's "Alexander's Ragtime Band," which first appeared in 1911, well after the important rags of Scott Joplin had been published. It was not a true rag that followed the style established by Joplin, but its jaunty rhythm and sing-along words made it a phenomenal success. The strong influence of minstrelsy could be appreciated in its lyrics because, with lines like "it's de bestest band what am, honey lamb," it called for delivery in the typical black-faced style. The two most successful recordings of the song were made by the black-faced performers Al Jolson and Harlan & Collins.

Berlin was one of the leading song writers of Tin Pan Alley and a lasting influence on popular music. He put new life into the sentimental ballads of the times of Paul Dresser. He played an important part in turning ragtime into commercial music with an international audience. He was one of a group of Jewish song writers who turned the sounds of minstrelsy into contemporary popular entertainment. The ragtime craze owed a great deal to the music of Joplin and the minstrel show, but the debt owed to the African American originators went unpaid. While Berlin and other song writers of Tin Pan Alley were turning out commercial rags by the hundreds, and pressing plants were producing hundreds of thousands of ragtime records, Scott Joplin was writing an opera that would eventually ruin him. His attempt to move ragtime from popular entertainment to a respectable art form failed.

The arrival of jazz music

The commercial development of jazz provides an example of how African American music was coopted and transformed by the industry of recorded sound. "Jass" music, as it was first known, was the work of African Americans, who called it *rag* or *blues*. The origins of jazz go too deep and are too complicated to explain here, but they bore the imprint of African rhythms and emerged from a context of ragtime and blues. The first jazz music is said to have been played in New Orleans, but it is clear that it was being played all over the South, especially where musical cultures came together. Jazz bands contained cornets, clarinets, trombones, banjos, drums, and a piano. The music was improvised and had a percussive emphasis in that the beat stood out with a driving rhythm. We shall never know what it sounded like because it was not recorded.

The first band to make a recording of the new music was a group called The Original Dixieland Jass Band (ODJB), which moved from New Orleans to Chicago and then on to New York in 1916. Musicians from New Orleans had always travelled to seek more lucrative jobs, and this process reached a peak around the time of World War I. The Great Migration carried jazz pioneers such as Jelly Roll Morton, Sidney Bechet, and Kid Ory from New Orleans to Chicago and brought their music to a larger audience, but they were not recorded. It was the all-white ODJB which got a contract from a record company. In February 1917 they recorded their version of "Livery Stable Blues" in Victor's New York studios. This record and their live performances made a big impression.

Although these early recordings provide us with the first sounds of jazz, they do not accurately represent the way it was played at the time. The jazz recorded in studios in Chicago or New York was much different from the improvised music played in bawdy houses or creole dances in New Orleans.[8] It had to become less improvised and more formal to suit the strict time requirements of acoustic recording. Furthermore the percussive emphasis had to be removed because loud drum noises were too much for the recording stylus, making it jump from the groove. The recordings were often made with muffled drums or with no percussion other than drumsticks knocked together. The jazz that was committed to wax, and therefore made part of the historic record, was a shortened version of a raucous and unpredictable music. It was also the work of white musicians; black performers were rarely invited into recording studios at this time.

The jazz put on record was a diluted, commercialized music intended for a white audience. It was produced in recording studios in the cities of the Northeast. Even its name originated from the white musicians who copied it – when black musicians talked about jazz, they were not referring to a style of music. Unlike minstrelsy and ragtime, which were musical styles eventually transcribed onto records, jazz as we know it was the creation of the recording industry.

The success of the ODJB provided an opportunity for several other white bands to follow their journey from New Orleans to Chicago and then to recording studios in New York. One was The New Orleans Rhythm Kings, and as one of its musicians admitted: "We did our best to copy the colored music we'd heard at home. We did the best we could but naturally, we couldn't play real colored style."[9] Not for the first time had the industry of recorded sound adapted an original African American music for a wider audience and by doing so significantly altered its character.

Jazz came in many forms. It was played under various guises in many parts of the United States. The blues craze of the early 1920s, when female singers like Bessie Smith became famous recording stars, was really part of the commercial jazz produced by record companies as popular music. Blues could mean different things to different musicians and covered a wide variety of musical styles. Originally it reflected the collective experience of black Americans in the hard years after their emancipation. By 1900 it could be heard all over the Deep South, in tent shows and barrelhouses and in the music halls frequented by African Americans. The Great Migration brought it north and created a market for it in the cities.

Blues, like jazz, was an improvised music that was inconsistent with the time limitations of the 78-rpm disc record. The music had to fit within the 3-minute boundary of sound recording, although the original blues, as sung in the rural South, was not constrained by time or the technical considerations of the recording studio. It appeared in many forms and had many functions: work music, personal expression, and dance music for entertaining a crowd. Putting it on record shaped its structure and its sound, just like the sound of jazz had been influenced by recording.

The records identified as blues songs were far distant from the authentic blues of the Mississippi Delta; in fact, many of the blues records in the 1920s had very little in common with the real thing. Sophie Tucker, whose "Some of These Days" set the tone of this style of singing, was known as "the last of the red-hot Mamas." She was born Sonia Kalish in Russia. Even the recordings of Bessie Smith and Mamie Smith were not the blues of the rural South but polished versions of these songs that reflected their years of performing in vaudeville and their exposure to Northern audiences. One expert on the blues, Alan Lomax, wrote later that it was "unfortunate" that these singers were the first to have best-selling records, because for years afterwards it was their style and not the authentic blues that was copied by others.[10]

The record proved to be the means to shape music by its wide diffusion and the impact it had on other musicians. Jazz was literally being made up as it went along; it was going in as many different directions as there were musicians who played it. But the hit record pulled it all together and refocused musical energies along the lines drawn by the great performers. Even a mistake during a session, such as the time when Louis Armstrong dropped the sheet music to a song and had to improvise the words, could bring about a new style which was immediately diffused and copied. When Mezz Mezzrow and his circle of jazz-playing friends heard "Heebie Jeebies," they began to imitate Armstrong's scat singing by making up their own nonsense lyrics.[11]

Louis Armstrong's musical career reflects the legend of jazz. He was born in New Orleans and grew up immersed in that unique musical culture which brought together European, African, slave, and creole music. Armstrong first played cornet in the brass band of the orphans' home where he was placed and then in several marching and dance bands. He was part of the Great Migration out of the South at the time of World War I. His mentor, Joe King Oliver, left for Chicago in 1919 and soon called young Armstrong to join him.

As his reputation increased Armstrong moved to New York in 1923 – the musical center of the United States at this time, with approximately 2,500 speakeasies or cabarets. New York was also the center of the recording industry, and here Armstrong advanced his career as a star soloist with Fletcher Hendersons' band. In January 1925 he was hired to accompany Bessie Smith in a recording session in Columbia's New York studios. At this time Bessie Smith was at the peak of her popularity. Dubbed "Empress of the Blues," she had built a successful career on the basis of her recordings. Handbills advertising her shows prefixed her name with "Columbia Recording Star," and part of her stage show depicted her singing in a recording studio.[12] The January 1925 session produced five sides good enough for release. Among them was W. C. Handy's "St. Louis Blues," a song that was to become Bessie Smith's trademark recording.

By the end of 1925, Armstrong was back in Chicago, working at a variety of clubs and dance halls. His main place of work was the Sunset Cafe, a rowdy speakeasy with bootleg liquor, dancing girls, and a connection to the mob. He did some sessions for the OKeh Company to make some extra money, and several of these records, including "Potato Head Blues" and "West End Blues," are among the most important and copied performances in jazz.

The Louis Armstrong legend is inextricably linked with his recordings. Although he was famous in Chicago for his virtuoso playing, without records of his music he might have gone down in jazz history as just another excellent player – the fate of many less fortunate and unrecorded stars. His records made his name and set the direction of jazz music in the 1920s. The 50 or 60 songs cut by Louis Armstrong's Hot Fives and Seven's between November 1925 and December 1928 have been rightly called "one of the most significant bodies of American music."[13] Taken as a whole they record an amazing period of artistic growth as Armstrong moved away from the Dixieland style of New Orleans and created a mature jazz based on brilliant virtuoso performance. The musical vocabulary that Armstrong established in these recordings was the basis of numerous trumpet solos that followed; they helped shape the sound of jazz for the next decade.

The record had become a force of change in American entertainment. By responding rapidly to new music and putting it on records, the industry of recorded sound was accelerating the pace of change in popular music. This is one of the themes of August Wilson's play

Figure 5.1. Louis Armstrong and his Hot Five. (Institute of Jazz Studies)

"Ma Rainey's Black Bottom," which dramatizes the declining career of one of the original female blues stars. Ma Rainey's style represented the older country blues, which was slower in tempo and less melodic than the blues recorded by younger singers in the late 1920s. Louis Armstrong's records were fueling the demand for "hot" jazz, with faster tempos and pounding rhythms. One of Rainey's musicians concludes: "Times are changing. This is a tricky business now. You've got to jazz it up . . . put in something different. You know, something wild . . . with a lot of rhythm."[14]

Jazz brought some important changes to popular music in the 1920s. The lyrics of nineteenth-century songs had been cloyingly sentimental, and much of this nostalgia seeped over into twentieth-century music. Jazz and blues had a more cynical view of the world than the music of Dresser or Cohan, and its themes did not respect home, family, or motherhood. The view of women presented in the lyrics changed dramatically, for now there were more overt sexual references that focused on infidelity and promiscuity. Some lyrics were downright suggestive, reflecting the earthy realism of African American speech.

If there was one common feature to all recorded jazz at this time, it was that it was intended for dancing. The sentimental ballads and the comic songs of vaudeville had been performed to a more or less static audience. Broadway hits and music-hall songs owed a lot of their popularity to the fact that the audience knew the words and could join in. Jazz was different. It had a syncopated rhythm like ragtime and a percussive beat that invited the listener to dance. The popularity of jazz music encompassed a multitude of new dances. In the years before the war, Americans had taken dance to heart; it was taught in hundreds of dancing schools, and exhibitions of ballroom dancing drew large crowds. The younger generation delighted in finding new and preposterous dance steps: the Bunny Hug, Turkey Trot, and Grizzly Bear. The foxtrot was the most popular of all, and it was danced by nearly all parts of American and European society. Jazz music was ideal for foxtrots, and many recordings were labelled as such. As the 1920s progressed, the foxtrot was superseded by less dignified dances. The Charleston, which appeared around 1923, was frenzied and unfettered and perfectly reflected the pace of the "roaring twenties." Other popular dances, such as the Black Bottom, stretched the boundaries of good taste even further.

It was the dancing and the corresponding threat to the morals of youth that created controversy over the new popular music. Before jazz, music had not engendered strong feelings. It was considered to be entertainment and not a challenge to the establishment. Jazz, on the other had, was feared as a degenerative force that corrupted all who listened to it. Its opponents called it "jungle music," a reference to its African origins and also to the primitive power of its rhythm. A *Ladies Home Journal* article claimed that "jazz originally was the accompaniment of the voodoo dancer, stimulating the half-crazed barbarian to the vilest deeds."[15] Jazz was the first (but certainly not the last) African American music to be seen as a force of change in society.

The African American essence of jazz and blues might have been restrained by the record companies, but the rhythm was impossible to extinguish. It was at the bottom of all the popular dances of the twentieth century, from the Cakewalk to the Twist. Black music and dance played a very important part in the rapid expansion of the industry of recorded sound, for the great boom which began shortly before World War I and lasted into the 1920s was supported by a fascination with new dances. Ragtime and other crazes fueled the rising demand for records. In 1914 *Talking Machine World* proclaimed that "All America is dancing these days" and that demand for records was so great that the companies were lagging behind in their orders.[16] The new dances of the Jazz Age propelled record sales to even higher levels as the listening public became the dancing public.

Jazz became more than music on a record. It was part of a cultural package that included new clothes, hair styles, vocabulary, and outlook. It was this aspect of the music, along with the salacious dances associated with it, that aroused the consternation of the middle classes. The new woman of the 1920s had undergone a dramatic change from the nineteenth-century vision of womanhood. The typical "flapper" could be recognized by her short hair and dresses, her cigarette, and the music she danced to. She was no longer a belle but a vamp who exerted her independence "deep in an atmosphere of jungle music and the questioning of moral codes."[17]

The popular music of the Jazz Age

Although the new women and their fast young men have become the symbols of the 1920s, they were in fact a very small part of the market for recorded sound. The audience for the hot jazz played in speakeasies and dancing clubs was largely white and affluent: college boys, socialites, and flappers. The mass audience still flocked to the Broadway stage and to the music halls of the vaudeville circuits. In retrospect, there was very little of what we consider as jazz in the Jazz Age. Ballads, comic songs, and songs from Broadway musicals provided the material for the most popular recordings.

Al Jolson was called "The World's Greatest Entertainer" at this time after impressive performances at New York's Winter Garden theater and numerous music halls around the country. A black-faced performer who sang, danced, mimed, and told jokes in the best tradition of vaudeville, he made hugely successful recordings of the songs he sang on stage. From "Swanee," recorded for the Columbia label in 1920, through "Toot Toot Tootsie (Goo'bye)" (1922) to "Sonny Boy" (1928), Al Jolson proved that the old music-hall traditions, the minstrelsy, and the contrived Tin Pan Alley songs were still prospering in the Jazz Age, and you can see this in his performances in "The Jazz Singer."

To survive in the world of clubs, cafes, and dance halls in the big cities, musicians had to play all sorts of dance music, which included rags, blues, marching tunes, and the more sedate music heard in hotel lobbies. Jazz bands provided a variety of dance music to please their audience. ODJB's second record release was "Mournin' Blues," which was not a blues song but a foxtrot as the label indicated. Throughout the 1920s jazz came to mean all popular music with a syncopated beat. It was often submerged in the more polite and acceptable forms of popular entertainment, a world in which black jazz musicians had little place.

The most popular recording of the decade was Paul Whiteman's "Whispering," which sold over 2 million copies in 1920. A slow ballad, it owed little to jazz. Whiteman was the most commercially successful recording star of the 1920s with a string of hit records. He was a formally trained musician whose large orchestra played in the fine hotels of the big cities. His "symphonic jazz" (as it was called) was restrained and melodic – a far cry from the raucous noise which emerged from a dixieland record. He put a respectable face on the bawdy new music, arranged and played it with high levels of professional musicianship, and reaped the rewards. Whiteman's title, the "King of Jazz," was somewhat ironic, bearing in mind how far the music had travelled from its African American origins; yet, to his credit, he brought a disciplined and well-crafted sound to a very large audience and defined the sound of popular music in the 1920s.[18]

In 1924 Paul Whiteman gave a historic jazz concert at the Aeolian Hall in New York City, a venue normally reserved for classical music. The evening's entertainment was entitled "An Experiment in Modern Music" since the intent was to show the audience how far jazz had come since the strident sounds of the ODJB. The concert began with their "Livery Stable Blues" and ended with the composer George Gershwin playing a "jazz concerto" he had written for the concert called "Rhapsody in Blue."

Born in New York of Russian immigrant parents, Gershwin had assimilated many facets of jazz and blues into his music – the syncopation, the "blue" notes, and jazz harmonies. Perhaps that is why his music seemed to represent American popular culture so well. "Rhapsody in Blue" was a masterpiece, and its first performance was called "A Birthday for American Music."[19] It evoked musical images of American life, especially life in the big city. Gershwin wrote: "I hear it as a sort of musical kaleidoscope of America – our vast melting pot, our blues, our Metropolitan madness."[20]

It also illustrated the Americanization of popular music. Many in the audience at the Aeolian Hall that night thought that "Rhapsody in Blue" was the equal of any musical masterpiece written in Europe. It was truly emancipated from the formalism of classical music without losing any of its potence or nobility. The Aeolian Hall concert was a milestone because it heralded a wider acceptance of jazz-based music. Although by no means the authentic jazz of the South, recorded jazz had entered the mainstream of popular culture, and there was to be no going back.

In contrast to the ballads and music-hall songs which accounted for the majority of record sales, jazz and ragtime were unmistakably American. To song writers and record buyers alike, there was something in the rhythm of ragtime that reflected the American spirit and the optimism of the nation that had become the world's greatest industrial power. As Berlin said: "Syncopation is the soul of every true American. Ragtime is the best heart-raiser and worry-banisher that I know."[21] Here was a popular music that owed nothing to European influences and reflected a uniquely American musical tradition.

The Jazz Age, it should be remembered, marked the beginning of the United States' domination of world politics as well as its culture. Jazz was also called the folk music of the machine age, an age created in the laboratories and factories of the United States. It was in the rapid tempo of jazz that listeners heard a musical reflection of the fast pace of urban life in America, a lifestyle that was shaped by the forces of technology and industry. Irving Berlin noted in 1924 that "the speed and snap" of popular music was influenced by the changes wrought by the automobile: "All the old rhythm was gone and in its place was heard the hum of an engine . . . the new age demanded new music for new action."[22]

America on record

Prior to the phonograph, music was diffused by travelling singers and by the sale of sheet music. A popular song from a Broadway hit, for example, would find its way to the public ear by touring companies who took the production into the hinterland. This would stimulate the sales of sheet music and recordings.

Song writers depended on music-hall performers to publicize their songs and bring them to the attention of the public. A great star like Al Jolson could turn an unknown song into an overnight hit by a successful stage presentation. The more he travelled, the more publicity was given to the song. The railroad carried entertainers across the American continent, and the steam ship took them to Europe. In the days before radio and television, song promotion could be achieved only by personal appearances, and performers lived a life of constant travel.

The first entertainment that moved from America to Europe was the minstrel show, which appeared in London in the 1860s. For the rest of the nineteenth century, minstrel groups toured Europe. The Christy Minstrels, a well-known troupe of black-faced performers, received tumultuous acclaim when they appeared in London. Minstrel shows were very popular in England and could be seen in music halls in several cities. The appeal of the minstrel spread beyond Europe to Australia, where the audience of British immigrants found the same enjoyment in the show.[23] This was the beginning of the African American influence on the world's popular music.

European record companies made their versions of the ever popular coon songs. Fred Gaisberg taught Johnson's "Laughing Song" to an English singer, Bert Sheppard, and they made the first European copy of an American hit record. Minstrel songs were the basis of the first vocal performances on Berliner disc records in England.[24] Ragtime recordings came next as the ragtime craze reached Europe. The Cakewalk was introduced to England when the Broadway show "In Dahomey" opened in London in 1903. Bert Williams was feted everywhere as the show toured the provinces. He gave a performance by royal command at Buckingham Palace, which ensured acceptance of the Cakewalk and its ragtime music by all social classes in England and France.[25]

The sound recording proved to be a potent diffusor of music. As the Big Three extended their operations to the Far East, the Pacific, and Latin America, their records spread musical styles farther afield. There was hardly any place in the world where the sound of the phonograph or gramophone was not heard. Explorers took them to the two Poles and to the heart of Africa.

Fred Gaisberg was the first of many record producers who were instrumental in diffusing American popular music to Europe. He played a pivotal role in introducing the coon song to Great Britain and extending the influence of African American music far beyond the borders of the United States. But even he was astounded at the power of the recording as a diffusor of culture. He was later to write, "In the bazaars of India I have seen dozens of natives seated on their haunches around a gramophone, rocking with laughter, playing [Bert] Sheppard's laughing record."[26]

American troops in World War I served to bring new music to a European audience. A nurse who had served with American troops in France reported to *Talking Machine World* that sentimental and patriotic songs were not as popular as one might expect. The soldiers' favorite records were distinguished by their ragtime rhythm, and anything with syncopation was welcomed because "rag is the rage" with the troops in France. The first jazz band is said to have been a regimental band of a black army unit stationed in France.[27]

Personal appearances followed the export of records. The singer Elsie Janis went to Europe to sing for the troops and stayed in London long enough to star in her own show, "Hello America," which brought Londoners some of the latest American popular music.[28] The Original Dixieland Jass Band followed up their success in New York by going to London in 1919 and achieving a greater sensation than they had done in New York. They were followed by numerous other jazz bands in the 1920s. Jazz music had a powerful appeal to the European record market, which devoured the recordings made by American companies. In France there was a considerable following for what they termed "le Jazz Hot." Many American dance bands found a warm reception in the United Kingdom in the late 1920s. In Germany a popular novelty song which was all the rage in the United States became a hit in 1923 as "Ja, Wir Haben keinen Bananen Heute."

Although live performances attracted attention to the new American music, the recording established jazz in Europe. Disc records of Louis Armstrong followed the course established by the cylinders of George Johnson in spreading African American music to a wider audience. Louis Armstrong was already famous in Europe before he actually went there on tour and started playing – his records had preceded him. The tens of thousands who greeted him knew his music only through sound recordings. The well-to-do youth of London, Paris, and Berlin danced to imported American records and made it the height of fashion. Jazz records were not only a source of entertainment but also a powerful vehicle for the spread of American culture.

The music and the dancing spread with the sale of records. The visual images of talking pictures and illustrated magazines did the rest. The technology and the culture of the Jazz Age was exported wholesale to Europe, where it became a living reflection of the American experience. Malcolm Cowley wrote of Paris in 1929:

> Always, everywhere, there was jazz. . . . There were black orchestras wailing in cafes and boites de nuit, radios carrying the music of the Savoy Ballroom in London, new phonograph records from Harlem and Tin Pan Alley played over and over again.[29]

One could find flappers in Paris, London, or Berlin wearing the same fashionable clothes and doing the same immoral dances as their counterparts in New York or Philadelphia. There were even fashion-conscious young ladies in Tokyo listening to jazz records. All came from a tiny, affluent segment of the population. All revelled in their freedom, including the means to buy entertainment products from the United States. For many Europeans, especially the well-heeled elite and the university population, America was represented in exported films and recordings. What they listened to was America on record. And much of the music and dance diffused in this way had originated within African American culture and had travelled across the oceans embodied in the products of the international industry of recorded sound.

PART TWO
THE ELECTRICAL ERA

6. The machines

The history of technology is a relatively new area of study. Although writers such as Lewis Mumford and Aldous Huxley were examining the impact of technology on civilization in the 1930s, it was not until 1957 that a professional group was formed. As their prime source of evidence, historians of technology have machines – beautifully complex artifacts with the ideas of the times embedded in them. Historians of recorded sound have rich sources and do not have to travel too far to investigate them. Millions of players and records have survived. They can be found in museums and private collections all over the world, and often in the homes of elderly relatives.

What evidence can we uncover from an examination of these relics of the industry of recorded sound? The search for artifacts must begin at the Edison National Historic Site, an Aladdin's cave of old phonographs. Edison's old laboratory in West Orange, New Jersey, has been turned into a museum, and the machine shops, chemistry lab, and other experimental rooms are still there, looking much as they did when the great inventor was alive. There are phonographs in every part of the laboratory complex: amusement models, dictating machines, tiny players fitted into dolls, and concert phonographs which played huge cylinders.

On the third floor of the main laboratory building, there is one room of some significance to the historian of recorded sound. The only evidence that this was the first recording studio are the numerous recording horns strewn around the floor, long polished metal horns, enamelled horns with wide mouths, and horns that look like hats worn by witches. Each of these horns had a specific use in recording: the bell-shaped 14-inch brass horn was used for individual singers; the 26-inch japanned tin horn was best for banjo, violin, cornet, and band records; and the 6-foot-long horns were used for orchestras.

When the visitor enters the museum, an imposing machine called the kinetophone catches the eye immediately. This was basically a

Figure 6.1. The site of Edison's first recording studio, with recording horns strewn around. (Author)

phonograph attached to a film projector, but it is such a confusion of metal parts, belts, and wires that it is not immediately evident what it did. The kinetophone was the first commercial attempt to provide talking pictures, and its introduction in 1913 announced a new age of entertainment in America. It used large cylinders of over 4 inches in diameter and 7 inches in length. It was placed behind the screen in the movie theater, and the projectionist operated it with control wires and pulleys. Its large horn was supposed to project the sound to the audience sitting in front of the screen.

Although it made a great impact when it was first introduced, it died a painful death at the hands of theater audiences who howled in derision when the sound got out of synchronization. The project turned into such a disaster that Edison dropped the idea, but when looking at the machine now, one cannot discern that it was a failure. To the average visitor it tells the important story of the first talking-picture device. The real significance of the kinetophone is that it proved that acoustic technology was inadequate for talking pictures. It is also a rather painful reminder of Edison's failure to move from mechanical to electrical sound technology.

Among the talking machines gathering dust in Edison's old laboratory are some significant failures, which have as much relevance to the historian as his well-known successes. On the third floor of the main laboratory building, there was a line of old Edison disc players, which were pushed up against the wall and could hardly be seen in the gloom of the attic. One machine, which at first glance appeared to be an ordinary disc player with its upright wooden cabinet and enclosed speaker, revealed a special turntable designed for Edison's longer-playing discs. On the shelf above it was a small film projector. Small spools of film were stacked on pegs next to it.

This was the successor to the kinetophone. It was another of Edison's attempts to join sound and image together into what he hoped would be the greatest consumer product of his age. This forlorn machine could have been the ultimate home entertainment center, but unfortunately it did not succeed. Edison was years ahead of his time in seeing the potential of recorded sound and images coming from one compact machine in the parlor, providing "honest workmen with grand opera" as he imagined it.[1] What an idea! We now know that this dream did not become reality until video tape recorders were perfected and mass-produced in the 1980s. Edison was a little off the mark when he imagined that this device would provide opera for the working classes rather than recordings of soap operas and football games, but the concept of this product was exactly right. This machine should be the starting point of any history of video recording, but it will probably be relegated to a footnote, if it is mentioned at all.

To start at the beginning of the story of recorded sound, the visitor has to go underground, into a special vault constructed during World War II to protect the secrets of America's greatest inventor. Underneath the laboratory yard is the place where the most valuable artifacts of Edison's long career are kept. His experimental notebooks are stored in a massive safe, behind an imposing armored door like the ones used in banks. Most of this underground vault is taken up with lines of shelving containing documents, including the millions of

Figure 6.2. The young Edison in Mathew Brady's Washington studio, April 1878. (ENHS)

letters sent to Edison. There are also hundreds of machines sitting on shelves, and each one marks an important invention or a significant commercial development.

One of the first tinfoil machines is stored here, preserved in its specially made wooden box. A small metal cylinder resting on an axle and connected to a hand crank, it has metal mouthpieces at either side. It is hard to recognize the beginnings of a great industry in such a small device. Nearby is a patent model of the device that Edison

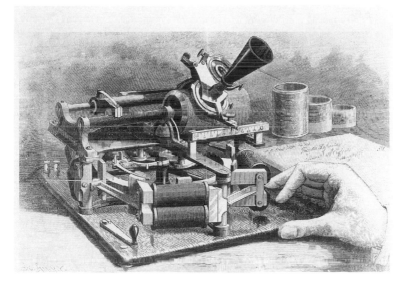

Figure 6.3. The new, improved phonograph of 1887. (From *Scientific American*, Dec. 1887)

took to Washington right after its invention. It is simple and elegant, not so much a machine as the embodiment of an idea. At one end of the axle is a flywheel to give an even turning motion. The cylinder with tinfoil wrapped around it sits on the middle of the axle, and resting on its shiny surface is the mouthpiece assembly with its recording stylus and diaphragm. At the other end of the axle is the hand crank that the young Edison holds, somewhat tentatively, in the photograph made in Mathew Brady's studio in 1878.

Moving along the shelves of the vault we come to the "perfected phonograph" of 1887, the first of many tries to turn the invention of 1877 into a commercial product. It is a substantial piece of machinery. Unlike the tinfoil phonograph, the works are so complicated that it is not immediately obvious that it is a talking machine, or "Edison's Wonderful Phonograph," as the *Scientific American* described it. The bottom of the device is a circular assembly of metal with coils of wire at each corner – this was the electric motor which turned the cylinder. A metal top plate held the feed screw which moved the recorder/ reproducer assembly along the wax cylinder. The user turned the recorder/reproducer assembly until it rested on the wax cylinder,

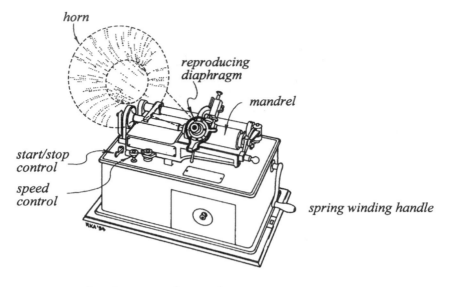

horn

reproducing diaphragm

mandrel

start/stop control

speed control

spring winding handle

A spring-motor phongraph

checked the position of the stylus on a scale inscribed on the metal, and moved a switch to start the electric motor.[2]

The first thing that strikes the casual observer is that operating these machines cannot have been easy. The user had to turn a small screw to regulate the speed of the motor to get an even turning rate. Then he or she had to carefully bring the recording stylus down onto the turning cylinder. It might be necessary to adjust several screws on the diaphragm assembly to make sure that the stylus sat exactly in the groove. As the recorder cut into the soft wax of the cylinder, special care had to be taken to ensure that the thin sliver of wax cut out of the groove fell into the shavings pan underneath and not into the machinery. If this happened the wax quickly clogged up the works.

Edison's next phonograph is more compact and businesslike. The M models of the 1890s were rectangular boxes of wood with all the works – the same feedscrew, cylinder, and recorder/reproducer assembly – sitting on a metal top plate. Underneath the plate and hidden in the wooden case was a compact electric motor. The distinguishing feature of this model was a governor on the top plate, which helped regulate the turning speed of the cylinder.

When comparing the Edison phonographs of the 1890s with a modern disc player, one is immediately impressed with the substance

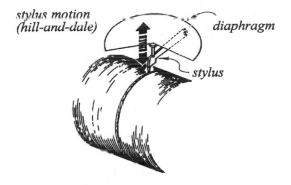

Acoustic reproduction

and workmanship of the early models. Solid, finely crafted machines, with handsome hardwood cases and polished brass fittings, they represent a different ethos from the mass-produced plastic and aluminum boxes containing electrical circuits which now pass as talking machines. Weighing at least 50 pounds, these phonographs were hand-built to Edison's high standards of workmanship and were intended to last a lifetime. They were not cheap; with prices ranging from $150 to $200, only the very rich could afford one.

These machines were intended to be the high-tech playthings of the upper classes, recording their music or speech. The sound that came out of this talking machine was normally the voice of the owner or his friends. It also preserved the fine music he made at home. The phonograph was more than an entertainer; it could save voices for posterity, providing an aural record of the passing of generations far better than a list of names in a family bible – "the tone pictures of a lifetime" from child's prattle to the "last feeble utterings of the death-bed," as one advertisement put it.[3] To the technically minded Victorian worthies who purchased these machines, it must also have appealed to their vanity to make records of their thoughts over the years, and surely anyone so farsighted to purchase one of Edison's phonographs would have important words to preserve forever.

The key to turning an expensive and complicated device into a consumer product for the masses is hidden beneath the top plate. The

Figure 6.4. Colonel George Gouraud being interviewed by a reporter in 1888. (ENHS)

power source was the means to reduce the price, weight, and complexity of the phonograph. The inventors had been drawn to the spring motor very early on – Edison had investigated it in 1878 – but nobody had solved the problem of ensuring uniformity of speed as the spring ran down and its power decreased. It was not until the 1890s that several important patents were filed for spring motors with governors that controlled the speed of rotation.[4]

This advance was quickly incorporated into a new type of talking machine which was smaller and easier to operate than previous designs. Edison's 1896 models were built around spring motors. Many of the features of the top works, such as the governor and adjustment screws, were removed. A simple belt drive replaced the gearing and regulator. The new model came equipped with the "automatic" reproducer, which was counterbalanced to adjust its tracking pressing as it ran along the groove.

A simple funnel-shaped horn was attached to the reproducer to amplify the sound. There were two main controls: a start–stop switch which activated the drive, and a screw to retard or accelerate the speed of cylinder rotation – it was still necessary to set the speed to get the right pitch. The user had to wind up the spring and place the reproducer stylus in the groove. Significantly, a recorder could be bought as an extra, an indication that the function of the machine was moving from recording music in the home to reproducing pre-recorded sounds.

This model came complete for about $100, which was still a very high price and much too expensive for the average consumer. Edison's next effort was the Home model, based on a much smaller spring motor which reduced its weight by almost 20 pounds. It sold for $40, bringing it into competition with the low-priced spring-motor machines of his chief rivals, the Columbia and Victor companies.

Eldridge Johnson's redesign of Berliner's gramophone was sold as the Trade Mark model of 1897. Priced at $25, this product competed with the popular cylinder players such as the graphophone made by the Columbia Company. Applying the spring motor to disc players was harder than applying it to the cylinders because the motor had to propel the reproducer across the wider diameter of the disc – in the Berliner machine there was no feed screw; instead the spiral groove guided the stylus along.

A price war erupted at the end of the nineteenth century as companies sensed a market for cheap machines. In 1898, Edison's experimenters redesigned the basic spring-motor model to bring its price down to $25. It was stripped of all but the essentials and was appropriately called the Standard model. It weighed only 17 pounds, and its price of $20 undersold the popular $25 Columbias. Yet prices were dropping as fast as new companies entered the market. Edison's final shot was the $10 Gem introduced in 1899, a tiny (7-pound) machine that could play only records. It competed with the Columbia Company's popular Eagle cylinder player, which also sold for $10. These models were cheap, but not cheap enough to compete with machines such as the $7 Euphonic.

A smaller version of the gramophone was soon introduced to match Edison's Gem model. This tiny disc player, aptly named the Toy, was the bare essential of turntable, crank, and reproducer, which sold for only $3. Although $5 or $10 was still a lot of money for a working man (it might equal a week's wages), the dramatic decrease in the price of machines and records was critical in achieving higher levels of sales.

The scaling down of the talking machine and the subsequent reduction of its cost helped create a mass market for recorded sound.
The artifacts of this process are by no means as impressive as the
earlier machines made for the wealthy, and their value to collectors
is much less. A Home or Gem model can be purchased today for
around $250 to $350, but a class M electric of the early 1890s brings
up to $4,000.[5] Yet the low-cost models are important artifacts. Edi-
son called them "the machine for the millions," and this is their significance. They enabled the phonograph to become a consumer good
in the twentieth century.

Cylinder versus disc

The industry of recorded sound was a high-tech arena in which business organizations competed with one another to improve the reproduction of sound. The history of this struggle is essentially one of
competing technologies, in which constant innovation brought forth
new and improved products. Unlike the electrical or automobile industries, where innovation abounded but the basic format remained
the same, the talking-machine business experienced the rivalry of
completely different technological systems: cylinder versus disc, disc
versus tape, and acoustic versus electrical reproduction.

The Smithsonian Institution in Washington contains artifacts produced by some of Edison's rivals in the world of recorded sound,
including some graphophones built by Bell and Tainter. The museum
also displays experimental equipment from the Volta laboratories,
and most notable are the large, glass discs used in experiments to
record sound photographically – an idea that was to come to fruition
long after the graphophone was forgotten.

The Smithsonian also has a major collection of the work of Emile
Berliner, including many of his early gramophones. Wonderfully simple, the small disc sits on a revolving pedestal which is connected to
a turning wheel. A thin piece of leather runs around the wheel and
connects to another wheel which has a crank attached. A black tin
horn perches precariously on the recorder/reproducer assembly, which
rests on the disc. The stylus and diaphragm work the same way as
the Edison version, but they are attached to the side (instead of the
center in Edison's machine) so that the assembly's edge rests against
the record.

A very important difference between the Edison and Berliner versions of the talking machine was the different way the wave form of the sound was cut into the groove. Edison used the vertical "hill and dale" motion, while Berliner's cut moved from side to side "laterally." As the competition between cylinder and disc heated up, proponents of each system engaged in fierce arguments about the merits of vertical versus lateral cut. One side claimed that gravity favored the up-and-down motion, while the other countered that it made it harder to move quickly and thus catch the sounds at the extremes of the frequency range.[6] Moving from side to side was said to be a less traumatic path for the stylus to take, but the resulting pressure on the sides of the grooves could break them down. Edison's supporters claimed that the cylinder and feedscrew arrangement gave a reproduction of even pitch all the way to the end of the record, while the more crowded grooves at the center of the Berliner disc caused inferior reproduction.

The method of cutting the groove into the record was only one of the many differences between talking machines at the turn of the century. Berliner had talked of the future of recorded sound in terms of the standardization of machines and the interchangeability of records as early as 1888. And he was completely right. Yet 20 years after he made this speech, there was a confusing number of different options for the prospective customer. First there was the choice of cylinder or disc player. Discs were available in either lateral or vertical cut. Each company's cylinders came in different sizes and were recorded to a different number of grooves to the inch. If you bought a record made by one company, you were lucky if it played on the machine of another.

Recording speeds were determined by whoever was operating the machine. The 70 rpm of the Berliner gramophone was decided by trial and error; it gave the longest play on a 7-inch disc without sacrificing sound quality. Other speeds used for commercial records ranged from 50 to 120 rpm, and it was not uncommon for one company to employ several different speeds in its record production.[7] The listener had to match the recording speed on the playback machine, because a slight change in speed, say from 78 rpm to 83 rpm, brought a noticeable change in pitch.

Difficulties of matching recording speeds was just one problem that the public faced in operating talking machines. The main problem was that the playback usually did not sound much like the original.

Looking back to the early phonographs and gramophones, E. C. Wente of Bell Laboratories concluded that "the surprising thing is not that the quality of reproduction is poor, but that reproduced sounds were at all intelligible.[8] As the listening public got over the novelty of recorded sound, their expectations increased. In other words, they expected to recognize the voice or piece of music on record. It was no longer good enough just to be able to hear a sound. Improving sound quality was the chief goal of the inventors and corporate laboratories. Competing technologies in the talking-machine industry were focused on improving the sound and giving one machine the commercial advantage over another.

At West Orange, Edison started at the sound's point of origin – the stylus – and experimented with many different shapes and sizes. He found that the harder the stylus, the clearer the sound, which led him to a permanent jeweled stylus of sapphire or diamond in contrast to the sharp metal points of the Berliner stylus.

Next to be considered was the stylus and diaphragm assembly, and one of Edison's favorite pastimes was to redesign the mechanical linkages between them. He also liked to experiment with different materials for the diaphragm. He discarded thin pieces of metal for a thin sliver of mica or glass, fixed in a circular frame with a special rubbery material. The diaphragm had to provide a sensitive response to sound waves without too much distortion as it vibrated. Viscous, "gooey" materials held the diaphragm in the frame and dampened its movement as it responded to loud or high notes.[9]

Several miles to the south of Edison's laboratory, Johnson experimented on the same things. He redesigned the stylus/diaphragm assembly around a mica diaphragm dampened by rubber gaskets. His attention was on the diaphragm assembly and its container – called the *soundbox* – and the hollow connecting tube, or *tone arm*, which took the sound to the horn. In 1903 he ingeniously constructed a tapered tone arm which connected soundbox and horn and amplified the sound on its journey along the airtight passage from the diaphragm to the horn. Johnson also designed an ingenious pivot and bracket for the tone arm that allowed it to move across the disc without bearing down too hard on the stylus in the groove.[10]

The next priority of the inventors, after improving the sound quality, was to increase the volume of playback. There was little doubt that the public wanted louder volume from their acoustic machines.

Once horns replaced eartubes, the reproduction of the phonograph had to compete with all the other noises heard in the living room. Portable machines became popular around the time of World War I, and recorded sound could then be enjoyed in the open, but with an even noisier sonic background. Finally, the dance crazes increased the demand for more volume, for instead of sitting quietly and listening, the customer now wanted to whirl around the room to the accompaniment of recorded dance music.

Edison's machine was at a disadvantage in this respect, because his first priority was clear articulation, and the disc was known to play louder than the cylinder. The first option to bring greater volume was to increase the scale of the whole system – from groove to amplifying horn – but this was rejected as impractical. Next several amplifying devices were tested in which compressed air or some mechanical means was used to assist the diaphragm as it moved in response to sound waves, much like power-assisted brakes and steering on a car. This idea was incorporated into a machine called the Auxetophone, but it was not widely adopted.

One way to increase volume was to make the reproducer bear down with more pressure (called *tracking force*) as it ran along the groove. This achieved a louder reproduction but only at the expense of more record wear and louder surface noise. A much simpler way of producing more volume was to increase the size of the horn. This is the most noticeable part of any talking machine of the turn of the century. Many are quite beautifully decorated, and some were modelled to look like the petals of a great metal flower. Underlying these artistic efforts was the pressing need to use the horn to improve the performance of the acoustic system of reproduction. Theoretical and empirical methods were used to find the right size and shape of the horn, but it took the power of vacuum tube amplification to satisfy the customers' requirement for more volume.

The next goal of research and development was to increase the playing time of the record. This was not just a matter of getting a little more for the money: the 2-minute duration of playback of the first cylinders and discs put the user in the position of constantly tending the machine, putting one record after another on it. This was a consideration that became important only after the initial novelty of recorded sound wore off. For real music lovers, as distinct from the people who did not mind what they heard as long as they heard something, the short playing time deprived them of the enjoyment of listening to their favorite pieces of classical music, because only a very short amount of it could be put on a record. A hundred years later, when attention spans are notoriously short, a 2-minute piece of music seems a ridiculously brief span of entertainment.

The length of playback was determined by the spacing of the grooves and the length of the groove as it snaked around the disc or cylinder. The standard Edison cylinders at the turn of the century could play for only about 2 minutes, while 7-inch discs could play a little longer. Longer cylinders and larger discs were introduced in the twentieth century. The disc had an advantage because it was easier to increase its diameter without making major changes to the player. Discs of 10, 12, and 14 inches were available in the first decade of the twentieth century; these discs could play for about 4 minutes.

The playing time of a record could be lengthened without enlarging it by cutting more grooves per inch into it. This approach depended on a smaller tip for the stylus and a recording medium that was hard enough to hold more grooves. Crowding the grooves closer together ran the risk of the stylus breaking down the thin walls of the groove and scratching across the record.

The phonograph and its record is a good example of a technological system in which each element is dependent on the other. A change in one part of the machine required a corresponding alteration in another part. Every improvement in the mechanics of reproduction, from heavier soundboxes to sharper styli, had to be matched by improvements in the chemical composition of the records or the benefits might be wasted. The need to increase volume and extend playing time put a premium on finding an improved record medium; wax compounds had reached the end of their potential by the first decade of the twentieth century.

At this very time, and by a lucky coincidence, there were several important innovations in plastic materials. The replacement of soft waxes by celluloid and phenol resins brought significant improvements in the quality of recorded sound. Reproduction was louder and clearer. The harder recording medium allowed more grooves to be squeezed onto a record and brought a few extra seconds of music. Although the machines are very impressive, the most important artifacts of the history of recorded sound in the early twentieth century are the cylinder and disc records made out of early plastics.

The technology which decided the struggle between cylinder and disc formats was not embedded in the machines but the records, and perhaps the most important feature of the records was the music on them and not their chemical composition. With numerous new and improved products on the market, and each one claiming higher fidelity, the often confused customer was forced to choose between technical innovations that he or she usually did not understand. Salesmen found that the public preferred discs not so much because of better sound quality, which was hard for the untrained ear to determine, but because discs were easier to handle and took up less storage space. Customers reported that disc players were easier to operate than cylinder phonographs because it required less care and dexterity to lower a stylus onto the disc.[11]

Simplicity of operation, ease of storage, and the slightly louder volume of the disc were the critical factors in its ascendancy over the cylinder. Thomas Edison's obsession with continually improving the sound reproduction of the phonograph was more the result of his own perfectionism than feedback from the marketplace, and it was probably difficult for him to comprehend that the listener might prefer the disc not because it sounded better but because it was easier to store. The attention of Edison's engineers and historians of technology was always focused on the performance of the machine and the various technical elements in the system of reproduction. How ironic that these were secondary considerations to the potential customer examining phonographs and gramophones in the showroom. It was the small matter of where to put the records and how many could be squeezed into a small space which often made the difference.

It is significant that the final victory in the battle of cylinder and disc was achieved not so much by a technological innovation but by a change in the look of the talking machine. Little consideration had been given to its appearance since the advent of the spring-motor models in the 1890s. The basic configuration of the cylinder or disc works sitting on a metal top plate of a rectangular wooden box (containing the motor), and attached to a horn was the standard. The major cosmetic differences were the kinds of horns available, from the basic tin funnel shape to the enormous, gaudily painted "morning glory" horns, which had to be supported by a special attachment. Whatever horn one purchased it still dominated the line of the machine, adding to its bulk and providing an unsightly dust collector.

Figure 6.5. Advertisement for the Victrola. (Courtesy of General Electric)

There had been several attempts to re-route the horn through the interior of the player, but none made any impact until Victor introduced its Victrola model in 1906.

The Victrola was Victor's most successful product and one of the most influential talking-machine designs of the twentieth century. It was the work of Eldridge Johnson, who assembled all the technological advances of the previous decade and put them into a completely new package. The Victrola's spring-driven mechanism had Johnson's tapered tone arm connected to a horn which increased its diameter at a constant rate, reproducing the mechanical amplification of sound in the same manner as a musical instrument. Yet instead of sitting on top, the horn turned down underneath the turntable and faced the listener through the louvered doors of the cabinet. The Victrola had a totally enclosed mechanism – including the horn. It was designed to look like a fine piece of furniture, with its function artfully concealed beneath the polished wood cabinet.

The name *Victrola* might have been inspired by the Aeolian Company's *Pianola*, the most successful player piano on the market and a well-recognized brand name that denoted a musical instrument of high quality.[12] The piano had been the main source of music in the home before the mass production of the phonograph. Yet its size and expense limited it to the parlors of the well-to-do middle classes, and it had become a symbol of affluence and good taste.

For the many Americans who wanted first-class music in their parlors, the time and effort required to master a musical instrument was a drawback. The manufacturers of pianos found a technological solution to this problem in the player piano, a mechanical alternative to the piano that read holes in rolls of paper to activate the piano's hammers. With a common heritage in the punched strips of tape of automatic telegraphs, the player piano and the Victrola met the need for a handsome machine that could produce fine music at the touch of a lever.

Priced at $200, the Victrola was aimed at the luxury market. Its main selling point was the way it looked and the fact that it would be a suitable addition to other pieces of fine furniture in the home. Its concealed horn did nothing for the quality of its reproduction, and in fact it had a smaller horn than the lower-priced table models. But this mattered little to the thousands who bought it. Once a piano had graced the parlor of the middle-class home and gave it an air of refinement and culture. Now a fine Victrola and a collection of the exclusive Victor Red Seal records made the same statement.

It became fashionable to own a Victrola. It was so popular that it became a household name for any talking machine. Dancing to the music played by a phonograph or gramophone was called a "Victrola Party." Even today those lucky enough to own an antique disc player in a fine wooden cabinet will often refer to it as a "Victrola," whatever the make. The Victrola overturned existing ideas about what a talking machine should look like and established the basic design of disc players for the next 20 years.

The bad news from Edison's sales force was that America was "Victrola Crazy," and sales of cylinder machines were dropping sharply.[13] The immediate and smashing success of the Victrola caused a shock wave that ran through the laboratories and offices of the talking-machine world. At West Orange, the aging inventor embarked upon a final, desperate experimental campaign to revive the cylinder format, but the Edison Amberolas could not stem the tide, and plans were quickly made to bring out a disc machine.

Although the West Orange works maintained production of cylinder models until the 1920s and Edison continued to experiment to perfect his phonograph, the introduction of an Edison disc player in 1913 was notice that the cylinder was on its way out as a viable technology. Touted as Edison's greatest achievement, the Diamond Disc marked the high watermark of the acoustic phonograph. Nowadays it is remembered for the purity of its tone and the brilliance of its reproduction – the result of the very hard condensite record and the diamond stylus. However impressive the machines and the claims made by its creator, the Diamond Disc line was a commercial failure. For all its beauty and faithful reproduction of music, the Diamond Disc machines are significant only for what they tell us about the pitfalls of introducing a new audio technology.

Although the lateral cut had become standard for most disc records, Edison chose to remain in the hill-and-dale format. It was impossible to play a lateral cut record on a hill-and-dale machine and vice versa, so owners of an Edison machine could buy only hill-and-dale cut records, and owners of Victrolas could not play Edison Diamond Discs. This deprived the Diamond Disc player of a library of pre-recorded music to play on it. Edison's attention was, of course, on the machine and not the records, which proved to be his undoing. His business managers soon saw that the lack of software, pre-recorded discs, was discouraging people from buying the hardware, the disc player.[14] The failure of this technology provided an important lesson which several other manufacturers were to learn the hard way during the twentieth century.

Although universal reproducers were devised after World War I to allow a listener access to both vertical and lateral cut records,

Figure 6.6. The Diamond Disc record, "A product of the Edison laboratories." (Author)

they came too late for the Diamond Disc to mount an effective challenge to the Victrola.

In 1914 about 23 million discs were manufactured, compared to only 3 million cylinders. Edison continued to make cylinders throughout the 1920s for the millions who owned phonographs, but he was almost alone. Retailers who stocked cylinder machines had a harder job selling them after the introduction of lower-priced Victrolas. By the time of World War I, the cylinder record was considered old-fashioned, which was fatal in an industry that prided itself on being at the cutting edge of technology.

It was a widely held belief that disc records sold best in cities and cylinders remained the favorite in rural areas. There is not enough

Figure 6.7. A farm family in Skidmore, Missouri, and their Edison cylinder phonograph in the 1890s. (ENHS)

proof to support this distinction, although cylinder machines were normally cheaper than discs. When black and white rural folk began to ask for "them plate records" instead of cylinders, the end was in sight.[15] The postwar depression administered the final blow to Edison's cylinder business, and hardly any were sold after 1923.

By the late 1920s Edison's phonograph was in deep trouble. Even the name was out of fashion. There had been a time when every small manufacturer had produced a talking machine with a name that ended in *phone*: the Manophone, Operaphone, Artophone, Compactophone, and even the Ediphone. The success of the Victrola changed this because *ola* became the most popular suffix. The introduction of Victor's line of Orthophonic models in the 1920s, which played electrically recorded records, made *ic* the desirable suffix, and machines now required a name ending in *phonic* to sell. The competition was able to depict the phonograph as an obsolete technology, and the name given by Edison to his favorite invention became a disadvantage in selling it.[16]

The Edison phonograph format devised in 1877 came to an end in 1929 when he ceased manufacture, and although his dictating machines continued to use an extended-length cylinder in the 1930s, the general public soon associated recorded sound with the revolving disc. Yet Edison had given them more than 30 years of sound reproduction with his cylinder, and the name *phonograph* lived long after the machines were forgotten. It was used indiscriminately as a term for the talking machine in the United States (as it is in this book), and it still stands for the technological system that mates stylus with the spiral groove of the record. An examination of the front of any home stereo will prove this, for there is always a button or knob with the word PHONO next to it – a reminder of the great contribution that Thomas Edison made to the technology of recorded sound.

7. Competing technologies

The competition between cylinder and disc, and lateral and hill-and-dale cut, had been fierce, but it paled in comparison to the threat of a new technology which appeared in the mid-1920s. Not since Edison's invention of the phonograph had the American public been so excited about a new entertainment technology as it was about radio. "In all the history of inventing nothing has approached the rise of radio from obscurity to power," announced one popular magazine.[1] The "radio craze" was a devastating blow to an already depressed industry which had barely survived the postwar depression of the early 1920s. It was not a threat of improved reproduction but of a new method of delivering the same entertainment. The music heard on the radio was free, and the listener had access to a library of music that was beyond the resources of all but the most determined record collector.

Radio had been originally conceived as a method of telegraphing without wires; by the early twentieth century, it was used to send messages to ships at sea with Morse code. But in the same way that telegraphy gave way to telephony, the wireless telegraph developed into a technology that could transmit the sound of speech through the air to millions of homes. Some inventors saw beyond the point-to-point transmission of radio messages to the transmission of music to an infinite number of listeners. The independent inventor Lee De Forest must be given the credit for the idea of using radio waves to broadcast information and music, although he was not the first to play music over the air waves. Reginald Fessenden, who had once worked for Edison at the West Orange laboratory, had achieved that feat in 1906 with an experimental transmission from Brant Rock, Massachusetts. De Forest's dream of broadcasting, the "invisible empire of the air" as he called it, was demonstrated in an extraordinary experiment carried out in 1910 in New York City. De Forest set up listening stations, much like those imagined by Bellamy more than 20

136

years earlier, and transmitted live music from the Metropolitan Opera to them.[2]

The talking-machine industry was unmoved. A radio broadcasting system required large amounts of capital and the control of numerous patents. There were too many small companies competing with one another. Experienced businessmen like Edison saw no commercial future in the technology. For once, Eldridge Johnson of Victor agreed with him: "The radio industry is going to be fighting over patents for years. We are not going to put out a radio."[3] Nobody could have expected the intervention of the United States government, which stepped into the business in the aftermath of World War I and negotiated a peace treaty. The formation of the Radio Corporation of America (RCA) in 1919 pooled the important patents, which were largely in the hands of General Electric, American Telephone and Telegraph (AT&T), and Westinghouse – all large, integrated companies with an impressive track record of introducing new technology.

The first radio sets were made up of components that were bought separately and then assembled into a receiver. They ran on batteries, and the listener used eartubes to hear the sound – just like the early phonographs. Westinghouse and RCA soon brought out simple single-circuit receivers. The weak sounds that came out of these early sets convinced the talking-machine companies that radio had no future as a provider of music in the home. Yet by 1921 there were over 250,000 radio sets in the United States. Yearly sales increased to 400,000 in 1922, and the number of broadcasting stations exceeded 200.[4] The first radio boom had begun. There was a noticeable decrease in the sales of pianos, sheet music, and talking machines.

The industry of recorded sound saw radio as a competing technology which threatened to replace their products in American homes. This adversarial relationship led them to prevent their artists from broadcasting, thus depriving radio of a pool of performing talent. The Victor and Edison companies released comic records that parodied the awful noises coming out of radio loudspeakers and missed no opportunity to criticize the sound quality of broadcasts.

Yet the idea of radio followed on the success of the talking machine. The "Radio Music Box," as it was first called, was seen by David Sarnoff of RCA as "a household utility in the same sense as the piano or phonograph."[5] The Big Three had brought Americans together in their homes to listen to music and had spent millions of dollars to convince them that this was a desirable and worthwhile way to spend leisure time. The great advantage of radio was that it brought this "Victrola Music" into the home for free.

By 1923 the radio boom seemed to be running down. In terms of the reproduction of music, there was no comparison with the sound of records. The commercial radio stations could offer only a small selection of music, and most of their programming was taken from records. The talking-machine industry hoped that listeners would tire of the poor sound quality and limited repertoire of radio, forgetting that it had overcome the same disadvantages in the 1880s and 1890s.

After disappointing sales in 1923 and 1924, both competing businesses looked to the vital Christmas season of 1924 for recovery. Whereas all the talking-machine manufacturers could offer was a change in the design of their cabinets, the radio makers brought out greatly improved receivers in self-contained units – they too had grasped the importance of creating a consumer product which would go into the home as a piece of furniture. "Almost everybody immediately bought a radio set," remembered one Victor employee, and all phonograph manufacturers suffered as consumers rushed to purchase improved radio sets. During the "radio Christmas" of 1924, there were 200 companies marketing radio equipment and no sign that public enthusiasm for it was about to diminish. The industry of recorded sound felt the dark cloud of impending doom settling over it. Victor suffered a decline in sales of 60 percent in 1924, and sales of Edison phonographs dropped more than 50 percent.[6]

Radio's development as a commercial technology followed the same path as the phonograph, but it occurred at a much faster rate. In less than 5 years, it had moved from technical novelty in the hands of a few enthusiasts to a major force in home entertainment. Advances in technology had been matched by lower prices and improved programming. Radio captured the imagination of the American public, and in living rooms all over the country, phonographs and gramophones were abandoned for another talking machine.

The situation of the recorded sound industry became desperate as sales declined steadily. The executives of the Big Three, who had once scoffed at the idea of radio and its "tinny" sound, were now ready to learn from their competitors. The appeal of radio was not just the novelty of "listening in" to voices and music that were somehow travelling invisibly through the air. The electronic amplification of music carried out by the radio's vacuum tubes brought a new sound to American ears – a booming, brilliant sound that could fill up a room.

While Edison and Johnson scorned the radio sound, American consumers were delighted with the increase in volume and the much deeper bass notes. Electronic amplification had a special quality that Americans took to heart and soon wanted to hear from their phonographs. The sound did not come from the depths of the acoustic horns but boomed out from radio loudspeakers. It was not as delicate and as well articulated as the reproduction of an Edison Diamond Disc, but it was loud enough to dance to, and its raucous volume suited the music of the Jazz Age.

Throughout the 1920s the phonograph and gramophone manufacturers had been aware of the listener's desire for greater volume from their machines. The success of radio forced them into a desperate search to find a way of increasing the volume of reproduction. Special attachments were sold to add onto acoustic phonographs to make them sound like radio, but these were only gimmicks. The search for more volume and the "radio sound" inevitably led to the same vacuum tubes which received the broadcast signal and amplified it. The industry of recorded sound could not beat radio, so they joined it, adopting the technology which produced the "radio sound." Nowadays we would use the term *electronic* to describe the process of turning sound into minute currents of electrons and amplifying them, but in the mid-1920s this term had not yet been coined. *Electrical recording* was the name given to the new system.

The electrical era of sound recording

The next stage of recorded sound technology was again the product of research on the telephone. The work of Edison, Bell, and Berliner on turning speech into electric currents had been taken up by the corporate laboratories of the telephone industry. Bell's variable-resistance telephone, Edison's carbon button transmitter, and Berliner's microphone had been the starting point of several experimental programs carried out by Western Electric – the research arm of AT&T – as part of the strategy to improve telephone service and extend the reach of its messages. Although committed to wired telephone communication, the telephone companies also took an active interest in wireless telephony (radio) because of its potential to provide transcontinental communication.

Although the problems they faced were the same, the laboratories of the telephone companies were very different from those of the inventors of the nineteenth century. Instead of broadly educated generalists, they acquired some of the best young brains in the country, recruiting them from the leading universities. Advanced degrees in science were now a prerequisite to work in a research laboratory. Instead of a handful of experimenters working around the clock in Edison's old Menlo Park laboratory, the telephone laboratories hired hundreds of highly trained technical personnel and put them to work in large teams. Research and development was placed within the context of the business strategy of the companies and made responsive to corporate control. The independent inventor who founded his own companies and kept control of the technology he developed had not entirely disappeared – Lee De Forest was one of them – but he was overshadowed by the large companies and their better financed industrial research.

The most important research program for AT&T was the extension of long-distance telephone service; this was the tool to crush the independent telephone companies. The Western Electric research staff searched for a means to amplify telephone messages to send them over longer distances. After examining magnetic and electromechanical devices, they decided that electronic amplification promised better results. This drew them to examine the newly developed vacuum tube, which was based on Lee De Forest's critical invention of the three-element triode or Audion in 1906. AT&T purchased the rights to De Forest's Audion, and Dr. Harold Arnold led a team at the Western Electric laboratory to turn it into a reliable amplifier.

Electronic amplification was a valuable technology with several commercial applications. One was a public address system which used amplifiers and loudspeakers to fill an auditorium with sound.[7] The amplifier was also a useful tool in the laboratory. The development of precise instruments for measuring sound was given a boost, for now the weak currents produced by the first electrical transducers could be amplified. Western Electric had developed highly sensitive microphones, notably the condenser microphone patented by E. C. Wente in 1917, whose output was so small it had to be amplified by vacuum tubes. The study of speech and hearing was given a new precision, because amplification could be used to distinguish sounds beyond the sensitivity of the ear.

In pursuing the goal of improving the telephone, Western Electric scientists were involved in the study of sound and its transmission along telephone lines. They uncovered new knowledge about the nature of sound and its conversion into electric currents. The availability of precise equipment to measure, amplify, and filter electric currents was of immense value. They could now break down electric speech into its component frequencies and use this data to analyze sound transmission.[8]

These experiments required a means to record sound in order to study it under laboratory conditions; each test message had to be saved like every other experimental result. Acoustic recording was not accurate or precise enough to do this job. There were two options available to them: improve the old acoustic phonographs, or develop a new system based on their mastery of converting sound into electric currents.

A cursory study of acoustic recording was enough to direct them along the latter path. While Thomas Edison was to devote most of his productive career to perfecting the phonograph, it was clear to a younger generation of experimenters that this technology had reached the limit of its usefulness. The two scientists leading this project at Western Electric, Joseph Maxfield and H. Harrison, preferred to use the microphones, amplifiers, and electrical filters on hand.

The system of electrical recording developed by Maxfield and Harrison exploited their knowledge of sound transmission to develop electrical analogies to the mechanical system of hearing. Their system used a condenser microphone to pick up the sound and change it into varying electric currents, an improvement on the way that the telephone mouthpiece turned speech into electricity. A vacuum tube amplifier increased the strength of these currents and used them to drive an electromechanical recording cutter that made a groove in the record. The cutter was balanced to move precisely within a magnetic field, and as the varying currents from the amplifier influenced its movement, it transcribed their wave forms onto the disc.

On playback, the movement of the needle in the groove acted within the magnetic field of the electrical pickup to reproduce the varying currents that carried the sound signal. These currents were in turn amplified by vacuum tubes to drive a loudspeaker. Electrical recording owed a lot to the basic system of telephone transmitter and receiver, which acted like the microphone and loudspeaker, and the newfound power of amplification.

Electrical recording not only had the benefit of the radio sound, it also gave a much wider and more faithful reproduction of the range of sounds heard by the human ear. The great advantage of using an electrical equivalent of sound waves was that the diaphragm in the microphone required only the smallest movement to record a wide range of frequencies, while the diaphragm in the acoustic reproducer moved in a direct physical relationship to the sound waves. The microphone diaphragm moved about one-tenth the distance of the acoustic diaphragm to record the loudest sounds, and its weight was one-twentieth of the Edison recorder. The microscopic movement of the electrical diaphragm meant that it could provide a uniform response to all extremes of the sound spectrum and little of the distortion of the acoustic method.[9]

The Western Electric researchers began to make experimental recordings in 1920. Like Edison's experimenters in the 1880s, they brought musicians to the laboratory to record them. They also gave considerable thought to the chemical basis of the recording medium and to the acoustics of the studio. They visited the studios of phonograph companies and talked with their engineers about their experiences in studio recording.[10] In 1922 they achieved recordings good enough to invite prominent members of the talking-machine industry to listen to their work: Emile Berliner visited the lab, as did Walter Miller, Edison's recording chief.

By 1924 the system was far enough advanced to take to the recording studios of the Victor and Columbia companies and cut some demonstration records. The executives of the Big Three companies were impressed but not impressed enough to immediately acquire the new technology. Their attention was on the radio threat, and they were loathe to abandon the old system and a massive inventory of acoustic machines and recordings.

Yet times were bad and getting worse; radio cut even further into the audience of the Big Three during 1924. Victor and Columbia capitulated and installed the new equipment in their studios to make test recordings. The first were made in Columbia's New York recording laboratory in 1924 by Sam Watkins, a Western Electric engineer. Joseph Maxfield supervised the recordings made in Victor's Camden studios in 1925. This was a time of experimentation, and much of it was trial and error as the equipment was adapted for commercial use. Watkins operated the electrical recorder in the Columbia recording sessions, and it performed well enough to be permanently installed.[11] When Bessie Smith came to Columbia's New York studios in 1925, she found she had to sing into a Western Electric microphone instead of the old recording horn. A new era in recording had begun.

The results of the first electrical recordings were impressive: the records captured a much wider range of the sound of music, and the overall sound quality benefitted from more control over the loudness of each sound. Although it was possible to play an electrically recorded disc on an acoustic machine, it often sounded too loud and strident when compared with the old records. Maxfield and Harrison designed a new acoustic machine to complement the increased volume and frequency range of electrically recorded discs. They calculated that an acoustic horn would have to be around 9 feet long to adequately reproduce all the sound frequencies of the new records, so they experimented with a horn which increased in size exponentially from the soundbox to the outer rim of the horn – bringing a level of amplification far superior to the straight horn. They devised the reentrant (or folded) horn, in which the longer passage along the airtight channel from the soundbox through the coiled horn (up to 6 feet long in some models) produced a level of reproduction that suited the wide range of frequencies captured in electrical recording.[12] The new machine was introduced by the Victor company in 1925 as the Orthophonic.

Playing one of the new records on an Orthophonic was a revelation to listeners accustomed to acoustic reproduction: the dramatic increase in volume, the clear sibilants, and most of all, the amazing reproduction of bass notes. The Orthophonics set the standard in acoustical reproduction. Backed by advertising which rightly claimed that their sound was vastly superior to any other machine, they sold very well. Victor obtained orders for $20 million worth of machines during one promotion. After surviving 2 years of declining sales, Victor recovered in 1926 to one of the most profitable years in its history, making an estimated $7 million profit, which eradicated the $6.5 million loss of the previous year.[13] The Orthophonics maintained Victor's preeminent position in the phonograph industry.

Victor made an agreement with RCA to install radio sets in some of their phonographs. Victor was joined by Columbia and Brunswick, who quickly introduced electrically recorded discs and amplified machines to play them. The first all-electric player, with amplifier, loudspeaker, and electrically powered turntable, was introduced by the Brunswick Company in 1925. Instead of the diaphragm, soundbox, and hollow tone arm arrangement – the assembly that had been the focus of attention of experimenters during the acoustic era – there was now a heavy magnetic pick-up at the end of a solid moving arm. The hollow tone arm which had once collected and amplified sound now had the more mundane job of supporting the magnetic pick-up as it moved across the record.

At first glance this new type of player looks exactly like the old acoustic models it was supposed to replace: the same ornamental cabinets, the same fine woods, and the same upright Victrola shape. A revolution might have taken place inside the works, but this is not evident from the outside. There were good reasons not to give the all-electrics an entirely new look. The manufacturers had large stockpiles of cabinets on hand when electrical recording threw their business into turmoil; rather than discard all this expensive wood, they put the new technology into old casings.

Manufacturers were also reluctant to make too many changes in their product for fear it would devalue their considerable inventories in acoustic sound and frighten off customers. Western Electric had developed electrical recording in secret, and Victor and Columbia did not announce their decision to adopt the technology with a fanfare of publicity. Yet the secret of electrical recording could not be kept for very long; by the end of the 1920s, most record companies were using the new process. Most of the manufacturers had acquired a license from RCA and were producing record players with vacuum tube amplifiers.

The Edison company was the last of the Big Three to make the transition to electrical recording. Edison resisted the new technology with some pride while desperately trying to improve acoustic recording. Yet the days of the phonograph were numbered, and even Edison was forced into electrical recording before the end of the decade with the introduction of the Edisonic models.

The exterior of the talking machine might not have changed much, but inside was an amplifying unit, with its vacuum tubes, and other electrical devices. The mysterious innards of the talking machine had been transformed from polished brass and oiled gear wheels to wires and glowing bulbs. Hiding behind the gauze cloth at the front of the cabinet was an innovation of some importance. The dynamic loudspeaker, which turned the output of the amplifier into sound, had already helped make the radio set into a desirable consumer product. It replaced the earphones of the early models in the same way that the acoustic horn replaced the listening tubes of the phonograph. The loudspeaker was part of the Western Electric system of electrical recording and had been developed in their laboratories. It was a transducer, just like the microphone, because it reversed the process begun by the microphone by turning the amplified electrical currents back into sound waves. Like the microphone, its critical moving part was a moving diaphragm acting within a magnetic field.

In 1925 C. W. Rice and E. W. Kellog of Western Electric laboratories designed a moving coil transducer, in which a coil of wire was placed within a magnetic field and moved in relation to current passing through it. The coil moved a thin, rigid cone attached to a large diaphragm, which re-created the sound wave that had moved the microphone diaphragm at the other end of the system. This new loudspeaker worked so well that virtually overnight all other types disappeared.[14] Western Electric first used this device for their public address system and it was soon applied to radio sets and phonographs.

The loudspeaker freed the user from earphones and could fill a room with loud music. Controlling the volume of reproduction was a welcome novelty for the owner of an electric machine. The volume control was symbolic of the new power provided by vacuum tube amplification. In the acoustic machine there was not much volume to control; it was more a matter of dampening the sound by mechanical means. The Victrola had a set of louvered doors in front of the horn that could be opened and closed. The Diamond Disc player had a ball of soft cloth which could be inserted into the mouth of the horn, either by hand or in the more expensive models by a cable attached to a lever, to lower the volume by gradually suffocating the sound, or "putting a sock in it."

Some designers of acoustic players realized that listeners like to control the sound of the playback and had provided knobs to be twiddled and turned. There were mysterious "tone modifiers" such as the one attached to the Manophone of the Delpheon Company. A silk cord held by the listener, it was supposed to "transmit your personal feelings" to the instrument. The company assured potential customers that this was a machine that you could really play. How this actually worked was never explained. The important point was that the listener could imprint his or her mood onto the reproduction of music, a feature that in the acoustic era was more psychological than technological.[15] The Vocalion model of the Aeolian Company also came with a string attached, and it too was advertised as the "instrument of personal expression."

The volume control on the electric machines was all business. It was like the one on radio sets, a round knob made of a tough Bakelite plastic. It could increase the power of amplification until the loudspeakers began to rattle. Turning up the volume control was the initiation into the electrical era of sound reproduction for the listener.

The shift to electric recording and reproduction gave the industry of recorded sound the means to compete with radio. *Talking Machine World* was quick to blame the slump of 1924/1925 on a failure to innovate in the face of a new technology and was optimistic that the new sound of recordings would win back an audience that had been lost to radio and motion pictures.[16]

Some talking-machine companies even joined the enemy and began making radio sets. By the end of the 1920s, they were producing radio/phonograph combination sets, which housed both radio and phonograph in the same cabinet and employed a common vacuum tube amplifier. Instead of the acoustic horn, the sound came out of the radio loudspeaker. These sets were first marketed in 1928, and 81,000 were sold. The following year 218,000 were sold, giving the impression that these machines might be the mass-market product of the 1930s.[17]

The combination of two competing technologies in one consumer product provides a fitting conclusion to the struggle of radio and talking machine. What once had been perceived as a fight to the death turned out to be a beneficial relationship in which both technologies could flourish. The rise of radio did not mean the demise of the phonograph and the end of recorded sound as some feared – only the beginning of a new phase in mechanized entertainment in which the two coexisted. By placing the phonograph in front of a broadcasting transmitter, radio pioneers like Reginald Fessenden had brought together two powerful technologies which were to influence popular culture in the twentieth century. Theirs was to be a symbiotic relationship in which they complemented rather than competed with one another.

Much the same had occurred with the competing technologies of talking machine and piano. Those who had predicted the downfall of the piano after the introduction of the phonograph had been proved wrong, for in 1914 a record 323,000 pianos were produced. Although this number was less than the 514,000 talking machines produced that year, it was clear that the piano was not doomed.[18] The popularity of record players had been exploited by the manufacturers of player pianos, which also provided music automatically. Americans did not replace playing the piano with playing records as the advertising campaigns of the record companies had suggested. Nor did they desert recorded sound for radio; both benefitted from an increased interest in music in the age of mechanized entertainment.

Talking pictures

The electrical method of sound reproduction did more than mark a stage in the technology of recorded sound; it brought together sound and image, permanently fusing their interests and uniting their technological development into one thread. It also brought about a powerful new entertainment industry. New methods of recording and reproducing sound had been developed for several commercial applications, and the most profitable field for the new technology was not in the talking-machine business but in motion pictures.

Talking pictures had been an important experimental goal since the introduction of the first film camera in the 1890s. Edison's original idea for motion pictures was as a visual accompaniment for recorded sound: the sound was the important thing. From the 1890s onwards, numerous inventors attacked the problem of synchronizing sound and image, using acoustic, electrical, and photographic methods of sound recording.

The advent of electrical recording was an important event in these research programs. At the Western Electric laboratories, it was recognized at an early stage that the new method of recording had a commercial application in films. By 1922 most of the elements of a system of talking pictures were available to them: electrical recording from microphones, amplification of the sound, and its reproduction

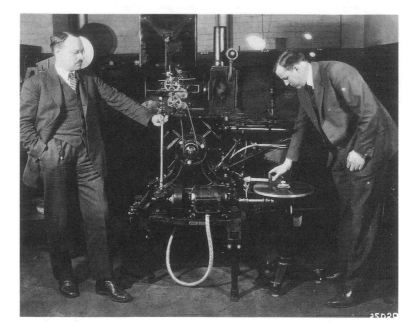

Figure 7.1. Stoller and Pfannenstiehl pose next to the Western Electric disc player attached to a film projector. (Courtesy of AT&T Archives)

in theaters over loudspeakers. The only thing lacking was the means of synchronization. Western Electric had considerable expertise in speed control and synchronization of electric motors. These techniques had been developed in research on multiplex telegraphy and the transmission of pictures over wires. In 1923 two experts were transferred to the teams working on film sound to develop a method of synchronization.

Henry Stoller and Harry Pfannenstiehl used separate electric motors, which drove the film camera and disc recorder, and coupled them in the same circuit to achieve synchronization.[19] The recorder transcribed sound onto an oversized 16-inch disc (often called a *platter*) which rotated at 33⅓ revolutions a minute. Although reproduction at this slower speed was not as clear as that from a disc revolving at 78 rpm, it was judged good enough for film sound, and it did last for the required 10 minutes. The recorder was started as the camera began to roll. The stylus was placed at the beginning of the groove, which was on the inside of the disc, and it moved outward to the edge. After filming and processing, the disc and the reel of film were loaded onto Stoller and Pfannenstiehl's playback machine, which joined film projector and disc player. The operator matched a mark at the beginning of the disc with one at the start of the film and started playback in both audio and visual modes at precisely the same time.

During 1923 Western Electric experimenters tested the complete system and made some short talking films. As the grand old man of the talking machine, Thomas Edison was invited to the laboratory to see the latest development of his invention. The engineers noted that he seemed impressed by their work, although he can hardly have been pleased to see that his system of acoustic reproduction was now clearly obsolete.[20]

Once the executives of AT&T had overcome their reservations about entering the sordid and unstable world of motion picture production, the Western Electric research teams were given the green light. They worked furiously to perfect the system and begin its commercial exploitation. Speed was of the essence because they knew that they were not alone in this field. Talking pictures had attracted the attention of many inventors who hoped to strike it rich. Far more dangerous to Western Electric were the other large companies with research laboratories that had been drawn into electronics by the development of radio. Corporate giants such as GE, Westinghouse, and RCA were also interested in finding commercial applications for vacuum tube amplification.

Western Electric's closest competitor was the independent inventor Lee De Forest, who had succeeded in putting the sound track onto the film itself. In the sound-on-film system, sound waves from a microphone were converted into electrical impulses that modulated the light given off by a special lamp. These varying levels of light were then photographed on film to make the sound track. As the developed film was run back through a projector, a lamp sent a beam of light through the sound track to re-create the pattern of photographed light. These were received by a photoelectric cell that converted the varying intensities of light to varying intensities of electrical impulses. These in turn were amplified and converted back into sound waves which powered a loudspeaker.

Lee De Forest began experiments on this technology after he sold his Audion to AT&T. He demonstrated it in 1923 and made over a thousand short Phonofilms, which were shown in small theaters, but he did not succeed in persuading any of the major film producers to adopt his idea. De Forest had shared the secrets of his Phonofilm with another inventor, Theodore Case, who improved the sound-on-film technology and tried to sell it to film companies. Case finally found an interested party in Fox Film, a company in the second rank of film producers with ambitions to grow larger. William Fox had begun his career as the proprietor of a nickelodeon – a small storefront film theater – and had gradually built up his company to encompass both film production and exhibition. Because sound on film was an experimental technology, he decided to employ it to make short newsreels which were shown before the main feature – a much easier technical challenge than musical shorts or full-length feature films.

At the same time that Fox was trying out the De Forest Phonofilm equipment, the giant General Electric Company was working on a sound-on-film system based on its Pallo-Photophone device, which produced a pattern of varying width on the film. This technology had first been employed to make special "Light Ray" records for the Brunswick Company, but these experiments met with little success. As one of the parent companies of RCA, GE had the full support of RCA's David Sarnoff, who committed his company to assist in its technical development. Western Electric also had a foothold in this technology. Their system used a light modulated by sound waves to record a pattern of varying densities on the film. There were three competing technologies of sound on film available in 1923: the De Forest Phonofilm, General Electric's variable area, and Western Electric's variable density. The race was on to bring sound to the movies.

Western Electric decided to concentrate their efforts onto sound on disc. Although sound on film had many advantages, it was a completely new technology that was going to require new methods of manufacture and new techniques in operation. On the other hand, the disc format was well established. The 16-inch records were to be pressed in Victor's Camden plant, which had 20 years of experience. Western Electric executives reasoned that the familiarity with disc technology would ease the transition to sound.[21]

In 1924 representatives of several large film companies were invited to watch a demonstration of sound on disc. They were not enthusiastic. They had seen numerous other sound systems over the years, and none of them had been successful. In 1913 Edison had prematurely announced that he had perfected talking pictures, but his acoustic kinetophone had been a resounding failure. The sound-on-disc system demonstrated by Western Electric did no more than supply canned music to a projected film. The film exhibitors already had professional musicians in their theaters who could do the job much better than recorded sound.

Silent movies had never been watched in silence because there was always a musical accompaniment, from a single pianist in a nickelodeon to 100-piece orchestras in large movie palaces, to provide music and sound effects to heighten the drama on screen. Film makers commissioned a great deal of music to accompany their films, and several popular songs had made their mark as theme songs for motion pictures. The leaders of the film industry were much more interested in avoiding the payment of royalties on film music than automating the process of sound accompaniment of film.[22] They had a large investment in silent films and were unwilling to abandon it for a new and untried technical novelty.

It was therefore left to a smaller concern to see the advantages of Western Electric's system and manage its commercial introduction. The Warner brothers had started in the nickelodeon business in Newcastle, Pennsylvania, at the turn of the century. Sam ran the projection machine, Jack sang in the pit, and the eldest brother Harry ran the business. From these small beginnings they moved to Hollywood and produced their first feature film in 1918. By 1925 they were building up a distribution network of film rental services and movie theaters to market the growing output of their Sunset Boulevard studios.

Warner Bros.' initiation into the new technology of electric amplification came when they built a radio station. They saw that this important new form of entertainment could also be used to advertise their films. Sam Warner heard about Western Electric's new technology from radio experts he consulted. He told his brothers that electrical recording could be married to a public address system of amplifiers and loudspeakers to fill up their theaters with sound. Their business strategy was to replace the professional musicians in theaters, enabling their smaller exhibitors to provide the kind of musical accompaniment that was heard in the big picture palaces. It was never Warner Bros.' intention to make a synchronized sound track to motion pictures; all they wanted was an orchestral accompaniment of re-

Figure 7.2. Making talking pictures at the Manhattan Opera House in 1926. The film camera is in the booth on the right. (Courtesy of AT&T Archives)

corded sound. In the words of Harry Warner, the chief executive of the company, "Who the hell wants to hear actors talk? The music – that's the big thing about this."[23]

The Warner Bros. film company made an agreement with Western Electric in 1925 to introduce the sound-on-disc system. They formed a joint company, the Vitaphone Corporation, and built an experimental sound studio in Brooklyn where the system could be developed further.[24] The music for their first talking picture was all important. Three prominent composers were commissioned to write the film score for "Don Juan," and the music was recorded by the New York Philharmonic Orchestra in the Opera House in New York City, which had been hastily converted into a recording studio – Western Electric's recording equipment was crammed into a cubicle close to the stage.

Recording the sound track was a long and arduous process that took months of work. Distracting noises from the outside interfered with recording, and there was the old problem of keeping the recording needle from overcutting into an adjacent groove when the music reached a loud crescendo or when a deep bass note made the needle jump from the disc. Warner Bros. and Western Electric technicians had to iron out the problems in the equipment as they went along.

The first Vitaphone program was not ready until August 1926. The response to "Don Juan" was enthusiastic but not overwhelming. The audience was fascinated with the sound, but the film industry executives who were present at the premiere still had their doubts about the commercial potential of sound pictures. To them it was still a novelty.

The biggest film companies – Loew's/Metro Goldwyn, Universal, Paramount, First National, and Producers Distributing Corporation (United Artists) – resolved to do nothing. They agreed to stay out of negotiations to purchase equipment until all the various methods of putting sound on film and disc had been fully evaluated. In the meantime radio appeared to be keeping Americans at home and away from movie houses. On nights that popular radio programs were broadcast, receipts from theater attendance dropped alarmingly.[25] By 1926 it was clear that something had to be done to ward off the radio threat.

There was no doubt at Warner Bros. what the course of action should be. They continued to make short Vitaphone films, which contained synchronized speech and music, at their Brooklyn studios and released several in the first half of 1927. Betting everything on the commercial success of sound, Warner Bros. shipped Vitaphone equipment to the West Coast to set up a sound stage to make feature productions. Harry Warner had already purchased the rights to a successful Broadway production that would be the next full-length Vitaphone feature.

"The Jazz Singer" was a sentimental play about a cantor's son who left the Jewish ghetto to make a career on Broadway. He abandoned the traditional music of his family and religion for the new, popular music of jazz. Although a great success, he returned home as his father was dying to reunite with his family. Al Jolson was signed in the lead role. He was perfect for the part, since his own life story reflected the story of the play. In 1926 he was at the apex of his career. As America's most successful vaudeville performer, Jolson had forged a close

Figure 7.3. Al Jolson in a famous pose from "The Jazz Singer" with the microphone just above him. (Courtesy of AT&T Archives)

relationship with his fans in the theater; he had the ability to communicate with them from the stage like no other music-hall star.[26] The talking film was to enable him to reach an even larger audience.

Unlike "Don Juan," "The Jazz Singer" was to have synchronized songs in addition to background music. Although they had made several shorts with synchronized sound, the Warner brothers were still a little unsure if their experimental sound equipment would do the job, and they were even more doubtful about its impact as entertainment. During filming, the unpredictable Jolson ad-libbed a line he had made famous on the music-hall stage: "Wait a minute. Wait a minute. You ain't heard nothing yet!" It sounded fine on the playback, and Sam Warner kept it in the film. Jolson's big speech came during his rendition of "Blue Skies." After the first chorus, Jolson stopped singing and turned to his mother: "Did you like that Mama? I'm glad. I'd rather please you than anybody I know of. . . ." The final film had only a few short sections of synchronized speech and music before it lapsed into silence and the familiar intertitles which printed out the dialogue on the screen. Yet it was the synchronized words of Jolson that brought the house down at showings of "The Jazz Singer." Jack Warner remembered that the audience was not prepared for what he called "the emotional surprise" of Jolson talking to them from the screen. He watched them jump to their feet cheering, "as though they had been prodded with an electric stick," and knew that the talking picture had arrived.[27]

In the weeks that followed the premiere of "The Jazz Singer" in October 1927, Warner Bros. mounted a national press campaign to attract attention to their "Supreme Triumph." Despite lukewarm reviews, theater attendance for the film grew rapidly. In 1928 the film began to set records for the length of run, and it finally grossed the unprecedented sum of $3 million. By the end of the year, the returns from the "The Jazz Singer" and other sound films convinced Warner Bros. to shift all their film production into "talkies."[28]

In the same year that Warner Bros. released "The Jazz Singer," William Fox demonstrated the improved Movietone system of sound on film to the press in several newsreels. When Charles Lindbergh set off to fly the Atlantic alone and created the greatest news story of 1927, Fox's Movietone cameras were there to record not only the sight but the sounds of that historic event. A few months after Lindbergh's triumphant return to the United States, Warner Bros. announced the premiere of "The Jazz Singer." Exactly 50 years after Edison's invention of the phonograph, the talking picture had become a reality.

With the success of the sound-on-disc system assured, Western Electric formed Electrical Research Products Inc. (ERPI) to market the technology to all of the film industry – after it had renegotiated the exclusive contract with Warner Bros. to use sound technology. It then made a cross-licensing agreement with Fox to get access to sound-on-film technology. All the large film companies took out licenses from ERPI in 1928 and began to make talking pictures. The process of wiring up film theaters for sound moved ahead very rapidly. In 1928 more than 1,000 installations were made. Yet the pace of innovation in talking pictures was accelerating, and the sound-on-disc technology that achieved such a brilliant success in 1927 was to have an extremely short commercial life.

The basic impracticality of using sound on disc was a result of the difficulties of synchronizing disc player and projector. There were too many things that could go wrong in the projection booth, and even the slightest misjudgment in lining up the beginning of the reel of film with the disc could ruin synchronization and the whole performance. Discs were easily broken, lost, or mixed up and played in the wrong order. Even as early as 1928, it was clear that the future of talking pictures was sound on film – easy to operate and almost foolproof in synchronization.

The two optical systems of varying density and varying area were quickly applied to movie making. General Electric's variable-area system was used successfully in 1927 for RKO's World War I drama "Wings" and the first feature produced with the Western Electric variable-density track was made in 1929. The advantages of sound on film were quickly evident; the knotty problem of synchronization was solved immediately because both sound and image were on the same piece of film. One set of film was used to record the sound track, another held the images, and the two were married in the printing stage. ERPI began to license sound-on-film equipment, and most of the major film producers adopted it, even Warner Bros., which quietly discarded sound on disc in 1930.[29]

Despite the abandonment of sound on disc, AT&T still managed to dominate the technology of talking films. In the annual report of 1929, AT&T could boast that Western Electric equipment was being used to make 90 percent of the sound films in production.[30] An examination of the credits of many old movies will often reveal that it was a "Western Electric Recording." The strategy of the telephone company to develop sound equipment for movies had met with unqualified success, just as their electrical recording system had transformed the industry of recorded sound.

The introduction of electrical recording in films and talking machines marked the end of the era of the heroic inventor. The story of talking pictures begins with the ideas and ambitions of independent inventors – Bell, Edison, and De Forest – and ends with organized research programs in company laboratories. The same held true for recorded-sound technology. The work once done in private laboratories and attics was now done in corporate research laboratories. Innovation was now in the hands of great companies who found that their expertise in basic science could be exploited to move into new businesses such as phonograph records and talking films. The independent inventor simply did not have the financial clout to introduce a new technology in recorded sound by the end of the 1920s.

Electrical recording also sounded the death knell for many small companies in recording and film making. This was not a cheap technology. Western Electric exacted a high price for their recording technology, including an 8 percent royalty on gross revenues for sound films, and not all could afford it. Converting to talking pictures was not merely the acquisition of new equipment – there were numerous technical problems to be solved before it worked properly, and the whole process of making films had to be recast. Only large film producers had the resources to manage this change. Their engineering staffs worked with the corporate laboratories that had developed the equipment to eliminate the inevitable teething troubles of sound on disc.

Silent film makers hoped that talking pictures were just a novelty that would soon wear off. At first the talkies' sound quality was so poor that many critics comfortably predicted their early demise.[31] But such progress was made in adding sound to pictures that by 1930 film making had changed significantly, and so had the motion picture industry. Although several small companies continued to make silent movies into the 1930s, they played to smaller and smaller audiences.

Electrical recording is a good example of a rapid and complete technological change. It swept away acoustic recording in a few years. In the film industry the transition was even more swift and dramatic. Here was a complicated technology in several different forms, a confusing patent situation, and a mass of different formats and standards. The legal battles that were anticipated between the competing systems of sound for film, and between ERPI and the film producers, failed to materialize.[32] After years of hesitation and indifference, Hollywood took the plunge into sound; by 1930 the task of conversion was complete. The silent film disappeared almost overnight, and with it went the great investment in that technology and the livelihoods of hundreds of actors and musicians. Only Charlie Chaplin managed to keep making silent films in the 1930s. The future was in the hands of large film studios and their talking films.

8. Empires of sound

The move to talking pictures required a massive construction program. The cost to rebuild Hollywood's studios ranged from $23 million to $50 million. When compared with the estimate of the value of the original studios, which was around $65 million, this was a staggering amount of capital. Film producers had to borrow millions of dollars to make the conversion to sound. The recovery of these fixed costs pushed them into making the most of their resources by mass-producing films.[1] Although the adoption of these manufacturing techniques had begun before World War I, the transition to sound in the film industry gave it more impetus, pushing the producers to standardize their output and exert more control over production. Sound shaped the way they made films and determined what kind of films they made.

Sound also had a profound effect on the film exhibitors, the businesses which showed the films made by the producers. They were faced with the expense of re-equipping their theaters with special projectors to show talking pictures and installing amplifiers and loudspeakers to reproduce the sound. Depending on the size of the theater, this job could cost over $20,000, and this made it too expensive for small businesses that were often forced to sell out to a larger organization. The independent exhibitors were swallowed up as sound became the standard.

The history of the American film industry is punctuated by struggles between exhibitors and producers. Synchronized sound shifted the balance of power to the film producers, who were encouraged by the prospects of talking pictures to buy theaters and wire them for sound. The studio system that flourished during the Golden Age of Hollywood in the 1930s and 1940s was established by these fully integrated film companies that had moved into sound.

The process of forward integration by film producers into exhibition had begun well before the coming of sound, but the enormous

158

income from talking pictures accelerated the process. The talkies captured the public's attention and created one of the most profitable
periods in the history of Hollywood. This boom gave Hollywood an
atmosphere approaching the enthusiasm of the Klondike gold rush.
The lead was taken by Warner Bros., who took the lion's share of
the spoils of talking pictures. The company made $14 million in 1929,
a $12 million increase over the previous year's profits. Warner Bros.
acquired the Stanley theater chain of 250 exhibitors in 1929 and also
took over the First National studio. Its Sunset Boulevard studios now
made films for 650 theaters. Fox acquired the Poli chain of theaters
and gained control of West Coast Theaters.[2] The two pioneers in
sound had quickly become a major force in exhibition.

Warner Bros. followed the success of "The Jazz Singer" with another Jolson film in 1928. Entitled "The Singing Fool," this was another part talkie: Jolson's singing was interspersed with silent film.
Although ticket prices were set at $3.00, the highest price yet asked
for a film admission, people flocked to see it. It was one of the most
profitable films of the 1920s and 1930s, taking in over $5 million. It
was also the vehicle to make international hits of two of the songs
showcased in the movie. "Sonny Boy" and "Rainbow Around My
Shoulder" were recorded by the Brunswick company and became million sellers. Their release was timed to coincide with the opening of
the film, and such was the demand for records that the Brunswick
factory had to work around the clock to keep pace with orders.[3]

The enormous success of Jolson's films for Warner Bros. pointed
the way for the rest of the industry. Beginning with part silent and
part talking pictures, the producers began to increase the sound component of their films, especially the music. In 1929 *Billboard* reported
that there were fifty musicals under production: "100% all-talking,
all-singing, all-dancing" films. One of these productions was a $2
million musical spectacular called "The King of Jazz," starring Paul
Whiteman and his band.[4] It was one of the first films to use a brand
new technicolor process, another innovation which film producers
hoped would attract moviegoers.

The ability to add sound to film naturally encouraged the studios
to make the most of synchronized dialogue and background music.
The musical play was an ideal vehicle for the new technology, and
film producers hurried to New York to buy up the rights for Broadway productions. The need for a supply of songs and singers had

become apparent when the Vitaphone company began making talking pictures in 1925, and it quickly made an agreement with Victor to use some of its recording artists.[5] With the musical stage of Broadway in precipitous decline in the 1930s, the motion picture industry became the major consumer of music. Film producers moved into the music publishing business. Warner Bros. bought up seven major concerns, including the catalogues of Harms, Chappel-Harms, and Widmark and Sons. MGM acquired Robbins Music, Leo Feist Inc., and Miller Music. Now they no longer had to pay fees for the music they used in film making. As one film executive said, "It is necessary for us to be in the music business . . . we have got to control the music situation."[6]

Successful film producers set out to create integrated media empires covering the production of both film and music. Films had become a most effective way of promoting music. Audiences that had once left music halls humming songs were now leaving movie theaters with film music ringing in their ears. When they went to record stores, it was film themes and songs that they wanted to buy. Columbia advised its dealers that "each week the tune studded talking movie leaves customers of yours with impressively presented theme songs echoing in their memories."[7] Film companies wanted to own the music that their movies had made into hits. They also wanted to collect royalties from the radio stations that played this music and the phonograph companies that recorded it.

The theme song was usually a commissioned piece of music that became the aural trademark of the film. Record companies also released individual songs from films which might become hits if the film was popular. The practice at this time was for several companies to record different versions of the same song. The songs from "The King of Jazz," for example, could be found on different labels by different performers, but only Columbia could claim to have the original version performed by Paul Whiteman, who was under contract to them.

In the acoustic era it was not possible to perfectly re-create the sound an audience heard at a music hall because of the limitations of the recording process. Electrical recording could duplicate the songs heard in film theaters. Much of the music used in films was pre-recorded in special studios rather than recorded live on the sound stage, and these recordings could be used as masters to press duplicates. Columbia could therefore advertise recordings of the songs heard in "The King of Jazz," as "played exactly as it was heard in the movie."[8]

After acquiring music publishers, it was a short step to take over record companies, the next profit source of the music business. Warner Bros. bought Brunswick Records in 1930. Now the company owned the music performed in its films and issued records of them. Their films, their songs, and their records were promoted by their radio station. As a result of this expansion Warner Bros. went from a small company with capital of $10 million in 1927 to a media giant worth $230 million in 1930.[9]

The other major entertainment empire was RCA. The widespread diffusion of the Western Electric sound-on-disc and then sound-on-film systems gave AT&T a commanding presence in film making that its great competitor RCA could not ignore. The commercial success of the Western Electric variable-density technology did not persuade General Electric and RCA to give up on their variable-area system. The management of RCA, led by David Sarnoff, decided that if no film-producing organization would use their system then one would have to be created. In 1927 RCA bought the tiny Film Booking Office of America, which had produced about fifty low-budget films in 1926. Next Sarnoff bought an interest in the Keith-Albee-Orpheum chain of vaudeville and movie theaters. These holdings were merged with several other independent film producers which Sarnoff had acquired to form Radio-Keith-Orpheum (RKO) in 1928. The GE/RCA sound-on-film system was organized into the RCA Photophone division. It now had a film production company to make its talking pictures and about 200 theaters to exhibit them.

The technological origins of RKO can be appreciated by watching the opening credits of its pictures. The corporate logo is a large radio pylon sitting on top of the world. In writing resembling an electric spark, the credits proclaim an "RKO Radio Picture." At the end of the credits, a small RCA logo appears on screen to certify that the picture was made with the RCA Photophone system. RKO was soon to join Warner Bros., Fox, Paramount, and Loews/MGM in the big league of talking-picture producers.

RCA also moved into the music business by purchasing two music publishing companies. In 1919 it took over the Victor Company, the leading member of the Big Three and a force in recording technology. Victor was a large company, and RCA could acquire it only with loans from GE and Westinghouse. The new company was called RCA Victor, a manufacturer of radio sets, radio-phonograph combination sets, and records. RCA now had the great plant that Johnson had built up at Camden, research laboratories, recording studios, and the impressive Victor catalogue, which included some of the finest classical recordings available. It also owned the trademark "His Master's Voice" and the image of Nipper listening to its master.

With the Edison company in decline, the only real competitor to RCA Victor in the record business was Columbia. The depression that followed World War I had hurt Columbia, forcing it into receivership and divesting it of its British branch. The newly reorganized company acquired the Western Electric recording system but had trouble paying for it. Louis Sterling, who now owned the British Columbia company, acquired the American parent in order to gain access to electrical recording. Sterling embarked on an ambitious program of using the new technology to build up a classical record library, and he slowly returned the company to prosperity with the proceeds of record sales.[10]

With the merger of RCA and Victor looming, Columbia looked to enlarge its operations with a foothold in either film or radio. In 1927 it invested in a small radio network, the United Independent Broadcasters, to obtain air time to promote its records. The new organization was called the Columbia Phonograph Broadcasting System. Entertainment had become big business in the 1920s, and it was large corporations that now held sway in the record and motion picture industries.

Brother, can you spare a dime?

The reorganized industry of recorded sound made a slow recovery from the postwar depression. Although annual sales increased slightly every year from 1925 to 1929, there was no comparison with the explosive growth of the radio and motion picture industries. Yearly sales of the talking-machine business remained in the $70 million range, but continuous pressure to lower prices forced profit margins down.

The vacuum tube had brought the new product that the industry desperately needed, but despite dramatically improved fidelity, the all-electrics did not have the same impact on the market as Edison's

Home models or Johnson's Victrola. They were too expensive to become an item of mass consumption, and the millions who had bought spring motor players did not rush to their dealers to exchange them. Electrical reproduction had increased prices: The Brunswick Panatrope cost $350, and the top-of-the-line Victor and Edison machines cost over $400. In the late 1920s this could also have purchased a Ford Model T.

Edison was often quoted as blaming the Model T for the demise of the industry based on his phonograph, and it was true that the automobile was the most attractive of all the new consumer goods available in the 1920s.[11] Yet the fickle, fun-loving Americans of the Jazz Age were tempted by a host of new entertainments – radio, talking films, speakeasies, miniature golf, and amusement parks – and there was a limit on how many dollars they could spend on enjoying themselves. A successful new entertainment often caused a depression in an older one. While Warner Bros. bathed in the triumph of "The Jazz Singer" in 1927, sales of sheet music slumped. As Hollywood musicals grew vastly popular, attendance for Broadway stage plays declined.

Despite these problems the entertainment industry put on a brave face and did its part to give the 1920s its aura of optimism and carefree hedonism. Their products set the tone of the "roaring twenties" with successful songs like "Blue Skies," which was promoted on record, radio, and the movies. It first appeared in a Broadway musical, it was sung by Al Jolson in "The Jazz Singer," and it continued to be recorded through the 1930s. The lyrics summed up the business euphoria of the 1920s – for investors there was nothing but blue skies on the horizon.

This was certainly the attitude of the stock market at this time, and some of the high-flying stocks were linked to the industry of recorded sound. Companies such as AT&T and RCA had provided the growth stocks for the bull market.

The stock market crash in October 1929 provided a symbolic end to a decade of self-indulgence and excess. The good times were now over, and a completely different period was about to begin, a depression so long and deep as to challenge the faith of even the most ardent believers in the capitalist system. The companies that had once appeared too powerful to succumb to any downturn in the economy were now threatened, and the value of their stock plummeted. RCA's common stock had increased to 114 during the great bull market, but by 1932 it fell to 2.[12]

The Edison phonograph business was one of the earliest casualties of the Depression. Just 2 days after the Wall Street crash of October 30, 1929, Thomas A. Edison, Incorporated, ceased manufacture of recorded-sound products. Edison was forced out of the industry he had created with his invention of the phonograph. It would be wrong to blame this disaster on the Depression, for the decline of Edison's phonograph business had began well before 1929. He had paid heavily both for his opposition to electrical recording and for his reluctance to desert the cylinder format. By the time his misgivings about the "radio sound" had been overcome, and a new line of electronic Edisonic machines had been introduced in 1928, it was too late. People had stopped buying Edison phonographs and records.

After the stock market crash of 1929, a soon to be familiar pattern of plant closings and bank failures dominated economic life in the United States. All manufacturers found their sales dropping alarmingly as fear and falling incomes reduced demand for goods. The industry of recorded sound had spent millions of dollars convincing the American consumer that pre-recorded music in the home was a necessity of life rather than a luxury. The dramatic fall in demand was a reminder that it was a luxury and one that worried consumers *were quite willing to give up. After a disappointing sales year of 1929*, in which only $75 million of machines and records were sold, total sales dropped to a new low of $46 million in 1930.

The outlook for the radio business was just as depressing. In 1930 total sales of radio sets dropped 40 percent from the year previous, from $500 million to $302 million. Half the radio stations in America were losing money.

Yet the depression that was ravaging the American economy did not affect the earnings of the film industry. The boom that had begun with the introduction of talking pictures in 1927 showed no sign of dissipating. In fact 1929 was the best year the motion picture industry had ever experienced. Average weekly attendance in movie theaters had climbed from around 70 million a week in 1928 to 115 million in 1929 and maintained an average of 125 million a week in the first half of 1930. At this time every person in the United States over the age of 6 went to the movies once a week on average.[13]

There were more technological innovations in the pipeline. Technicolor promised to bring brilliant, lifelike color to films. In 1929 Fox introduced a wide-screen, sound-on-film process called Grandeur Films, an appropriate term for some of the ambitions of film producers. Profits for the eight largest film producers were over $50 million in 1930, and the crowds who queued for films like "All Quiet on the Western Front" were a sign that the public had not grown tired of the novelty of talking pictures.[14]

The year 1931 brought a different story. Hundreds of banks went under, thousands of factories were closed, and millions became unemployed. The United States was now in the grip of the worst depression in its history. The film industry, which had been considered to be depression-proof, had finally run out of paying customers. The great boom of talking pictures that had fueled massive expansion turned into a bust. Financially overextended and deep in debt, many of the leading companies soon faced bankruptcy. By 1933 four of the eight largest film makers were losing money, and nearly one-third of all movie houses had been shut down.[15]

The winter of 1933/1934 marked the lowest point of the Depression. It was said that President Hoover had promised Al Jolson a medal if he could find a song to lift the spirit of the nation.[16] But the feeling of the times was best summed up by the singer and band leader Rudy Vallee, who popularized a song entitled "Brother, Can You Spare a Dime?" – a comment on the grim realities of the Depression. Vallee was radio's first matinee idol. He hosted the Fleischman Hour on NBC – one of the most popular radio shows of the 1930s. Listeners who tuned in could listen to him singing about the economic malaise of the United States – a far cry from "Blue Skies." The song's voice is that of a veteran of World War I, someone who had built railroads and erected factories in the 1920s but was now unemployed, hopeless and begging for money.

The talking-machine companies had built millions of phonographs and gramophones and duplicated hundreds of millions of records. Now their factories and recording studios stood silent. The sales figures of 1931 told a story of total disaster, dropping from the $46 million of 1930 to $16.9 million. Many more manufacturers and record companies had gone bankrupt.

The Depression affected the sales of ethnic and race records first, because their audiences were devastated in the economic downturn. African American artists were among the first to be dropped by record companies when sales dried up. Black music now went underground as musicians had to find other work to survive. Even well-established stars such as Bessie Smith found their recording work drying up. She neatly summed up the situation: "Nobody want to hear blues no more. Times is hard. They want to hear novelty songs."[17] She was soon glad to accept $50 for a recording session when once she had commanded the fee of $3,000.

The number of record releases slumped. Monthly sales of a thousand or so units could make a recording a hit, compared with the tens of thousands required to make a hit in the booming 1920s. As record sales dropped even further, recording activity was cut down to the absolute minimum – only to complete contractual obligations of signed artists. RCA Victor issued no catalogue at all in 1931, and many of its big-name recording stars were dropped. The management was now frantically cutting costs wherever they could and told studio engineers to cut down recording to one take per selection.

Musicians like the young Benny Goodman, who made a living by playing in recording sessions, found this work ending. Recording engineers found themselves out of work. Happily there were plenty of opportunities for sound technicians on the West coast, where talking pictures were still being made. Discharged employees from the record companies joined song writers, script writers, actors, and agents in the long train ride cross-country to the golden hills of Hollywood.

With record sales at an all-time low, and little hope for the future, it was now possible to purchase record companies at bargain-basement prices. Herbert Yates, an aggressive entrepreneur who had made a fortune in movies, now saw an opportunity to build an entertainment empire by acquiring bankrupt record companies. As owner of the Consolidated Film Laboratories, Yates had taken over film companies which had been unable to pay their bills. He operated several film studios such as Republic Pictures, the producer of cheap cowboy films and "B" movies.

Yates acquired the American Record Company and its record presses in the old Scranton button works. He then went on a buying spree in the record industry, taking over many small companies. Their products were cheap copies of popular songs, traditional music, and novelty records that were sold to chain stores and mail-order houses. The records were usually smaller than the 10- and 12-inch, full-priced records and made out of cheaper materials such as waxed paper, chemically covered paper, and metal. They sold from 25¢ to 50¢ a-piece. The small labels were most concerned with keeping costs to a minimum and therefore avoided recording copyrighted music with well-known stars. Country music and traditional songs sung by unknown performers was their forte. The "hick disc," as *Variety* magazine called it, continued to be popular in rural areas during the Depression.

Some labels, such as Conqueror, were reserved exclusively for the large mail order operations who sold inexpensive records to the rural market. Record companies such as Cameo, Medallion, and Oriole obtained masters from larger companies and used them to stamp cheap copies. These labels were easy prey in the Depression years, and one by one they were acquired by Yates and consolidated into his American Record Company (ARC): Banner, Cameo, Conqueror, Melotone, Pathe, Perfect, OKeh, Romeo, and Vocalion. ARC acquired Brunswick records from Warner Bros. in 1931, giving it a prestigious label with some well-known recording stars, including the Mills Brothers and Bing Crosby. Brunswick became ARC's prestige line, each record selling at 75¢ while the rest of its records sold at 35¢.

Yates was not the only entrepreneur building an empire of record companies. In Europe the Depression had the same effect on the talking-machine industry, and sales plummeted. Louis Sterling had plans to develop an entertainment conglomerate in Europe, and his Columbia organization acquired several phonograph companies. Columbia competed with the British arm of the Victor company, His Master's Voice, to dominate the European recording industry. With sales of records dropping 90 percent in 1930–1931, Sterling amalgamated Columbia and His Master's Voice to form Electrical and Musical Industries (EMI) in 1931. Sterling added more European companies to this combine, including Odeon and Parlophone, until he operated in nineteen different countries ranging from the United States to the Far East. EMI was now the largest record company in the world.[18]

Fear of anti-trust action in the United States led Sterling to sell the American Columbia company to Grigsby-Grunow (the radio manufacturer) in 1931; a few years later it was sold to the American Record Corporation. By 1932 ARC had become the largest record company in the United States, with sales of 6 million units.

These records were destined for the counters of variety stores and rural mail delivery. They might have been cheap and inferior recordings, but they accounted for 60 percent of total unit sales. The market for premium classical recordings had dried up. RCA Victor sold only 3 million units in 1932 (including the sales of its low-priced Bluebird records), and the rest of the industry accounted for only 1 million units. The slide continued into 1933. With total sales at only $6 million, the American record industry had reached its lowest point.

The depressed state of the industry attracted more foreign investors, who saw an opportunity to acquire record companies cheaply. After failing in his attempt to take control of Columbia (before it was sold to ARC), the English investor Ted Lewis decided to buy pressing plants and studios in the United States and set up an American subsidiary of his Decca company in 1934. Lewis persuaded Jack Kapp, who had run the Brunswick company for ARC, to manage the operation. Kapp was not only an experienced record company executive but he also brought many of Brunswick's recording stars with him, including Bing Crosby. The business strategy of Decca was to lower the price of all recordings to 35¢ a disc. This compared with the $1.00 premium discs and the standard 75¢ popular recordings offered by Victor, Columbia, and Brunswick. Instead of a market that had been divided between cheap (35¢) and premium ($1.00) products, Decca set out to equal the best of the competition's recordings with 35¢ discs.

The emergence of Decca and the American Record Company as the two leading companies in the United States was a result of their strategy of lowering the price of records. Herbert Yates and Ted Lewis were not inventors in the mold of Edison or Johnson and could not be called music lovers; they were hard-headed businessmen who restructured the industry to suit the depressed times. Lewis had been attracted into the business by the high sales of several American recordings in Europe. Al Jolson's "Sonny Boy" and Gene Austin's "My Blue Heaven" had sold millions of units worldwide. Lewis saw that an American record company could provide the music for an international entertainment conglomerate.[19]

Decca quickly established itself as the major producer of popular records, especially those destined for juke boxes. Recorded sound weathered the Depression of the 1930s with the help of coin-slot players in public places, just as it had done in the depression of the 1890s.

The introduction of electrical recording had brought significant improvements to the coin-slot machine, for amplification and a dynamic speaker could project sound to every corner of a bar or soda fountain. It now came with discs and a sophisticated record changer.

The first automatic record changer was patented in 1921; it was followed by many different devices to play more than one record at a time. The failure to develop a long-playing record in the 1930s made these mechanical contrivances the only way that the music lover could enjoy long periods of entertainment without constantly tending the machine. The Capehart Company was the leader in manufacturing record players for home use which could play several discs at a time. Some of their models could even play both sides of a record!

The first modern coin-slot machine with electronic amplification and a multi-record changer was produced in 1927 by the Automatic Music Instrument Company (AMI). AMI was joined by J. P. Seeburg, Rudolph Wurlitzer, and the Rockola Manufacturing Company in devising coin-slot machines with advanced record-changing mechanisms which could select from twenty or twenty-four discs.[20] The penetrating playback and booming bass made the most of electrical amplification and the large dynamic speakers. For listeners during the 1930s, juke boxes gave them the highest level of sound reproduction outside the movie theater.

At the end of the 1920s, only around 50,000 of these machines were in use, but the repeal of prohibition in 1933 brought about a dramatic change in social life as Americans flooded back to bars and clubs. No self-respecting drinking establishment was without one. The juke box had its linguistic origins in the South, where dancing or "jooking" to records was a popular pastime. Small drinking establishments with only recorded sound as their musical entertainment were called *juke joints*. Here patrons could dance to blues or country music. During the 1930s the number of juke boxes in use rose to a high of 500,000, and they could be found in taverns, pool halls, restaurants, hotels, cafes, bus stations, and even beauty parlors. More than half of the nation's juke boxes were in the South.[21]

The store of records in the nation's juke boxes required changing every week, and by 1936 over half of all record production in the United States was destined for them. In 1939 juke boxes consumed about 13 million discs a year, mainly loud dance music and suggestive

Figure 8.1. Teenagers admiring a Wurlitzer juke box in 1942. (Library of Congress)

novelty songs.[22] The Depression had moved the focus of the recorded-sound industry from providing music to be enjoyed in the home to cheap public entertainment.

Radio days

The radio was now the home entertainer; it proved to be the most resilient part of the entertainment industry during the Great Depression. Radio stations survived by selling air time to commercial advertisers. The cheap radio set, the small table model, proved to be the mass consumer good of the electronic era. There were about 12 million radios in American homes in 1930; this number nearly doubled by 1935. By comparison in 1933 there were only about 500,000 of the new electric record players, the majority of them in radio-phonograph combinations. At this time the average price for a radio receiver was $35, and one was in 60 percent of all American homes. The American family listened to about 5 hours of radio a day.[23]

The reason that the American public turned to the radio in the dark days of the Depression was not merely because the music and entertainment was free. It was somehow more comforting to be part of the invisible radio audience, listening either to the late night broadcasts of dance bands or to the fireside chats of the newly installed president. Radio created a national audience and molded national values and beliefs in a way that no other medium had been able to do.[24] It was the great communicator of the Depression era, and the great events of the times – whether it was the crash of the *Hindenburg* or the Japanese attack on Pearl Harbor – came to Americans over the radio.

The forces of the Depression had the same effect on the radio industry as it had on movies and records, for only the largest operations had the financial strength to survive. The telephone technology that had fathered the electronic era made its mark on radio by facilitating the creation of radio networks. Telephone engineers had successfully used their lines to link performers in front of a microphone to a broadcast transmitter in a radio studio. These remote transmissions, employing the telephone company's "wires," were often used to make broadcasts from hotel dance floors and clubs. Long-distance telephone lines could be used to send radio programming across country and link individual stations into a larger network. AT&T had a monopoly of the wires and used them to connect stations with its own WEAF operation in New York City in an experiment it called "toll broadcasting." Each program was sponsored by an advertiser, who paid a fee to bring its message into thousands of homes. This successful venture pointed the way to the future for commercial radio. It also underlined the powerful presence of the telephone companies in broadcasting.

The activities of AT&T were closely watched by RCA. In 1926 an agreement was reached with AT&T to lease its lines to a new corporation of radio interests. The National Broadcasting Corporation was the brainchild of David Sarnoff of RCA. In addition to RCA, its financial sponsors included GE and Westinghouse. AT&T retired from the radio business and sold WEAF to NBC as the flagship station of the new network. WEAF provided programming for local stations who joined the network. The latter got the high-quality programs from the entertainment capital of the country, and NBC's sponsors had the means to advertise their products to millions. As one advertising executive noted: "American businessmen, because of radio, are provided with a latch key to nearly every home in the nation."[25]

NBC leased AT&T's long-distance lines for a fee of $1 million a year. In 1928 it began coast-to-coast transmission to sixty-nine affiliated stations. Eventually it operated three great radio networks over the American continent. Its only competitor was the Columbia Phonograph Broadcasting Company. Under the leadership of William S. Paley, the corporation was reorganized as the Columbia Broadcasting System (CBS) in 1929.

CBS and NBC radio grew steadily during the Depression. In 1934 CBS had 100 affiliates, for which it provided 16 hours of programming a day. Most of the larger broadcast stations joined the networks, leaving only the smallest stations independent. By 1937 the networks spoke for 210 of America's 685 stations but accounted for 88 percent of the total broadcast wattage.[26] Network radio dominated the airwaves and the diffusion of popular music in the United States.

Although the phonograph companies printed "Not Licensed for Radio Broadcast" on the labels of their records, that did not stop radio stations from playing them – recorded sound was the cheapest way of programming popular music and had been employed as such since the earliest days of radio. From the viewpoint of the phonograph industry, this was piracy of their product, but as it did bring new songs to the attention of a national audience, it could be seen as free promotion of a recording. The rise of the radio networks did not bode well for the record companies, because the two networks had a policy against using "canned music" in their programming.

Although the pre-recorded disc was shunned by network radio, the disc record format did have a place as a means of recording sound. Radio broadcasters were committed to live music and entertainment, but the cost of hiring performers was too great to sustain this policy throughout all of their programming. Recording and reusing their programs was an economical way to get the most out of the money spent on live performances. As radio grew in popularity during the Depression, so did the amount of recording carried out in broadcast studios. Radio stations were to become major users of recorded-sound technology in the 1930s. Most of their recordings were made on discs, because this was an efficient and convenient way to record programs and then mail them to other stations.

Special recording equipment was used to make transcriptions of radio programs. The term *transcription* was used to distinguish it from the inferior sound quality of "mechanical reproduction," which referred to playing commercial 78-rpm discs on the air. Transcription allowed a local radio station to broadcast a show whenever it desired rather than take it from the network link. Distributing these recordings by mail to stations across the country enabled a sponsor to broadcast a program simultaneously across three time zones. The first show to be syndicated in this manner was the hugely popular "Amos 'n Andy" comedy show. This radio version of a minstrel show was first broadcast in two 5-minute segments with a commercial break. Each segment was recorded onto a 78-rpm disc and despatched across the country.[27]

Radio programs were not the only materials transcribed, because it did not take long for advertisers to realize that the pre-recorded disc was the ideal means to spread their messages across the nation's air waves. A sponsor would support the recording of both entertainment and their advertising on one disc, and these were distributed to radio stations.

The 78-rpm disc format had the disadvantages of poor sound quality and short playing time. The Western Electric system of 16-inch discs revolving at $33\frac{1}{3}$ rpm solved both these problems. When sound on film began to replace discs in film studios, many of the discarded disc recorders were picked up by transcription services eager to meet radio's voracious demand for recorded programs.

Transcription companies were founded to sell recorded programming. They maintained large libraries of specially recorded music and complete radio programs. The World Broadcasting Service, formed in 1929, licensed the Western Electric recording technology. By 1936 at least 350 radio stations had contracts with the four largest transcription services: the Standard Radio Library, the RCA/NBC Thesaurus Library, the C. P. MacGregor Service, and the World Broadcasting Service. By the end of the 1930s, these services had built up a market of $10 million. Unlicensed transcription of live performances had also reached large proportions as radio stations used disc recording machines to build their own libraries of transcriptions.[28]

As the primary means to record sound, the disc record played a vital part in the radio system. It saved not only programming but also the advertisements – the foundation of the commercial broadcasting networks. In 1935 paid advertising on CBS and NBC exceeded $48 million, and over 10 percent of all programming was devoted to commercial messages. As the networks extended their reach, and sponsors sought an even greater audience, recorded programs became ever more useful to them.

The pre-recorded discs made by record companies did not entirely disappear from radio stations, because they continued to be a cheap source of music programming that could be picked off the shelf whenever it was needed. The success of the 1935 radio show "Make Believe Ballroom" established the format of announcers playing records and talking to the audience between the songs. Martin Block of station WNEW in New York carried out imaginary conversations with band leaders and singers in between their records. "Make Believe Ballroom" was a great success and aired twice a day in the important New York market. Transcriptions of the program soon went into syndication.

The recorded-sound industry emerged from the Depression on the coattails of radio, which had promoted its recordings to a national audience. The slogan of the record companies was now "The music you want, when you want it."[29] Consumers with a little more money in their pockets now bought their own copies of the recordings they had heard on radio or juke boxes. Sales of all types of music were on the increase, not only popular songs but also classical music. Total sales of records and talking machines for 1935 accounted for only $9 million, but the next year the figure jumped to $31 million, an indication that the worst of the Great Depression was over.

In 1938 about 33 million records were sold. The Big Three record companies were now RCA Victor, Decca, and Columbia/ARC. RCA Victor held the lead with sales of 13 million discs, Decca was a close second with sales of 12 million, and Columbia/American Record Company sold 7 million discs.

In an ironic turn of the tables, the mighty Columbia Broadcasting Network bought out the American Recording Corporation to obtain the name and plant of the Columbia Phonograph Company. CBS paid only $700,000 for ARC, a sum much smaller than the $2.5 million paid by Louis Sterling for the Columbia Record Company in 1925. In 1927 it had been the record company that had bought the radio organization, but recorded sound was no longer the profitable business it had once been. Now radio was king of the entertainment industry.[30] The voice from the radio set had now surpassed the voice from the screen as the most important factor in promoting recorded music.

In addition to the record-pressing plants, the acquisition of the Columbia Phonograph Company brought CBS a prestige record line, a roster of classical musicians, some important stars of popular music, and the modern recording studios of Brunswick Records. Columbia introduced premium red-label recordings at 50¢ each and began to challenge Victor's dominance of the classical music market. Now two of the Big Three record companies – RCA Victor and Columbia – were closely associated with radio organizations. They were now empires of sound: huge, integrated business organizations based on the reproduction and transmission of sound.

The Great Depression helped accelerate the process of consolidation in the entertainment industry brought on by the introduction of electrical recording. By the end of the 1930s, the companies involved in making talking machines and records were no longer independent organizations devoted to recording sound but parts of larger businesses that embraced several technologies and manufactured several kinds of products. RCA Victor sold a broad range of electrical goods, from industrial control systems to car radios, in addition to records and radio-phonograph combinations. Decca was involved in electrical manufacturing, and CBS was primarily focused on radio. Recorded sound no longer stood on its own as a distinct product – the wonderful talking machine – but existed as one component in a much more sophisticated world of entertainment.

9. Swing and the mass audience

In the 1930s popular music was created within the interlocking systems of record production, film making, and radio broadcasting. A newly recorded song required extensive promotion on radio and in movies to bring it to the attention of the record-buying public. Al Jolson was the first of many entertainment stars to move from vaudeville to movies and then to radio. Throughout the 1930s the leading figures in popular entertainment – such as Rudy Vallee, Bing Crosby, and Fred Astaire – were active in recording, films, and radio. They reinforced their images in the three media and used film and radio to plug their songs. Overseas record and film sales brought their music to an international audience. The great sales networks created by Edison and Johnson could not compare to this.

The beginning point of this extended technological system was the ubiquitous microphone. In recording studio, film stage, or dance hall, it picked up the sound of a performance and turned it into the electrical currents which ran through the empires of sound. Wherever a big band played, it could be connected to this national network by a radio "wire" – the cable that ran from the microphone on the bandstand to the local radio station, which then broadcast the performance nationwide. A transcription machine in the broadcast studio made a permanent record which could be played later.

Radio exposure was vital in marketing a recording, because the networks brought music to all parts of the country. A wire installed in the famous "Cotton Club" in Harlem brought Duke Ellington's band national exposure, as it did for Cab Calloway. Even local radio programs could attract promoters and sponsors. The story of the discovery of Count Basie's band is worth retelling. Basie's sets at the Reno Club in Kansas City were sent over the wire to the experimental radio station, W9XBY. The independent producer John Hammond heard a broadcast late one night on his car radio and was so impressed that he drove to Kansas City and offered a contract to Basie.

Thus began the recording career of one of America's most influential big bands.[1]

A star of the entertainment industry of the 1930s had to master several different media to reach the mass audience. After several years of singing in clubs and dance halls, Bing Crosby caught the attention of Paul Whiteman and secured a spot on Whiteman's radio program in 1929. Crosby's mellow baritone ideally suited the new technology of electrical recording and amplification. He crooned softly into the microphone, and the machine did the rest – bringing an intimate, subtle sound to the listener. Unlike the performers from vaudeville and music halls, singers in the electrical era did not have to project their voices to reach the audience. Stars from the acoustic era, such as Al Jolson or Bessie Smith, found their declamatory style of singing outdated. A new generation of radio "crooners" was soon to dominate popular music.

Bing Crosby was signed by the newly formed Columbia Broadcasting System in 1931 to star in a series of radio shows. The success of these broadcasts brought more lucrative commercial sponsorships, longer programs, better time slots, and a larger audience. Millions of radio sets were tuned in to his "Kraft Music Hall," an hour-long variety show of music, talk, and comedy which established Crosby as one of the most popular radio personalities of the 1930s.[2] With corporate sponsorship, Crosby's music reached the ears of millions, and he used the reach of network radio to promote his recordings on the Brunswick and Decca labels. Soon Crosby was being mobbed at personal appearances, and his records regularly became best-sellers.

Crosby followed the career paths of other successful radio entertainers and made the move into motion pictures. He appeared in musicals, comedies (notably the "Road" series with Bob Hope, another radio performer who appeared in films), and even some serious dramatic pictures. A song introduced by Bing Crosby in a movie would soon find its way onto the shelves in record stores and into the racks of recordings held in radio studios. His recording of "I'm Dreaming of a White Christmas," one of the best-selling records of all time, was written by Irving Berlin for a musical called "Holiday Inn," but it was the movie starring Fred Astaire and Bing Crosby that made the song a hit. The single, taken from the sound track, was released by Decca in October 1942 and over the years sold over 30 million copies.[3]

Radio went from being a rival to films and records in the 1920s to become an important ally: RKO was part of the great RCA empire, which included the NBC radio network; the Paramount film studio had a large interest in the CBS network; and several film studios operated their own broadcast stations. From "Amos 'n Andy" onwards, radio personalities made the important transition to films. The radio variety show was imitated in several films, such as Bob Hope's "Big Broadcast of 1938" for Paramount. In return, film stars appeared on radio to promote themselves, their films, and the products of their commercial sponsors. Popular radio shows, such as "The Lone Ranger" (CBS), were turned into films. In 1932 NBC opened a radio studio in Hollywood which produced hundreds of hours of programming about motion pictures and film stars.[4]

The sharing of star performers and their music among radio, film, and records was mutually beneficial. Film studios owned much of the rights to the music (the result of their acquisition of music publishers), and collected substantial royalties from radio stations and record companies, who in turn benefitted from the promotion of music in films. The American Society of Composers, Authors, and Publishers (ASCAP) had been formed in 1914 to protect the interests of song writers. During the 1930s it worked to ensure that the songs of the music publishers it represented would dominate network radio and motion pictures. Film musicals were the premier showcases for new music, but all types of films, from westerns to romances, contained catchy songs. For big studios like Warner Bros., MGM, and Paramount, the choice of film music was determined by their large interests in music publishing. They did not miss an opportunity to plug a song they owned in their films.

The extended system of broadcasting and duplication of recorded sound brought popular music to every part of the United States through a national network of radio stations, chains of movie houses, and record stores. The first musical product of the empires of sound was called *swing*. During the 1930s and 1940s, this jazz-inspired dance music dominated popular culture as completely as the large integrated corporations controlled the world of entertainment.

Swing as a popular music style denotes the rise of the big bands. By the end of the 1920s, the raucous and unpredictable "hot" jazz of small Dixieland groups was being replaced by a fixed repertoire of music from larger and more rehearsed dance bands, who usually played in the softer "sweet" style. The popularity of ten- to fifteen-piece orchestras, such as that of Paul Whiteman, was built on intricate ensemble playing. The improvisation and hectic activity of hot jazz was tempered to appeal to a wider audience. In the 1930s jazz bands mastered the carefully arranged section playing in which each part of a large band – the brass, reed, and rhythm sections – played off one another in complex patterns. The introduction of electrical recording played a part in this transition because it could reproduce the subtler sounds of sweet jazz. Where volume had been the major criteria of vocals in the acoustic era, the microphone could pick up every nuance of the voice. In the 1930s vocalists were chosen for their impeccable intonation.

Electrical recording was not solely responsible for this shift in musical style; Paul Whiteman's band predated the electronic era by many years, and his greatest hits were acoustically recorded. Yet the use of sensitive microphones made it much easier to make better records of groups of musicians. Electrical amplification of the sound also brought across the powerful dance rhythm of swing, and playing a record on a home player or juke box at maximum volume enabled the listener to actually feel the power of the music as it blared from the speakers.

Several large dance bands were responsible for bringing swing into national prominence: Duke Ellington, Fletcher Henderson, Count Basie, Cab Calloway, Jimmie Lunceford, and the Casa Loma orchestra. The musician most closely identified with swing music was the clarinet player and band leader Benny Goodman. His rise to fame is testament to the importance of radio in promoting popular music. Goodman began his career as a journeyman musician in small bands and as a session man in New York recording studios. He had been struggling to make ends meet when he was signed up to play on the network radio program "Let's Dance" in 1935. This program was broadcast across the continent from the giant NBC studio 8H in New York – making up a 3-hour program in each of the three time zones. Three bands were signed to play dance music through Saturday night: Xavier Cugat played Latin-influenced dance songs; Kel Murray was responsible for popular, "middle-of-the-road" tunes; and Benny Goodman played jazz to those who stayed up late.

Saturday night had never been a good slot for radio advertising because it was traditionally a time when Americans went to the mov-

Figure 9.1. Dancing to the music of a juke box in the 1930s. (Library of Congress)

ies, but the sponsor of "Let's Dance," the National Biscuit Company, hoped that dance music would keep people at home and tuned in to advertisements for their new Ritz crackers.

Goodman's radio broadcasts were well received and brought him the coveted recording contract with Victor Records – a sign that he had arrived in the world of music. After the radio series was completed in 1935, Goodman and his band embarked on a national tour. Their East Coast performances met with lukewarm response, but when the band went west they played to a much more receptive audience. The time difference in broadcasting "Let's Dance" from New York meant that West Coast listeners did not have to stay up so late to hear Goodman's sets at the end of the broadcast. Many in the audience at the Palomar ballroom in Los Angeles had heard Goodman's sound on the radio and then purchased his records. When they heard it live, they reacted with so much enthusiasm that the performance bordered on uproar. The triumph at the Palomar ballroom put

Goodman at the forefront of popular music and heralded the beginning of the swing era.[5]

Swing encompassed a broad range of musical styles which spanned the distance between hot (fast and rowdy) and sweet (softer and more melodious) playing. At one end of the swing spectrum were the blues-based bands such as Count Basie's orchestra. Basie's singers, such as Jimmy Rushing, had a style of performing that reflected the blues and jazz of the early 1920s. They were called *blues shouters*. At the other end was the softer, mellow sound of Guy Lombardo and his Royal Canadians. Sweet and inoffensive, this type of music brought an escape from the worries of the Great Depression.

Swing managed to appeal to the tastes of young and old. A large part of Benny Goodman's audience consisted of teenagers, the "bobbysoxers" who danced in the aisles at his concerts. Swing meant different things to different people, but the important thing to the empires of sound was that it appealed to millions of Americans.

Benny Goodman's success came at a time when many dance bands were riding the wave of swing's popularity. His achievement was that his interpretation of the music fitted the requirements of network radio and satisfied a large and diverse audience.[6] Although Goodman was a highly competent musician and an inspired band leader, his elevated position as "King" of swing is somewhat misplaced. He might have helped popularize the music, but he did not create it. Like many other white jazz musicians, he found a style and an audience by adapting African American music for wider consumption by predominately white listeners. He followed the precedent set by the Original Dixieland Jass Band in 1917 and Paul Whiteman in the 1920s. The great irony of swing was that while the wildly successful bands of Goodman, Artie Shaw, the Dorsey brothers, and Glenn Miller were defining it to a mass market, its true pioneers – who also happened to be black – were struggling to make a living.

The mechanization of entertainment had created a system of mass production of films and recordings which had to be sold to the largest possible market. During the 1930s radio had created a mass audience for recorded music but in doing so had to leave out some of the diversity of national culture. The rise of the radio networks introduced the commercial consideration of appealing to the many while offending the fewest. The mass production of standardized amusement required that the diversity of national culture be honed down to the essentials: in much the same way that Henry Ford's Model T automobile came only in black, the music and film of the empires of sound represented the white experience in America.

The businesses wired into the national entertainment network represented a vast investment of capital and technology. They were committed to the status quo. They played the music to attract the most listeners and commercial advertisers. In the South and West, they did play country and western music, which could be considered an ethnic music of rural folk, and local stations tried to reflect the musical tastes of their audiences, but on the whole the music broadcast from coast to coast was very "middle of the road": commercial, upbeat, and inoffensive.

Record stores, radio stations, and film theaters were a potent force in the dissemination of popular culture, which made it even more important to exert centralized control. In his novel *Mumbo Jumbo*, Ishmael Reed imagined the popular music and dance of the 1920s as a virus of African culture – the germ of the Jazz Age – that spread rapidly across the United States and transformed all who listened to it. Called "Jes Grew," it was as "electric as life" and characterized by ebullience and ecstasy. Alarmed by its impact on youth, the leaders of society took steps to contain it, especially in view of the speed with which it traveled on record and over the radio: "if Jes Grew slips into the radiolas and Dictaphones all is lost."[7] At the end of the novel, the establishment creates a great depression to end the threat, the same depression which in reality ended the recording of black and ethnic music.

The popular music which emerged in the Depression was a highly commercial, formulaic sound which was aimed at the mass audience. As several music critics have pointed out, swing was a diluted version of the hot jazz of the 1920s, and it was not until this form of jazz had been "thoroughly sterilized and sanitized by the white imitators" that it became commercially successful. Musically, swing was soon stagnant and bereft of new ideas as Duke Ellington once commented, but it had won over a huge segment of the population. With the exception of Ellington and a few others, the majority of the most creative jazz players of the 1930s were not heard on popular radio programs.[8]

Although excluded from the air waves, many black musicians scratched out a living playing in small bars and clubs. The sales of race records had virtually died out in the Depression, but the need for records for juke boxes provided work for a small number of jazz musicians and blues singers. On one occasion John Hammond persuaded the Brunswick company to record some small jazz bands to provide recordings for juke boxes in black neighborhoods. These sessions brought together several musicians from Count Basie's band and an inexperienced young singer called Billie Holiday.[9] The combination of Holiday's voice, Lester Young's saxophone, and Teddy Wilson's piano playing has never been equalled. Yet these were cheap records hurriedly made in unrehearsed recording sessions. They used uncopyrighted music and tired-out arrangements, but many of these recordings have been acclaimed as jazz masterpieces.

Although the empires of sound excluded many forms of music from the air waves, they did make an effort to bridge the gap between high and low culture. This task had been started by the record companies in the first years of the twentieth century to increase their sales of classical music. The radio networks took it up in the 1930s to head off the growing criticism of the low quality of their programming. The Women's National Radio Committee was not alone in complaining, "The radio must take the place of the concert hall, the opera, the lecture forum. . . . It has given us instead a parade of vaudeville."[10] The networks responded with programs of symphonic music. Weekly broadcasts of the great conductor Arturo Toscanini on NBC cornered a surprisingly large audience and made the name of the maestro known all over the country. Broadcasting from the same studio used by Benny Goodman for "Let's Dance," Toscanini conducted a series of memorable performances in 1937 and 1938. These programs introduced a higher class of music to the national audience. About 10 million American families tuned in weekly to broadcasts of classical music and opera in 1938/1939. A *Fortune* magazine poll of 1938 claimed that 39.9 percent of the population, including "negroes, poor whites, farmers" had heard of Toscanini.[11] This was a testament to the power of network radio.

Highbrow music on the radio stimulated sales of classical records. Victor and Columbia had the best catalogues and prospered accordingly. Nevertheless it was the unprecedented popularity of swing that was the major factor in the reinvigoration of the industry of recorded sound at the end of the 1930s. In 1939 total record sales were 50 million, and about 85 percent of this was swing records.[12]

The record companies found that the young were a very important market for swing. Although it took several hours of part-time work to come up with the 50¢ for a disc, thousands of teenagers were buying them. Swing had become the central facet of a youth culture which covered music, dance, dress, vocabulary, courtship, and social ritual. Many of the new customers for records were young women: the "bobbysoxers," who wore a uniform of short white "bobby sox," white buck shoes, pleated dresses, and blouses or sweaters. They did the "Jitterbug," the "Suzie Q," and the "Big Apple." They were "hep-cats" who followed their favorite band with a devotion unknown since the golden age of the silent cinema in the 1920s. The leading band leaders became celebrities.

Swing had become an entertainment industry by 1940, and for the first and last time, jazz music had found a mass audience, which was composed of the young and the old, urban and rural dwellers, black and white. When Benny Goodman joined "long-haired musicians" and played to the cultivated audience of Carnegie Hall in 1938, swing had reached even the most discriminating music lovers and bridged the gap between popular and classical music.[13]

As many as 450 "name" bands were active at the end of the 1930s, and each one had to distinguish itself from the rest. Each band had its own uniform and signature tune. The most successful swing musician produced a simple, distinctive sound that was reduced to an easily recognized formula, and in doing so sold millions of records.

After years of struggling in the music industry, and limited success in tours and recordings, Glenn Miller finally found the "sound" he had been looking for. The prominent leads of his clarinet and saxophone sections in recordings such as "Chattanooga Choo Choo" and "In the Mood" made his music stand out in the crowd. In 1940 *Billboard* began its "Best Selling Retail Records" weekly chart, a national record survey which counted sales of recordings. The first certified gold record was Glenn Miller's "Chattanooga Choo Choo," which sold 1 million copies in the first 6 months of its release in 1941.[14]

The advent of the million-selling record was a sign that the industry of recorded sound had recovered from the ravages of the Depression. Its products were bought by millions, and the profits from swing fulfilled the promise of the early 1920s, when it appeared that the business had a bright future. In addition to a highly popular music which increased sales of records, the industry had also produced inexpensive disc players for the home.

These were electrically powered turntable units with a tone arm containing a magnetic pick-up and stylus. The idea was to hook them up to the family radio set, which amplified the sound and reproduced it on its loudspeaker. These "plug-in" record players were symbolic of the changing position of the phonograph. Once a free-standing machine in the middle of the parlor, it was now an adjunct to the radio, an attachment to supplement the daily fare of news, drama, and music broadcast over the air.

A plug-in set was introduced by the Columbia Company; the Radiograph sold for $55, which was still fairly expensive during the Depression years of the 1930s. In 1934 the RCA Victor Company introduced its Duo Jr., which at $16.50 was competitively priced. Even cheaper copies followed, and by the end of the decade, the price had dropped to around $10.[15]

Rising sales of machines and records at the end of the 1930s reflected the return of prosperity to the United States. The outbreak of World War II played a decisive role in the recovery, because the United States became the arsenal of democracy, and unemployment declined as output soared and wages rose.

War had much the same effect on the recorded-sound industry in 1940 as it had in 1917. The manufacturers found some of their raw materials in short supply, especially the shellac which was the major ingredient of records. It soon became dangerous to cross the Atlantic, as German submarines repeated their campaign of sinking merchant ships. The United States government employed the facilities of the industry to contribute to the war effort: their factories made munitions, their laboratories carried out secret war research, and their recording studios produced patriotic songs and propaganda messages.

The great demand for popular entertainment during the war years provided a stimulus for recorded music. The mobilization of the United States for war took millions of men out of the work force and placed them in uniform. Musicians were no different, and their departure for the front stripped the dance bands of their players. Things got so bad that some bands considered hiring women in place of men, just as they had replaced men in factories and offices, but this alternative proved to be unacceptable for most band leaders.[16] The solution to this problem was to replace musicians with a machine – a process which had been going on since the introduction of the phonograph.

The radio networks were forced to drop their opposition to canned music as their studio musicians were called up. In 1940 a series of court cases brought a ruling that property rights to a recording ended when it was sold. This opened the floodgates for the commercial record to become the mainstay of radio broadcasting. It was also the beginning of the rise to prominence of the radio announcer who played recordings on the air, the so-called disc jockey. Martin Block's "Make Believe Ballroom" now had twenty-three sponsors and a national audience. He was receiving about 12,000 letters a month in 1943.[17] During the 1940s an estimated 75 percent of all programming on American radio came from records.

The war years marked even greater inroads of recorded sound in everyday life because popular music played an important role in maintaining morale on the war and home fronts. World War I had shown that war increased the demand for music, and as soon as the United States entered World War II, the record companies released a stream of patriotic and sentimental songs: "Remember Pearl Harbor," "I'll Be Seeing You," and "God Bless America," which had been written for an earlier war but became a national institution after Kate Smith recorded it for Columbia in 1939.

The empires of sound faced new tasks during the war. Their products were meant not only to entertain but to inform and educate. Propaganda played an important part in keeping the entire American population devoted to the war effort. Recorded messages exhorted war workers to increase output, provided information about war bond sales and scrap metal drives, and tried to persuade the public to cease dealing in black-market tires and gasoline. In addition to pressing millions of copies of Glenn Miller's songs, the companies also made discs entitled "This Is Your Enemy" and "You Can't Do Business with Hitler" for broadcast over the radio and public address systems.[18]

Music was deemed to be highly important in maintaining the morale of troops serving overseas. The Office of War Information began a program of recording music for the troops to be played over public address systems and the Armed Forces Radio Network. A selection of popular songs was recorded onto oversized (16-inch) discs much like the ones used in radio transcription. They revolved at 33⅓ rpm and could play much longer than the 78-rpm shellac commercial discs. The music on these records was recorded in conventional studios or was taken from other recordings. Many were recorded in the same way as radio transcriptions – with a wire from a live performance or broadcast studio linked to a recording facility. Millions of these V discs, as they were called, were shipped to American troops all over the world.

One of the most popular programs on armed services radio, and one that was transcribed and distributed on disc, was "Command Performance." The idea was that servicemen could request music and entertainment, and the staff of the show did its best to broadcast it on Armed Services radio. Naturally most of the requests were for swing, but significantly many soldiers asked to hear the everyday sounds of American life: the sizzle of a steak being fried, the wail of horns in San Francisco harbor, or the noise of traffic in New York City. The success of this program underlined how recorded sound evoked powerful memories and created strong and lasting emotions. Canned music and sound effects reminded American servicemen of home.

Although the troops overseas enjoyed a variety of music, from blues to country and western, swing was the common denominator. It maintained its position as the dominant popular music throughout the war. It is probably not much of an exaggeration to say that the United States swung through World War II. The big-band sound provided the background music to one of the great dramas enacted in the twentieth century; its driving, well-disciplined sound perfectly reflected the energies of a nation involved in total war. It was heard in service clubs, shipyards, and airfields. Reveille in swing time was played to American troops stationed in England. The music of Benny Goodman, Tommy Dorsey, and Glenn Miller had a vast audience in Europe, where both sides in the conflict listened to the latest dance tunes. Even the Germans and Japanese broadcast American popular music in their propaganda messages.

At home, Americans listened to swing on the radio and on record. It was played to them while they worked. They could tune to big-band broadcasts while driving their cars. They danced to it in halls and juke joints, and they experienced its amplified sound in movie theaters. The empires of sound had made this music the core of mass entertainment. As one historian of jazz wrote of his own experience: "These people not only danced to swing, they ate to it, drank to it, necked to it, talked to it and frequently just listened to it. It was everywhere."[19]

10. High fidelity at last

Despite the depressed economic environment of the 1930s, the technology of the electrical era was continually improved. The concerted attention of well-financed corporate laboratories, the exchange of ideas between the three business endeavors employing recorded-sound technology (talking machines, radio, and talking pictures), and the international diffusion of technology across the Atlantic were the forces of this endeavor.

The film industry led the way in improving the electrical recording system devised in Western Electric's laboratories. One element of this system which benefitted from the diffusion of ideas from one business enterprise to another was the dynamic loudspeaker.

The great movie palaces built in the late 1920s contained thousands of seats, and very large loudspeakers were required to fill these auditoriums with sound. The loudspeakers also needed to catch every note played by large orchestras and to convincingly re-create the sound of gun shots or melodramatic screams. Consequently the leading edge of loudspeaker design was in film theaters. Research carried out in Western Electric's laboratories was supplemented by the more practical work of the engineering departments of film companies. Western Electric staff found themselves working for film producers, making up loudspeakers in studio workshops. They experimented with various configurations of transducers and with the baffles and sound insulation of the cabinet.[1]

In 1931 the first three-way speaker systems were introduced in which sound was divided up into high, middle, and low frequencies, and each band was sent to three different transducers in the loudspeaker, each one designed to work best with that part of the sound spectrum: the large "woofer" for the bass, a mid-range driver, and the tiny "tweeter" for the treble. This technology eventually diffused to the talking-machine industry and by the 1960s was incorporated into the loudspeakers used in home stereos.

189

The Western Electric system was exported to film producers and record companies in Europe, where it was eagerly examined. European operators had every incentive to improve it; the license fee paid to Western Electric was motivation enough to develop their own electrical recorders based on Maxfield and Harrison's pioneering work but without infringing on their valuable patents. Only the amplifiers, developed in Bell Labs and constantly improved during the 1930s, were left untouched in foreign laboratories.

Arthur Haddy was working for Crystalate record company, a small concern which imported some of its masters from the Cameo Company in the United States, when he first saw the electrical recording equipment developed by Maxfield. Haddy thought it looked like "a load of junk" and immediately set about modifying it. He was not the only Englishman re-engineering Western Electric equipment. Alan Blumlein of the British Columbia company made significant improvements to the recording cutter, which turned the varying currents of electricity produced by the microphone back into movement, guiding the cutting stylus as it engraved the sound signal into the groove. Like many other engineers, he reduced the weight of the cutter by removing some of its mass, especially the iron heads of the large magnets used to create the magnetic fields. His design employed the moving coil in a magnetic field system, which worked in basically the same way as the moving coil transducer in a loudspeaker. This improvement replaced the balanced armature cutters then in use.[2]

A moving coil cutter was also developed by Arthur Keller of Bell Labs in the United States. This innovation began as a device to measure the depth of a vertically cut groove. Keller also applied the moving coil concept to the pick-up that translates the wave form back into electrical currents, which are then amplified and reproduced by the loudspeaker. In Keller's design, a minute coil attached to the pick-up stylus regenerated the sound signal.[3]

Although Edison had pioneered the use of permanent jeweled styli with the Diamond Discs, the majority of electric pick-ups in the 1930s employed the replaceable metal stylus developed by Berliner. Diamond styli were used in radio transcription machines, and this was clearly the path to better reproduction. Engineers experimented for years to discover the optimal shape of the stylus, one that would sensitively respond to the wave forms in the groove without disfiguring them.

As styli were made smaller and more responsive, the device that turned its microscopic movements into electric currents had to become more sensitive. The large pick-ups based on the electromagnetic principle were replaced by lightweight piezoelectric pick-ups which used a crystal instead of magnets. More sensitive pick-ups required more precise tone arms to carry them across the record and ensure steadier tracking in the groove. The new pick-ups produced a lower output and therefore had to be matched with more sensitive and powerful amplifiers. As engineers developed one part of the system, they found that they had to improve all the other elements, too.

The lighter pick-ups and tone arms exerted less pressure on the record and reduced the power requirements of the turntable motor. This made it possible to replace the heavy gear drives with rim-driven turntables. During most of the 1930s, gear and belt drives transferred the turning motion to the turntable in ways which had not changed much since Edison applied electric power to his phonograph. The introduction of the idler wheel or rim drive in 1938 marked a step towards more simplicity and lower cost. This was widely used in turntables of the 1940s and 1950s.[4]

The most advanced disc players of the 1930s were smaller and more efficient versions of the all-electric models of the 1920s. The process of reducing size and increasing efficiency had been carried forward from the nineteenth century. Tiny styli could sit in smaller grooves, and the smaller the groove, the more sound that could be put onto a record. Engineers on both sides of the Atlantic worked to encode more sound signals onto a given piece of recording medium in their efforts to increase playing time and record on more than one channel.

Engineers at Bell Labs experimented on binaural (two-channel) sound in the late 1920s. They made records with two microphones connected to two cutters, which were mounted side by side over the revolving disc. The disadvantage of making two grooves instead of one was that the recordings took up twice as much space; even with a 16-inch disc, this was impractical.

The long life of Edison's hill-and-dale cut format provided another option for these experiments. The vertical cut had virtually died out after he left the phonograph industry, and the lateral cut of the Western Electric system became the standard in both records and film sound tracks. Yet vertical cutting did have some advantages in reducing the signal-to-noise ratio, and it was widely used in transcription machines in broadcasting. In 1932 Bell Labs developed a superior transcribing machine with a vertical cut which reproduced a range of frequencies much greater than the disc cutters used in record studios.[5]

One approach to stereophonic sound came from a combination of the lateral and vertical formats, each carrying a channel of sound. Blumlein's experiments in EMI's laboratories successfully employed lateral and vertical cuts to get two channels of sound into the groove. In 1931 Blumlein was assigned a significant patent in the history of recorded sound, which covered several types of stereo system, including the carrier-wave principle, which uses multiplexing to carry two signals, and the lateral and vertical cut combination in the same groove.[6] This last idea was to be the basis of stereo sound. In the United States, Keller had the same idea and developed his own lateral/vertical system.

The only problem with this approach was that lateral and vertical cuts produced slightly different-sounding recordings, and there was bound to be an element of "cross-talk" between the vertical and horizontal motions of the pick-up. Instead of the 90-degree difference between lateral and vertical, Keller and Blumlein realized that a 45-degree difference would balance the two channels perfectly.

The 45/45 system, as it was known, used two cutters adjusted at 90 degrees from each other to cut a separate signal into each wall of the groove of the recording: one at an angle of 45 degrees from the surface, and the other at an angle of 135 degrees. Each channel of sound was inscribed into a side of the "V" shaped cut. Blumlein and his assistants in EMI laboratories made test recordings of "My Fair Lady" which proved that high-fidelity stereo was possible. When the executives of Bell Labs listened to these records, they were greatly surprised; the Americans thought that they were the only ones investigating binaural sound.

Although stereophonic reproduction of music was successfully developed in the 1930s, it was not turned into a commercial product and mass-produced like the Western Electric electrical recording system. The reasons for this are not hard to find: both Europe and the United States were in the middle of a depression, and it was hard enough to find customers for monaural recording. As Keller was to point out, selling two of anything was a disadvantage during a depression.

Perhaps it was for this reason that the spring-motor acoustic model remained in many parlors for the duration of the Depression. This machine usually had a reproducer designed to play electrically recorded discs, which gave the listener the benefit of the higher frequency range and clearer reproduction of the electrical era. Still, playing a record still meant turning a winding handle, fitting the steel needle into the pick-up head, sliding the metal lever on the turntable, and carefully lowering the tone arm onto the record – a ritual which had been taught in American homes since the turn of the century. Despite the technological leap forward of electrical recording, the acoustic record player survived the 1930s and 1940s. In many houses the old upright acoustic machine was still there in the 1950s, and I doubt if I am the only one of my (baby boom) generation who grew up winding the crank of the family phonograph.[7]

One of the most popular talking machines of the 1930s was the portable acoustic player, which had been in production since World War I. Inexpensive and convenient to play, it suited the energetic lifestyle of the younger generation. Portable acoustic models were still being made in the 1940s – nearly 50 years after they had been first introduced. In 1939 RCA Victor offered the Victrola O-10 model, a compact spring-motor machine for the bargain price of $9.95.[8]

Despite reductions in price, the cost of moving into the new electrical technology was still too much for many Americans. Impressive technical advances did not necessarily translate into more customers. The composer Serge Rachmaninoff noted the "astonishing improvements" in records that would not disappoint the most discerning listener, but he also pointed out that when the sound quality of records was poor (in the 1920s), sales were at an all-time high, and when the quality of recordings was improved (in the 1930s), sales were at an all-time low.[9]

The long-player (LP)

Although the general public was not interested in advanced technology of sound recording, there were still customers for it in the film industry and business community. These two markets were most concerned with extending the playing time of records because businessmen and film producers needed longer recordings.

The 2- and 3-minute barriers were broken in the early years of the

Figure 10.1. This advertisement shows how recorded sound can augment a modern lifestyle. (Courtesy of General Electric)

twentieth century, when the 100 grooves to the inch of recordings was increased to 200. The laboratories of the Big Three managed to extend the playing time to 7 and 8 minutes in the 1920s. Western Electric labs pushed it to 10 minutes to match the duration of the reel of film, but exceeding this mark confounded all comers in the 1930s.

Edison announced a long-playing record in 1926, a 12-inch disc with 40 minutes of reproduction, but once again he had anticipated rather than perfected an important innovation. Despite the improvements in the record surface, it often failed to reproduce sounds in the higher frequencies and suffered from low-volume reproduction. In 1931 Bell Labs developed an experimental 10-inch, long-playing record with 300 grooves cut to the inch to replace the 16-inch disc used in the Vitaphone film sound system. The Victor company introduced a 78-rpm shellac long-player (LP) in the same year, but it had poor fidelity and high surface noise, and there were few recordings to choose from.[10] Lacking a long-playing record, all record companies could do was package several 10- or 12-inch discs in a paper and cardboard binder – hence the name *album* for long-player – and hope that classical music lovers did not mind constantly changing records.

Businessmen and film producers could not be expected to be so understanding, and both quickly deserted the disc format for other methods of sound recording. The film industry moved to photographing sound on film, and the manufacturers of dictating machines turned their attention back to the pioneering experiments of magnetic recording on steel wire.

The amplifiers which powered electrical recording systems were also applied to the wire recorders based on Valdemar Poulsen's patents. Several small companies produced electric dictating machines using wire as a recording medium in the 1930s. The varying currents of electricity produced by the microphone were stored as magnetic fields on a metal wire. Although these machines could record about 30 minutes of sound on the reel of wire, the quality of reproduction was poor, and the wire was difficult to work with, often becoming tangled or breaking. Another disadvantage of steel tape and wire was that they were both fairly expensive materials. The recorders used a lot of metal to record a signal because the wire had to run past the recording heads at great speeds. Experimenters tried using strips of metal and coated metallic surfaces onto belts, discs, and drums. They also attempted to coat powdered magnetic material onto paper tape, but not with much success.

Commercial wire recorders were used in businesses and in radio stations as a means of making transcriptions. The Brush Development Company of Cleveland, which had built up a business in manufacturing piezoelectric pick-ups, brought out the "Soundmirror" machine using steel tape in 1937. This was the work of the German emigré S. J. Begun, who designed the Lorenz recorder, which was used as a transcription machine by German radio stations.[11]

The telephone companies had also investigated magnetic recording as a means of conveying pre-recorded messages – a mundane but necessary service which could replace expensive human operators. Bell Labs devised the Mirrorphone, a magnetic recorder using steel tape, to give weather reports to telephone callers. This was the extent of the commercial application of magnetic recording in the United States on the eve of World War II.

Recorded sound had an important part to play in military operations. The phonograph had been invented to save telephone messages, and in time of war it could record the wired or wireless communications of the enemy. The secret projects to break the codes of the German and Japanese relied on saving these messages for future crypto-analysis. Secret audio surveillance was carried on in all theaters of the war and on the home front, where the telephone messages of Japanese spies in Hawaii were recorded on disc. The FBI eavesdropped on every call made between Honolulu and Tokyo, including one on December 5, 1941, in which the disposition of the fleet in Pearl Harbor was discussed.[12]

Although the disc recorder was used in these surveillance campaigns, the short duration of its playing time and the fragile discs were not suited to the task. Wire recorders had the advantage of longer playing time and virtually unbreakable recordings. In peacetime they had found limited use in recording business messages and radio broadcasts, but in war they were widely used by the armed forces. Although their reproduction did not sound quite as good as discs, they could stand a lot more rough handling. When American troops stormed the Normandy beaches in 1944, the scene was described by war correspondent George Hicks from a navy ship. His firsthand account was recorded on the spot by a wire recorder and later broadcast to the American radio audience.[13]

The Brush Development Company and the Armour Research Foundation, the only American organizations committed to magnetic recording, benefitted from large orders from the military in the 1940s. Their wire recorders were built by several outside contractors, including GE, and were used by war correspondents and intelligence officers. Contracts issued by the Naval Research and Development Department in the early 1940s stimulated interest in tape recording; before the end of hostilities, the Brush Company had made overtures to the Minnesota Mining and Manufacturing Corporation (3M) to experiment with thin tapes coated with ferro-magnetic powder as a recording surface.[14]

The sound quality of magnetic recorders was very poor until alternating-current (a/c) bias systems were introduced in the 1940s to reduce the signal-to-noise ratio and distortion. The principle of a/c bias recording had been patented by W. Carlson and G. Carpenter of the Naval Research Laboratory in 1927, yet tape and wire recorders continued to use Poulsen's method of direct-current magnetization. Not until German engineers rediscovered a/c bias and began to magnetize with high-frequency currents was the distortion and noise common to all kinds of wire and tape recording reduced.[15]

Most of the experimentation with the tape format was done in Germany, where the electrical manufacturing company AEG cooperated with the giant chemical concern I. G. Farben to develop a tape recorder. In magnetic as well as acoustic recording, the first generation of independent inventor/entrepreneurs had been replaced by the organized research of large companies. The laboratories of AEG and Farben developed a tape (made of paper or vinyl acetate) covered with a fine, uniform layer of brown iron oxide. This was to be the future of magnetic recording.[16]

The totalitarian state created by Adolph Hitler was a great consumer of propaganda messages, and tape proved to be the ideal medium to carry this material. A tape recorder installed in a radio station could send out an unlimited amount of propaganda. The great technical advances achieved by the Germans were not appreciated until the last months of the war, when several tape recorders were captured. The chaos of war brought about a diffusion of this technology because the German machines soon were being examined in the United States and Great Britain.

The AEG Magnetophon had an electric-motor drive and a high-

quality vacuum tube amplifier. The iron-oxide coated tape made by
I. G. Farben slid past the recording heads at the high speed of 30
inches per second. What impressed the American engineers most
about the captured Magnetophons was the clarity of their sound reproduction. It was better than sound on film, almost as good as discs
(not counting the high-performance transcribing machines built by
Western Electric), and in a completely different league from the wire
recorders previously available.[17] It was also a much cheaper method
of recording than discs. The arrival of the German machines in the
United States increased interest in magnetic recording and proved to
be an important addition to the work already accomplished by the
Brush and Armour companies.

Wartime research also played an important part in the development
of electrical recording. Full Frequency Range Recording (FFRR), devised by Arthur Haddy in the 1940s, showed the direction that disc
recording was to take. FFRR was the product of a wartime government contract from the British Ministry of Defence to develop disc
recordings of submarine noises to train the sonar operators of the
Royal Navy and Coastal Command. Defeating the German U-boats
in the Battle of the Atlantic had become a matter of life or death for
the British government. As it was vital for these operators to be able
to distinguish between the noises of friendly and enemy submarines,
the specification called for a frequency response of 14,000 cycles, a
range far greater than that of any existing recording system.[18]

Sound waves can be measured in terms of their frequencies – the
number of cycles made by the wave every second (cps). The deep bass
sounds are in the low frequencies, and the high notes are at the other
end of the spectrum. The human ear has a range of nearly 20,000
cycles per second, from 20 cps to around 18,000 cps. The acoustic
phonograph could pick up frequencies only within the narrow band
from around 200 cps to 3,000 cps. The electrical recording system
extended the range from 130 cps to 4,200 cps. The introduction of
improved microphones and the moving-coil disc cutters gradually
moved the top part of this range to 8,000 cps.[19]

With all the resources of a desperate government behind him,
Haddy was able to increase the frequency range to span 80 cps to
15,000 cps. He used the moving-coil cutter that had been invented
by his countryman, Alan Blumlein, and made it even lighter and more
responsive. The carefully designed elliptical stylus rode along the side

of a smaller groove instead of sitting on the bottom. Haddy, like many experimenters before him, found that advances in recording had to be matched by a better record surface. He revised the procedures of electroplating masters and making duplicates to make sure that the extra high frequencies recorded onto the master would survive during the manufacture of millions of duplicates. Although not as visible as the innovations in pick-up and stylus, the duplicating process was as important in the 1940s and 1950s as it had been in the first decades of the twentieth century. Improvements in plating masters were necessary to ensure that the wave forms in the finer groove would be faithfully reproduced on the duplicates.

FFRR was commercially introduced in 1945, and the response of recording engineers was unanimous: it was described as "sensational" and "miraculous." FFRR took the disc format to a new level. It was most noticeable in recordings of large symphony orchestras with the sound of soaring string sections.[20] The Decca recordings made by the FFRR process and released on the London label in the United States just after the war were the first indications of the possibilities of significantly improved reproduction from a shellac disc. They were a sign of things to come.

A revolution in sound

The history of recorded sound in the twentieth century was punctuated by two world wars that brought significant changes to the industry, technology, and audience. It is often said that wartime accelerates the pace of technological development, and World War II would seem to prove that point. Such influential new technologies as radar, jet propulsion, electronic computers, and atomic power all came out of this conflict. The field of recorded sound was no different, for several important innovations appeared shortly after the war. Magnetic tape recording, the vinyl microgroove record, and the stereophonic reproduction of sound were all commercially introduced after 1945.

These innovations marked the technological high point of the electrical era of recorded sound. In the 1950s new talking machines which played different types of records were in wide use. The old shellac 78-rpm records were replaced by 45- and 33-rpm discs, which were lighter, more durable, and sounded better. The magnetic tape recorder was the first break from the stylus and disc format established by the gramophone in the nineteenth century. Instead of placing the stylus in the groove of a disc, the user threaded a thin strip of tape through a recording head. Simpler and more flexible than discs, magnetic tape offered significant improvements in recording.

The rapid advance of magnetic recording technology during World War II illustrates the powerful influence of wartime demands on the pace of innovation. With the captured German Magnetophons as a basis for research and the availability of 3M magnetic tape (a red oxide formulation on a plastic base), several American manufacturers were encouraged to introduce magnetic tape recorders. Most of these companies were new entrants to the field of recorded sound. They were small, entrepreneurial organizations, often based on the technical talents of one or two engineers. The Magnecord company was formed by five engineers of the Armour Research Corporation. They designed a recording machine for use in radio stations. The Ampex company was established by the Russian engineer Alexander Poniatoff in 1944 to make precision electrical equipment for the military. After the war he looked for a new product and was inspired by the Magnetophon to develop a tape recorder.[21]

In 1948 Ampex put its model 200 professional recorder on the market. It could be used in recording studios to make master recordings, and it offered superior performance as a transcription machine in radio stations. Brush produced the BK-401 tape recorder and sold many to musicians and broadcasters. The radio networks' aversion to canned music and programming had been overcome during the war years, and the American Broadcasting Company (ABC) network bought twelve of the new Ampex 200s.

Bing Crosby played a part in this transition to magnetic recording. Long weary of broadcasting his show live every week, Crosby evaluated all methods of sound recording, including transcription disc, sound on film, and the new tape recorders. He put together his own show in 1946 after completing his contract for Kraft, and ABC was so pleased to acquire it that it gladly reversed its previous opposition to broadcasting recorded programs. At first Crosby used radio transcription recorders to save the performance onto 16-inch discs, but unfortunately the editing required to make up the program produced unsatisfactory recordings. Crosby's staff conducted a blind test of available recorders and decided that magnetic tape recording best fitted their needs.[22]

Crosby decided to finance the introduction of the Ampex machines. His high profile in the entertainment industry and ABC's groundbreaking purchase of tape recorders helped break down the resistance to broadcasting recorded programs. Although the sound quality of tape recordings was not as good as recordings made with disc cutters in experienced hands, it was cheap and flexible and could be used by comparative novices. Within a short time the tape recorder was standard equipment in radio stations. ABC's purchase of Ampex machines was quickly followed by a purchase by Capitol, a new record company founded in 1942 by two song writers (Johnny Mercer and Buddy DeSylva) and the record retailer Glenn Walichs. Magnetic recording now had a foothold in the record business.

Magnetic recording was the first of several innovations introduced in the late 1940s. Taken as a whole these technologies created significant changes in the world of recorded sound, changes so drastic that some historians have described "a revolution in sound" in the postwar period.[23]

This so-called revolution in sound came at a critical time for the industry. In 1945 those company executives with long memories must have been uneasy at facing the transition from war to peace, bearing in mind the calamitous postwar depression of the 1920s. Swing music was in decline because the public was tiring of it, and it was expensive to maintain large bands. The mass market for popular recordings created by swing was fragmenting. Although sales of classical and children's records were encouraging, popular music sales were stagnant; this forced the majors to search for a new musical formula to take the place of swing.[24]

Would the industry of recorded sound revert to the Depression conditions of the 1930s when the war was over? The danger signs were not long in coming. Record sales were disappointingly flat after the war. About 100 million discs were sold in 1941, the year the United States entered the war. By 1947 this number had reached 325 million, only to fall to around 250 million in 1948, a 20 percent decline in terms of constant dollars.[25] New and improved technology, based on "the legacy of war research," was to be the weapon of the industry as it struggled to regain the mass market for recorded sound.[26]

The manufacturers of talking machines had always made exaggerated claims about the technology of their products. They continued to pledge the same things to listeners that the inventors had promised for the first acoustic machines 50 years previously: the high-frequency "overtones," the "natural color" of music, wearless records, and of course "high fidelity" of the recording to the original performance – a term which had already been overworked by the time of World War II. Although the rhetoric of the manufacturers was high-tech, their products were hardly innovative. "The new miracles of war research" were the same 78-rpm players with impressive names: the "Golden Throat" loudspeaker system, the "Magic Brain" automatic turntable, and the "Magic Tone Cell" pick-up.

While the talking machine in the family room had not changed much during the 1930s, its major competitor in home entertainment had changed. The introduction of FM (frequency modulation) radio broadcasts in the late 1930s, with their exceptional fidelity and lack of static, acted as a spur to the engineers in the phonograph industry who recognized that the surface noise and frequency range of disc recordings could not compare with FM radio.

The first shot in the campaign to transform the tired technology of the electrical era was the microgroove record, a long-playing record which built on the advances in recording achieved in the 1930s. This new product required a set of interrelated innovations: a tougher recording medium to hold a smaller groove, smaller and more precise cutting styli to cut more grooves per inch, and sensitive electromagnetic pick-ups on the player matched with high-gain amplifiers.

The composition of the recording medium on the surface of the new record was all important. All previous attempts to crowd more grooves on the record had failed because the shellac surface could not hold the smaller grooves and all the sound information inscribed onto them. Although we call them *shellac records*, shellac was only one element in a complicated mix of materials, which included fillers (such as slate and limestone), binders, lubricants (to cut down on friction as the stylus moved along the groove and to ease the removal of the blank from the stamper), and abrasives (to grind the point of the stylus to conform to the shape of the groove). Shellac constituted only 13 percent to 15 percent of the record, the main ingredient being the filler which was bonded together by the shellac. The state of Indiana had the best reserves of limestone for filler, and it became the center of American record production, producing 75 percent of the material used in records.[27]

In most home record players, the reproducing stylus was a steel needle, and the surface noise which accompanied its ride down the groove was a result of its contact with all the ingredients of the record. The signal-to-noise ratio (which indicates how much extraneous noise there is in reproduction) of an average shellac record was around 25 decibels, which means a very noisy playback. This ratio compares the difference between the playback noise and the highest signal level the system can produce without distortion. A decibel (db) measures differences in loudness; 3 db is normally the smallest difference apparent to the ear. The higher the signal-to-noise ratio, the better; a high ratio indicates that the surface noise is not drowning out the music you want to hear on the playback.

Much of the unwanted noise heard on a 78-rpm shellac disc was the sound of the disc surface being worn away: the weight of the magnets in the pick-ups put a heavy tracking force of between 100 and 200 grams on the metal needle and pushed it down hard on the shellac. On a typical Victor machine, the downward pressure was estimated to be 50,000 pounds per square inch. A shellac disc lasted only a short time under such punishment; average life was between 75 and 125 plays.[28] In a sense the surface noise was welcome in that it drowned out a lot of other more annoying noises on the record. Blisters on the surface and hard particles and impurities from the record ingredients produced the ticks, pops, and loud snaps that are instantly noticeable when listening to old 78s or to the sound tracks of movies made with the Western Electric sound-on-disc system.

Vinyl resins were introduced by the Union Carbide Company in the 1930s and marketed as an unbreakable material for things like cabinets for radios and parts of telephones. Now called PVC, vinyl materials can be found everywhere, from weatherproofed clothing to fountain pens. Like their distant ancestors, the phenol resins used in Edison's Diamond Discs, they could be molded while hot and then hardened into a permanent surface. In addition to being hard enough to take the record groove and virtually unbreakable, vinyl had the advantage of very low absorption of moisture in humid conditions, a problem which had caused warping of cellulose acetate discs.[29]

The first vinyl records were made from a copolymer of vinyl chloride and vinyl acetate, a harder and finer material than shellac. This meant that more grooves could be pressed into them – a vital consideration in a long-playing disc. To achieve a playing time of 30 minutes, the groove has to be nearly half a mile long. Instead of the normal 80 to 100 grooves cut per inch, the new long-player was cut with 224 to 260 grooves per inch. The bottom of the groove was only 0.001 of an inch wide – roughly three times smaller than the grooves of a shellac disc; hence the term *microgroove* to describe these records.[30]

Because vinyl contains no abrasives, a permanent jeweled stylus with a synthetic sapphire or diamond was employed for the microgroove system. Engineers developed pick-ups with a tracking force of 10 grams, which was at least ten times lighter than the ones used on shellac records. The innovations in moving-coil record cutters were applied to the pick-up. Instead of being permanently attached to the tone arm, the pick-up now came in the form of a removable cartridge; usually it held one stylus for 78-rpm discs and another for microgroove discs. The benefits of the new record material and pick-ups could be heard in the vastly improved signal-to-noise ratio. A ratio of 30 db was very good for shellac, but with the vinyl records the ratio rose to 55 and 60 db.

The LP was developed in the laboratories of the Columbia Company under the direction of Dr. Peter Goldmark. Like Edison, Johnson, and Haddy before him, Goldmark wisely spent some time improving duplicating techniques for the new records. He visited the Columbia record plant at Bridgeport and was appalled at the dirt and lack of concern about foreign particles introduced into the duplicating process.[31] The technique of electroplating masters with gold, silver, or graphite had not changed much since Edison's time, but the microgroove records required a higher standard of quality control.

Columbia succeeded where Edison and RCA Victor had failed, because it devised a marketing plan which covered the provision of recordings and players. They collaborated with the Philco Company to bring out a cheap plug-in player that sold for $29.95. It was a turntable, cartridge, and tone arm in a plastic clamshell-like casing. The slower playing speed made it very important to cut down the noise of the turntable and eliminate variations in the turning speed, both of which are more evident at slower speeds. The rubber idler wheel was ground to perfect circularity and the turntable carefully centered.

Philco used a crystal cartridge, a lightweight tone arm cushioned in rubber, and a metal stylus with a 6-gram tracking force.[32]

The provision of master recordings of longer pieces of music was a critical part of the marketing plan, because the history of recorded sound had shown that a new player required suitable records to support it. It was pointless to market LPs without a tempting collection of recordings. Columbia took the time to assemble a library of longer recordings in the new format before introducing it to the public. The practice of making safety backup copies of master records on acetate 33⅓-rpm, 16-inch transcription discs proved to be an enormous advantage, since Columbia's engineers had only to copy from these masters. Less fortunate recording engineers had to copy four or five 78-rpm masters and edit them together onto one disc.[33]

All the years of research and planning came to a climax in 1948 when Columbia executives announced the long-playing record to the press. They claimed that their product took "the musical world by storm." It was an invention that "revolutionized the recorded music industry."[34] It was depicted as a totally new technology, despite the fact that the long-playing record had a history that went back to the Western Electric sound-on-disc recorders of the 1920s. The idea of long-playing records certainly was not new, nor was the 33⅓-rpm speed, nor the 12-inch disc; all had been employed in the 1930s. The development of the LP was shaped by long experience with transcription machines.[35] Even the wonderful new recording medium, vinyl plastics, had been employed as transcription discs for radio and for "V" discs during World War II in order to survive the long journey to the front.

The real challenge of introducing a new format for a pre-recorded disc was not the technology itself but the process of persuading record companies to adopt it. Edison had proved that it was futile to establish a new standard in records and try to maintain a monopoly over it. His Diamond Disc venture had been crippled because the players were not able to play other manufacturers' records. Columbia had to bring all the other record companies into the new microgroove technology. After their engineers had established the standards of the new record, from depth of groove to thickness of disc, Columbia's management had to persuade the rest of the industry to adopt these standards.

Figure 10.2. Three formats for records and players: the old 78 rpm, and the two new microgroove formats. (Library of Congress)

Columbia must have felt confident in 1948; the system worked well, and all record producers knew that there was a market for the long-playing disc, especially among lovers of classical music. As there were no other competing technologies on the market, the Columbia executives felt that it would not be too difficult to get the 33⅓-rpm standard accepted. But they miscalculated the reaction of RCA, long the rival of Columbia in the record business and a company that prided itself on being the leader in new technology. Had not RCA developed the first LP and numerous other important innovations?

Company pride did not permit RCA to go along with the Columbia microgroove records; hence the introduction of their own microgroove 45-rpm disc. RCA was also in a position to provide a large selection of popular recordings in the new format. They produced a small plastic turntable and pick-up unit which could play only 45-rpm records. It sold at the bargain price of $12.95.

The "battle of the speeds" which followed was a disaster for all concerned – confused customers who delayed their purchases, pointless duplication of programming on several different formats, and expensive, overcomplicated turntables. By 1950 there were four speeds to choose from: 78, 33⅓, 45, and 16 rpm – the latter was the newest format, which promised full-length operas, stage plays, and books on even longer-playing records. The so-called record wars that erupted between CBS and RCA hindered the introduction of microgroove technology, because it made consumers uncertain of the outcome. The result was a slow transition to microgroove records.

Despite the claims of Columbia and RCA, the microgroove record did not sweep all before it. There was considerable resistance to microgroove records from consumers, because they had to buy new turntables to play them. Record dealers saw microgroove records as disrupting their business and decreasing the value of their inventories. It was not until 1954 that several of the major record companies began to send 45-rpm singles to radio stations instead of the heavier shellac 78s.[36] Vinyl did not completely replace shellac until the late 1950s, and it was still possible to buy 78-rpm records in the 1960s.

The introduction of magnetic tape recorders followed the same slow and cautious path. This was not an absolute technological change like talking pictures. The disc recording system was a tried and proven technology which represented a considerable investment of expertise. Engineers in recording and radio studios were too prudent to abandon this technology as soon as tape was introduced, and many regarded magnetic recording with suspicion. For the first few years of use, tape machines were operated in studios alongside disc recorders, in much the same way that soundmen had used disc and tape systems together in the early years of synchronized movie sound.[37] Tape recorders were adopted throughout the industry in the early 1950s, but it took at least a decade to phase out the trusty disc recorder. In film studios the transition to magnetic tape was also slow, a result of the large investment in optical methods of sound recording and the stock of skills in applying it to sound stages.[38] In practice the revolution in sound was carried out at a leisurely pace.

The audiophile and stereo sound

There was one group of listeners who immediately and unconditionally adopted microgroove technology. In a survey carried out soon after the LPs were introduced in 1948, it was found that customers tended to be of above-average income and interested in classical music. One sample found that 38 percent of the purchasers already had a collection of more than 500 records. Most buyers made special trips to their dealers for special demonstrations, but half the sample said that they had made up their minds about purchasing the system before they entered the store! Here was a group of people who were devoted to collecting and listening to records and who were willing to pay any price for improved sound reproduction.

At the time of purchase, these customers said that the long-playing feature was most important to them, but when they were interviewed some months later, they thought that better sounding records was the main benefit of microgroove technology.[39] The improvement in reproduction was hard to resist. The bloated, indistinct sound of the postwar consoles, with their booming bass and muddy trebles, could not compare with the new long-playing microgroove records. Much of that reassuring, regular "swish" of 78-rpm shellac discs had been consigned to history by the quieter LPs.

The enthusiastic response of audiophiles to the LP made it clear to the industry of recorded sound that there was a considerable market for what was termed *high fidelity* – a standard of reproduction greatly superior to the old 78-rpm shellac disc. *High fidelity* was a term that had been used and overused from the 1930s onwards. It referred to the faithfulness of the machine's reproduction of the original music: wide frequency response, flat frequency response (in that all sounds are reproduced at equal levels), wide dynamic levels, and low distortion and noise. It did not necessarily begin and end with a wide frequency range – the range of sound from highs to lows that the equipment can reproduce without distortion – although this was often the measuring stick of high fidelity. It also covered the ability to clearly reproduce the extremes of volume (from soft to loud) without distortion.

The new records sounded so much better than the old that the expectations of music lovers were raised. Listeners who purchased sophisticated equipment to listen to the best of classical music now saw (or, more precisely, heard) that the old dream of bringing first-class music into the home exactly as it had been played – first articulated by Thomas Edison – was now possible. Audiophiles became advocates for higher and higher fidelity.

It would be easy to imagine that this goal was the guiding light of the manufacturers of phonographs, but surprisingly it was not. The revolution in sound had been aimed at stimulating the stagnant post-war market for recorded sound. Once this had been achieved by microgroove records, there was no reason to continue innovating; the "battle of the speeds" had demonstrated how disruptive this process could be – and how dangerous to profits. The manufacturers decided to rest on their laurels and enjoy the boom in sales created by the changeover from the 78-rpm to 33-rpm format. This was as far as they wanted to go, and they argued that the consumer could not discern and therefore did not care about any more improvements in reproduction.[40]

The crusade for higher fidelity was therefore the work of an army of amateur phonograph builders. In the 1950s building amplifiers and loudspeakers became a very popular hobby. Stores which sold radio components began to stock parts which could be assembled into home players. Their customers were often servicemen who had been trained to operate electronic equipment during World War II and had maintained an interest in it. Some of the engineers who had also worked in wartime electronics founded small companies to provide the components. After the decimation of the Depression, there were only about thirty concerns producing audio equipment, but in the 1950s this number increased dramatically as new companies entered the business, many with the aid of GI loans. These were start-up companies established by inventors and entrepreneurs – the same kind of people who had founded the industry of recorded sound in the 1880s and 1890s.

MGM film studios employed two experts in loudspeaker design, Robert Stevens, who later founded Stevens Manufacturing, and James B. Lansing, who founded Altec and then JBL. Another important innovator in loudspeaker design, Henry Koss, formed KLH and then Advent. Avery Fisher founded the Fisher Radio Corporation, a manufacturer of advanced sound equipment. In the immediate postwar years, he sold a few high-quality radio-phonograph components sets, ranging in price from $800 to $1,000.

Several small manufacturers made amplifier kits that could be assembled at home with a soldering iron and screwdriver. The enthusiast followed the instructions, scrutinised the circuit diagram, soldered the parts onto a plain metal chassis, and hoped for the best. It took time, patience, and some electrical knowledge to make these things work. Separate tuners could be assembled to receive radio broadcasts. The price range went from the cheap kits made by the Heath Company, which sold for about $50, to $100 high-wattage amplifiers with several tubes. Pre-amplifier kits, which had volume and tone controls, were sold separately. Many companies sold loudspeakers, either complete or in kits. Many audiophiles built their own systems out of these component parts.

The purchase of a reel-to-reel tape or wire recorder completed the system. While some companies concentrated on making professional studio recorders in the years after the war, others put out smaller models for home use. These basic machines came complete with amplifiers and microphones. For the first time it was possible to record sound in the home with comparative ease. The home phonograph conceived by Edison in the nineteenth century had become a play-only machine by the 1930s. There were disc recorders available which used the same technology of "acetate" discs and cutters found in recording studios. Companies like Presto and Audio Devices marketed "instantaneous" discs, which could be played back on any home 78-rpm disc player after recording. The problem with these recorders was that operating them required all the care and skill used in professional studios. The home user had to choose the right cutting stylus, position it properly on the disc, adjust the depth of the cut, and control the thread as it was cut from the groove.[41]

Magnetic recording offered the same advantages to the amateur that it had brought to the recording studio: ease of use, longer recording time, and editing capabilities. It was eagerly acquired by a postwar generation interested in recording, and tape and wire recorders became a popular fixture in business offices and schools as well as homes. Tape was easier to handle than wire, which had a tendency to break and often knotted up when rewinding. Audiophiles took tape to heart and provided a market for recorders made by Magnecord, Fairchild, and Rangertone. Cheaper models were made by Webcor,

Wilcox-Gay, and Revere. All these companies had concentrated on magnetic recording, but they were soon joined by others who had once been committed to discs, such as RCA and Presto. Several other companies – Reeves Soundcraft, Audio Devices, Orradio and 3M – provided blank reels of tape. By 1953 the number of tape players in use exceeded a million, and the major record companies, led by RCA and Capitol, began to market pre-recorded tape.[42]

Tape was the format to introduce stereo sound into the home. It was much easier to put two channels of sound onto separate bands of 1/4-inch tape than crowd them into the groove of a disc. Webcor introduced a popular conversion kit that converted mono tape recorders into stereo; this was followed by stereo tape players in the late 1940s (notably the Magnecord of 1949) and pre-recorded stereo tapes in 1953. The availability of stereo tape revived interest in binaural sound. Recordings of FM radio programs on stereo tapes became a popular method of demonstrating high-fidelity equipment, replacing the disc in an unsettling precedent for the record companies.[43]

It was clear to the audio industry that the number of audiophiles and high-fidelity enthusiasts was growing and that they were also becoming more knowledgeable about the technology of recorded sound. Existing magazines about electronics and audio were selling more copies, and new ones were unveiled to meet the demand for technical information. Terms like *wow and flutter, total harmonic distortion*, and *equalization* were used by customers as well as salesmen at trade shows.[44]

Audio shows and fairs had been held in major American cities from 1949 onwards. What began as a trade show for manufacturers and retailers soon turned into a jamboree for high-fidelity enthusiasts. The scene was described by Roland Gelatt, himself an audiophile and historian of the phonograph:

> gadgeteers of dubious musical sensibility delighted in employing their expensive equipment to cleave the ear with piercing piccolos and growling double basses such as never were heard in a concert hall. Bizarre recordings of thunderstorms and screaming railroad trains were concocted for those to whom high fidelity reproduction was an end in itself and not a means to musical reproduction.[45]

Not every audiophile wanted to go this far. The introduction of stereo sound had brought the goal of faithful reproduction of an actual concert performance within reach. Now the listener had two channels of sound which could be positioned at will to re-create the impression of music reverberating from all sides, as it did in the concert hall. The tone and balance adjustments of the amplifiers (or pre-amplifiers) gave a measure of control over reproduction which had never before been enjoyed by the home listener, who could now manipulate the amplitude of chosen frequencies in the same way that the recording engineer fine-tuned the equalization controls on his professional console.

Interest in stereophonic sound gave a boost to the sales of magnetic recorders and pre-recorded tape. In 1957, $7 million was spent on pre-recorded tape in the United States. RCA had become the largest user of 1/4-inch tape in the country, recording 6 million feet a week.[46] The time had come for record companies to develop a competing stereo product or leave the high-fidelity market to tape. Those companies with a strong interest in classical music knew that they had to record in stereo or risk losing their best customers. EMI and Deutsche Grammophon had decided to move over to the tape format if no stereo disc could be developed.[47]

Although the basic idea of the stereo disc had been worked out in the 1930s, there were still some important problems to be solved, not the least of which was the stereo format to be developed. The 45/45 concept of Blumlein and Keller had been advanced the farthest in research and development, but it was by no means the only system available. The vertical/lateral idea had a following in Europe and was promoted by several large companies, including Decca in England and Telefunken in Germany.

A demonstration in New York in 1957 compared a vertical/lateral player designed by Arthur Haddy of Decca with a commercial 45/45 system developed by the Westrex Company of the United States, a subsidiary of AT&T and the successor to ERPI. The results of the test showed that the latter had the advantage of dividing binaural sound between two identical cuts in the record, while the vertical/lateral cuts were made differently and required adjustment of specific frequencies (equalization) to sound exactly the same.[48] A tentative agreement was made to pursue the Westrex system.

Before stereo had any kind of commercial future, there had to be agreement by manufacturers and record producers on the standards chosen for the stereo records. Which channel was to go on which side of the groove? Which kind of cartridge would best reproduce the complex movements of a stylus in a stereo groove? How could a record be made so that it could reproduce two channels on a stereo system and still be played on all existing mono players? There were many questions to be answered, and each one had to be incorporated into a set of standards. The unhappy consequences of the "battle of the speeds" were still fresh in the memory, and a similar conflict had broken out among manufacturers of tape recorders over the speed at which the tape passed over the recording head: 3¾, 7½, 15, or 30 inches per second. In an industry marked by ferocious competition, there were plenty of barriers to reaching an agreement on a stereo standard.

The issue of standardization was important enough to be recognized by Emile Berliner as early as the 1880s. It is not only a technical matter, because the interchangeability of records and players is critical to selling them. Perhaps because we now enjoy complete standardization, we tend to overlook the mighty efforts required to achieve it. It would be a different matter if we could only play Victor records on an RCA player or if each company's records sounded different. For all its importance, standardization of recorded sound products is an invisible technology: it can only be heard.

During the 1930s one of the main hurdles to standardization had been overcome by the universal adoption of the 78-rpm standard. Yet other standards were still unresolved, including the invisible standard of recording levels embodied in the recording curve, which describes the boosting or reducing of bands of sound frequencies in recording.

Recording has to be done from a base reference point – a point that establishes how loud the recording will be, and how each part of the frequency range will be reproduced. The recording engineer is concerned with saving the sounds in the minute groove of a revolving disc; for this reason, recording each part of the frequency range at the same level is impractical. To squeeze the full range of frequencies into the groove usually requires the bass notes to be reduced and the treble to be strengthened. Thus the highs and lows are recorded at different levels.

Normally the higher frequencies are recorded with "constant velocity," which means that the amplitude decreases with the increase in frequencies. Below a certain point, the so-called "crossover" point, the lower frequencies are recorded at constant amplitude, at which

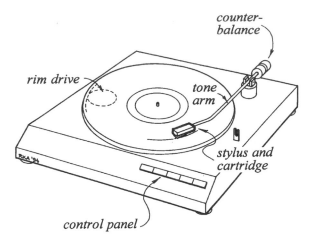

counter-
balance

rim drive

tone
arm

stylus and
cartridge

control panel

An electrical record player

all frequencies are recorded at the same level. Called the *recording curve*, this process corresponds to increasing and lowering the tone controls on your stereo as you record. This is fine for your own equipment, but if you are recording masters intended to mass-produce duplicates, the other recording studios have to know what you did so that their recordings sound the same.

American companies began to use constant amplitude in recording in the 1930s, and each company used its own recording curve with a different crossover point. The result was that audiophiles had to carefully match the tone controls of their machines with the recording characteristics of each record they played.[49] The lack of a common recording curve was a barrier to standardization and to achieving higher levels of fidelity.

The Record Industry Association of America (RIAA) assumed responsibility for promulgating standards after 1945. It had established the standard for microgroove records and for the equalization used in recording on them – the recording curve. Many records lost part of their high frequencies as the groove came near to the end of the record; to compensate, the high-frequency response could be increased as the arm moved to the end of the record. At the lower frequencies, deep bass sounds were attenuated during recording in order to prevent the cutting stylus from jumping the groove and cutting into the adjacent groove.[50]

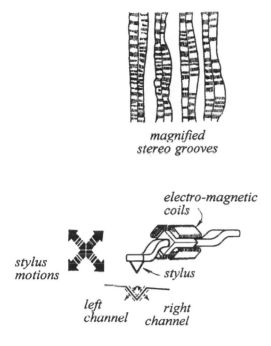

magnified
stereo grooves

electro-magnetic
coils

stylus
motions

stylus

left   *right*
channel   *channel*

Electrical reproduction

In the 1950s each studio continued to use its own recording curve; in many cases one company might use different standards for different recordings. Adding to this confusion were the standards adopted by other organizations, such as the National Association of Radio and Television Broadcasters. The adoption of a common recording curve meant that a record made by any company would be recorded to the same standard as all the others, and that every disc played on the home player would (in theory) have the same emphasis on the high or low frequencies. The recording curve cannot be seen on the record nor is it evident on the record player, where it resides within the electronic circuits of the amplifier. The equalization circuits are activated when the PHONO button is pushed.

In December 1957 the Westrex stereo disc system was formally adopted as the American standard by the RIAA, and the critical step had been taken in the commercial introduction of stereophonic sound. The first stereo records were put on sale in the same year: the revolving disc was back in the market for high fidelity. Although the introduction of stereo sound was hailed as a great innovation by the industry of recorded sound (which never missed an opportunity to make such claims), the Westrex 45/45 system had its origins in the 1930s – like most of the other well-publicized "miracles of war research." The important postwar innovation had been the agreement on standards for the stereo disc.

The home stereo

The stereo record was not intended for the mass market, and sales were not high. Yet the audiophile now had a reason to build a suitable playing system, which stimulated sales of audio components: a precise turntable, made by companies such as Garrard and Dual; one of the new dynamic pick-ups, sold by Pickering, Fairchild, and Audak; and two matched loudspeakers to reproduce two channels of sound.

Audiophiles had always used speakers which were scaled-down models of the speakers used in movie theaters – large bass woofers and trumpet-like tweeters, which projected sound great distances but were overwhelming in the home. The invention of the dome-shaped tweeter by Roy Allison and the acoustic suspension enclosure by Henry Koss brought very high performance into a small box. The latter innovation sealed the low-frequency transducer in an enclosure small enough to use the trapped air as a stiffener. This dispensed with the large bass woofers needed to deliver low-frequency sounds. The new loudspeakers were small (less than 2 feet high), efficient, and affordable. Several new companies such as Acoustic Research, Advent, and Allison Acoustics marketed "bookcase" speakers, which were the basis of many home stereo systems.

Twin speakers encouraged manufacturers to go back to the console shape of player – a long, flat box – which had first appeared in the 1920s. In the new consoles, loudspeakers were incorporated into the ends of the rectangular cabinet. The same period cabinets were still in vogue: the "Hepplewhite" (Stromberg-Carlson) and "Chippendale" (Philco and RCA Victor), which were guaranteed to "blend perfectly with your lovely furniture." It was still fashionable to conceal the working parts and the identity of the talking machine behind wooden doors. The Victrola idea was still the creed of the talking machine.

Neat little bookcase speakers tempted some manufacturers to move them away from the console and thus recast the look of the home phonograph. At last, form could follow function, and the home stereo of the 1960s had a more modern look. The sparse, Scandinavian style became fashionable. Made out of light-colored wood, these were long low boxes with a clean, uncluttered line and separate speakers. Replacing Mediterranean-style cabinets in oak or pecan veneers was a new look influenced by the component systems of hi-fi enthusiasts in which aluminum and other metals replaced wood. The component sets made little concession to style. They were purely functional, going just one step further than the bare-metal chassis of Heath kits. They came in aluminum cases with black metal tops and aluminum and chrome fronts. The only hint of wood was a slice tacked on to each end of the metal boxes of the components. Instead of a wooden door, the front of the unit was now a mass of control knobs, small lights, switches, and a backlit channel selector for the radio. Instead of the single volume knob there was a complete set of treble, bass, balance, and loudness (which increased the bass at low volume) controls. There were enough switches and knobs to satisfy the most demanding button pusher. Instead of masquerading as a piece of furniture, the component system unashamedly announced its function with an array of dials and switches that reminded one commentator of the cockpit of a B52 bomber.[51]

The shift to a more functional look for the home record player was supported by a truly revolutionary technology – a technology which had emerged, unsung, from the "legacy of war research" and which was to have a profound effect on the industry of recorded sound. The demands of war had channeled scientific research into areas of strategic importance, such as electromagnetic computing machines (to break codes) and radar. Scientists used the same sort of vacuum tubes found in the home phonograph. Although the performance of vacuum tubes had been improved considerably since the 1920s, they were still far from satisfactory. They were expensive, prone to breakdown, and very fragile. They generated a lot of unwanted heat in the heart of electrical equipment. It was said that you could read a newspaper by the light coming from a bank of vacuum tubes in an audio amplifier. You could never be sure when one would fail, but you knew that it would burn out sooner or later.

The invention of the transistor in Bell Labs in 1948 constituted an advance in electronics equal to the invention of the vacuum tube, which it was eventually to succeed. It not only replaced vacuum tubes in radios, phonographs, and all sorts of electrical equipment but did the job more efficiently and more reliably. Transistorized technology helped put a stereo, rather than just a talking machine, in every American home. It was one of the main factors in bringing high fidelity within reach of the average consumer.

It should come as no surprise to the reader that this breakthrough was the result of research into telephony and that it occurred in the same laboratories that had produced electrical recording. John Bardeen and Walter Brattain of Bell Labs invented the first point-contact transistor in 1948. They demonstrated that a piece of semiconducting material, a slice of germanium crystal, could amplify or control electric current. Further inventions produced devices where the transistor effect took place within the layers of germanium. These earlier transistors were used to amplify current. Their first commercial application was to amplify sound in smaller and more efficient hearing aids.

A major application for transistors was the control and amplification functions carried out in electronic equipment by vacuum tubes. Substituting a transistor for a vacuum tube increased reliability, decreased price, and most of all saved space: the transistor was the means to reduce the size and weight of the talking machines on a scale that would have amazed Edison and his generation of engineers.

The first audio product to show the effects of transistor miniaturization was the radio. In the 1930s and 1940s, a portable radio with vacuum tubes was the size of an airline carry-on bag. Transistors required less voltage and therefore could be run from smaller batteries. In 1954 the first transistor radio was introduced by the American Regency Company (with a Texas Instruments transistor). It was followed in 1955 with the model TR 55 from the Tokyo Telecommunications Engineering Company using a chip of their own design. It carried the brand name Sony.

The Sony Company, as it was renamed in 1957, began its long association with recording sound with the manufacture of tape recorders in postwar Japan. Akio Morita, one of its co-founders, had been introduced to recorded sound by the family Victrola and its Red Seal records. American music was very popular in Japan after the war, and the young company had survived by fabricating phonograph motors and pick-ups. The success of the tape recorder led to more audio products and the transistor radio. Sony engineers worked to reduce its size even more. By 1957 they had produced a radio small enough to fit into a shirt pocket – the original idea of Morita and his partner Masuru Ibuka.[52]

The transistor radio became an item of mass consumption as millions were manufactured. By 1959 there were 12 million in use; soon there were more radios than households in the United States.[53] By scaling down the size and reducing the cost of radios, manufacturers had found an unlimited market for them. One of the major users of transistor radios was the young, who carried them around as a portable source of sound. Transistor radios brought them rock'n'roll and played an important part in promoting popular music in the 1960s. They ensured that Top 40 radio programming continued as a potent force in promoting popular music.

Once the transistor radio was seen to be a commercial success, the application of this technology to audio equipment quickly followed. Not only could a transistorized amplification unit reduce the size of the talking machine, it could also reduce its cost. As more transistors were made, the unit priced dropped. Equally important was the smaller size and lack of heat buildup, which made it possible to put transistorized amplifiers, tuners, and pre-amplifiers on top of another without fear of overheating. Manufacturers could scale down professional equipment and bring it within the purchasing power of the home listener, bringing high fidelity to all.

As early as 1961 transistorized phonographs were introduced for home use. An amplifier, tuner, and turntable were crammed into one unit. The basic configuration was a square box with a lid hinged to the back that lifted upwards, electric motor and drive positioned underneath the turntable, and the speaker in the front section. This basic shape was common to most of the cheap players from the 1920s to the 1950s, when it was incorporated into such popular models as the ubiquitous "Silvertones," sold in the Sears catalogue. Wood was still the preferred material, for the manufacturers of record players tended to shun the Bakerlite plastics which were so popular with radio makers. The quality hard woods found on a nineteenth-century phonograph were rarely seen in the postwar table-top players, when cheap wooden composites were used, often with a cloth covering. The transistorized player used plastics instead of wood, which helped reduce its price.

The new look of the phonograph was not merely the result of the technology of transistors and enclosed speakers. It also reflected the new shape of the market for recorded sound, in which teenagers played an important part. The console models like the Victrola or Orthophonic were intended to go into the living room. They were for family listening; adults would choose the music and operate the machine. In the 1960s the phonograph was often played for the enjoyment of the young, and its size and shape came to reflect its position in the youth culture. No longer an imposing piece of furniture in the parlor, the phonograph was now to be found in the childrens' rooms or college dormitory. It had to be portable, because American teenagers were constantly on the move in their pursuit of happiness.

The steady improvement in transistors and solid-state electronics brought smaller and cheaper record players ideally suited to the youth audience for popular music, who were buying 45-rpm vinyl discs in record numbers in the 1960s. The tiny transistors were attached to a circuit board on which the wiring connections were etched onto copper-coated plastic. These printed circuits were first used during World War II and were soon employed in the automated assembly of electronic devices. Transistors, capacitors, and other devices were attached to these circuit boards to produce a miniature solid-state replacement for the bulky metal chassis which held vacuum tubes and transformers. A tiny solid-state board could be fitted under a turntable unit, which was only 2 or 3 inches deep, to give it the amplification power for the phonograph and receive AM broadcasts for the radio. These small portable units could be made just a little bigger than the 7-inch, 45-rpm disc they played. They came encased in a variety of colored plastics and were sold for under $30.

The home stereo became an important part of the consumer lifestyle of the 1960s, a machine that everyone wanted in the home, like the television set. While the desire for perfect high fidelity still inspired a generation of audiophiles, stereo reproduction of recorded sound became a basic requirement for all talking machines. Manufacturers were ready to meet this need, especially the Japanese companies such as Sony and Panasonic (the trade name of the Matsushista Corporation), who took the lead in low-priced stereos.

Sony had followed the success of its transistor radio with the first all-transistor television in 1960 and continued to reduce the size and price of its products. What Sony and its fellow Japanese electrical manufac-

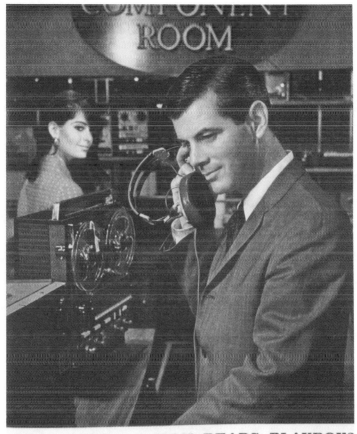

WHAT SORT OF MAN READS PLAYBOY?

Figure 10.3. Listening to one of the new high-fidelity tape recorders in an audio store. (Reproduced by Special Permission of *Playboy* magazine. Copyright ©1967 by Playboy)

turers exploited was the desire for portability in mechanical entertainment: television and radio were the technological necessities of American life, and the nineteenth-century maxim of one in every home was no longer enough. The Japanese devised smaller and cheaper machines to go into the kids' rooms, the kitchen, the car, and the boat.

In the 1960s they offered a range of home stereos priced from $150 to $400, all with two way speakers (tweeter and woofer) and auto matic turntable. Most of these units were made out of plastic and came

Figure 10.4. The line of Sony stereos in 1969, priced from $179.95 to $319.95. (Courtesy of Sony Corporation)

in a rectangular box with the speakers separate. What had started as a luxury good for the technically minded elite in the 1960s became a mass-produced consumer good in the 1970s. High-fidelity sound was now within the reach of college students and apartment dwellers.

11. Rock'n'roll and the revolution in music

What effect did the revolution in sound have on the music that was recorded? For technological determinists, those who believe that technology is the wellspring of change, the postwar innovations appeared to have an immediate impact on the world of music. A few years after the introduction of tape-recording machines and microgroove discs, a new type of popular music burst upon the scene. Often described as a force of dramatic change in American history, the product of an enormous cultural revolution, rock'n'roll became the most influential popular music of the twentieth century. Rock'n'roll was by no means "the only revolution in the 80-year-old history of the American record industry" as some have claimed, but it made a much greater impact on American society than an earlier revolutionary form of popular music – jazz – and its effect lasted much longer.[1] Rock as a musical style and a way of life moved effortlessly into film and television, dominating the cultural landscape for decades.

It had a dramatic new sound, an electric sound, which was characterized by the ringing tones of electric guitars amplified through loudspeakers. Electrification had not only been used in the recording process; the electric pick-up and amplifier had replaced the acoustic soundbox of the guitar with unlimited power. The sound of the crashing power chords of the electric guitar was to become the trademark of rock'n'roll.

Yet it was more than the guitar sound that made rock recordings different. There was an edge, that special reverberating echo, that can be heard in such quintessential rock'n'roll records as "Heartbreak Hotel" (Elvis Presley), "Be-Bop A Lula" (Gene Vincent), and "Summertime Blues" (Eddie Cochran). The sound of guitars and voices was changed in the recording studio to give these records a dimension different from recordings of other popular music.

It was not difficult to find a link between the revolution in sound recording and the new sound of rock'n'roll; the music came hot on the heels of the tape recorder and the microgroove disc. In fact the 7-inch, 45-rpm disc provides us with the prime artifact of rock'n'roll; much smaller and lighter than the 78, its much larger center hole created a different shape. It was the format for rock'n'roll. The brightly colored labels prompt us with the names of the legendary performers and the companies that recorded them: Elvis Presley on Sun, Buddy Holly on Coral, and Chuck Berry on Chess.

Rock'n'roll is important not only for the changes in the sound of popular music but also for the changes it brought in the music industry. It was the product of independent record companies – business organizations that had almost died out during the 1930s. The technology of electrical recording had favored the larger companies, and the Great Depression did the rest. Very few of the independent operations survived the Depression; those that did, such as Commodore, used the facilities of the major record companies to master and press recordings for specialized audiences for jazz or classical music. During World War II, a shortage of shellac to make records and a recording ban of the musician's union cut down record production to the bare minimum, eliminating many of the surviving independent companies.

Of all the new sound technologies made available after the war, magnetic recording has been hailed as the most important force of change. Some historians saw the professional tape recording machines as an important tool for small, independent companies in their efforts to compete with the big studios. Once recording had required costly facilities and complicated disc cutting machines, but now anyone could do it with an inexpensive tape recorder. It has assumed some importance in the history of rock'n'roll: "The ubiquitous tape recorder freed recording from its dependence on the arduous and complicated studio procedure . . . and made the process considerably more flexible, mobile, and inexpensive." The skills of the recorder were no longer required because an amateur could operate one. In short, "Tape was a boon to the hitherto depressed folk."[2]

There can be no doubt that independent companies were the vehicles to bring a new popular music to Americans. As small, locally run concerns, they recorded for a local audience. They adopted the policy of recording "ethnic" music that was originated by the big companies in the 1920s and abandoned by them during the 1930s. Yet they were not high-tech organizations that quickly adopted the latest technology. On the contrary, they were distinctly low-rent, low-tech operations that made do with old equipment.

The independents could not afford to be on the leading edge of technology. On the whole they came into record production from the promotion or musical side of the business. They were not technically oriented. They used secondhand equipment: old microphones, worn-out disc presses, and old acetate recording lathes obtained from a radio station or bought cheaply from another company. This equipment could be quickly installed in a garage or storefront. The independents were firmly established in the 78-rpm shellac record format. In fact, the shift to microgroove records caused them great additional expenses in production that they would have preferred to avoid.[3]

Most of the independents who influenced the development of the new music of the 1950s emerged in the 1940s – long before the introduction of professional tape machines. They recorded with acetate disc cutters. They leaned heavily on radio for production as well as promotion. Radio studios often provided recording facilities for the independents, and often a friendly local radio station might be persuaded to loan out its microphones, amplifiers, and transcription recorders.[4]

Innovations in tape recording certainly made it easier to set up a recording studio and make master records; in the early 1950s, when many more independent companies were formed, it was an important factor in opening up the industry. Yet in the critical period of the late 1940s when the new music emerged, the technology used by the independents was, by financial necessity, the old one of recording on acetate masters and having them pressed into shellac discs. The progenitor of rock'n'roll was rhythm and blues, which was released on 78-rpm discs. Most of the early rock'n'roll records – including Elvis Presley's historic singles made for Sun Records – were available on the 78-rpm format. The new music was on the old technology.

The great business problem facing the independent record manufacturers was not in the studio, in sound recording, but in distribution. Here was where the national distribution networks of the major companies really counted – "major" denoted companies based on ownership of presses and a system of warehouses, wholesalers, and record jobbers. The majors were part of the empires of sound and used their corporate connections to promote their songs by getting them played on the radio, including them in Broadway musicals, and incorporating them into the sound tracks of Hollywood movies.

The majors emerged from the war all-powerful and unchanged. Capitol and Mercury (which was formed in Chicago in 1947) were the only new entrants to the record business with the resources to press and market their products. It was rumored that Mercury used the power of organized crime to force its recordings on retailers and juke box operators.[5] The rest of the independents had to make do with hand-me-down presses or send their masters to be pressed in another company's plant. The record producer then loaded the boxes of discs into the back of his car and hit the road. It was a struggle to get their product on the shelves of record shops and on the play lists of radio stations, but these were the critical considerations in getting the hits which powered the popular record business.

The rise of the independents

Jazz and rock'n'roll emerged from the social and economic turmoil caused by the United States' involvement in world wars. In both conflicts, there was a great migration of African Americans and a new injection of their music and dance into popular culture. When this happened after World War I, it resulted in the commercial introduction of jazz. The next war brought employment opportunities for African Americans, after the hard years of the Depression, and they moved up the Mississippi valley to industrial cities of the Midwest, such as Chicago and Detroit. They travelled to Southern California to work in aircraft factories. All these new city dwellers enjoyed a brief period of prosperity; with money in their pockets, they created a small but dynamic market for records – just as they had done in the 1920s.

The major companies did not completely desert their race catalogues during the Depression. RCA maintained its subsidiary Bluebird Records, and Columbia still had OKeh Records, but their attention in the 1940s was on the older styles of country blues and gospel. They failed to notice new types of music emerging in the postwar period, especially the Be Bop style of modern jazz and the electrified blues coming from the cities of the Midwest and Northeast.

Independent record companies appeared in cities to serve an audience whose musical tastes were not met by the majors: Apollo (formed

1943) and Jubilee in New York; Savoy in Newark (1939); Excelsior (1942), Jukebox (1944), Modern (1945), Imperial (1945), and Specialty (1945) in Los Angeles; King in Cincinnati (1944); and Chess in Chicago (1947). Many of the entrepreneurs who founded these companies had their base in record retailing or in artist management. Some ran bars or nightclubs and converted their halls into makeshift recording studios. Others operated strings of juke boxes, a very important outlet for popular music. These operations were usually owned by middle-class whites, with the notable exceptions of Trumpet Records (Jackson, Miss.), Red Robin (Harlem), and Duke-Peacock Records (Houston), which were formed by black entrepreneurs who moved from the retail business into record production.[6]

There were also independent record companies who specialized in country and western, jazz, and classical music. King Records was one of the few independents who had a foot in both blues and country music camps. Savoy Records produced gospel, Be Bop, and some of the pioneer rhythm and blues records. Folkways and Vanguard Records were established in 1948 to promote folk music; they were followed into this growing field by Elektra in 1950. Verve was founded by the promoter Norman Granz in 1949 as a jazz label. The entrepreneur George Golden formed Tico Records in 1948 to provide Latin and mambo music to the Hispanic audience of New York.[7]

One of the most influential independent companies, and the one most in tune with changing black music, was Atlantic Records, founded in 1947 by Herb Abrahamson and Ahmet Ertegun – two music lovers who just wanted to record blues and gospel music that could not be found on any existing label. In contrast, the Chess brothers had little appreciation or understanding of the music on their records – they were in it for the money, and as soon as they realized the potential audience for Chicago bar blues, they rushed to record it.[8]

Several types of African American music, all of which were built on the foundation of the blues, emerged in the cities of the northern and western United States after World War II. The term *rhythm and blues* (R&B) was coined to describe it, a broad grouping that encompassed the smooth sounds of the West Coast jump blues, the boisterous performers of the blues shouters (who often fronted big bands), the vocal harmonies and gospel inflections of groups of singers, and the electrified guitar sound of musicians like Muddy Waters and Howlin' Wolf – the Chicago blues of city life. It had once been called *race music*, but after the war the businessmen who assembled the popular music charts referred to it as rhythm and blues (R&B) so that it would not offend white listeners. It was the fusion of these several styles of R&B with elements of country music that brought about rock'n'roll.

The independent record companies took the lead in recording the new wave of R&B performers and produced what we now hear as the first rock'n'roll records. Although it is difficult to reach a general consensus on the first record of the new style, Wynonie Harris' "Good Rockin' Tonight," released in 1947, is a good choice. A seasoned blues singer, Harris had begun recording in 1944 when he sang in front of Lucky Millinder and his orchestra for Decca Records. After pocketing his $37.50 recording fee, he moved on. His next records were for the small Apollo and Aladdin independent labels. "Good Rockin' Tonight" had first been recorded by Roy Brown for Deluxe Records of New Orleans, and Harris recorded it for King Records of Cincinnati soon after.[9] Harris had an exciting stage show and shouted the blues in the big-band style. His influence can be seen in many rock'n'roll performers, including Elvis Presley, who recorded "Good Rockin' Tonight" for Sun Records in 1954, his second record release.

Another veteran of the big-band era who made a lasting impact on the evolution of rock was Big Joe Turner, who had begun recording in the late 1930s on the Vocalion label. He embodied the style of blues shouters that went all the way back to Bessie Smith. By 1950 Turner had released over fifty records, for large and small companies, and had enjoyed some success on the rhythm and blues chart. In 1951 he signed with Atlantic Records and in 1954 recorded "Shake, Rattle and Roll" in a radio studio in New Orleans.[10] This was a sizeable hit.

Neither "Good Rockin' Tonight" nor "Shake, Rattle and Roll" made any impact on the *Billboard* pop charts – the barometer of popular music in the 1950s. The first rock'n'roll record to enter these charts was "Crazy Man Crazy" by Bill Haley (on the independent Essex label) in 1953. Haley had begun his musical career as a country and western performer, but deserted the music and his cowboy outfits to concentrate on rhythm and blues that teenagers could dance to. His cover version of "Shake, Rattle and Roll" was a huge success and sold over a million copies in 1954. The rock'n'roll movement was on its way.

By recording music that the big companies felt was not commercial enough for the mainstream of popular music, the independents took advantage of the changing tastes of the record-buying public. They scored hit after hit on the *Billboard* popular-music charts. Companies like Atlantic expanded on the proceeds of hit records and gradually built up informal distribution networks across the country. The old system of record stores allied to one of the Big Three was replaced by a much more diverse marketing arrangement in which discount houses, record clubs, and rack jobbers (entrepreneurs who maintained racks of popular records in supermarkets and drug stores) distributed records.

Many more independent companies were formed in the 1950s as the profits from rock'n'roll began to trickle down in the music industry. They were appearing all over the country and especially in the South, in such unlikely places as Mississippi, Alabama, Louisiana, and Tennessee. Rock'n'roll was moving the center of the recording industry away from New York City. A borrowed, battered "Concertone" tape recorder and an empty room might be enough to establish a studio. Muscle Shoals in North Alabama was the site of several studios which were to make their mark on rock'n'roll. Numerous small companies thrived in Memphis and New Orleans, and each one hoped that it might produce that million-seller record.[11]

These newcomers liked to think of themselves as rebellious young companies challenging the old order of the empires of sound. The fact that rock'n'roll was the music of youthful rebellion neatly fitted this analogy. Just as the power and emotion of rock was a reaction against the bland, polished music of the older generation, the recordings of the independents went counter to the conservative tastes of the majors.

From 1948 to 1955, the four major companies – Columbia, RCA Victor, Decca, and Capitol – placed over 75 percent of the hits on the *Billboard* top-sellers chart. In the first period of rock'n'roll, from 1954 to 1958, the so-called Big Four no longer dominated sales of records. In 1958 their releases accounted for only 36 percent of the *Billboard* charts, which were now full of the releases of independent companies like Atlantic and Chess.[12]

By 1960 there were around 3,000 record labels in the United States, of which only about 500 were operated by established companies. The rest were *one-shots*, the work of an entrepreneur who found a

Figure 11.1. An early recording studio in Muscle Shoals, Alabama, in 1951, with a wire recorder. (Grace Johnson)

likely singer or song, bought a few hours of studio time, and paid a factory to press a thousand records. It cost only $150 to rent an independent studio for 3 hours and $100 to have a master tape recorded and edited. A 7-inch disc could be pressed for 11¢ apiece, and after paying for a license fee from the American Federation of Musicians, the whole venture could be financed for less than $1,000.[13]

The one-shots joined the output of the majors and the independents in vying for space in record shops and radio time. With an average of 120 singles and 75 albums released each week during the 1960s, there was a mighty struggle to get a record noticed. Promotion was critical, and the key to promotion was radio exposure. The interdependence of phonograph and radio, which had been established in the 1930s, remained a vital thread in the history of recorded sound.

Many of the pioneer record producers of the rock'n'roll era had begun their careers in radio and obtained their technical know-how in broadcasting. In the 1940s recording studios were full of radio equipment, operated by engineers who had come from radio. Radio experience provided not only technical skills but an appreciation of the changing audience for popular music. Sam Phillips was not the first radio disc jockey to move into record production, and Bill Haley was not alone in leaving radio for live performance.

Although much less visible and glamorous than the technology, the business relationship of record producer and radio disc jockey (or deejay) was far more important in the rise of rock'n'roll than tape recorders or microgroove records. The radio, especially AM radio, was the critical technology in promoting the new music, and the re quirements of radio dictated the form of the rock'n'roll single – most noticeably in its short playing time, which gave more opportunities for commercials during the program.

Rock, radio, and television

The new popular music of the 1950s was a media phenomenon, and its growth was part of the interaction of the mass media. The emergence of rock'n'roll is best understood within the context of the changing entertainment business after the war when the empires of sound were faced with technological, economic, and legal challenges. After 1945 the independent company returned in the film and record business, and a new technology emerged to challenge the status quo. Radio and films faced a serious competitor in television, itself a prod uct of the laboratories of the big corporations. Once perfected it quickly replaced the existing mechanical entertainers in American homes. Radio was now considered to be the obsolete technology, and just like the phonograph in the 1920s, it had to find a way to coexist with the powerful newcomer. Radio had to adapt to survive.

As television now dominated the middle ground of family enter tainment, radio stations had to seek out new audiences – not the mass audience, which was quickly lost to them, but the segmented ethnic and youth audiences. The time was ripe for local stations to replace the narrow, middle-of-the road programming which had dominated the networks' air time during the 1930s. African Americans in south ern cities and northeastern urban ghettos, who had started the R&B boom by clamoring for blues songs with a dance beat, were an important new market for radio. In the 1940s many urban stations began to realign their programs to suit a predominately African Amer ican audience. Like the independent record companies, they were largely owned by whites but the records they aired were directed towards blacks. Stations such as WDIA (Memphis), WLAC (Nashville), and WRKD (Los Angeles) broadcast R&B, blues, gospel, and jazz. By 1954 there were 700 radio stations in America aimed at the black market.[14]

A major factor in the rise of the independent record companies was the decline of the radio networks – a key element in the empires of sound. The end of their monopoly allowed smaller business organizations to access the air waves. Independents now had a chance to promote their records on local radio.

As a consequence of these changes in the broadcasting industry, blues and country music were heard more often after the war. They could be heard as far away from their southern and western roots as California and New England. As in World War I, the global conflict in the 1940s helped spread musical styles on record. Many GIs got their first taste of regional music listening to V discs or Armed Services Radio. At home, good-looking young male crooners had become the stars of popular music, but, significantly, the Armed Services Radio polls found the country and western singer Roy Acuff to be more popular than Frank Sinatra. Zenas Sears, a New Englander who became the leading R&B disc jockey in Atlanta, first heard blues and gospel while working with black troops in Burma. He was one of the GIs who returned home with a taste for "black" music.[15]

Local radio stations, like local record companies, were much more sensitive to their audience's changing needs than the majors or the networks. In the early 1950s much of their youthful audience wanted to hear R&B. Even in cities such as Birmingham, Alabama, considered to be the most segregated community in the United States, white radio played black music, although it could not be promoted as such. The "Atomic Boogie Hour," hosted by Tom Umback, began to program R&B music in the 1940s. Umback was white but tried to sound black. His audience consisted of the large black population of Birmingham and a broad range of white listeners in the 15 to 25 age bracket.[16] Station managers avoided hiring African American disc jockeys and were concerned that their play lists not appear to be "Negro-oriented," but nevertheless they did play black music, ranging from the traditional country blues of the Mississippi Delta to the new electrified blues coming out of Chicago and Detroit.[17]

In the 1950s radio play constituted the main form of promoting a record. The Top 40 format dominated the nation's most important radio markets, and the company which placed its records on the play lists of key stations had a better chance of making them hits. The practice of *payola* (a contraction of *pay* and *Victrola*) was widely used to get airplay. The independents had an especially close relationship with the local disc jockeys and juke box operators – both had to be bribed to use their records.[18]

While the majors had to sell records in the hundreds of thousands to turn a profit, it only took a sale of a few thousand records to recoup the costs of production of the independents. With sufficient airplay the small company could have a local hit that would bankroll further operations. It might even hit the jackpot and enter the *Billboard* charts, the dream of every one-shot operator, and bring in $50,000 or $75,000.

Radio was both the promotional tool and the antenna of the record business. The term *rock'n'roll* was coined around 1951 by a disc jockey from Cleveland. Alert to telephone requests and the sales of records in local stores, Alan Freed responded quickly to the growing appeal of R&B and turned his show into a showcase for the music. Such was the success of his "Moondog's Rock and Roll Party" that in 1954 he moved to New York and a much larger audience. The program climbed to the top of the ratings chart as rock'n'roll became more and more popular. Freed was America's most influential disc jockey until the payola scandal disgraced him in 1959.

Unlike public performances and studio recording, the air waves were not racially segregated. Whites could tune into "black" stations with ease and then cross the color bar invisibly. After listening to R&B music on their radios, the next step was to buy the records, and those who found it impossible to buy them at their local retailer because they did not stock "Negro" records frequented stores which did stock the products of the independents. The companies themselves learned from their distributors that white teenagers were buying records aimed at the adult black audience. In the early 1950s the Southern distributors for Atlantic records began to report that "white high school and college kids were picking up on the rhythm and blues records, primarily to dance to."[19]

The collaboration of the local radio stations and the independents brought about the miracle that the majors had been hoping for since the last days of World War II: the discovery of a dynamic new market for recorded music. The fascination with rock'n'roll reinvigorated the sagging figures for record sales in the United States. In 1955 there was a 23 percent increase in constant dollar sales over 1954. In 1956 sales went up another 25 percent and continued to rise every year until 1960.[20]

These figures reflect sales of all sorts of music. Rock'n'roll records were only part of the popular-music catalogues of the record companies, and it should be kept in mind that American teenagers made Pat Boone as well as Elvis Presley recording stars in the 1950s. Like Presley, Boone had started his career making covers of R&B songs on the independent Dot label, only his renditions were much safer copies than Presley's.

From a purely commercial point of view, sales of singles constituted only about half of total sales of records at this time, and the rest was in the LPs which were totally dominated by the majors with their strengths in classical and Broadway music. Despite his string of fifteen Number 1 hits in the 1950s, Presley did not sell as many records as Frank Sinatra, who had moved to the LP format and who became the most popular recording artist of the rock'n'roll decade in terms of total dollar sales. The sound track albums of Broadway plays and films were the blockbuster hits of the 1950s – the original cast album of "My Fair Lady" sold 13 million records – and this served as evidence that future profits would be found in the LP.[21]

Perhaps it was for these reasons that a few of the majors moved to coopt rock'n'roll as soon as it appeared. Bill Haley was signed by Decca records in 1954 after the success of "Crazy, Man, Crazy." RCA Victor bought Elvis's contract from Sam Phillips in 1955; thereafter his records were marketed nationally, and his reputation grew out of its base in the South and West. Rock'n'roll records appealed primarily to the young, and it was their tastes which began to influence popular music as the demographic peak of the baby boom made young record buyers supremely important. Their dollars ensured that radio and the record industry would prosper in the age of television.

Some of the majors hoped that rock'n'roll was just a flash in the pan and thought that if they ignored it, it might go away. But as soon as it became clear that R&B records were yielding hit singles, the majors began to copy or "cover" them. Covering was an old practice in the recording industry; white musicians had been copying black music and adapting it for a mass audience since the 1890s. It was a cheap way to produce records. Most of the first rock'n'roll recordings were covers of earlier R&B hits, including Presley's "That's All Right" which was based on the 1947 blues recording made by Arthur "Big Boy" Crudup. The majors became so adroit at covering that they often beat the original recordings from independents onto the charts.

This process was nothing new in the industry of recorded sound: small companies had always taken the risk of recording new music, and the larger companies, who played a predatory role, swooped down to cash in on any new fad. Covering extended beyond "black" music: when country records enjoyed an increase in popularity in the mid-1950s, the majors released diluted versions of "hillbilly" standards aimed at a general audience.[22]

The covers often removed or changed the more blatant sexual references of the lyrics to make the songs more palatable. Bill Haley's "Shake, Rattle and Roll" is a good example. The original lyrics sung by Big Joe Turner included:

> You wear low dresses, the sun comes shining through,
> I can't believe my eyes, all of this belongs to you.

This was changed to:

> You wear those dresses, your hair done up so nice,
> You look so warm, but your heart is cold as ice.[23]

Where rock'n'roll referred to sexual activity in the original recordings (its origins are to be found in jazz lyrics of the 1920s), it soon acquired a more sedate meaning as dancing.

As they appropriated rhythm and blues to sell more records, the major record companies produced a less abrasive version of it, applying their sophisticated studio techniques to the songs. They also carefully groomed the performers because they appreciated the importance of the music's image. The story has often been told of Sam Phillips' search for a white singer who could put over black music. The search ended when Elvis Presley walked into his Sun recording studios. If Phillips had been concerned with selling records alone, the color of the performer's skin would not have mattered much, but he knew that public appearance was vital for record promotion.

The image of the music grew more important as television replaced radio as the mass medium. Presley's appearances on the Ed Sullivan Show on CBS were the key to his phenomenal rise to national prominence. This program was a televised variety show which encompassed acts that differed little from the vaudeville shows of the 1890s to the newest, and, most startling, music. At its peak the Sullivan show was watched in 50 million homes, and its Sunday night broadcast was incorporated into the family ritual of middle-class America. It did not matter that the television cameras showed Elvis only from the waist up – the energy and thinly veiled sexuality of his performance came over on the small screen and instantly created the first rock'n'roll star.

The power of television in promoting music had been demonstrated as early as 1954, when an unknown singer performed "Let Me Go Lover" in a TV drama. Although the record had made little impact when it was released the year before, it quickly climbed to the top position in the *Billboard* charts after the broadcast. Country music had also been promoted on the large and small screens: in the popular cowboy movies of the 1930s and 1940s, and then in the 1950s when television revived this genre. The Davy Crockett craze of the 1950s began with a motion picture and spread to a successful TV series. The "Ballad of Davy Crockett" was released in 1955 and went on to sell more than 7 million records on about twenty different labels.[24]

The first popular-music showcase on television was "Bandstand," which aired in 1952. It showed filmed performances which accompanied each record played. The renamed "American Bandstand" first appeared on national television in 1957 on the ABC network. It aired from 3:00 to 5:00 P.M. every day, just in time to be watched after school. The studio audience now had a bigger part on the show as teenagers danced to the songs. Frequently, the stars appeared in person to be interviewed, but in essence the program was a televised dance party. The recordings it showcased were given national exposure, which promoted the careers of several teen idols, including Fabian, Frankie Avalon, and Paul Anka, who were more notable for their good looks than their music.

The look had become a factor in creating the stars of rock'n'roll. The process was satirized by Stan Freberg in a song called "I Was on My Way to School," in which a producer grabs an unsuspecting teenager to sing in a recording session. The kid argues that he can't sing, but that doesn't matter; he is pushed in front of the microphone and told to sing the first thing that comes into his head: "I was on my way to school. . . ." Reality was not far from this. Fabian was only 15 and had no singing experience or musical training when he was asked to audition: "He was terrible. The Company signed him."[25]

The visual drama of rock'n'roll performances was an important part of its hold over the youth of America. Like jazz and swing, the music had a distinct look as well as sound, but rock'n'roll was much more visually exciting. During the 1930s and 1940s, the film industry had produced visual versions of popular songs. The 3-minute "soundie" shown in theaters before the main feature was an early film version of the music video. They were well-produced short films, but the static nature of big-band performers, who sat on chairs on the bandstand and did not move about much, produced uninteresting images.

This could not be said of rock'n'roll. Here was music with an overt sensuality and more than a touch of rebellion. It was based on the propulsive rhythm of African music, and it incited movement. The energy and raw excitement translated easily into powerful images, and that is precisely why the original R&B musicians were rarely allowed to perform their songs to a white audience – this would have placed an intolerable strain on the already tenuous color line in America.

The empires of sound had effectively excluded African Americans from the air waves and had depicted them in degrading terms in motion pictures. *Billboard* reported in 1943 that "Radio still has the rule that a Negro cannot be represented in any drama except in the role of a servant or as an ignorant or comical person." Most commercial sponsors were worried that black performers on their programs would present their products unfavorably to the white audience; "Negro talent" on a Pillsbury flour–sponsored program would brand it as "nigger flour."[26]

If rock'n'roll was to make the high ground of popular culture, which was dominated by the visual image of television and films, the look as well as the sound had to be "covered" by acceptable white artists. Instead of the original African American performers, or the first leather-clad white copies, film and television promoted a group of clean-cut young white singers as the new stars of rock'n'roll. Better dressed and less threatening than their predecessors, they were to bring rock'n'roll to the national television audience and ensure its dominance of popular music.

Rock and the film industry

The rise of television had a damaging effect on motion picture atten-dance, because families replaced the weekly trip to the film theater with the daily watching of television. The great film studios, which had constituted the core of the empires of sound, also faced a legal threat to their monopoly powers of film production and exhibition. In 1948 the U.S. Supreme Court decided an anti-trust case which forced the major studios to divest themselves of their theaters, effec-tively breaking up the monopoly power of the old film studios. But they were free to move into record production, and in the 1950s United Artists, Paramount, 20th Century Fox, and Columbia pictures formed their own record companies. (Columbia's Colpix company was no corporate relation of the Columbia record company, which was owned by the CBS radio network.) Despite the changing business environment, the links between the record companies and the film industry remained as strong as they had been in the 1930s and 1940s: Warner Bros. had their own record division, MGM formed its record company in 1946, and Decca Records acquired Universal Pictures in 1952 and was affiliated with the Music Corporation of America (a film talent agency).

The film industry, like the radio stations, was forced out of the middle-of-the-road audience by television and likewise began to ex-plore new markets. The youth audience was an important element in this strategy, and film producers were quick to cash in on the popu-larity of rock'n'roll.

In 1955 MGM released "Blackboard Jungle," a film about the problem of juvenile delinquents in inner-city schools. It provided some pretentious social comment and a model of delinquent behavior and dress that was eagerly assimilated by teenagers. It also had a catchy theme song, "Rock Around the Clock" by Bill Haley, which became the anthem of the new youth culture. Although it was recorded in 1954, it did not make an impact on the public until it was featured in the film a year later. Haley did not appear on screen, and his song was only partially played during the opening credits, but it was enough to propel "Rock Around the Clock" to the Number 1 position on the *Billboard* charts, a place it occupied for 24 weeks.

Haley followed this triumph with a movie entitled "Rock Around the Clock," which basically told the story of his band. Rock'n'roll had its own version of the American success story. An unknown artist or band was "discovered" (in this case by Alan Freed), a best-selling single was recorded, and numerous public appearances were made for a rapturous teenage audience. The ultimate act in this drama, and the sign that true fame had been achieved, was the nationally broadcast television show.

Haley appeared in another rock musical in 1956 called "Don't Knock the Rock." It was followed by a slew of similar films in 1957 as the big studios rushed to cash in on the craze: "The Girl Can't Help It," "Mr. Rock and Roll," "Disc Jockey Jamboree," "Rock All Night," "Untamed Youth," and "Rock, Rock, Rock." Scores of rock'n'roll movies were made in the decade after 1955.[27]

Elvis Presley made his first movie in 1956, just after he signed with RCA records. His second film, "Jailhouse Rock," was released in 1957 – a year in which five of his recordings reached the top of the charts, including the single of the same name. Although television had brought him national celebrity, it was film which made him a world-wide star. "Jailhouse Rock" told the story of a young man who left jail to find fame and fortune in popular music. It was the 1950s version of "The Jazz Singer" and the twentieth century retelling of the Horatio Alger "rags to riches" story. In some ways it mirrored Presley's own meteoric ascent from truck driver to rock star. Spurned by a big record company, Vince Everett (played by Presley) set up his own independent company. Many stock figures of the popular music business were depicted in the film: the juke box operator, the record promoter, the crooked record company executive, and the friendly radio deejay who "broke" the song on the air.

The songs for "Jailhouse Rock" were specially commissioned for the film and written by the professional song writers Jerry Leiber and Mike Stoller. As was the practice with making Hollywood musicals, they were recorded before the shooting began, and Presley mimed to the songs as he was filmed on the set. The pre-recorded music was later added to the sound track. As usual, the movie served to promote songs which were released on record when the film opened.

One scene in the film showed hundreds of copies of Vince Everett's record moving from presses to record stores and then into the hands of frenzied teenaged girls. This was a potent image in the new visual culture of rock. The million-selling 45-rpm single was the latest chapter in the American dream, but it did not mark the apex of the popular singer's career. In both "Rock Around the Clock" and "Jailhouse Rock," the hit record figured prominently in the rise of the rock'n'roll star, but it was only a stepping stone to television and the movies.

Both television and film exploited rock music without compromising the traditional control they exerted over the performance. Live music was substituted by singers miming or "lipping" to their records. Although some performers considered it artistically dishonest to pretend to sing the song, the audience did not care because they were accustomed to the recorded sound rather than the live performance. As the vehicle of rock'n'roll, the record was the original performance – the primary experience. As Carl Belz has argued, the performance in the rock'n'roll era was in fact a reproduction: an imitation of the record.[28]

Radio, television, and films made rock'n'roll big business, and the music that flooded the air waves was a pale, commercial dilution of the original R&B sound of the early 1950s. By 1959 the spontaneity and vitality of rock'n'roll had dissipated. What had once been acclaimed as a fresh and exciting sound that challenged the status quo was now a predictable element in the industry of recorded sound, which now encompassed television as well as film and radio. When it came to television and film exposure, there was no doubt that the image was more important than the music. Bill Haley had been one of the pioneers of the new sound, but as a balding, middle-aged man, he quickly disappeared from the picture. The growing importance of the visual media in rock'n'roll diluted its musical content and undermined its stance as the music of youthful rebellion.

The empires of sound had managed to coopt the movement. Rock'n'roll had become just "rock," and soon all kinds of popular music came under this heading. The historian of popular music Charlie Gillett concluded that the industry of recorded sound, "with typical sleight of hand, killed off the music but kept the name," for "a softer substitute" had replaced the original.[29] The revolution in popular music was over.

Rock in the 1960s

The music might have died in 1959, in the words of singer Don McLean, whose record "American Pie" described the decline and fall of rock'n'roll, but its audience was very much alive and growing bigger.

The vast potential of the "baby boom" market, the demographic surge after World War II, was still untapped. About 76 million men and women were born between 1946 and 1964. This was the generation that received "Kiddie Players" for birthdays and Christmas (6 million of these were sold in 1952) and played special children's records on them. They were also the first generation of American youth to be raised on television. Visual images played as important a part in their culture as the TV set did in their leisure time. By the 1960s they had entered the affluent society and become "a leisure class of professional teenagers," with the money to buy their own records.[30]

Ten years after Bill Haley and Elvis Presley brought new excitement to popular music, the Beatles revived a business that had again begun to flounder in formulaic and mediocre recordings. The Beatles were signed to the English Parlophone label, a subsidiary of the giant EMI concern. Their first recordings were offered to Capitol Records in the United States as part of an arrangement with EMI, who owned an interest in the company. Capitol declined to exercise its option, and subsequently the first American releases of the group were pressed by Vee Jay, a black-owned company formed in Gary, Indiana, in 1953 to record blues and gospel.

The pleasant popular songs "Love Me Do" and "Please Please Me" made little impact on the American market, but "I Want to Hold Your Hand" was an immediate hit, reaching the top of the *Billboard* charts in January 1964. "I Want to Hold Your Hand" was made with the American audience in mind; this was the "American sound" with which Brian Epstein, the manager of the Beatles, was going to infiltrate the largest market for records in the world.[31] EMI had to put a great deal of pressure on Capitol Records to release the single, and they were probably as surprised as anyone by its success. The independent companies who had been struggling to sell Beatles records quickly reissued them, and by March of 1964 the Beatles held the top five slots on the *Billboard* charts, a feat that has not yet been repeated.

The Beatles did for popular music in the 1960s what Elvis accomplished in the 1950s: they popularized a new sound to the mass audience and dramatically increased record sales. They did a lot to revive sales of popular music and the bottom line of the large corporations who produced it. Around 1960 sales of recordings in the United States had begun to decrease from the peaks reached during the first heady years of rock'n'roll. The British invasion was part of the reinvigoration of popular music in the 1960s, a second wave of rock'n'roll. The Beatles had sold about 76 million albums and nearly 40 million singles in the United States by 1977.

They also created a new star image in popular culture. Celebrities were an important part of rock'n'roll, and rock stars were considerably different from the previous stars of Hollywood in that they were not remote, inaccessible figures above the ordinary, but adolescents just like the kids who idolized them.[32] Although the Beatles looked and sounded a lot different from the rockers of the early 1950s, the formula for their star appeal was much the same – ordinary working-class youths, who with luck and talent had been touched by the magic wand of stardom. While Elvis Presley had been somewhat rebellious and threatening in his early days, the Beatles were well groomed and endearing. Their image was as carefully calculated as the "American sound" of their first recordings. As had Presley's, their appearance on the Ed Sullivan Show was a turning point in their careers, and they wasted no time in moving into films: "Help" and "A Hard Day's Night."

It was no surprise that the Beatles would engender a wave of imitators who copied both their sound and look. The Monkees were the first to be billed as America's answer to them. The group was formed to act in a television show loosely based on the format of the Beatles' successful movies. The four young men who portrayed the Monkees were not expected to play on the records; these were to be made by real (but anonymous) musicians in the recording studio. Each member of the group was chosen on the basis of looks and "personality," a comment on the growing irrelevance of musicianship. Like the rest of pop America, the Monkees mimed their songs on TV. Their records sold surprisingly well. They achieved a string of hits in 1966 and 1967, a testimony to the power of television in marketing a record. When the show was canceled in 1968, little more was heard of them.

Columbia Pictures was responsible for the Monkees' concept, and the records were released on the Colgems label, a subsidiary of the film studio. Unlike the first wave of rock'n'roll, the rock music of the 1960s enriched the big corporations. The British invasion was the work of the majors who reacted rapidly to the inrush of British bands by buying the rights to release recordings made in the United Kingdom and by grooming American groups who had the British sound.

The larger companies, with their international connections, were better positioned to acquire British groups for recording contracts and market their records internationally. But most important, only the integrated concerns could create the visual images which were vital to promoting popular music.

Television had made the image an important part of entertainment. The great radio networks – ABC, CBS and NBC – had become television networks and had branched out into other media operations, including recording. Television had been incorporated into their businesses and was now used in the promotion of their products. Film producers like Universal, Warner Bros., and MGM had added television to their varied portfolio of media interests. The empires of sound had changed with the times.

12. The record

Previous chapters have described how the recording became a new consumer product, a status symbol that conferred good taste on the listener, and a vehicle for the diffusion of American popular culture. It could also serve as a cultural artifact. Thomas Edison toyed with the idea of using the phonograph to record the voices of Victorian worthies, in order that their words of wisdom could be saved for posterity, but the program was forgotten when the commercial potential of recorded music was discovered. It was left to the academic community to use recorded sound to save a people's cultural heritage.

Anthropologists took Edison phonographs out west to record the songs and music of the American Indians. J. W. Fewkes of Harvard University made the first records in the 1890s. The phonograph played a vital part in preserving the musical folklore of America, creating ethnomusicology as a separate branch of anthropology. Ethnomusicologists travelled the continent, from the frozen north to the steamy jungles of central America, in search of the musical folklore of the indigenous population. They recorded Eskimos, Indians, and the descendants of the Maya. While the gramophone and the disc took over the commercial recording business, anthropologists preferred the spring-motor phonograph because it was sturdy and stood up to the demands of field work.[1]

Native American music was sporadically recorded by the record companies: Emile Berliner made some recordings of Indians in the 1890s, Victor made some more around 1905, the Gennett Company distributed records of Hopi Indians in 1925, and Edison committed the sounds of the Seminoles to wax record in 1926 so that future generations could study them.[2]

In the early years of the twentieth century, a heavy Edison machine was again tied onto a saddle and taken out to record the ethnic music of the far West, but this time it was cowboy songs that were to be saved on the phonograph's cylinder. John Lomax had obtained a fellowship from Harvard to collect Western folk songs. In 1908 he set out on the first of many trips. He recorded in cow camps, dugouts, and saloons, persuading reluctant cowboys to sing into the phonograph. He lamented that the first blues he ever heard disappeared quickly, "gone with the Texas wind," because the singer shunned the clumsy horn.[3]

Although popular legend usually depicts a frontier inhabited solely by whites, African Americans played an important part in opening up the West, and there were many black cowboys. In his hunt for frontier ballads and Western folk songs, Lomax was able to record their music, especially the blues. It was, in fact, a black saloon keeper in San Antonio who sang "Home on the Range" for him in 1908. Once the song had been recorded on the Edison cylinder, Lomax replayed it for a music teacher, who wrote out the music. "Home on the Range" was included in Lomax's book "Cowboy Songs and Frontier Ballads," which was published in 1910. It became a well-loved song enjoyed by millions, including President Franklin D. Roosevelt, who said it was his favorite.[4]

It became John Lomax's life work to find and preserve the folk music of America. With his son Alan, Lomax contributed 10,000 songs to the Archive of the American Folk Song, which they established at the Library of Congress in Washington. Lomax's long career as a ballad hunter took him to the Deep South, where he recorded spiritual music in churches and work songs in penitentiaries. He discovered important blues singers, like Big Bill Broonzy and Leadbelly (Huddie Ledbetter), and brought their music to a small but appreciative audience.

Unlike other people who had been able to commit their history to books, African Americans did not have a written record of their trials and tribulations in the New World. Their history and their culture had been preserved in their music – in gospel and in blues. The first of their music to be recorded was dixieland jazz bands and the classic blues of the female singers like Bessie Smith in the 1920s. But this was commercial music sung by professional entertainers, and it reflected the urban experience. The country blues of the South was largely ignored by the record companies, until the unexpected success of Mamie Smith's "Crazy Blues" alerted them to the potential of the African American market for records.

Encouraged by the huge profits of Mamie Smith's records, the

OKeh Company aimed their recording program at the northern urban ghettos and the cities of the New South. The catalogue was called "race records" instead of the more unsightly "Negro records," which had been common in the nineteenth century. Instead of minstrels in black face and vaudeville performers, this series was going to feature the real thing, because it was intended for the black audience. Many other companies followed suit and started their own race catalogues.

Record companies had already sent their recorders to distant cities to set up their machines in hotel rooms and rented halls to capture the best of European music. Now they sent their men to Chicago and Atlanta, to Memphis and New Orleans, and through the Mississippi delta. Paramount recorded several legendary blues men, such as Blind Lemon Jefferson and Charlie Patton. The replacement of the clumsy acoustic phonograph by the microphone made their job much easier. With electrical recording systems rented from Western Electric, the field recording teams took to the road and set up their equipment in office buildings, churches, and skating rinks. In large cities such as Memphis or New Orleans, they rented studios.[5]

The blues craze also encouraged the companies to record gospel and country music. In 1923 OKeh sent its field team to Tennessee, Kentucky, Virginia, and the Carolinas to sample the authentic folk music of America's rural South. OKeh's recording manager Ralph Peer made the first contacts with performers who were to become important figures in country music. Soon the larger companies followed; it was evident that there was a market for "hillbilly" records among the working classes. The first country song to become a best-selling record was "Blue Yodel," sung by Jimmie Rodgers, the "singing brakeman" who had been strongly influenced by the black music he heard while working on the railroad. Several more best-selling records for the conservative and cultured Victor Company in the late 1920s proved that music on the periphery of popular entertainment could produce commercial recordings.[6]

The numerous independent companies formed after World War I did their part in recording America's musical diversity. The OKeh Company was the pioneer in recording the cajun music of the French-speaking Acadians of Louisiana. Their 1925 recordings of this unique musical style were not put on the market. The first cajun recording released was of an accordionist called Joseph Falcon, whose "Alons a Lafayette" was distributed by Columbia in 1928. Falcon had been

Figure 12.1. Field recording of the blues in the 1940s, for the Library of Congress. (Library of Congress)

persuaded by George Burrow to go to New Orleans and cut some records to be sold in Burrow's store. Burrow's check in payment for 500 records was required to overcome the objections of the studio managers, who were reluctant to record this unusual music.[7]

The policy to record ethnic music devised by the large companies in the first part of the twentieth century was responsible for preserving a broad swath of American regional music. The same policy that produced recorded music for the Swedish and Finnish enclaves of the Midwest also provided the Spanish-speaking communities of the Southwest with their native music, and so on. For the most part these recordings served a narrow market niche and, with the possible exception of Hawaiian music (with its distinctive guitar sound), they did not affect the direction of popular music in America.

African American music was different. It was recorded more frequently than any other type of ethnic music. All in all, the blues was the most recorded folk music of America, and the total number of recordings greatly exceeds the totals of every other type of ethnic or regional music.[8] While the majority of ethnic music records remained in the collections of immigrants, or on shelves in the Library of Congress, the music of black America came alive on recordings and spread its influence far and wide.

The two uniquely American contributions to modern music, jazz and rock'n'roll, were the result of the diffusion of African American influences. Jazz and rock'n'roll were incubated in the grooves of recordings and launched by the sale of the records. Here were two musical forms that were not written down but drew their energy from the spontaneous expression of the musicians. The record was the only way to save it. Like jazz before it, rock music styles had evolved as musicians listened to recordings and copied what they heard. Learning from recordings therefore represented the musical education of the first wave of rock musicians, just as it had inspired the generation of jazzmen who followed in the wake of the Original Dixieland Jass Band (ODJB).

Legend has it that the first jazz band to be offered a recording contract by the Victor Company was the Original Creole Orchestra, a group led by the cornetist Freddie Keppard. Keppard turned down the offer, and the opportunity for jazz immortality, because he was frightened that if he made a record it would be easier for other musicians to "steal his stuff."[9] The ODJB had no such reservations, nor did Louis Armstrong, whose recordings became a textbook for future jazz musicians.

Louis Armstrong and Bessie Smith had learned their music the hard way: listening to live performances and honing their skills on the road. The generation of young musicians born at the turn of the century had an easier route. By the time this group reached puberty around World War I, the recording industry was reaching the peak of the acoustic era, and all sorts of records could be purchased, including blues and jazz. Many homes had pianos by the 1920s, but it was the introduction of the phonograph into American parlors that opened up vast musical horizons. Benny Goodman grew up in Chicago at the time that jazz was first played there. In 1921 his father bought a secondhand phonograph, and the Goodman boys became avid listeners. Benny Goodman was 16 when Armstrong made the famous Hot Five series of recordings in the late 1920s, and around 20 when Fletcher Henderson and Duke Ellington released dance-band records that defined swing music. These were the models for Goodman's musical development.[10]

The record producer John Hammond grew up in a comfortable upper-class home. His parents had a Victrola and a collection of Victor Red Seal records, but Hammond was drawn to the Columbia Grafanola of the servants' quarters, where he listened to jazz records. Reflecting on her experience, Billie Holiday concluded that "I guess I'm not the only one who heard their first good jazz in a whorehouse." As a child running errands for a brothel keeper, Billie Holiday was drawn to the fine Victrola in the front parlor. The records of Bessie Smith and Louis Armstrong had the most effect on her, especially Armstrong's recording of "West End Blues." She later said that these two recording artists were her main musical influences.[11]

Louis Armstrong's records were the beginning of several careers in music. His version of "West End Blues" had the same powerful effect on another youthful music lover as it did on Billie Holiday. The music critic and author Leonard Feather first heard the song in a record store in Kensington, London, in 1929, and this began his lifelong involvement in the world of jazz.[12]

As the first great soloist of jazz, Louis Armstrong showed the artistic potential of the music to a whole generation of aspiring musicians. The jazz player Howard McGhee remembered the impact of a Louis Armstrong recording: "one of his famous records – 'West End Blues' – I heard that, I says, Goddam, this is bad."[13] Louis Armstrong's recordings of the 1920s might have been the most influential in the history of popular music, because they reached so many people. As Evan Eisenberg has argued: "with Armstrong the phonograph began to do a job more remarkable than storage . . . live music and paper composed music would now mimic records." Armstrong was now "the voice of the phonograph, the voice of the invisible man."[14]

The younger generation who listened to the records of ODJB or Armstrong were privileged in that they gained access to a music that had once been the preserve of the fortunate few who lived in New Orleans or other big cities. Recordings made blues and jazz accessible to the whole nation. Growing up in Arkansas, a state with no blues tradition and few players, Big Bill Broonzy had little opportunity to hear the blues. He learned how to play by listening to records.[15]

Even for those kids in the big city who did not have the money to attend stage shows, there were cheap records. And if they could not scrape together the 35¢ to actually buy them, they could be enjoyed for free in the listening booths of record shops – until the patience of the proprietor ran out. In Seattle, Washington, far from the musical centers of jazz in Chicago and New Orleans, Bing Crosby listened to it in the demonstration rooms of the Bailey Music store.[16]

Edison and the other inventors thought that there were great opportunities for recorded sound in music education, and they sold special machines and records to schools. Some band leaders of the swing era, such as Woody Herman, heard their first jazz on records in high school, but many more picked it up by casual listening. As jazz trumpeter Dizzy Gillespie noted, "each musician is based on someone who went before." The recording made it easy to copy music, whether it was blues or jazz or gospel. Theo Phelps started a choral group in Mississippi in the 1930s, which later included Willie Dixon. Phelps remembered that "We'd hear a gramophone record and if it was good we'd pick that record up and sing it exactly like we heard it."[17]

For Lester Young, one of the most talented saxophone players of the big-band era, the difficulty was choosing which record: "I had a decision between Frankie Trumbauer and Jimmy Dorsey, you dig, and I wasn't sure which way I wanted to go. I'd buy me all those records, and I'd play one by Jimmy Dorsey and one by Trumbauer."[18]

The explosive arrival of Be Bop on the postwar jazz scene demonstrates how a new style could spread through recordings. The work of a small number of jazz musicians led by Charlie Parker and Dizzy Gillespie, Be Bop was a musical avant garde with a completely new vocabulary of sounds and significantly new harmonic ideas. In one sense, it was a reaction against the immaculately arranged music of swing. Because it was improvised, it could not be written down easily. Nor was it copied easily. One aficionado followed Parker around, preserving his solos on a wire recorder, but for those who were unable to go to the clubs in New York City where Parker and Gillespie played after-hours, there were a small number of 78-rpm records. These were produced by independent labels – Savoy, Dial, and Spotlite – who were taking a chance on a sound that was a cacophony to ears accustomed to swing. But to the true believers, Be Bop was the wave of the future. Red Callender remembered: "We used to play those records – we'd get into a room and live with them all night. It was unbelievable. Something from outer space . . . we actually wore those records out, wore the grooves out."[19]

Recordings played an important part in keeping the black musical tradition alive in hard times. The Great Depression and the consolidation of the recorded sound industry in the 1930s severely curtailed ethnic recordings. Only the large record companies were to survive. The output of their smaller subsidiaries devoted to race music dropped sharply but did not completely cease. Victor's Bluebird label, Columbia's OKeh subsidiary, and the Vocalion label of the American Record Corporation gradually returned to field recording in the late 1930s, when the worst of the Depression was over.

Although their output of records was much less than the great diversity produced in the 1920s, they did contain some historic and influential recordings. During the 1930s the real blues, the purest reflection of the African experience in America, was committed to record. The reputation of Robert Johnson, the King of the Delta Blues, rests on the slim foundation of just over forty recordings made between November 1936 and June 1937. Although millions have listened to his music, very few people actually saw him play. Only eleven of his songs were released during his lifetime, yet his influence on the modern Chicago blues and on rock'n'roll is unending and comes entirely from his records.

Johnson began playing in Mississippi during the 1930s. He came to the attention of the American Record Company through H. C. Speir, who ran a record store in Jackson. Johnson auditioned at Speir's store and was soon on his way to a recording studio in San Antonio, Texas. The list of sessions in this studio on the days he worked there gives an idea of the diversity of regional recording: W. Lee O'Daniel and His Hillbilly Boys, Hermanas Barraza con guitarras, The Chuck Wagon Gang, The Hi-Flyers, Zeke Williams and His Rambling Cowboys, and The Light Crust Doughboys.[20]

Much has been written about Johnson's influence on modern rock guitarists such as Eric Clapton and Keith Richards, but in the 1930s and 1940s, it was young blues men like Muddy Waters who were listening to his records and assimilating the sounds of the Delta blues. Born in 1915 in Mississippi, McKinley Morganfield learned how to play the blues guitar by copying what he heard on the records of the great blues players. He moved to Chicago and as Muddy Waters made recordings from which other young men would learn to play the blues. The survival of the blues as a musical style in the 1930s owed a lot to recordings, for blues was not played much on the radio and not seen on the silver screen. The blues musician and writer Willie Dixon noted that "the only way you would hear a blues is to go by the Barrelhouse because they were playing it there on records."[21]

Elvis Presley and his generation got their musical education from recordings, either from the records they bought themselves or from the records played on the radio. He reminisced that "I'd play along with the radio or phonograph, and taught myself the chord positions. . . . I dug the real low-down Mississippi singers, mostly Big Bill Broonzy and Big Boy Crudup, although they would scold me at home for listening to them." The stage performances of such R&B performers as Wynonie Harris completed the indoctrination of the young Presley. Harris' record producer, Henry Glover, claimed that "When you saw Elvis, you were seeing a mild version of Wynonie."[22]

Recordings brought the sounds of black music to rock'n'rollers like Elvis Presley and Buddy Holly. Scotty Moore (who played guitar behind Elvis Presley) had learned a lot from the playing of Muddy Waters and Howlin' Wolf on record. Records also brought country and western music to singers such as Chuck Berry, whose first Top Ten hit "Maybellene" (initially called "Ida Red") had an unmistakably country sound.

The British invasion

Learning from records was not restricted to American musicians. The recording was the means to convey American music to Europe and school musicians in sounds that they could not hear live. Imported records played a very important role in disseminating new styles.

While the Depression of the 1930s severely curtailed the production of blues and jazz records in the United States, the European market remained. A small but vocal European audience for hot jazz helped support American musicians by their insatiable appetite for new recordings. At the lowest point of the Depression, when few jazz records were being made in the United States, the independent producer John Hammond contracted with the British Columbia Company to produce records for them.[23] From the 1930s onwards, collecting American jazz records became a passion for a small group of Europeans, "a lonely, private passion" as the writer Ian Whitcomb recalls. But the possession of a treasured 78-rpm shellac was more than just entertainment: "by owning rare records they owned jazz themselves."[24]

Europeans took jazz a lot more seriously than Americans; they were the first to consider it an art form worthy of scholarly study. The first magazines and books on jazz were written in France.[25] The European music press kept a close eye on the American recording industry. Readers of the British magazine *The Gramophone* in the 1930s could read about the latest reissues of jazz records, find out about changes in the personnel of the big bands, and enjoy detailed reviews of recordings that were soon to be made available in the United Kingdom. They could also hear some of the finest American musicians in person, such as Duke Ellington, who visited London in 1934. Union disputes over employing American musicians in England limited tours to individuals instead of bands; subsequently the main vehicle for promoting jazz music was the record.

Swing was as popular in Europe as it was in the United States. The big-band sound was everywhere, either on American recordings or from European bands who imitated Glenn Miller or Benny Goodman. How did these musicians learn how to duplicate the complex sound of the big bands? One critic provided the answer: British bands, he claimed, were "reduced to slavish note for note facsimiles of American bands . . . filched from an American band's recordings." A letter to the editor of the *Melody Maker* asked "Must We Always Ape America?"[26] The short answer to this question was "yes." There were no indigenous musical styles to match swing or blues. Jazz was an American music, and its overbearing popularity in Europe determined that Europeans would listen either to American recordings or to live performances of bands copying the music they heard on records.

In the years immediately following World War II, American cultural exports reached a peak. Popular recordings and films swamped Europe, and it was hard for European companies to compete with the slick, professional imports. Mass production of entertainment in the United States gave American companies the benefits of economies of scale and allowed them to undercut their European competitors. Following the success of films and recordings, American television programs found a receptive audience in the 1950s. The term *cultural imperialism* was coined to describe this invasion of the European entertainment industry; as the German film director Wim Wenders pointed out: "The Americans colonized our subconscious."[27]

The vehicle for this colonization was the record. In the 1920s it had brought jazz to Europe, and 30 years later it brought rock'n'roll, when its effect on young people closely followed the precedent of jazz. Rock'n'roll appeared first on records:

> It was heard in the vacant lots of the new British coffee bars where, although filtered through a distinctly British atmosphere of boiled milk and beverages, it remained demonstrably alien and futuristic – as baroque as the juke box on which it was played.[28]

Rock'n'roll records encompassed a whole youth culture, which included dance, dress, and vocabulary. In the 1950s English youth could purchase American-style black jeans – the better to imitate the posing of rock stars like Elvis Presley and Gene Vincent and film stars like Marlon Brando, whose sneering stance was imitated on street corners all over the United Kingdom.

The ready availability of American records in the United Kingdom was the work of the empires of sound. Most of the majors began to release not just jazz but their popular recordings in Britain after the war, either through their English subsidiaries or through arrangements with the big European companies like EMI. Capital, Brunswick, RCA, and Coral records were soon available in record stores. The first Top 10 charts were published in England in 1955 and reflected a dominance of all types of American popular music, from Rosemary Clooney to Tennessee Ernie Ford. The first Bill Haley record entered the charts in January, and in December "Rock Around the Clock" on Decca's Brunswick label became the first single to sell more than a million copies in the United Kingdom. It opened the floodgates for the recordings of Elvis Presley, The Platters, and Gene Vincent.[29]

The showing of a few key films, "Blackboard Jungle," "Rock Around the Clock" and "The Wild One," completed rock'n'roll's conquest of the United Kingdom. These motion pictures validated the new youth culture, and the song "Rock Around the Clock" became a teenage national anthem. The effect of these films on English youth was much greater than their impact in the United States; scenes of mayhem and riots followed performances of "Rock Around the Clock." Normally sedate English teenagers, now depicted in the press as "rhythm crazed gangsters," could be seen marching along main streets of towns all over the country shouting "we want rock!"[30]

The accusations of "jungle music" which had been levelled against jazz in the 1920s were revived. The same dire consequences were predicted for "the jungle beat of rock'n'roll . . . stimulating savage, animal emotions in the minds of millions of our young people."[31] This claim did nothing to cool the ardor of youth, nor did it discourage them from buying the records and joining the rock'n'roll movement.

After the major American labels began to issue their popular records in Europe, the independents followed them by making licensing agreements with English companies. In 1954 the British music press discovered a new type of American music called rhythm and blues. One record by a performer named Wynonie Harris was selling well. English readers were informed that this music was "the choice of Negroes" in the United States and that it appeared on new labels such as Apollo, Savoy, and National.[32] Decca and EMI were the first to issue recordings from the independents, licensing master recordings from Atlantic, Dot, and Tamla Motown. Chuck Berry, the Miracles, Little Richard, and Fats Domino could soon be heard in English record shops.

These records had the most impact on the music of the Beatles, and many other British rock groups formed in the early 1960s. McCartney and Lennon were only two of hundreds of English musicians who learned their trade and developed their style from recordings. In the case of the Beatles, it was R&B records – "your B sides, all the 'shots of rhythm and blues,' and all the lesser stuff we helped bring to the fore." According to Bob Wooler, who was a deejay in the Cavern Club when the Beatles started their career, it was their ability to capture the excitement of black music which propelled them to the top of the Liverpool music scene.[33] In the early 1960s the Beatles repertoire was dominated by R&B material: Chuck Berry, Roy Orbison, and the Marvellettes.

American music in all its forms found an audience in Europe. Records produced during the folk revival of the 1950s inspired British folk singers and skiffle artists like Lonnie Donegan to emulate the sound of Leadbelly and Woody Guthrie, artists whose music had survived on record since the 1930s. Donegan's recording of "Rock Island Line" – a folk song attributed to Leadbelly – made both the British and American Top Ten charts in 1956. It started the skiffle craze in England, which was the incubator for many future rock groups. The attention of the press was on the riotous tours of Bill Haley and Gene Vincent, but the performances of bluesmen like Big Bill Broonzy in

England had an equally powerful effect on the budding musicians in the audience.

The presence of regional American music in the musical upbringing of many English performers cannot be underestimated. It is revealed in the lyrics of a song written by Van Morrison, who began his long musical career in a group called Them, covering blues standards such as "Baby Please Don't Go." Morrison sings of a window cleaner in Ireland who returns home on his lunch break and listens to records of Jimmie Rodgers:

> I heard Leadbelly and Blind Lemon
> On the street where I was born,
> Sonny Terry, Brownie McGee,
> Muddy Waters sing "I'm A Rolling Stone."

He could also have listened to the historic recordings of Robert Johnson or Muddy Waters or Big Bill Broonzy. Although not in general release, they were available to those who wanted to listen. Ian Whitcomb encountered the blues from records: "In that other country I knew all the words of 'Never Trust a Woman' by age ten, and a garbled version of 'Shotgun Boogie.'"[34] These kinds of records were responsible for a new wave of rock'n'roll that began in England and then swept across the Atlantic.

The so-called British invasion of the 1960s neatly reversed a trend that had been established right after World War I – now it was English popular music that was exported to the United States. The cultural overthrow of American popular music by the Beatles and the Rolling Stones was not without irony, for their inspiration was American recordings. Here were young men from the English provinces, or from the respectable suburbs around London, singing about Memphis and New Orleans and numerous other places that they had never seen. They sang of the African American experience – not from their own lives but from their immersion in recordings.

Like the Original Dixieland Jass Band before them, the Beatles owed a great debt to black music. John Lennon admitted to feeling a little uncomfortable when African American artists were on the same bill as the Beatles: "It seems to be their music, and I feel sort of embarrassed. . . . They can do these songs much better than us."[35] Unlike the ODJB, the Beatles had rarely heard the live performances of the music that inspired them.

Rock'n'roll brought the recording to preeminence. Unlike other popular music that evolved from live performances, rock'n'roll emerged from styles diffused and blended through the medium of recordings. In the early part of the century, the record had been a byproduct of music publishing, a lucrative little sideline. In the new order of rock'n'roll, sheet-music sales and public performances followed a successful recording. The hit record – the million-selling, 45-rpm single – was the driving force of popular music.

The inventors had envisaged the recording as a reflection of the sounds and music of their society. They could not have imagined its power to diffuse culture. Yet exports of records helped to define the culture of rock'n'roll. They were part of the "sacred artifacts" which represented the new youth movement:

> the quiffs [a hair style], the drapes [clothes], the Brylcreem and the "flicks" – it came to mean America, a fantasy continent of Westerns and gangsters, luxury, glamour and "automobiles".[36]

The record was supposed to follow in the wake of a great musical career, not create it. But all this happened in the 1960s. Paul McCartney of the Beatles put his finger on it when he said that the "record was the thing. That was what we bought, that was what we dealt in. That was the currency of music: records."[37]

13. The studio

The place where records are made is usually called a *studio*, but in Edison's day it was often called a *laboratory*. The Big Three companies used this term to give their customers the impression that sound recording was constantly being improved, which it was. The first recording studio was established in Thomas Edison's West Orange laboratory in 1888. It was on the top floor of the main laboratory building, a large open space under a vaulted ceiling. During the frantic campaign to perfect the phonograph in 1888, Edison's men hauled a piano up there and used it for experiments on recording. At first this work was carried out in the open space of the room, but soon the recording phonograph was enclosed behind a wooden partition, with only the horn showing through it at head height. The musicians crowded around the horn, while the experimenters and their machinery remained out of sight behind the acoustic barrier – an important physical distinction had been made between artist and technician. Absolute silence was maintained while the recording was made. The first steps towards the recording studio had been taken.

Another common term used to describe a studio was *recording room*; usually this is exactly what it was, a room in the factory or offices of a record company. The first gramophone recording studio was over a shoe shop on 12th Street in Philadelphia. When Fred Gaisberg went to England, he set up the studio for the Gramophone Company in the basement room of its offices in London. The recording room for the United States Phonograph Company in 1892 was a loft over a meat packing house.[1]

Even these humble spaces were a great improvement over the hotel rooms, penny arcades, and parlors that had acted as recording facilities for the first group of entrepreneurs engaged in producing commercial records. In the early 1890s, penny arcade operators and travelling phonograph exhibitors needed pre-recorded cylinders and discs, and they made records by the dozen wherever they could. One

Figure 13.1. An early Berliner recording studio with a gramophone on the right. (Library of Congress)

of Fred Gaisberg's first jobs in the record industry was to round up performers, load up machines, and provide piano accompaniment to the sixty or seventy recordings made in one day – all for $10 a week![2]

It was not until the first years of the twentieth century that the Big Three began to establish custom-built studios in New York City, the musical center of the nation. These facilities supplemented the recording laboratories established within the great factories of the Big Three. Artistic concerns were now being taken into consideration and more attention given to the comfort of the performer and the convenience of recording. Most of the studios were large rectangular rooms. The Victor studio at Camden, for example, was a room 16 × 22 feet with a ceiling of 11 feet, 6 inches.

The recording machine now stood isolated in its own room or behind a frosted glass partition. Special materials or drapes were placed on the walls to limit the reverberation of sound. Edison's studios were built with little or no reverberation – they were made *dead* or *dry*, as

Figure 13.2. An acoustic studio with a horn connected to an enclosed recording machine. (Courtesy of EMI Music Archives)

it was called. Because Edison liked to hear each instrument distinctly, the recording horn was placed close to the musicians, which gave the "forward" sound that he preferred.[3]

Edison's recording expert Walter Miller said that in the early days of sound recording, neither artists nor experimenters really knew what they were doing – they advanced by trial and error.[4] There were no meters to guide them and no way to tell if the music entering the horn of the phonograph would re-emerge on the playback as a recognizable reproduction. Acoustic recording was difficult to control and impossible to predict: a performance that sounded wonderful live might not sound as good on record, in fact it might not sound like it at all. Playing back a recording meant rerunning the reproducing stylus in the soft wax groove, which eradicated the original. Usually the recorders made a test recording, sacrificed it in playback, and then shaved off a layer of wax to make a new surface on the recording blank. They adjusted the machine to suit the voice of the performer before the song was repeated.

The main considerations in adjusting the machine were the composition of the diaphragm in the soundbox and the size and shape of the recording horn. Several types of diaphragm were on hand in the studio: very thin ones, which were more sensitive to soft sounds and low notes, and sturdier ones, which could stand up to high volume. Choosing too thin a diaphragm could result in a blasting of the sound, but a thicker one might fail to vibrate sufficiently to capture the high notes. The decision about which one to use was made on the basis of experience and an intuitive feel for the way a voice or instrument would sound as it was reproduced from the soft wax of the cylinder. The recorder maintained his own recording cutters and kept his trade secrets.

Making a recording required an unusual mix of scientific precision and craft skills, because recording in the acoustic era was as much art as science. The recorder had to understand the workings of the machine and the materials at hand: the quality of the voice, the thickness of the mica diaphragm, and the temperature of the soft wax of the cylinder. None of these factors remained constant. Numerous types of diaphragms and wax were used, and each produced a different sound. Making the right judgments in setting up the equipment and placing musicians around it took years of experience. These were craft skills which could only be learned on the job.

The recorder had to position the singer and the accompanying instruments around the horn to achieve the best balance of sounds. The challenge was to place the musicians so that each of them could be heard distinctly and the loud instruments did not drown out the soft ones. Stringed instruments were normally placed close to the horns, with brass instruments placed farther away. The distance from the horn was varied according to the pitch of the instruments. Wooden boxes were used to elevate the upright piano into the mouth of the horns; in some studios a complicated system of bleacher seats arranged musicians in tiers before the horns.

The recorder also had to be able to gauge how a sound would reproduce and coach the musician accordingly. This was often a sensitive matter, because it was easy to become discouraged by the sound playing back from the phonograph. The great bass Pol Plancon was not the only artist who shouted "That is not me" when he heard his recorded voice.[5] A vital part of studio work was instructing the artist how to sing or play in a manner that could be best reproduced by the machine. Tremolo was thought to disturb the path of the needle in the groove and was usually avoided. Dramatic increases in sound or pitch jarred the recording needle, forcing it out of the groove. One recording guide advised the performer to "avoid singing with too much expression."[6]

The practice often employed for a female soprano was to station a studio assistant behind her to move her away from the horn as she hit the high notes. This task required perfect timing and some diplomacy. One singer remembered:

> We had to sing carefully into the very center of a horn to the accompaniment of an orchestra that invariably sounded out of tune. . . . As one approached the climax, or high note . . . one was gently drawn back from the horn, so that instead of a ringing high note one sounded as though one had suddenly retired into the next room.[7]

The recording rooms were far from ideal places to sing; in fact, from the performer's point of view, it was the worst possible acoustic environment. It is no wonder that so many of them "dried up" before the impersonal recording horn, deprived of the sounds coming back from the auditorium and the comforting presence of an audience.[8]

A good recorder not only had to balance artistic and technical judgments but also needed to be both musical director and psychologist. Gaisberg was a master at relaxing nervous performers, who had justified misgivings about entrusting their voices to the machine. The recorder had to contend with "gramophone fright" while keeping in mind that he was being paid to produce a set number of recordings within a short time period.[9] Even the great divas were expected to produce six to ten masters in a 2-hour session. There was little time to repeat takes. The recorder who did not return to company headquarters with the required number of masters found himself in trouble.

The basic unit of recording was the "take" of a performance, which lasted only as long as the playing time of cylinder or disc. The recorder had to keep one eye on the clock and pace the song accordingly. A stop watch or clock became an indispensable part of studio equipment, and countless perfect recordings had to be rejected because they exceeded the 2- or 3-minute mark.

While modern studio practice is to record and playback until a satisfactory recording is made, the acoustic recording room had a

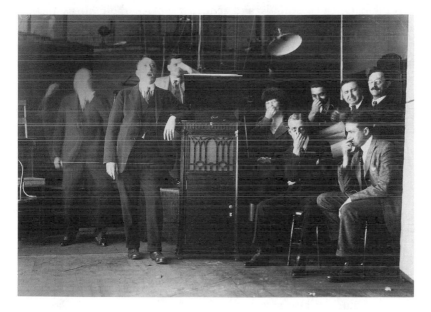

Figure 13.3. An Edison recording committee having some fun, listening to a typical record player of the 1920s. (ENHS)

different objective. In the days before the duplication of masters by molding, the studio was the place to mass-produce recordings rather than make one faultless master. Recording was an arduous process that required patience and most of all stamina. It was not unusual to make forty or fifty cylinders of one song in a day. It was not comfortable work. The wax record was sensitive to temperature, and most studios were heated to keep the wax soft. Performers were soon in their shirtsleeves as they shouted into the horn.[10] Some studios had banks of horns connected to several recording machines to facilitate the mass production of master records.

Each record company had its own philosophy of recording based on the available technology and shaped by the commercial objectives of the business. Edison considered himself a musical purist and wanted to hear the sound of each instrument clearly – a consequence perhaps of his deteriorating hearing. Edison records favored single voices accompanied by pianos or violins but were not as effective with large groups. Victor recordings usually did a better job of capturing the sound of larger numbers of musicians. Their recorders strove for a good balance of sounds and tended to place their horns farther away from the performers, even though this could make the sound more indistinct. Their studio had more reverberation, which brought more naturalness and a brighter sound. In their assessments of the competition's records, Edison's staff often commented that Victor and Columbia recordings had more "pep," which probably referred to their better reproduction of middle and lower sound frequencies, which Edison sometimes sacrificed to emphasize the high frequencies.[11] Some record producers went for volume at all costs and were willing to abandon clear articulation for a loud sound.

Electrical recording

The Western Electric process of electrical recording was eagerly adopted because it finally gave some measure of control over volume and tone. The microphone also permitted the recording of large orchestras and brought to life instruments that had been quiet or completely absent during the acoustic era – the drum, the violin, and the bass. The piano also sounded a lot better; its thin tone on acoustic records was replaced by a more realistic sound.[12] The increased frequency range of electrical recordings permitted more of the sound of each instrument and voice to be inscribed on the wax disc, bringing forth a fuller, richer, and, above all, louder sound.

Gone were the days when the recording engineer had to cram as many musicians as possible around the recording horn and restrict the sounds that might force the cutting needle from the groove. The cumbersome horn was replaced by the microphone, which freed sound recording from the cramped little rooms full of perspiring musicians elbowing their way to the horn.

In the era of electrical recording, the most important element was the microphone. Its sensitivity in turning sound into electrical currents determined to a large extent what sort of sounds were picked up and how they were recorded. In the old days of acoustic recording, the loudest and most strident sounds had been recorded and only these hard "tinny" sounds could be reproduced on phonographs and gramophones. Recorders who had learned their trade in acoustic studios were often accused of having "tin ears" – a direct reference to the metal horn.[13]

The first microphones were based on the carbon button transmit-

Figure 13.4. The electrical recording studio in 1925. A large, spacious room with only one microphone! (Courtesy of AT&T Archives)

ters developed by Berliner and Edison for telephones. They came in many forms: the Western Electric disc-shaped microphone, which was suspended in a metal circle, the "soup plate" model of much larger dimension, and the cylindrical "tomato can." These lacked the sensitivity to reproduce all the elements of music and speech.

During the 1920s and 1930s Western Electric's laboratories produced new types of microphones which improved pick-up capabilities and brought more flexibility in recording. Their electrical recording system employed a condenser microphone, which was much more responsive than the carbon version. All microphones had a diaphragm like the ones used in telephones and acoustic phonographs, but in this case the diaphragm was part of a variable condenser or capacitor. It was attached to a back plate with a small air gap in between. High-voltage current was applied between the plates; as the diaphragm moved in response to sound waves striking it, the capacitance between it and the back plate changed and produced a voltage proportional to the sound. The small capacitance changes of the microphone re-quired an amplifier to strengthen the current. A production model, the Western Electric 394 condenser microphone (also marketed as the RCA type 11A), became the basic tool of sound recording in film, radio, and record studios in the 1920s.[14] It was a dramatic improve-ment over the old carbon microphones, which had the same trouble capturing the sibilant "S" sounds as the acoustic horns and also tended to "freeze up" during a sudden increase in amplitude or pitch.

The Western Electric system was certainly more sensitive to sound than the old acoustic horn, but it was equally sensitive to heat, hu-midity, and vibrations. In high humidity the condenser microphones shorted out or went "noisy" with unwanted sounds. In field trips to the South in the heat of summer, they often failed. Recorders had to remember that they were now using fragile electrical equipment in-stead of the robust horn.

The advent of electrical recording, although bringing dramatic changes to the studio, did not make the skills of the acoustic era obsolete. The recording horn was gone, but now there was the prob-lem of placing the microphone. The recorder still had to exercise his skills in assembling musicians around the microphone and creating the right balance of sound in the studio. A wrong balance would make some instruments sound louder on the playback while others were not heard.

The availability of meters to measure the peaks and lows of a re-cording was a help in estimating the balance, but it did not completely replace the old system of trial and error. Each session began with a test cut and a playback just like in acoustic recording. After the play-back the engineers might reposition the instruments, and the perform-ers might rehearse a passage. The great advantage of the new system was that the recording could be heard over loudspeakers as it was made, which gave a clear idea of the balance of sounds and the amount of reverberation picked up by the microphones.[15]

The Western Electric system still cut the sound signal into a re-volving wax record, and the operator had to carefully monitor the cutter. Sudden increases in volume or pitch could still force the cutting head to jump into an adjacent groove despite the provision of sound meters on the new equipment. The recorder had to be aware of the heat and humidity that affected both the composition of the wax and the acoustic properties of the studio. Recording in the electrical era still required a mix of technical proficiency and artistic awareness. The miracle of electrical recording could not, and did not, replace the years of experience that were necessary to make sound judgments in the studio.

Several other elements of the acoustic era were transferred to studios using electrical equipment: the acoustic isolation of the machine from the performer, the use of a red light or buzzer to indicate that recording was going on, and a special room for artists to calm their nerves before entering the studio.[16]

The main change brought about by electrical recording was an increased awareness of the acoustic properties of the studio. The sensitivity of the microphone picked up much more of the room's reverberations and other ambient noise. The early trials of the Western Electric equipment in Columbia's New York studios forced engineers to resort to heavy drapes and even a tent hung over the performer to dampen the reverberation.[17]

The introduction of electronic amplification in the 1920s did not lead to the abandonment of the knowledge accumulated in acoustic studios. Far from it, information about the construction of studios and their acoustic properties was diffused from the old acoustic rooms to new studios using the microphone. The "dead" studio – with little or no reverberation – had been developed by recording engineers from the phonograph industry. Their example, and in some cases their assistance, helped the pioneers of electrical recording install wall coverings (such as horsehair or cowhair) and ceiling hangings to limit reverberation and absorb the higher sound frequencies.

The explosive growth of radio broadcasting in the mid-1920s created many makeshift studios on roofs, in hotels, and in spare rooms in department stores and office buildings. These were quite primitive compared with the large studios constructed by record companies, but they still picked up unwanted sound bouncing off walls and ceilings; this reverberation muddied the reproduction of speech and made it difficult to discern individual sounds. Broadcasters looked to the previous generation of studio designers in their attempts to limit reverberation. The refitting of the WJZ radio studio in New York City was based on the advice of Walter Miller of the Edison laboratory.[18]

Electrical recording changed the manner in which recordings were made and the place where this work was done. It also affected the relationship of those who worked there. The studio had always been

Figure 13.5. An early radio broadcast studio. (Courtesy of EMI Music Archives)

the preserve of the technician, and introducing more complicated machinery made his position even more important. Those responsible for the artistic content of the recording were much less influential in the new hierarchy of the studio.

When the first Western Electric recorders were brought to film studios, their operators (soon called *soundmen*) took charge of filming. The soundman was the one who started the take, and he was the one who approved it, not the director or the actors. Douglas Fairbanks, Jr., remembered that "He was a magician. . . . He was like Merlin, or the Wizard of Oz and a bit of a faker in some ways because he was experimenting himself at that time."[19] He also had the power to stop the action if he was not satisfied with the sound quality, and he often did. In radio work, the engineer stayed in the control room while the musical director moved back into the studio to have closer contact with the musicians. NBC put the engineer in charge of the production and made him responsible for the broadcast.[20]

In the studios of the record companies, the "recorder" was now the "recording engineer." No longer a mechanic or experimenter but a specially trained employee of Western Electric, he was schooled in the workings of the equipment and procedures that had to be followed. He consulted dials and meters and made fine adjustments by turning knobs or pulling switches on the recording consoles. Some of them wore white coats and maintained a professional demeanor.[21]

The division between the work of recording and musical arrangement had been nebulous or even nonexistent in the acoustic era. Fred Gaisberg acted as recorder, musical director, and business manager of his sessions. In the electrical era these functions were divided up and formal distinctions made between technical and artistic tasks. On one hand was the engineer, who operated the equipment, and on the other was the musical director, who hired the performers and arranged the music. The former concentrated on his meters and kept the dynamic range of the recording within the capabilities of the equipment. The latter decided on tempos and arrangement. Although it was important to have a good rapport between the two, it often broke down because artistic and technical considerations did not necessarily coincide.

The schedule of the studio was determined by the recording manager. The Western Electric equipment represented a considerable investment, and time was money in the studio. Adherence to a strict schedule of recording in the electrical era made the studio clock even more important. The workday of the studio was divided into 3-hour sessions which extended from early in the morning to late at night. Each session was expected to produce four takes good enough for mastering.

Many musicians in recording studios were paid by the session and were treated as artisans who were responsible for only one part of a complex product, which indeed they were. They were expected to follow orders and get the job done as quickly as possible. This attitude is dramatized in August Wilson's play "Ma Rainey's Black Bottom," which takes place in a recording studio in Chicago in the late 1920s. The recording manager made it clear what his priorities were: "I'm not putting up with any Royal Highness ... Queen of the Blues Bullshit! ... I just want to get her in here ... record those songs on that list ... and get her out. Just like clockwork."[22]

For many jazz and blues players, the record session was a quick way to make some extra money: musicians still depended on the income from live performances. Many studio groups, like Louis Armstrong's Hot Fives and Sevens, were quickly organized from available musicians who rarely performed together outside the studio. There was little time to practice or arrange the songs. They might make two or three different versions of the same song, one with vocal, another with trumpet solo, and so on. The musicians spent the afternoon or morning hours recording, picked up their $25 or $50 fee, and went on their way.

The recording manager usually selected the songs to be recorded and decided which artist would record them. He had final approval of the take and decided what takes should be mastered. Once a master had been chosen, a matrix or master number was inscribed on the soft wax of the disc or cylinder. This number served to identify the recording through the process of duplication and manufacture. The Big Three companies usually used a recording committee of executives to decide which masters to release, because commercial as well as technical factors had to be considered.

Only the greatest stars in the classical rosters of Victor and Columbia had a say in interpreting the music and deciding which take should be released. The work was done at their convenience, and it was sometimes carried out in their homes rather than at the company's recording studio. This practice was ended as the empires of sound took control of recording and placed it within the context of corporate strategy. In the studios of the electrical era, the musician was only an employee who followed the instructions of the man in the control booth.

The recording studio was, after all, part of a system of mass production, and as such its output had to be coordinated with the other factors of production. The electrical method of sound reproduction was quickly adopted in record production, radio broadcasting, and talking pictures. It set in motion technological and economic forces which produced common methods of recording sound. Just as there was a unity of technique in operating the Western Electric equipment, there was also a unity of purpose in the business strategies devised to exploit it. The term *studio system* is usually used to describe the dominance of four or five large companies in the film industry during the 1930s and 1940s. The goal of the system was mass production of films and complete control over all aspects of production. In the larger context of the film, radio, and record businesses, the studio system was the means to increase production and bring this work under corporate control.

Sound recording technology and technique

Al Jolson's cry of "You ain't heard nothin' yet, folks" in "The Jazz Singer" perfectly summed up the technical developments in the decade following the introduction of electrical recording. During this time several important development paths were established by engineers improving sound recording: the use of multiple microphones and mixing of their output, the editing of recordings including re-recording of different sound tracks, and the stereophonic reproduction of sound.

Improvements in equipment or in technique that were developed in one type of studio were easily transferred to another. The radio broadcaster learned from the recorders of the Big Three who worked in acoustic studios. The development of electrical recording called on experience gained in radio broadcasting. Western Electric engineers carried out an analysis of studio design based on the operation of AT&T's radio station before they built their own experimental facilities.[23]

By the late 1920s broadcast engineers of the radio networks had accumulated an important stock of knowledge about operating microphones and amplifiers. They had some of the newest equipment and the best facilities. They had moved from rooms big enough only for a piano and an announcer to large complexes of several studios, some large enough to accommodate the radio orchestras assembled by the networks. Some broadcast facilities contained several recording studios which could be used separately or together. The NBC studios built in 1927 in New York represented the state of the art at that time. They contained eight separate studios (four of them two stories high), and each one had its own control room.[24]

Radio studios began to employ a control booth from which the conductor directed the musicians in the studio and the technician mixed together the signals from several microphones and supervised the disc cutter.[25] Another important precedent was established in radio drama, in which each character spoke into a separate microphone. The use of multiple microphones was to become one of the most important techniques of sound recording. It moved from radio to film and then to recording studios.

The dissemination of technical information was aided by close association between parts of integrated business organizations and the formation of professional associations. The Academy of Motion Picture Arts and Sciences was set up as a clearinghouse for information about the new technology of talking pictures. Although it is best known for awarding the "Oscars," it also held classes to train the employees of the major companies and formed a committee to establish technical standards. Several engineering societies, such as the Society for Motion Picture Engineers, acted as clearinghouses of information and producers of technical standards. Above all, the movement of skilled personnel facilitated the diffusion of technology. The soundman on the film set used microphone techniques developed in broadcasting and had often learned his trade in radio.

Of all the studios using electrical recording, the sound stages of the film producers presented the most complex sonic environments and posed the toughest challenges for the sound recorder. Throughout the 1930s film sound was at the leading edge of the technology, and many of the innovations pioneered in film making were diffused to record studios.

Sound brought many changes to film production. In the silent era the main concern was light. Film studios tended to be makeshift affairs of wood and glass, and a great deal of filming was done outdoors to make the most of the California sunshine. Film making at this time was anything but silent, as the director Frank Capra remembered: "people yelled all the time. The director had his megaphone . . . the cameraman might yell at his grip at the top of his voice, or someone might be building on the set next door, hammering and sawing."[26] The Western Electric equipment could not discriminate among the sounds it picked up: the whirring of the camera, a squeaking director's chair, or the thuds of the film crew walking about.

Film studios were quickly crammed with heavy drapes and blankets to eliminate unwanted sound. The introduction of the sensitive microphone forced film makers to enclose their sets and build a controlled environment in which to shoot films. The new electrical recording system could be used inside only, for the sensitive condenser microphones picked up extraneous noises and were seriously affected by wind. Film making was now confined to a sound stage, an enclosed building which was designed to facilitate the requirements of sound recording. A typical stage might be 60 feet high and 200 or 300 feet square. Thick walls kept out unwanted sounds, and dense wall coverings provided the sound absorption necessary to cut down on reverberation. They had to be totally soundproofed to eliminate outside noises. The heat generated by the lights required that the sound stage be air-conditioned, and in the hot California summers, gallons of water were extracted from the studio every hour.[27] It was an enclosed, electrically powered world in which the soundman was king.

Film making now required absolute silence. Capra remembered: "now you had to work in the stillness of the tomb. If you belched or coughed you'd wreck a scene. You had to watch what you ate and drank." Light was a secondary consideration to sound, and film lighting had to be changed to accommodate the requirements of recording. The hum of arc lights created a background noise on the disc playback, which led film makers to use incandescent lamps instead.

The need to soundproof the set had an immediate and deleterious effect on film making. To cut down on extraneous sound, film cameras were encased in a soundproof booth in which the cameraman worked in oppressive heat. The camera was now imprisoned. It was restricted to long takes, and there were few cuts from take to take. The actors were forced to crowd around the microphone, which was artfully concealed in a vase of flowers or a table lamp on the set. The first talking pictures were full of ponderous dialogue and static shots of one or two actors. Directors succumbed to the temptation of using sound effects to heighten the drama, deafening the audience with breaking glass and gun shots. The results were far from entertaining.

The marvel of talking pictures did not necessarily mean a better picture or a more entertaining spectacle. It could, in fact, be argued that sound did nothing to improve the artistic content of films because film making was now a captive of the bulky, immobile machines which recorded the sound. The dialogue coming from the screen was far from satisfactory. One critic complained of the "scraping, screeching, rasping" sound that blurred the speech of even the most articulate stage performer brought to the film studio. The recordings made by the Western Electric process were better suited for music than speech. It was often difficult for the audience to discern a male from a female voice, and if there was more than one person talking on the screen, it was not easy to tell where the sound was coming from.[28] Keeping the two parts of a dialogue separate and audible proved to be difficult with a single condenser microphone connected to a recording turntable.

Film makers soon liberated their equipment from the shackles of sound and learned to incorporate sound recording into their art. The sound booth for the cameras was replaced by the *blimp* – a smaller container which could be moved around. As soon as this arrangement was put onto wheels and run along rails, the camera regained some of its mobility. Some manufacturers began to redesign their film cameras to make less noise. The Mitchell Company produced its BNC (noiseless camera) line that was to become standard equipment in film making for 50 years.[29] The most important innovation on film sets was the simple mechanical expedient of attaching a microphone to a boom and swinging it above the heads of the actors. The microphone caught the sound but did not get in the way of film cameras. Many of the new employees struggling with these booms had come from radio, where performers had stayed in one place. Now they were moving targets.[30]

The need to move the microphone around put a premium on mobility and light weight. The condenser microphone had the drawback of large bulk (because of the attached amplifier), and it was superseded in film studios by the dynamic microphone. This had a diaphragm within a magnetic field; as sound waves moved it, it generated current by its motion within the field. There were two basic types of dynamic microphones: the moving coil and the ribbon. In the moving-coil design, a diaphragm attached to a coil moved in relation to sound waves and produced a voltage which was proportionate to the velocity of movement in the coil. The 1931 Western Electric type 618 moving-coil microphone did not need an amplifier connected; it could transmit through a cable to the mixing console without sound loss. It was the perfect choice for a boom microphone.[31]

In the ribbon type of dynamic microphone, a conducting ribbon was suspended in a magnetic field, and differences in sound pressure on each side of the ribbon caused it to move and vary the electrical current produced by the ribbon. It was sensitive to the direction of the sound as well as its amplitude and pitch. The ribbon design was developed by Harry Olson in the RCA labs and became the first bi-directional microphone used in studios in the 1930s.[32] Since the sides of the microphone were dead to sound, two actors situated at the front and back of the microphone could record a dialogue with little distracting reverberation. This was especially useful in radio studios. The RCA 77 series of ribbon microphones introduced in 1933 brought a discernible improvement in capturing the sounds of speech.

Unlike their colleagues in recording studios who had only to capture the sound of musicians playing together, where the blend or balance of sound was the main consideration, the soundman had to pick up noises and dialogue spoken on different parts of the set. The introduction of more sensitive directional microphones gave soundmen more flexibility in recording sounds. They could pick up discrete sounds from each actor and give the sound track a spatial quality, helping the audience to distinguish the origins of the sounds they heard. At the end of the 1920s, two or more microphones were commonplace on sound stages, and the soundman now sat at a mixing console and adjusted the volume of the input of several microphones. He tried to keep the two parts of a conversation separate, and if one actor spoke from across the room, the volume of his voice was changed proportionately.

Mixing was the way that the sounds were balanced before being recorded onto the disc. The RCA mixing console brought together the different sound inputs and allowed technicians to adjust the amplitude of each track in the overall mix. This became an important tool in creating film sound.

In film making there were three types of sound to be recorded: dialogue, music, and special effects (the noises of telephones, doors, and automobiles). Each was made differently and perceived differently by the audience.[33] For example, in Warner Bros.' "Public Enemy," made in 1930 with the Western Electric Vitaphone system, the film opens with the Vitaphone orchestra playing the introductory theme. Then the camera moves about the city while the audience hears the sounds of street cars, footsteps, and noises from a bar room. These sounds rise and fall as the camera sweeps by. Then the talking of two characters is gradually increased in volume to catch the audience's attention. Later in the film the sounds of police whistles, gun shots, and screeching tires of the getaway car add drama to the narrative.

In the first talking pictures, all music and dialogue was recorded live on the set. Several cameras were kept rolling, and the film was cut to suit the dialogue captured by the Western Electric recording machine. In addition to the microphones on the sound stage, there were also microphones for the musicians, who played behind the cameras. Music would be played simultaneously with the action and recorded directly onto the single disc. Yet it was not always possible to have an orchestra standing to the side of a stage; consequently some scenes were shot without sound, and a pre-recorded sound track was added later. These "wild" shots were not projected with synchronized sound but with background music. This practice was commonplace in the first years of talking pictures, when only part of the movie would have synchronized sound.

If the actor on the set was not able to sing or deliver his or her lines as required, another performer would speak off-camera into a microphone that recorded the song directly onto the disc. The actor on the set mimed the song. This practice was used from the very beginning of talking pictures.[34]

The problem with the disc format was the difficulty of editing the sound track. Once the engineer had started the camera and disc recorder in simultaneous operation, it was not possible to stop and re-record a section, because both camera and recorder were kept rolling for the 10-minute duration of the reel and the disc. Once a recording had been made, it was impossible to go back and make changes, because this would upset the synchronization. Any break or splice in the film would also ruin synchronization.

The move to sound on film brought back some flexibility to the sound stage, because the film could be edited. Pieces of film (with its accompanying sound track) could be cut and rejoined without upsetting the synchronization. An editing machine for sound film, the sound or Hollywood moviola, was introduced in 1931. The editor passed lengths of film through the machine and watched the image through a magnifying lens while listening to the sound. The moviola simplified editing and helped to reduce the long static takes that had characterized the first talkies.[35]

Despite the flexibility of sound on film, the editor still had to keep with the sound recorded on the edge of the film: both sound and image had to go together. It was soon realized that filming and recording did not have to be done at the same time, because parts of the sound track could be added later in a process called *dubbing* (from doubling or copying), which involved making a recording of a recording.[36] Yet the limitations of the Western Electric equipment made this difficult and usually unsatisfactory. Dubbing could be accomplished by joining two disc players together, but disc-to-disc dubbing had the problem of increased noise on the final recording. This meant that synchronized dialogue and the background music were rarely heard together in the films of the early 1930s unless they were recorded simultaneously on the set.

The incremental improvement of all parts of the technical system of making sound pictures, from more sensitive and directional microphones to better quality film stock, gradually brought sound quality to a point where engineers could re-record without great sound deterioration.

The development of noise-suppression techniques was the critical part of this process. The surface noise of disc or sound on film combined with extraneous sounds produced a high level of distracting noise on the sound track, which increased alarmingly during re-recording. This noise was usually concentrated at the high end of the frequency range. Engineers at Bell Labs began to attenuate the strength of signals at chosen frequencies, basically adjusting volume of different sounds by increasing or decreasing the amplitude of chosen bands of frequencies. This practice, now known as *equalization*, enabled the frequencies where troublesome noise was found to be increased during recording and decreased in playback. This technique was so effective that it tempted film makers to use periods of silence in their movies.[37]

Another important technique in film sound was *compression* in which the amplitude of the sound was reduced at the time of recording. Soundmen were faced with the problem of recording a volume range of 60 to 80 db on the sound stage with a medium that could accommodate a range of only 40 to 50 db. In addition, the dynamic range of studio recorders was usually much greater than the reproducing equipment in the theater. Engineers devised compression techniques which limited the peak areas of volume and could be used to subtly diminish sounds across the whole range.[38] Equalization and compression were to become important techniques in the reduction of unwanted noise in all types of sound recording.

Soundmen developed the technique of dubbing to join different recordings into one sound track. They started by adding music and sound effects to sections of film, but the process was developed to restructure the sound track completely. Their emphasis moved from recording the sound on the set to editing it in re-recording studios after the film had been shot. When a sound problem arose on the set, the answer was "we'll fix it in the re-recording" instead of stopping everything and trying it again.[39]

The technique of adding a different sound to an existing shot developed very rapidly in film studios. Silent films had a large foreign audience that film producers were loath to give up when they began making talking pictures. If a producer wanted to exhibit the film in a foreign market, he had to make two versions of each shot, one in English and one in the foreign language. This expensive procedure was made obsolete when soundmen mastered the techniques of re-recording, which allowed a film to be dubbed into another language after it had been shot. A new set of actors would follow the action on the screen in a re-recording studio and read from the script in whatever language was desired. This new sound track was then mixed with other tracks containing music and sound effects.

The movie sound track is an assembly of many different sounds, from dialogue recorded on the set to pre-recorded "canned" sound effects added later. At the end of the recording process, the soundman might have to mix together as many as sixteen different tracks into the final composite sound track. The film musicals of the 1930s posed the most difficult problems of mixing and editing sound. In addition to the music, dialogue, and sound effects of closing doors, ringing telephones, and so on, there was also the sound of a full orchestra and many steel-shod shoes tapping in unison to be recorded. The musical was the quintessential Hollywood product of the 1930s, and its success and longevity owe a great deal to the skill of the sound recorders and editors.

As it was inconvenient to keep an orchestra on the set, film producers had their own studios to record the songs for their musicals. The musicians played from a complete score that was often specially composed and arranged for the film. Several microphones were placed at strategic locations in the studio, some at the front of the orchestra to record the soloist and strings, others farther back to catch the wind instruments and percussion. Even after the introduction of directional microphones, soloists were acoustically insulated from the rest of the orchestra with screens.[40]

Re-recording engineers mated the sounds of the orchestra with the dialogue recorded on the set and added in sound effects from their libraries of sound. This rough sound track was run through the mixing consoles of the re-recording studio. This was the time to correct any errors in synchronization and enhance parts of the sound track for dramatic impact. They could record new vocals or instrumental music after filming, with the musicians playing to a projected film. The dubbers became so proficient that they could make up a perfect recording of a song out of sections of many different takes of a less than perfect performer.[41]

Re-recording techniques put control of the making of films into the hands of the technicians, who were much more malleable and inexpensive than actors and actresses. The soundman worked on the film set to record dialogue; the production mixer worked in his own studio fitting different sounds to images; and the dubbing mixer, or re-recording engineer, worked at his console to add and subtract from the final sound track. The sound track was constructed after the film had been shot, and it was the film editors and sound engineers who shaped the final print. The film that went to the theaters was as much their product as it was the actors', who were often justified in asking the soundman, "What have you done to my picture?"[42]

Taken as a whole, the development of recording techniques in film studios was motivated by the desire to control completely the sound heard by theater audiences. Technicians gradually removed all unwanted sounds. Their microphones were more selective in what they picked up, and extraneous sounds could be reduced with their noise reduction systems. Most of all, the rapid advance of editing permitted them to eliminate sounds at will.[43]

Filming on sound stages brought a controlled environment for photography and sound recording, a hermetically sealed building in which every nuance of light or sound could be manipulated. Paramount Picture's "Holiday Inn" provides us with a rare glimpse of a Hollywood sound stage, and subtly reminds us of the difference between perceived reality and the illusion of the film set.

In the first part of the movie, we see the Holiday Inn, a rural retreat for harassed singer Bing Crosby, and listen to him sing "I'm Dreaming of a White Christmas." What the audience experiences is an illusion; a recording of Crosby's voice has been dubbed onto the film. What we see is him miming. When he hits the Christmas tree bell with his pipe, we do not hear that noise but a recording of the pure sound of a bell ringing. The scene was filmed on a set and the sounds added in later, but the audience accepts it as reality. In the second half of the film, Crosby visits Hollywood, where a movie is being made about the inn. We see the sound stage, with fake snow pouring down over the set, and the cameras, film crew, and boom microphone, which follows the heroine as the carriage moves her to the front door. The interior of the inn is the same, but now we see the film cameras and technicians. Inside the set, she starts to sing "I'm Dreaming of a White Christmas," and Crosby breaks in, at once destroying one illusion while acting out another.

The development of sound narration

After the initial novelty of talking pictures had worn off, audiences grew more sophisticated in their perception of sound. Those who paid for admission to the picture show expected more of recorded sound than those who listened to it at home on their phonograph or radio. Film producers were ready to invest in more realistic and complex sound tracks, and their technicians became masters of mixing and editing recordings.

In the early 1930s the main consideration for a film sound track was something that the audience could hear and understand; once this had been accomplished, the emphasis shifted to manipulating it for dramatic effect.[44] Sound can convey strong emotions. It can be used not only to tell the story but also to guide audience reaction to what is seen on the screen. This was appreciated by the silent film makers, who used the accompaniment of a single piano or full orchestra to set the scene and send appropriate signals to the audience: violins for romance, trumpets for drama, and so on.

Although sound films depend on dialogue to tell the story, hence the term *talkies*, nonsynchronous sound can play an important part in film narration. Sound can indicate the time frame of the movie, using music associated with specific time periods to suggest the dimension of passing time. A few seconds of hot jazz can effectively put the viewer in the time frame of the 1920s, for example.

Sound can be the invisible narrator, as in Fritz Lang's "M," where the child killer is heard but not seen. His off-screen whistling alerts the audience to his presence. As the story unfurls, the sound of the whistle becomes more ominous and alarming. "M" was made in 1930, when film makers were just coming to grips with adding sound to their films. The difficulties of producing synchronous sound with the Western Electric system, and their background in using sound in silent films, led these directors to use nonsynchronous sound to great effect; the results have been called *silent sound films*.[45] "All Quiet on the Western Front" (1930) used the sounds of warfare very effectively, although it should be remembered that these were not the actual noises of the front but rather recorded sound effects.

Sound can direct audience attention to one part of the action and, just like the focus of a camera, bring one part of the image into center view. For example, in "All Quiet on the Western Front," the camera shows us a group of soldiers marching through a town with the noise of the footsteps and the crowd watching them. As the camera moves back from this scene and shows us a school room in the foreground, the sound of marching soldiers slowly subsides as the noise of school-children rises to capture our attention. In this way the relative volume and pitch of sounds are altered to underline the movement of the camera.

Ears, unlike eyes, have no lenses to focus on or eliminate stimuli. They receive all sound simultaneously and indiscriminately. Yet we usually listen to one sound while phasing out others. Our ears act as frequency analyzers, picking out the bands of sound which we decide to listen to. The soundmen in the re-recording rooms began to usurp this function by making the audience concentrate on specific sounds.

During the 1930s the engineers at Bell Labs began to explore the spatial qualities of sound and investigate the way in which audiences heard it. It was discovered that the overall flat frequency response – a desirable property in the recording studio – made for an unnatural sound quality in the movie theater. Soundmen began to alter amplitude of selected frequencies, and in many cases low frequencies were strengthened to give a more natural sound.[46]

Our ears are very sensitive to the direction of sound, detecting time differences as small as microseconds. The time elapsed between reception in each ear tells us where the sound is coming from. Using sound as a means of establishing spatial differences was developed in radio, where only the aural sense of the audience could be manipulated. Radio technicians used changes in volume and reverberation to give distancing effects of sound. As a character walks away from our field of vision on the screen, we receive visual information which indicates where he is going. On the radio we have only aural clues – diminishing volume and echoes as the character moves farther away from the listener.

These techniques could be applied easily to film making. As early as 1929, J. P. Maxfield of Western Electric outlined the means to give a spatial effect to film sound. He recognized that the voice coming from the loudspeakers behind the screen should appear to follow the speaker around the set. The loudness and reverberation of the voice should change to give the monaural track a dimension of distance. The key, according to Maxfield, was to continually alter the ratio of intensity of direct sound to reverberated sound.[47]

This was first accomplished in films such as "Citizen Kane" (1941), in which radio techniques were brought to full fruition on the large screen. Orson Welles, who wrote and directed "Citizen Kane," had begun his career in radio with the Mercury Players, and his films were full of techniques used in radio: changing volume to give a spatial effect (such as the echoes in Kane's cavernous house) and overlapping dialogue to give a sense of realism, because in the real world we rarely hear just one voice speaking. Uninterrupted synchronous sound was used to bridge visual transitions in time: a cut from one shot to another brings us a new image but the unbroken sound track beneath it provides continuity from shot to shot. The narrator who speaks to the audience throughout this film was also taken directly from radio practice. The political speech that Kane makes in Madison Square Garden was put together from about a dozen recordings, and his voice was given an echo by adjusting the amount of reverberation on the dubbing console. Kane's final word, "Rosebud," was given its resonance by combining two tracks of Welles' voice, each with a different reverberation.[48]

The artistic and technical triumph of "Citizen Kane" showed how far film sound had travelled during the 1930s and the debt it owed to radio technique. Yet for all its subtlety and dramatic effects, film sound still came from one source. All the experiments in sound recording up to this time had concentrated on one channel of sound. Although film makers and radio broadcasters used numerous microphones and had become experts at mixing and editing sound tracks, all their efforts were reproduced on one channel. The important role played by radio personnel in film sound was also a factor in its limited perspective, because in radio broadcasts all the sound comes from the same place – the microphone. Complex film sound made up of many different tracks was still reproduced in theaters from only one sound source.

In real life, sounds reach our ears from many sources, giving a spatial quality to what we hear and enabling us to sense the location of its source. To achieve the illusion of perfectly natural sound, at least two separate channels of sound have to be reproduced. Ideally the sound from speakers behind the screen should follow the action as actors move across our field of view. It was the requirements of film sound that led scientists and recording engineers to grapple with the problems of recording two tracks of sound separately. In England, Alan Blumlein had started on such experiments after he saw one of the first talking pictures and left the cinema somewhat disappointed at the results. The search for binaural sound reproduction, now called *stereo*, had begun.

Bell Labs made experimental binaural recordings in the 1930s. In 1933 work was begun on a sound system intended for motion pictures that used three channels of sound. Three discrete recording systems of microphone-amplifier-loudspeakers were used to pick up and reproduce three channels, each with its own track on the film. The playback gave a sense of the spatial quality of sound experienced by the audience in a large concert hall. Each of the three sound tracks had its own amplifier unit and bank of loudspeakers. The system could reproduce a sound level equivalent to an orchestra of 2,000 musicians. When demonstrated at Carnegie Hall in 1940, it produced such stupefying levels of volume that the *New York Times* reported that the audience was at once spellbound and "a little terrified."[49]

Walt Disney was the only film maker who applied these new ideas to a full-length motion picture for commercial release. The sound track for his "Fantasia" was recorded on eight separate channels, which were mixed into three channels with a fourth control channel to enhance the playback.[50] "Fantasound" was duplicated in theaters with banks of speakers which were placed behind the screen and in the auditorium to surround the audience with sound. It represented the high watermark of recording technology of the 1930s.

Film sound had always been conceived as an accompaniment to images, but Walt Disney went all the way back to Edison's original plan for motion pictures and used images to illustrate sound. He engaged the well-known conductor Leopold Stokowski to provide the music for the film. "Fantasia" provided unforgettable animation to accompany the recorded music of Bach, Tchaikovsky, Beethoven, and Schubert. It premiered in 1940 to enthusiastic reviews, but it did not recoup the $2 million spent on its development. It required an elaborate, expensive system to reproduce it in theaters; for this reason it did not play in its original form in many places.[51]

"Fantasia" and "Citizen Kane" were masterpieces of motion picture technique. The Golden Age of Hollywood represented more than the creation of a perfect illusion; it marked a high point of recorded-sound technology in the service of this illusion. The Oscar given for best achievement in sound recording rewarded artistic as well as technical accomplishment. When we look at such classic films as "Gone with the Wind" and "The Wizard of Oz," we are not hearing the sounds as they occur in the real world but sounds made under the controlled conditions of the sound stage and re-recording room. The dialogue has the same brilliance and clarity as the technicolors, and the same artificiality. In a typical Hollywood production, we see a love scene on a cliff above a roaring ocean and hear only voices; even if the sounds of the wind and waves can be heard, the volume is tactfully lowered as the lovers speak.

The pursuit of the perfect illusion in films was to lay the groundwork for dramatic improvements in sound recording in record studios. The technical and artistic development of sound on film during the 1930s established the direction that the technology of recording sound was going to take for the next 50 years.

14. Perfecting studio recording

Diffusion of recording techniques from sound stages to the studios of the record companies was slow. The first time that several microphones were used to record a large group of musicians was in 1926 in the Metropolitan Opera House in New York to make synchronized recordings for Vitaphone films. Engineers from the Victor Company thought that one microphone placed in the auditorium was best, but the Vitaphone recorders wanted to use six: one each for strings, brass, woodwinds, basses, and percussion, and one for the overall sound. They made a recording of each setup and compared the two. There was no doubt that the multi-microphone technique produced clearer and more lifelike sound.[1]

This test did not lead to general use of multiple microphones in the recording industry; common practice in the 1930s was to place one microphone above the musicians. The transition to multi-miking came slowly. At first engineers employed two microphones for large groups and orchestras, one at the front and one at the back. Later they added other microphones to pick up the bass section or the soloists. This procedure was established in the large recording studios by the end of the 1930s, but recorders in smaller studios still used one or two microphones.

Studio recorders did not attempt to create several tracks of a recording and mix them together; and actually the single microphone recording can bring out all the sounds of a large orchestra. Benny Goodman's historic Carnegie Hall concert of 1938, for example, was recorded by one microphone over the band, which conveyed its sound to the CBS studios for transcription. The emphasis in the record business was on the realistic reproduction of a live performance, and once the recording had been made, there was little thought of altering it in any way to make it sound better.

Although the technique of re-recording was not unknown to the engineers in record studios, it was very rarely employed by them in

285

the 1930s. One notable exception was the remastering of some of Caruso's recordings done years after his death. Victor wanted to release some earlier recordings of the great tenor but was discouraged by the distant, tinny sound of the accompaniment. Engineers used equalization to isolate Caruso's voice and then re-recorded it with a new orchestral accompaniment added to the vocal.[2]

Equalization was a very useful technique because it could bring out the sounds which were drowned by louder instruments. Even musical purists such as the great conductors Leopold Stokowski and Arturo Toscanini were persuaded of the advantages of equalization by the sudden illumination of instruments which could not be heard clearly during the concert.[3] All musicians had become accustomed to the process of recording over and over again until a perfect take had been captured on wax, but this had not yet given way to a re-creation of the performance through dubbing numerous takes onto one faultless master – a practice that some considered to be cheating.

The fundamental difference between record studios and sound stages of film producers was the ultimate goal of the sound recording. The goal of making records was a truthful reproduction of music or dialogue exactly as it was heard; recorders wanted to capture the immediacy and excitement of the live performance. Film makers are in the business of illusion, and soundmen are given the task of creating one of a film's most important parts. The sound track of talking pictures was never an accurate representation of the sounds generated on movie sets; it was an artificially created composite designed to give the illusion of the sound accompanying the action on the screen.

Although studio engineers did not quickly adopt the techniques developed by soundmen, they did make considerable improvements to their work area. The studio went from a narrow, bare room with a phonograph at one end to a complex of electrical equipment and specialized acoustic spaces. Performers and technicians, who had once been separated by a thin wooden partition, now did their jobs in completely different work places separated by glass windows and linked only by electrical cables.

Studios of the major record companies were no longer single rooms but complexes of studios and control rooms. EMI's Abbey Road facility in London was the largest custom-built recording studio in the world when it was completed in 1931. It contained three performing areas: Studio 1 was a large auditorium intended for classical music

Figure 14.1. Studio 1 at Abbey Road in the 1930s. Several micro-phones are in use. (Courtesy of EMI Music Archives)

which could seat 250 musicians; Studio 2 was of medium size for dance and jazz bands; and Studio 3 was a small room built for small groups and accompanied vocalists. Over 4 miles of electric cable connected these studios to a central control room.[4]

By the end of the 1940s, the use of multiple microphones was commonplace in the large studios. Some were suspended from the ceilings, and others stood on stands in front of the musicians. Portable sound baffles were used to ensure that the microphones did not pick up the sounds of other musicians, a process known as *leakage*. On the walls were different kinds of materials to reflect or absorb sound. Abbey Road studios were built at a time when the heritage of the acoustic studios was still strong; subsequently it was made as acoustically dead as possible with little reverberation. After World War II, the wall coverings were torn down and a new, livelier studio acoustic created.[5] Each of the studios operated by the big companies in New York, London, and Milan had its own acoustic properties and a distinct sound that a recording engineer or musician could recognize.

Electrical cables ran from the microphones in the studio to a control room. A small glass window allowed the technician to see into the studio, and a telephone sat on the table next to him. The interior of the control room was packed with electrical equipment. The mixing console, with its impressive display of meters, switches, and circular control knobs, was the dominant feature. A rack of amplifiers running from floor to ceiling occupied one wall. A pair of speakers mounted in the control room allowed engineers to monitor the recordings. Other speakers connected to the same circuit were installed in the performing area so that the musicians could listen to the playback.

The technician sat at his console and altered the volume of sound coming in from each microphone. The mixing console was primarily a network of wiring, complete with switches and meters, built around a set of potentiometers (called *pots* or *faders*), which varied the loudness of the sound before it was recorded onto the master disc. Each channel of sound had its own VU (volume unit) meter, which provided continuous measurement of the microphone's output. The technician controlled the input of each microphone from his console, moving the fader control to alter the level of sound coming from the microphone.

Mixing was the critical element in determining how the music was recorded and how it sounded on the playback. The engineer had to balance the different sounds picked up by the microphones. There were no hard and fast rules as to what constituted a good balance; it was a unique combination of creativity and technical know-how. The great maestro Stokowski was one of the first conductors to record his orchestra with the Western Electric system. When he was told of the function of the mixer he replied: "You're paying the wrong man. He's the conductor and I'm not."[6]

The sound passed through the mixer to the recording lathe, where the sound waves were cut into a master disc. The lathe was a large, stable turntable with a very precise disc cutter carefully positioned over the revolving disc. Moving-coil cutters, based on the designs of Blumlein in England and Keller in the United States, were quickly introduced into recording studios and became the standard method of making disc records. The professional recording lathe usually came with a special vacuum-suction device to clean the swarf that came out the groove. Recorders used a microscope to view the wave forms of sound in the grooves of the disc.

During the 1930s a new form of master record was developed,

which used a layer of cellulose nitrate lacquer on a glass or aluminum disc. This was first done by the English inventor Cecil Watts in 1934. In addition to being a better recording medium – it had much less surface noise than wax – the *acetate* (as it was called) could be replayed immediately without any sound degradation. By the 1940s cellulose nitrate masters were commonplace in studios.[7] This basic idea was transferred to home recording machines using acetate "instantaneous" records.

Tape recorders were first installed in control rooms around 1947. They were operated alongside the disc lathes, because the output of the recorder still had to be cut onto the master disc. Tape recorders did not make better sounding recordings, but they did make longer recordings, and it was easy to edit them – all that was required to make an edit was a razor blade or nonmagnetic scissors and some adhesive tape. Ease of editing made it possible to make up a composite sound track of numerous recordings in the same way that the soundmen had edited pieces of sound on film.

Dubbing had been tried experimentally in the 1930s using two disc recorders joined together, but these efforts were hampered by the old problem of deteriorating sound quality. The introduction of Ampex tape recorders led to similar trials with tape dubbing. The leading figure in these experiments was neither an engineer nor a scientist, but a country and western guitarist named Les Paul. In the true Edison tradition, Paul was both a businessman and an inventor. His pioneering work in creating the solid-body electrified guitar is now enshrined in the Gibson "Les Paul" line of guitars. Paul was an early advocate of tape recording and had influenced his friend Bing Crosby in his decision to adopt the technology.

Crosby gave Paul an Ampex machine, and the guitarist began to experiment with it. Inspired by the dubbing techniques he had witnessed on Hollywood sound stages, Paul modified his tape machine to make recordings of recordings. He could then dub (or *overdub*, as it is called in the record industry) one track onto another. He accompanied his wife Mary Ford on the guitar while she sang the vocal. He then added several more tracks of his guitar playing to give more body to the recording. This can be heard on records such as "How High the Moon" (1951), which contained an unprecedented twelve overdubs.[8]

This innovation did not become common practice in recording studios in the 1950s. It was time consuming, and it took skill and patience to reduce the surface noise on re-recordings. The most that engineers accomplished was to divide the song into vocal and musical accompaniment and record each track separately. Recording sessions were still driven by the economic imperative to make masters quickly and efficiently; the goal of a good take in as short a time as possible had survived from the acoustic era. The system of corporate control of recording had remained unaltered by any change in technology.

The "artist and repertoire" (or A&R) man took over many of the functions of the recording manager and came to dominate not only recording but also the careers of the artists. He had the power to match songs with singers and decide which masters would be released. He hired the arranger or did the arrangements himself. He supervised the recording session and was responsible for its product. As one A&R man described the system: "The company would pick 12 songs for Peggy Lee and tell her to be at the studio Wednesday at 8, and she'd show up and sing what you told her." The artist was excluded from post-production work, which determined what songs would be released and how they sounded.[9]

The recording career of Frank Sinatra underlines the conflict that often existed between artist and A&R man. During World War II Sinatra's love songs had been immensely popular, but after the war his records did not sell as well. Sinatra attributed this decline to the A&R man at Columbia, Mitch Miller, who insisted that he record unsuitable material and novelty songs. Most performers were bound by contract to a record company, and Sinatra was obliged to record in the company's studios exclusively. When he moved to Capitol records in 1953, he was able to work in different studios with new arrangers and went on to make extraordinarily successful recordings again.[10] The product of the studio was determined not just by the technology but by the social organization of its use.

It was this social order that was challenged by the independent record companies, who were not encumbered by A&R men and had more flexibility in record production. The independents did not have a corporate hierarchy; the owner, record producer, promotion manager, and recording technician were often the same man. This made it easier to recognize and promote new talent, such as the stars of rock'n'roll.

The independents often used a group of in-house musicians who acted as session men, not only to play behind the recording artists but also to support them in the often intimidating work of producing hit records. Chess had the services of Willie Dixon – a singer, song writer, and bass player who played a major role in blending blues styles into more accessible R&B recordings. Dixon contributed some of the most famous songs of the Chicago R&B era and helped the singers interpret them in the studio. In addition to playing the bass guitar in the sessions, he also arranged the music and assisted in production. As resident Svengali of the Chess studios, he shaped the sound of the Chicago urban blues.[11]

The independents were usually much closer to their performers, both artistically and physically. The original recording studio of the Atlantic company was a room about 20 × 15 feet over Patsy's Restaurant on West 56th Street in New York City. The control room was no more than 3 feet wide and also served as the company's office. It contained a small four-channel mixer.[12] Another independent studio in New York was described by Oscar Hijuelos in his novel "The Mambo Kings Sing Songs of Love," the story of some Cuban musicians who came to the United States to make their fortunes in the 1950s:

> The studio was about the size of a large bathroom and had thickly carpeted floors with corkboard- and drape-covered walls, and a large window looking out on 125th Street. . . . Three big RCA ball microphones in the center of the room for vocals, another three for the instruments. . . . The horn players would stand to the side, the rhythm section – drummers and string bass and pianist – on another.[13]

A typical "hole-in-the-wall" studio of an independent record company, and one that played a pivotal role in the development of rock'n'roll, was the Sun studio in Memphis. Situated in a commercial section of Memphis, it was a room 30 × 18 feet lined with the white acoustic tile found in radio studios. A control room stood behind a glass window at one end. This was the nerve center of the operation, containing two large Ampex 350 professional tape recorders and two Presto acetate lathes to make 78-rpm and microgroove recordings. The owner and operator of the studio, Sam Phillips, worked the RCA style mixing console, with which he could mix the sounds from five or six microphones into a single-track, mono master.[14] Phillips did no overdubbing on his records, and indulged in no post-production editing. He set up his microphones, quickly checked the balance, and attempted to capture the performance on a single take.

Like most other companies in the record business, Sun used both tape and disc technology. Although tape recording had been adopted by independent studios like Sun, it played no part in the creation of the particular sound of those first rock'n'roll recordings. The distinct Sun sound was more a product of the inadequacies of the studio than a conscious effort to use technological means to shape the sound. Since no baffles were used in the studio, sound would leak from one open microphone to another. According to Phillips' assistant Jack Clement, this was the secret behind the hazy echo of the Sun sound.[15]

The echo effect gave recordings a hard reverberating dramatic sound. Echo was commonly used in recording studios at this time and was particularly popular in country music. It could be produced by double-tracking on tape (recording two tracks and then combining them with a split-second delay), or by varying the acoustics of the studio. Big studios had their own echo chambers and sophisticated devices to produce time delays and reverberation, but in small studios electronic manipulation of sound was not considered as effective as putting a microphone out on the fire escape.

The sparse sound of rock'n'roll owed little to magnetic recording and marked a step back rather than a step forward in the technology of recording. Multi-miking techniques and post-production dubbing were used in recording studios, but they were the preserve of the major companies in making classical and middle-of-the-road orchestral recordings. The FFRR system was helpful in recording Mantovani but not Elvis Presley. In achieving a stark and incisive sound, record producers like Sam Phillips were aiming at spontaneity rather than perfect reproduction of music. They were returning to the sense and sound of the raw jazz recordings made in the acoustic studios of the 1920s.

The important changes in the recording studio were cultural rather than technological. Musicians, record producers, and engineers were becoming equals as the strict hierarchy of the studio system was broken down. One musician who benefitted from this new relationship of artist and technician was Buddy Holly. As a teenager in Texas, Holly was well versed in country and R&B from listening to it on the radio. Holly got his opportunity in the wake of Elvis Presley's successful rockabilly recordings and achieved the dream of all aspiring musicians — a record contract with a major label. In January 1956 Buddy left Lubbock, Texas, for Decca's recording studios in Nashville with high hopes and a brand new Fender Stratocaster guitar with which he intended to make a musical career.

Holly's first sessions with Decca were complete failures. In the studio the record producers had their way, insisting that Holly not play his guitar because it would interfere with his vocals and muddy the sound. There was to be no rock'n'roll drumming. The arrangements were done in the country and western style, and the tempo was slow. The version of "That'll Be the Day" he recorded was restrained, rigid, and unappealing. The poor balance overemphasized the echo, and the supporting musicians could not be clearly heard. Decca soon dropped Holly, and the disillusioned young man returned to Texas.

The next recording of this song was to be much different. It was done in the studios of Norman Petty, an independent producer in Clovis, New Mexico. Petty had begun in radio and then made a living in free-lance recording and selling the masters to larger companies. Like many other local bands, Holly and his friends had made demos with him to use in promoting their music. Petty had a more relaxed atmosphere in his studio, where musicians were not billed by the hour but by the session, which could go on all day if needed. He let Holly record "That'll Be the Day" his own way, offering suggestions through the long practice sessions.[16]

With the tapes in hand, Petty then had to spark the interest of A&R men in record companies in New York. After suffering rejection from all the majors, he finally found one record producer who thought that the song had commercial potential. It was released through Brunswick, one of the lesser subsidiaries of Decca. "That'll Be the Day" hit the million sales mark in 1957 and launched a short but immensely influential recording career.

Buddy Holly was one of the few rock'n'roll performers who took an active interest in the technology of recording. He quickly mastered the studio techniques of making balances and mixing tracks, and he experimented with some of the new equipment such as echo devices. The tape recorder had begun to make an impact on the sound of popular music by the late 1950s. It was now being used more in the recording studio to dub and double-track. Double-tracking involved making two recordings of the same vocal and superimposing the second on the first with a slight delay, giving the vocal more density and depth. This can be heard in Buddy Holly's "Words of Love" of 1957, which gives the impression of several voices in harmony.

Musicians were becoming more familiar with tape recorders; many had purchased cheap reel-to-reel machines to record their own music. This was done to hear how a composition sounded and to provide the promotional demo. As a youth Chuck Berry had an interest in the technical workings of the phonograph and radio, which had provided his musical education. He bought a wire recorder in 1951 to record his own songs. A $79 tape recorder was his next purchase, which was used to make the demos that got him a session with Chess records. When he got to their studio in Chicago, he found it equipped with an Ampex professional recorder and a mixing console that could handle twelve microphones – an indication of the growing technical sophistication of the independents.[17]

The balance of power in the studio was moving from the engineers and record producers employed by the record company to the performers themselves. Many of the new hit tunes were written by singers who recorded their own compositions. The selection of material to be recorded was no longer the unquestioned preserve of the A&R man. Even the ownership of the music had changed. ASCAP's stranglehold on music publishing was broken in the 1940s when radio broadcasters, tired of paying high royalties to ASCAP, formed their own music publisher, BMI (Broadcast Music Incorporated). This company held most of the rights to the new music of the 1950s.

In the first part of the twentieth century, the song was everything, a property to be recorded by many artists and the source of profits through royalties. Sheet music was copyrighted and protected. The recording was now the important thing – the property and the profit maker. In the 1950s an artist like Chuck Berry or Buddy Holly would come to the studio with his own material and his own ideas about playing it. The song was his property. He might have to split the authorship with the owner of the record company or with the deejay who promoted his music, but he was still the source of the material he recorded.

The ascent of a rock star from obscurity to international fame was done on the basis of a successful recording. With little experience as performers, and only a demo to show for their musical education, young men such as Buddy Holly and Elvis Presley had quickly reached the top of their profession.

In his last recording sessions, Buddy Holly experimented with multi-tracking and other re-recording techniques. He brought in string sections and added their sound to his songs. Before he died in an airplane crash in 1959, Holly had popularized the two guitars, drums, and bass lineup of rock groups and pioneered the musician's role as record producer. He planned to build his own studio in Lubbock and make records there, but in the meantime he used a tape recorder to record his songs at home.[18]

The eventful musical decade of the 1960s began with few indications that the pioneering work of Buddy Holly was going to become common practice in recording studios. Only the independent record producer Phil Spector was creating popular music by employing the technological arsenal of sound recording. Spector had enjoyed a varied musical career as song writer, performer, and record producer before he formed his own record company. He successfully experimented with tape dubbing using batteries of drum kits, three or four pianos, and numerous musicians – all taped independently and then mixed together to produce what was accurately termed "the wall of sound." This effect was immediately evident on hearing his records. The music swells and fills up the entire spectrum of sounds. Layer upon layer of vocals, drums, and guitars converge to create a dramatic wave of music. Spector called it a "Wagnerian approach to rock & roll: little symphonies for the kids."[19] It marked the beginning of a decade of innovation in the recording studio.

The studio as an instrument

When the Beatles first entered Abbey Road recording studios in 1962, the transition from disc to tape recording was complete. The tape machine now stood in the control room, and the master recording was now a reel of magnetic tape. The Beatles first recorded on a two-track machine, which took the ten inputs from microphones and distributed them on two channels of recorded sound. In this way all the instruments could be put on one track and the vocals sung onto the other.

The two-track machine was considered a major advance over the single track in that it could record two tracks simultaneously in the studio or it could be used to add on a second track to an existing recording. A take of a song with guitars, drums, and vocals could be recorded on two tracks and stored. It could later be mixed down onto one track and the free track used to add strings or trumpets.

Despite advancing technology, little change had occurred in the social organization of the Abbey Road studio. Performers and technicians were still kept apart, and the control room, the nerve center of the operation, remained out of bounds for musicians. The machinery was firmly in the hands of the technicians and the record producer. The latter had the power to add whatever track he liked to the original track performed in the studio. Abbey Road had its hierarchy of technicians: tape operator (or "button pusher"); engineer, who did the microphone placement and balancing; and record producer, who not only managed the session but also acted in the same role as the American A&R man by arranging music and choosing musicians.

Like most of the studios operated by the large companies, Abbey Road remained committed to a strict daily schedule made up of 3-hour sessions. The record producer was still in charge of the recording session and the release of records. Musicians treated the studio as a work room in which their playing was under the control of the men in the glass-fronted room above them. When the red light came on, they started work to produce three or four acceptable masters within the 3-hour time limit. As one young rock musician recalled of his experience at Abbey Road, "We were totally overawed by it all. . . . All we had to do was turn up and get on with it . . . we did exactly what we were told." The technical side of the process was a mystery to them, and they did not dare enter the control room.[20]

This was also the position of the Beatles when they first started to record. Their producer played an active role in shaping their music in the studio, and it was often George Martin's ideas that turned a promising Lennon–McCartney composition into a best-selling record. Martin was not only a highly experienced engineer but also a musician who was expected to "tidy up" the playing of the young men in his studio. The Beatles listened to his suggestions about how a song should evolve and took his directions about how it should be played. Like hundreds of aspiring recording artists before them, they were simply working in the studio of a large corporation under the direction of a corporate employee. George Martin had the final say in what songs were recorded and what tracks were chosen for release.

Although it was acknowledged within the international record industry that in general the quality of British recordings was high, especially for classical music, their recording technology lagged behind that of studios in the United States. Record producers from Abbey Road were vastly impressed when they visited American studios. George Martin sat in on a Frank Sinatra session at Capitol studios and noted that in terms of equipment and recording technique, the Americans were far ahead.[21]

Many of the studios of the major American companies had been rebuilt in the late 1950s to accommodate the introduction of stereophonic sound. These studios were complexes of recording rooms of various sizes, and they carried out a wide range of recording. Capitol's Hollywood studios were redesigned in 1959 to provide several different facilities for recording. The newest electronic amplifiers and mixers, incorporating solid-state circuitry, were installed to mix in monophonic or stereophonic sound. Tape recorders were used exclusively to make master recordings. The studio complex of United Recording Corporation in Hollywood comprised three studios of 65,000, 27,000 and 3,000 cubic feet, respectively; two small studios for mono mastering (in which the master tape recording is transferred to disc master for duplication); one studio for stereo mastering; and a recording-transfer and mixing studio. There were five echo chambers.[22] The flexible facilities in this studio could be used for all types of commercial recording, including sound for motion pictures. Columbia's studio on 52nd Street in New York City was set up to make phonograph records and radio and television commercials – three important recorded-sound products of the 1950s and 1960s.

The transatlantic channels of technological diffusion that had brought so many innovations in recorded sound from North America to Europe included not only personal visits and the technical journals of recording engineers (the Audio Engineering Society was formed in 1948) but also the popular recordings made in the United States and released in the U.K. The double-tracked records of Buddy Holly and Phil Spector had alerted musicians and recording engineers alike of the infinite possibilities of tape recording. After listening to the Beatles' record collection, which went from rockabilly to Motown, it was clear to the Abbey Road staff that "the Americans must be cheating."[23]

The Beatles' recording career coincided with the rapid advance of recording technology. Four-track recording was introduced soon after their 1962 debut. It made re-recording much easier. Recording heads could now lay several tracks of magnetized sound on the 1-inch-wide strip of magnetic tape. Improved tape and advanced noise-reduction systems, which were based on the techniques of equalization and compression, made it possible to re-record many times over without losing sound quality in a sea of background noise.

Once the studio engineer had only been able to manipulate the amplitude of sound coming in from the microphones. Now he could also increase or diminish any band of frequencies, and do it during and after the recording – blending tracks of sound in the mixer and recording it onto multi-tracked tape. He could then record these tracks any way he pleased, drawing upon a vast reservoir of editing techniques developed in the film industry.

On a four-track recorder, each of the tracks was devoted to a vocal or a few instruments. The engineer used the first few takes to record the rhythm section of guitars and drums onto one track. When this was finished, he recorded several takes of the vocal track and mated the best one to the rhythm track. If no satisfactory take of the vocal was produced, he had to make up a composite vocal track using the best parts of several takes and editing them together. The two remaining tracks were used to add in more instruments or groups of strings or anything that might be needed to enhance the song.

With the sound of the three combined tracks playing in his earphones, George Martin might sit down at the piano and add (or overdub) a few notes on the fourth track. Later, he might overdub the sound of a tambourine or timbale. If he used up all four tracks, he could remix (or bounce) them down to three tracks and free up a track for overdubbing. The ease of re-recording on four-tracks encouraged the addition of larger groups of musicians (playing strings or brass instruments) to a recording. They could be assembled in a separate studio and their efforts recorded onto a track which would be later added to the song. In this way concert music began to seep into pop songs, as groups of musicians or even whole orchestras were brought into the studio to provide backing tracks or flourishes to be added at critical moments in the song.

The remixing process, where the tapes from the recording session were put through the mixing board once again, enabled the technician to alter the structure of a recording by adjusting the balance of its many parts. Instead of turning knobs he slid the faders up and down – another innovation passed on from film re-recording consoles – to compile the recording.[24] He could emphasize the vocals over the instruments or vice versa, bringing up the sound of one instrument or eliminating it altogether. Working from the basic set of sound tracks, the remixer could combine and recombine endless versions of the same song. George Martin often mixed one version of a Beatles recording for release in England and a different one for the United States.

By 1965 a significant change had taken place in the Beatles' recording activities. No longer excluded from the control room, they now played the decisive part in choosing the takes to be used and determining how they were mixed. They had broken the strict rules about studio time and now occupied the studio for all hours of the day and night. They used the studio as a place to write and rehearse as well as record. Most important, the Beatles now saw the studio as the place to create rather than to record sound. When they came to the studio, they were no longer playing live into the microphone but using recording technology to fabricate a song out of many different parts. Instead of bringing a pile of American records to the technicians and asking them to duplicate this sound, they were now telling them to re-create the sounds they imagined. Martin saw his role move from imposing musical discipline on them to realizing their musical ideas.[25]

Performers were taking artistic control from the record producer and A&R man and were free to do as they pleased in the studio, providing their records sold in the millions. The practice of recording in 3-hour units was breaking down. By the late 1960s a pop single might represent over 100 hours of studio time. Phil Spector's recording of Tina Turner's "River Deep – Mountain High" used up days of recording time and cost over $20,000 to make.[26]

When Simon and Garfunkel came to record in Columbia's studios on 52nd Street in 1967, they worked through the night, sometimes in darkness, recording track after track and layering them together into a complex sound. First Simon's guitar and then his voice was recorded. This was combined with a previously recorded rhythm track, which was made by a session musician. Garfunkel then recorded his vocal, keeping in time with Simon's voice as it came to him over the earphones. The engineers recorded track after track. When Simon was not satisfied with a phrase, he left it and moved along to the next, knowing that he could come back and record it at his leisure and then have it edited (or punched) in.[27]

Much the same procedure went on in the studios of the independents. Jerry Lieber and Mike Stoller, who wrote many of the most popular R&B songs of the 1950s, produced records for their Red Bird company. A correspondent from *The New Yorker* found them in the A&R recording facility on the fourth floor of a commercial building on West 48th Street. They were discussing the fourth take of a rhythm track made by guitar, bass, piano, and drums:

"Shall we go with this one?"

"It's the best," Stoller said. "There's a tempo pickup in the first few bars that we'll have to cut, but after that it settles down." With the rhythm section tape rewound, Stoller leads the horn section while the rhythm tape is played over the studio loudspeakers. This track is then replayed in the control room:

"It's coming, but the baritone [saxophone] should honk more. Bring up the saxes a bit."

"I can bring the bari up more than the tenors," said the engineer, as he moved the sliding controls on the mixing console, adjusting the sound of each instrument as it came in on its own track.[28] Lieber and Stoller, George Martin, and numerous other producers were using tape editing to produce perfect recordings. Other musicians saw the same technology as a means to change the sound of popular music.

The release of the Beach Boys album "Pet Sounds" for Capitol Records in 1966 provided an example of what could be accomplished with tape dubbing. It was an inspiration for many producers and musicians, especially the Beatles. Here was a record that went beyond the usual pop format of bringing together ten or twelve singles onto a 40-minute LP. "Pet Sounds" was a densely orchestrated recording which could only have been made in a studio. Brian Wilson of the Beach Boys, inspired in part by the Beatles' 1965 LP "Revolver," attempted to create something different in a pop album. He spent months mixing and remixing different tracks to come up with new combinations of sounds: guitar and electric organ, harpsichord and harmonica, and an electric oscillator to produce an unearthly distortion. He used synthesizers to create electrical analogs (or copies) of real sounds. He dubbed in unusual sounds over the music, including animal noises – hence the title of the work.

Brian Wilson showed that mixing and dubbing in the studio could be used to give a new electronic dimension to music. The Beatles were impressed. They turned Studio 2 at Abbey Road into a laboratory of new electronic sounds, putting tape recorders through all sorts of devious manipulation. They increased or slowed down the tape speed, played tape backwards, and spliced pieces of tape together randomly. Some of their methods to alter sound were simple: a piece of adhesive tape or cardboard stuffed underneath a spool of tape to disturb its path across the recording head, or a finger placed on the revolving tape capstan to slow it down and distort the sound.[29]

The Beatles and their technicians experimented with all aspects of studio practice. They drastically altered microphone placement to get different sounds; they used loudspeakers as microphones; and they played with the equalizers, limiters, and compressors on the mixing console to alter the sounds they recorded. They sought out unusual instruments to record, such as the electronic mellotone. Sound effects taken from the Abbey Road library of recorded sound were also dubbed in. On "Good Morning Good Morning" the sounds of sheep, cows, dogs, horses, and elephants were mixed in. Even the noise of an audience, complete with applause, was added to give the illusion of a live performance to an artificially created musical event.

By 1967 they were masters of the recording studio. They came and went at Abbey Road as they pleased, often working through the night. Four-track recording was no longer adequate for their musical ideas; subsequently they joined two four-track machines together to make an eight-track recorder.

The results can be heard on their "Sgt. Pepper's Lonely Hearts Club Band" issued by EMI in June 1967, almost 5 years to the day after their first test recording at Abbey Road. The distance that they had travelled in this short time is evident in the depth and complexity of this pioneer "concept" album. The technologies of tape recording and long-playing records had played a critical role in the production of a new sound of the recording studio and a new kind of popular music. "Sgt. Pepper" was acclaimed as an artistic triumph. In the press the Beatles were compared to Ellington, Chaplin, and Tennyson. This one record brought a new respectability to rock'n'roll, a style that had moved from raw dance music to something now acclaimed as art.[30]

For many listeners "Sgt. Pepper's Lonely Hearts Club Band" summed up the music and the sentiments of the 1960s. This psychedelic sound was as distinctive as the hot jazz of the 1920s or the swing of the 1940s. While jazz and swing records saved a live performance in the studio, the psychedelic sounds of the sixties were as much the product of electronic manipulation as musicianship, from the Beatles' misuse of tape recorders to Jimi Hendrix's feedback from the electric guitar. It was a sound based on the new technology of recording.

With studio technique at such a high level of development, it was not difficult to see the recording as a substitute for live music – the real concert in the auditorium could be replaced by an artificial concert contained on a long-playing record. "Sgt. Pepper" had been made to sound like a live performance, with taped audience noise and formal introduction, because the Beatles were tired of touring and wanted the record to stand in its place. They produced a recorded performance that could be enjoyed at home without the distractions of the screaming fans, a performance so complex and perfect that it could never be duplicated live.

The advances in the technology of sound recording had blurred the line between technician and performer. Technology did not completely replace the artistic act of creation; it changed it by increasing the contribution of technical skills. Making music and recording it became one indivisible act in the studio; hence the Beatles and many other artists could say that they made records rather than music.[31]

Technology and art in the studio

The recording techniques perfected at Abbey Road were quickly diffused to all recording studios; even the most precocious new band had ambitions to produce complex recordings. Few other records had the same influence on popular music as "Sgt. Pepper," because it spawned a host of imitations as rock groups disappeared into the studio to produce "concept" albums and "rock operas." The 5 months taken to record "Sgt. Pepper" had convinced some in the musical press that the Beatles had run out of inspiration; an album was expected to take only a few days to record. After all, the Beatles' first album "Please Please Me" had been completed in just one day. But after "Sgt. Pepper," many months and hundreds of thousands of dollars of studio time became the norm for a popular-music LP.

The so-called "progressive" rock groups had an audience of maturing baby boomers who were now the proud owners of transistorized stereo systems. The availability of low-cost stereo equipment played a critical part in the commercial success of progressive rock in the 1960s. Much of the studio wizardry of George Martin and the Beatles was lost if one played "Sgt. Pepper" on an old, low-fidelity monophonic unit. The rapid development of studio recording technique went hand in hand with the new capabilities of the home disc player, which made it possible for the listener to appreciate the more complex sound of progressive, album-based rock'n'roll.

Progressive rock had the attention of the record-buying public, an important outlet in FM radio, and the most extensive range of machinery yet available to musicians. Once six or seven microphones had been used for an entire orchestra; now four or five might be on the drum kit alone. By the end of the 1960s, it was not uncommon to have twenty-four inputs of sound coming into the mixer and sixteen outputs leaving it. Every channel could be subjected to many sorts of equalization, not to mention filters, pitch shifters, time delays, and multiple echoes.

Success in recording popular music did not depend solely on acquiring the most advanced studio technology. The distinct "sound" of a studio was the product of many factors, and not all of them were technical. Jerry Wexler, a producer working for Atlantic Records, achieved a string of hits in the 1960s using studios in Memphis, Tennessee, and Muscle Shoals, Alabama. Aretha Franklin and Wilson Pickett were among the artists he recorded there, and the ingredients which went into making their hit records included the craft of the studio musicians who worked in Memphis and Muscle Shoals and the skills of Wexler in producing the sessions.

Despite the astounding success of Wexler and other independent producers in regional studios, the emphasis remained on the technology. "State of the art" was the goal, and it was constantly advanced by the introduction of new machines for saving, manipulating, and reproducing sound. There were also electronic devices which actually created sound. The music synthesizer, a creator of artificial sounds, came of age in the 1960s. The secret of electric speech not only opened the way for the telephone and phonograph but also presented a means to manipulate electric currents to make music. The inventors who tried to create sounds electrically in the first decades of the twentieth century used oscillators to produce single tones. Although it was possible to make sound electrically, it was immensely difficult to make music with it, because the sound could not be modified easily. Robert Moog devised oscillators which were controlled by the amount of

Figure 14.2. Jerry Wexler at the mixing board, Muscle Shoals Sound Studio, 1979. (Courtesy of Dick Cooper. Copyright 1979 Dick Cooper.)

voltage and that could alter the volume, pitch, and overtones of the sound. The Moog synthesizer was commercially introduced in 1966 and was followed by more sophisticated models which could mimic a greater range of sounds.[32] Transistorized synthesizers could do even more, and (as usual in the transistor revolution) their price dropped so that more musicians could afford them.

The synthesizer was more than just an electrical instrument; it was part of the recording equipment. The most advanced synthesizers sent their output directly into the mixing console, bypassing the microphone and unheard by any human ear. The electronic synthesizer was the perfect tool for the creative recording engineer or musician. It was itself a recording device. The Mellotron, an early synthesizer, had a keyboard which activated analogue recordings of instruments and voices. The Mellotron could provide many sounds required in a recording session, but the transistorized synthesizers of the 1960s could provide any sound, making them up to order and saving them for future use.

The synthesizer and electric keyboard were soon indispensable in the modern studio. The numerous sources of sound coming from the performing area of the studio had grown so large that new mixing consoles were designed to deal with the growing number of inputs. Eight-track recorders had given way to sixteen-track and then twenty-four-track machines. Thirty-two tracks were introduced in the 1970s. The possibilities of tape editing and dubbing became endless. The interior of the control room became a densely packed collage of meters, switches, and controls. The recording studio was now the high-tech workshop of popular music.

In the 1970s it was not unusual to hear a record in which all musical instruments had been played by the same person and remixed together. The popular-music industry now embraced the same goals of artificiality and illusion that had made Hollywood the vanguard of recorded sound. Now the tables were turned, and it was film makers who copied the techniques of multi-track recording used in the studios of record companies.[33]

A long-playing record might have hundreds of invisible tape splices on it, where new material had been added to the master. Even "live" recordings were touched up in the remixing room to eliminate defects. Some engineers recorded the practice sessions of symphony orchestras in order to have material to edit into the final mix, if parts of the recorded performance were not quite right. It was not only technicians who edited the tapes; conductors and musicians had also begun to go into the control room and make their own corrections.

Yet recording with twenty-four channels instead of one did not necessarily mean a twenty-four-increment jump in sound quality. There was some disagreement among recording engineers about the value of multiple microphones. One remembered that during the 1960s he happened to listen to an early stereo recording made with one pair of microphones, and the clarity and naturalness of the sound amazed him; it was far superior to anything he had heard on a record. Constant remixing of numerous tracks of sound could just as easily take away from a performance as add to it. Instead of one take where everything had to be right, sessions were now based on constant playing and replaying of a piece of music. But after the second take of the same song, the decline in musicianship sets in as boredom takes over.[34]

Technology had provided total control of sound recording and promised perfection in saving a performance – but at the cost of losing spontaneity. John Hammond was not alone when he argued that high-tech recording had set back the record business 20 years. In his view the synthetically created sounds of the studio were a poor substitute for the live and naturally blemished performance.

In a long recording career that spanned Count Basie to Bruce Springsteen, Hammond picked a session from 1936 as the most perfect recording he had ever produced – despite primitive conditions and inadequate technology. It was made in a small hotel room, about 12 × 15 feet, with a group of musicians led by Count Basie. They began early in the morning after playing all night. There were six of them in the makeshift studio, and there was no room for Jo Jones' bass drum, which Hammond knew would probably force the needle out of the wax record, and so they did without. This was Jones' first session, as it was Lester Young's, but it is hard to believe this when you hear them playing.[35]

The initial sounds of the scratches and pops of the revolving disc are quickly forgotten as the first notes fill the loudspeakers. If there was time to think about the one microphone, the restricted range, and the lack of bass, it would probably detract from the enjoyment of listening, but all these factors are quickly overcome by the beauty of the performance and the realization that Hammond caught the moment, not just the music. If the musicians had been in a position to spend months in the studio perfecting these songs, who knows if they would have sounded any better?

Listening to the scratchy 78-rpm discs of the 1930s, it is not difficult to understand why so many people still avidly collect them. Some of the best performances of jazz and blues were recorded in the 1930s, before musicians had the luxury of editing out their mistakes. Technological perfection, the absolute highest fidelity of reproduction, does not necessarily mean more enjoyment of the music. The evaluation of any system of sound recording and reproduction is in essence a subjective process and, as Edison once commented, people hear what you tell them to hear and not what they really hear.[36]

Some music lovers in the late 1920s were distinctly unhappy with the brave new world of electrical sound recording. To them the new system produced a harsh, unwelcome sound. This attitude was best expressed by Compton Mackenzie – author, music lover, and editor of *The Gramophone* – who concluded that "the music itself is a mass of jangled nerves." Mackenzie was not alone mourning the passing of the "cool, dark beauty" of the acoustic era. He claimed (with some justification) that "the exaggeration of sibilants by the new method is abominable, and there is a harshness which recalls some of the worst excesses of the past." He then combined aesthetic revulsion with patriotism: "I don't want to hear symphonies with an American accent. I don't want blue-nose violins and Yankee clarinets."[37] Had Mackenzie uncovered a critical connection between the Western Electric recording system and the new sound of symphonic music? Did the new technology influence the interpretation of the classics? Probably not. What he heard was the emphasis put on the upper registers by recording engineers still enjoying the novelty of extended frequency range.

All in all, the technological advance of sound recording has had more advocates than detractors. Producers of classical records, notably Walter Legge at EMI and John Culshaw at Decca, saw that the advances in recording after World War II could make the production of records an art form in itself. Legge argued that the recording could be made superior to the live performance, the standard by which all performances were to be judged.[38] No one justified the benefits of recording technology more persuasively than the acclaimed classical pianist Glenn Gould. In 1966 he published some articles entitled "The Prospects of Recording" in which he argued that the recording should now supersede the performance. The goal of musical perfection was now attainable in the recording studio, where the musician could become "creatively dishonest" and produce music that far exceeded his capabilities in the concert hall. Gould argued that making music in the studio was better for the performer, because it brought him into closer contact with the listener who played his records at home:

> I discovered that, in the privacy, the solitude and . . . the womb like security of the studio, it was possible to make music in a more direct, more personal manner than any concert hall would ever permit.[39]

He envisaged a much closer relationship between performer and listener brought about by the recording and playback equipment, which brought more intimacy than the physical proximity of the concert hall. He argued that playing the recording produces a shared experience which brings a new immediacy in performance. The "new listeners" now had the power, if they possessed a first-rate stereo pre-amplifier, to use the volume and tone controls to usurp the function of the recording technician and tailor the recording to suit individual taste and mood. The "new composers" in turn could benefit from the breakdown of the division between composing and performing; they could supervise the recording exactly as they intended it to be. In short, Glenn Gould saw the triumph of science as reviving rather than stultifying art.[40]

Synthetic music and the punk revolt

Not all advocates of studio technology had motives as pure as those of Gould. The mechanization of sounds made it easier to mass-produce music and to downgrade (or even eliminate) the services of the musician. Machine-made sounds became more common in the 1970s, when the independent producer became a powerful force in popular music, not only as a record producer but also as a record creator.

This process can be seen clearly in the appearance of *disco*, the often despised but popular dance music which dominated the best-seller charts for most of the decade. Disco was produced in a studio and played in *discotheques*, where recordings entertained hundreds of milling dancers. Deejays used two disc turntables to ensure continuity of the music, and had equalizers and speed controls to manage the transition from one record to another. They used a public address system to sing or talk over the recorded sound.

Disco was a studio music created by record producers whose weapon of choice was the synthesizer. Dance music requires a steady beat, and most disco producers used a drum machine which artificially created the sound of drums. The machine was programmed to produce a beat indefinitely and had the capability to mimic a range of percussive sounds. As in the case of synthesizers, the first drum machines simulated sounds synthetically, but soon they were able to sample drum sounds by recording them. The sounds were held in the machine's memory and could be reproduced at will. Digital synthesizers made this job even easier. Models such as the Roland TR-707 became a fixture in many recording studios.

The producers had all the tools of the studio at their disposal: synthesizers and drum machines for the rhythm tracks, vocal tracks from singers or from other recordings, equalizers and compressors to manipulate the sound, and most important, mixing consoles to play around with all these parts until a satisfactory mix was obtained. As Juergen Koppers, Donna Summer's engineer, noted, "the whole arrangement is in the mix afterwards."[41]

Such was the importance of the mix that disco producers produced several of them for every hit song: 7-inch singles for general sales and radio play, and extended-play 12-inch discs for the deejays. Donna Summer's disco anthem "Love to Love You" was issued in 4-minute and 16-minute versions.

As in all popular dance music, disco required image as well as sound; this was achieved by the hit movie musical "Saturday Night Fever." In the time-honored tradition of the genre, "Saturday Night Fever" told the story of a young man who found fame and fortune, but this time it was as a prize-winning disco dancer and not as a jazz or rock star. This film and its best-selling sound track moved disco into the center of popular music, and such was its popularity that by the end of the decade, record shops now carried the 12-inch single.

Disco was not the only popular music based on the new technology of the recording studio. Electronic sounds began to influence musicians in the 1970s, bringing new styles such as techno-pop, industrial rock, and just plain "techno." The move back into the studio begun by the Beatles and the Beach Boys became a full-scale retreat. Successful pop groups such as Depeche Mode and Human League relied on synthesizers and drum machines to do most of the work and did not hide the fact that their sound was studio-derived. Numerous dance records were produced without a drummer or guitarist; only the vocals were the work of humans, and even those inputs were electronically enhanced. Techno-pop became so pervasive that some bands assumed robotic stage personas to complement the machine-made quality of the music. Devo sang "Are we not men? We are devo!" and proclaimed a new level of cultural de-evolution.

The popular music of the 1970s was often criticized as banal and overtly commercial when compared with the decades that preceded it. Rock'n'roll had made popular music the voice of youth rebellion in the 1950s and 1960s, but there were few traces of it left in the 1970s. The tight hold of the media conglomerates on the record industry had made the rock star the means to market their output rather than to challenge the status quo. Soft drink bottlers, brewers, and manufacturers of clothing also appropriated the sounds of rock'n'roll to sell their products.

Although it was produced by the most sophisticated technology yet applied to recording sound, pop music in the 1970s had become bland and predictable, as emotionless as the synthesizers that fabricated it. In a decade when people still looked backwards to "Those Fabulous 60s," popular music had lost its ability to shock or inspire.[42]

Resentment against the state of popular music was festering in underground bands in London and New York for much of the 1970s. Groups like the New York Dolls, the Ramones, and the Sex Pistols were formed as a way of protest against mundane popular music and its commercialization by multinational corporations. In their eyes, disco was as loathsome a product as a consumer society could concoct, and rock had become bland, bourgeois, and totally discredited. Punk music and dress were formed in a drastic reaction against the status quo of modern society, especially as it was manifest in the record industry. It was the result of another cultural exchange between the United States and Great Britain.[43]

The release of "Anarchy in the UK" by the Sex Pistols in 1977 brought a fresh sound to the public's attention and was the formal beginning of a new movement in popular culture. The Sex Pistols were the most highly publicized group in a new wave of nihilism that swept through teenage culture on both sides of the Atlantic. They were the vanguard of a loud and unapologetic movement which attacked popular music for becoming part of the establishment. "Anarchy in the UK" rediscovered the musical excitement that had once been felt by young people in the 1950s. It was a revolt against the megagroups, their arena concerts, and their over-produced recordings. What punk announced in a loud and discordant voice was that rock was dead.

Whereas the lyrics of R&B and rock'n'roll had heralded the arrival of the youth culture in the 1950s, punk reflected its decline and fall. Part of the words for "God Save the Queen" were: "No Future, No Future, No Future for You, . . . No Future for me."[44] Punk bands espoused social and political causes and illuminated topics such as racism, police brutality, and ineffectual government in their songs.

They even criticized the powerful role played by American entertainment in British society: "I'm So Bored with the U.S.A."

In addition to lyrics which were intentionally provocative, "Anarchy in the UK" achieved a new low point in musicianship. Several of the Sex Pistols could hardly play their instruments and did not try to give the impression that they could. The harsh sound of punk was deliberately amateur: a reaction to the high-gloss professionalism of recorded sound of the 1970s. The simple guitar, drums, and vocal lineup was used for maximum noise levels and dramatic impact. There was no suggestion of professionalism, because it would reek of the rock-music establishment. The punks played badly and were proud of it. Steve Jones of the Sex Pistols summed up their attitude with this often quoted line: "We're not into music. We're into chaos." Far from espousing technology, the punks rejected it. They proudly announced that their records were "lo-fi" and in "mono-enhanced stereo."[45]

Unlike other rock performers who had willingly abandoned the concert for the recording studio, punk groups saw the performance as paramount, and in many cases it turned into spectacle as the audience was taunted to participate in the mayhem. The violence of the shows reflected not only the anger of inner-city youth but the heritage of the first wave of rock'n'roll – punk brought back its excitement and spontaneity in a form that was even more threatening to middle-class America than anything it had experienced in the 1950s.

If punk bands set out to shock and enrage, they achieved this goal immediately. Groups like the Sex Pistols gained enough notoriety to ensure that their music would be heard. Their success, in both artistic and financial areas, encouraged the formation of thousands of punk bands – including the Clash, Souxsie and the Banshees, and the Buzzcocks – who were inspired by the Sex Pistols. The anti-professional stance of this *new wave* encouraged participation in the movement, because lack of musical ability was not a barrier but rather an advantage in breaking through the trite superficiality of popular music. The message was that anyone could make music, thus it followed that anyone could make a record. One punk magazine called *Sniffin Glue* sent out this advice to would-be punk musicians: "Here's one chord, here's two more, now form your own band."[46]

The recording studio did not have to be a high-tech establishment owned by a large company; it could be established anywhere there was a tape recorder. Nor did it have to be based in a major city. In a short time punk moved from the capital cities to the hinterland, and the influence of local music in the provincial centers led to many new derivations of punk: the "Manchester sound," the "Seattle sound," and so on.

One of the most important changes produced by the new wave was in studio technique, where the punk bands turned back the clock to the 1930s with a sparse, immediate, and unadorned sound. The Sex Pistols and their ilk rejected recording technology; they were distinctly low-tech and low-fi. Their recordings were as basic and unadorned as the music. Punk negated the movement towards synthetic creation of sound and extensive post-production construction of the recording. The punk bands went back to the single microphone, one or two takes, and no re-recording. There were no electronic synthesizers and no drum machines. Capturing the immediacy of the live performance was once again the goal of the recording; consequently 50 years of technological progress as thrown out. The punk sound was raw, un-balanced, and above all realistic. What you got on record was what you heard at the concert with all its flaws intact.

15. The cassette culture

As the phonograph approached its 100th birthday in 1977, Edison would have been well pleased with the progress of his favorite invention. The technology of electrical recording had been dramatically improved after 1945, and the range of frequencies reproduced by recorded sound had slowly increased: the microgroove record covered a range from 30 to 10,000 cps, and the stereo units of the 1960s extended the range far up into the high frequencies, around 15,000 cps. The modern phonograph captured most of the audible sounds of music and speech, with low levels of noise and distortion. The realistic stereo reproduction of sound, which had not even been dreamed of during the acoustic era, was made a reality in the 1960s.

These advances would have no doubt pleased Edison the inventor, but Edison the businessman would have been equally impressed with the low price and wide availability of this technology. High fidelity had been brought within the budget of the majority of Americans in the 1970s, and there cannot have been many families who did not enjoy the benefits of recorded sound in one form or another. The annual sales of audio products in the United States had risen from $1.7 billion in 1975 to $4.1 billion in 1979: $1 billion in pre-recorded cassettes, $1 billion in eight-track tapes, and $2.1 billion in discs.[1]

Despite all the technological advances and improvements, the basic talking-machine format determined by Edison and Berliner had remained unchanged. A stylus still ran along the groove and reproduced the analogue signal of sound modulated into it. Berliner's revolving-disc idea had stood the test of time and now dominated recorded sound despite the steady diffusion of magnetic tape. Whatever the advantages of tape, it still had not displaced the disc as the dominant format. The disc was still going strong in the 1970s and looked like it might last another hundred years.

The microgroove long-playing disc was perhaps the greatest achievement of the industry of recorded sound. Manufacturing such

313

a product required the highest level of precision and quality control; even the slightest imperfection was immediately evident to the listener. The record manufacturers could lay claim to the world's most precise mass-produced consumer product.[2]

The method of duplicating records had not changed much since Edison's invention of electroplating masters with gold dust in the 1880s and Johnson's application of this method to discs. The steps used in electroplating the master and making a matrix remained, only the tolerances had been made finer and every solution and procedure had been refined. The preparation of the lacquer master discs was carried out to the same standards of cleanliness required in satellite construction and hospital operating theaters.[3]

Cutting a sound signal into these discs was done with a specially heated stylus attached to a variable-pitch cutting lathe, which automatically varied the cut from 400 to 150 grooves per inch, depending on the frequency and volume of sound being recorded. Instead of the steady hand and experienced eye of the recorder, the modern cutting lathe used the infallible memory of a computer to adjust the pitch and depth of the cut.[4]

Edison and Johnson had been very proud of what they thought was the automation of record duplication, yet their specially designed machines required some human labor to operate and no small measure of skill to produce an acceptable duplicate. The fully automatic record press was developed during the 1940s, and 20 years later microgroove discs were made by machines which mixed the biscuit of extruded plastic and then forced it into an automatic press, combining the chemical and mechanical steps of making a record into one quick process. A computer within the machine determined the amount of force applied by the press and how long it would take to form a record. One of these machines could duplicate a 12-inch record in less than 30 seconds and make about 1,800 of them a day.[5]

Stereo discs were available to the public by the millions and at reasonable prices, which ranged from $3.98 to around $6.98 in the 1970s. Nearly every possible sound had been recorded onto LP discs: all the classics from Thomas Arne to Efrem Zimbalist; an unending volume of pop, rock, and easy listening music; the sound of every language on earth in either music, voice, or language instruction; the calls of the wild and the songs of birds and whales; the noises of machines from steam engines to jet aircraft; documentary discs of historic events; commercial recordings of sales pitches and product information; instructions to make, bake, and repair useful items; and the unnatural sounds of the music synthesizer.

Yet just when the revolving disc had reached the apex of its technological development and popularity in the 1970s, a new competitor emerged to challenge its place as the preeminent form of recorded sound.

The reel-to-reel, magnetic-tape format had its supporters in the stereophonic cadres of audiophiles and the legions of home recorders. Although a flexible and easily edited format, the reel of magnetic tape had one flaw – difficulties of handling. Threading tape through the narrow gate of a recording head and attaching it to the pick-up reel was a task too complicated for many users. A long-playing capability was certainly welcome, but the problems of identifying and locating selections on a reel of tape denied listeners the easy access to their favorite songs that discs had given them. These were not minor considerations; consumer difficulties with handling Edison's cylinders had played an important part in their downfall, and the wire recorder had succumbed to tape because of the same problem. Reel-to-reel tape was too cumbersome to be the format for pre-recorded music, which is why the revolving disc survived the challenge of magnetic tape.

Manufacturers of tape recorders were not the first to encounter the problems of handling long lengths of tape; film cameras and projectors had suffered from the same problems. Designers of dictating machines also had years of experience in overcoming the difficulties of loading tape in and out of a machine. The endless loop of plastic tape was one method of solving this problem. Another was the tape cartridge devised for film cameras, in which the film was enclosed in a plastic shell and ran around a single spool. The magazine load was found to be the simplest for the customer to handle. This format had been used in broadcasting to hold a short pre-recorded message or commercial; it could be inserted quickly into a player, and it came in a convenient plastic case. The Fidelipac system for broadcasters used a fixed length of tape on one hub – taking it from the inside and returning it to the outside of the hub. It could be played only in one direction. For the home user the cartridge has the disadvantage of being difficult to fast forward to a desired selection and impossible to rewind; it is time-consuming to access specific songs in a long program of sound.

Cartridges had also been developed for use in automobile sound systems, where portability and ease of operation were at a premium. The radio had opened up the new market of automobile sound in the 1930s, and after the war radios became standard in many American cars. Yet people wanted to select music while travelling, and several unsuccessful attempts were made to develop a disc player for automobile use. By the 1960s there were several tape-cartridge systems under development, including the four-track, continuous-loop cartridge based on the Fidelipac and the RCA "Casino" cartridge, which was about the size of a paperback book.[6]

In 1964 the Lear Company, a manufacturer of executive jet airplanes, approached the Ford Motor Company with a plan for a continuous-loop cartridge with four sets of paired stereo tracks. Ford bought the idea, and the Motorola company built the Lear stereo eight-track players, which were installed in Ford automobiles from 1966 onwards as a luxury option. RCA agreed to develop the software for the new product, providing hundreds of pre-recorded selections to go on the tapes – a very important factor in its commercial introduction.[7] The eight-track was convenient for the car driver because it could be inserted into the player with one hand. It was also manufactured for use in home radio/phonographs. Although millions of tape cartridges were sold to home users, it was not an entirely satisfactory product for them; it was difficult to access selections, and the sound quality suffered from wow and flutter from the tape transport, which distorted reproduction.

An important application for tape recording was in the dictating machines used in offices. Businessmen did not require the same standard of fidelity as the home listener; their concerns were convenience of use and portability. The Permaflux Scribe of the 1950s was a typical machine, employing magazines which had the tape running between two hubs.[8] The cassette had tape on two reels instead of one, which made it possible to rewind and fast forward with ease. Several European concerns had employed the tape cassette in small, personal dictating machines. In 1962 the Philips Company developed a cassette in which the tape was half as wide as the standard 1/4-inch tape and ran between two reels in a small plastic case. The tape moved at $1\frac{7}{8}$ inches per second, compared with the $3\frac{3}{4}$ on eight-tracks and home tape recorders. Its very slow speed put more words on the tape but paid the price in limited fidelity.

The Philips compact cassette was introduced in 1963. During the first year on the market, only 9,000 units were sold. Philips did not protect its cassette as a proprietary technology but encouraged other companies to license its use. The company required that all users of its compact cassette adhere to its standards, which guaranteed that all cassettes would be compatible. An alliance with several Japanese manufacturers ensured that when the format was introduced for home use in the mid-1960s, there were several cassette players available. The first sold in the United States were made by Panasonic and Norelco. They were quickly joined by other companies as the compact cassette took hold. By 1968 around eighty-five different manufacturers had sold over 2.4 million cassette players worldwide. In that year the cassette business was worth about $150 million.[9] The Philips compact cassette became the standard format for tape recording by the end of the decade.

Its name gives us a clue to its wide appeal. It is small enough to fit into a shirt pocket, yet it can still hold 45 minutes of music on each side of the tape. It is very easy to use – one has only to insert it into the player, usually by lifting up a lid, and press the PLAY button, the mechanism then engages, and the tape spools turn. The Norelco Carry-Corder of 1964, the first cassette player on the American market, was powered by flashlight batteries and weighed in at 3 pounds. It could record and play back and came complete with built-in microphone and speaker.

The cassette was a tribute to the role of plastics in recorded-sound technology. From the tensilized mylar tape on its plastic hubs to the special runners, guides, and spools which turn within a clear plastic shell, the cassette is made up of several different types of plastic. Since the development of the early phenol resin materials in Edison's laboratory around 1913, plastics in many different forms had played a bigger and bigger part in the audio industry. Not only were they used as recording medium, but they also made up the casings of record players and tape recorders.

The major drawback of the audio cassette was that it was a low-fidelity medium. It had a poor frequency response when compared with the disc, and its playback was marred by a loud and annoying tape hiss. The serious home listener could not be persuaded to accept it with these disadvantages, and the cassette was seen as a means of bringing portable sound to the less discriminating user – a tape version of the transistor radio.

Steady improvement of the sound of the cassette followed the same path as the revolving disc. Both were technological systems that responded to an approach which encompassed both the player and the recording medium. The manufacturers of magnetic tape, especially Japanese companies such as Sony, Denon, and TDK, devised new types of magnetic materials to coat onto plastic tape that could hold more magnetic information. They gradually improved the basic ferric oxide compounds with the addition of cobalt mixtures and then developed chromium dioxide as the magnetic material on the tape. This provided superior recordings. The next step was to replace metal oxides with tiny particles of pure metal, which permitted even more intense magnetization, increasing the frequency response of the cassette tape and helping to reduce surface noise. Then they had to improve the recording heads of the player to handle extra high frequencies.

Both disc and tape recording had benefitted from technologies developed in film sound, ranging from microphone placement to the design of loudspeakers, and the cassette was no exception. The techniques of equalization and compression were well-known methods of reducing noise in recording, which had first been investigated in the 1930s for film sound. They were based on altering the recording levels by increasing or decreasing the emphasis of chosen sound frequencies – a common practice in recording which had been used for several purposes, including compensating for the inadequacies of playback equipment. The widespread practice of altering recording levels – in essence the adjustment of the recording curve – had led to a standardization problem, but it also showed the way to reduce noise, especially in cassette tapes.

An improved method of reducing the noise of magnetic tape recording was developed by Ray Dolby, an employee of the Ampex Corporation. The Dolby A system was based on pre-emphasis of certain higher frequencies in recording and de-emphasis of them during playback. The system splits the signal into four audio frequency bands and raises the volume of some of the high frequencies – normally the quieter passages of music or conversation – to record these frequencies at higher levels than the other bands. Tape hiss is most audible at high frequencies, and the sounds at this level were the ones increased by the Dolby system to mask out the annoying noise. In playback these frequencies are reduced to their original levels by the exact amount that they were previously raised, and much of the background noise and tape hiss which is most evident during playback of the quieter passages is reduced because the sound signal overrides it.[10] If the sound recorded has sufficiently high frequencies to drown out the hiss, the Dolby system does not boost them.

Dolby had originally designed the system for recording studios. Dolby A was first employed at the Decca studios in England in 1966. He was persuaded to apply it to home cassette players, and the Dolby system was incorporated into them beginning in 1971. Although Dolby noise reduction was only one of several methods available, it had an advantage of easy application to existing equipment, avoiding costly redesign of the whole unit. The dramatic reduction of tape hiss with this system (Dolby claimed a reduction of 10 db in tape hiss, hum, and cross talk), combined with the higher-frequency response of chrome and metal particle tapes, finally brought high fidelity to the tape cassette and attracted the attention of audiophiles.

Cassette tape was dramatically improved in the decade after its introduction in 1963. It reproduced stereo signals, and its performance grew closer to the fast turning reel-to-reel units and the stereo disc. Japanese manufacturers led the way in incorporating the cassette into home stereos. The transistor and the cassette became complementary technologies; the cheap radio/phonograph combination soon came with a cassette player built in, which could record any output of the unit. By the 1970s the cassette player was incorporated into the high-fidelity equipment purchased by the more demanding home user. This was also the work of the Japanese manufacturers, who were led by Sony, Matsushita, and Nakamichi in producing cassette tape decks which could compete with the reel-to-reel units in sound quality.

Some home tape recorders of the 1970s, in both reel-to-reel and cassette format, incorporated technologies developed in the recording studio. One could record on four tracks and copy from track to track in the same way that recording engineers worked in the high-tech studio. The top-of-the-line models came with all the controls found on professional machines: VU and peak meters, several forms of noise-reduction systems, and various filters. Some units came with their own mixing consoles built in. The home listener could buy condenser microphones and monitoring loudspeakers exactly like the ones used in professional studios. The inventors had hoped that the phonograph would enable the Victorian gentleman to record the music made in his home, but now it was possible to turn a home into a recording studio.

A short time after the 100th birthday of the phonograph in 1977, the cassette tape began to challenge the disc format in total sales. The number of LPs sold gradually declined, while the sales of cassettes increased rapidly. By the beginning of the 1980s, the ratio of vinyl to tape sales was on the order of 6:4 and rapidly approaching parity. Record companies were issuing their product on both disc and cassette, and some were getting uncomfortable with the term *record* to describe their business.[11]

In contrast to the tape reel, the cassette could be attractively packaged – an important consideration in marketing pre-recorded music. Smaller and more durable than a long-playing disc, a cassette could exceed it in playing time and almost match it in sound quality. But most importantly it had a recording capability, which gave it the commercial edge over records and eight-track cartridges.

The cassette tape became the worldwide standard in tape recording. It was used nearly everywhere and for every purpose: demonstration records were now put on cassettes rather than acetate discs, promotional records were taped on them, and everyday recordings used in the home and car were on the ubiquitous cassette. It had become as interchangeable and widely used as Berliner had predicted for his disc record back in 1888. It was a global technology.

The cassette was at the heart of two of the most important new talking machines of the 1970s. The first was a portable stereo player with two-way speakers and powerful transistorized amplifiers. This brought together some of the critical innovations in recorded-sound technology of the postwar period. It not only had high fidelity but also came at an affordable price. It also brought a new level of noise nuisance – the aptly named *boom box* could blare out music approaching noise levels of 120 db at close range, which is equal to the deafening roar of a jet engine.[12]

The portability and low cost of the boom box made it difficult to avoid the oppression of amplified recorded sound in modern society: in the city, on the beach, even driving down the street – there was no way to escape it. More than any other machine, the boom box was associated with inner-city African American youth. A rapper called LL Cool J recorded a song about his machine: "I can't live without my radio, I don't want to offend other citizens, but I kick my volume way past 10." Aptly entitled "I Need a Beat," this song spoke for millions of teenagers.[13] The boom box became a symbol of black anger in Spike Lee's film "Do the Right Thing," in which the loud playing of this powerful machine caused a racial flare-up in a city neighborhood.

Rap and the machine

The cassette played a critical role in the development of *rap*: not only the most exciting new popular music of the 1980s but one in which revolutionary new uses were found for audio equipment.

Rap emerged from the black community and stood alongside such ghetto arts as graffiti writing and break-dancing. Although it could be argued that rap came at the end of a long road of underground black music, which started with the field hollers of the slaves, it was nevertheless heavily influenced by the music technology of the 1970s. It began in dance halls and clubs in New York and Brooklyn, where disc jockeys played records and talked to the crowd over the songs. They employed the common disco setup of two turntables and a mixer: one turntable could be used for rhythm and the other for the lead. The rappers also inherited the disco legacy of the 12-inch disc, but they soon added a dimension of their own. They began to use the basic turntable and amplifier setup for public shows. This scene was encountered in Harlem in 1977:

> A crew of sound brothers . . . troops down the hill with cartons of records, speakers, two turntables and a mixer. . . . Slammin their equipment in front of an old street lamp, their hands move slow, hooking wire and mics and testing a Gil Scott Heron drum beat on a technics turntable. BOOM/BLAST – "Yo this be DJ Hollywood rockin da turntables in da hood."[14]

The raw material of all this new music was the pre-recorded disc. Rap was built on altering existing sounds by superimposing other sounds and noises on them. The most dramatic innovation of the rappers was to use their turntables as musical instruments: they slowed down and speeded up the disc, they rubbed their fingers on the surface to produce tremolo, and they scratched the surface of the disc with the needle, not randomly but rhythmically – making it part of the music. During the 1960s the recording studio itself had become an instrument, fabricating the glossy complexities of progressive rock. Rap took this one step further and used simple playback technology to make the music. Rap finally made the phonograph into a musical instrument. The scratches and clicks which had been the bane of recording engineers for decades now became an integral part of the music.

Rap had its rhythmic conventions and a division of labor: the disc jockey concentrated on providing the music from records and altering the sound by scratching it, and the rapper or master of ceremonies (MC) talked over the sound and made the rhymes. Rap performers had exotic names which indicated the dual nature of making the music: "Grandmaster Flash and the Furious Five," "Eric B. and Rakim," and "Run-D.M.C."

The first rap single to make any impact on popular music was "Rapper's Delight" by a group called the Sugar Hill Gang on their own independent Sugar Hill label in 1979. Based in part on the riff of the 1978 record "Good Times," by a disco group called Chic, it received little airplay on radio. Although dismissed by the major record companies as a fad and "too black" by radio stations, the Sugar Hill records are now seen as the vanguard of the new movement, in the same way that "Rock Around the Clock" heralded rock'n'roll.[15]

The Sugar Hill releases were too professional and too entertainment-oriented to satisfy many rappers, who were more concerned with the underground spontaneity of dance parties than making commercial dance records. The rapper Fab 5 Freddy concluded: "People weren't capturing the essence of hip-hop that was at the parties with the scratching and all that."[16] Rap and hip-hop was underground music in that it was produced locally and not immediately coopted by the media conglomerates and marketed on records. Although the record was the source of the music, the music was not put on records because that was the preserve of corporations with their recording studios and stamping presses.

The format of rap and hip-hop was the cassette tape. It was easy to record, and everybody knew how to do it. The wide availability of double cassette decks made it even easier to re-record and copy songs. The cassette was the ideal vehicle for a noncommercial music made by teenagers. Hardly any rappers had access to a recording studio, but everybody had a boom box, and the universal practice of home taping had diffused the essential skills of recording. Rap was similar to punk in that it was a low-tech sound, although this was more the result of lack of money and sophisticated equipment than the conscious decision to subvert the technology of the studio.

Once the rap song had been recorded on a cheap, transistorized cassette deck, there remained the old problem of distributing it. Rap was ignored by black stations, who stayed in the more predictable arena of gospel, soul, and funk. It was also avoided by all the major record companies. The rappers duplicated tapes on dual cassette recorders and marketed their own songs in the urban ghettos of the Northeast. Instead of nationwide distribution networks, rap musicians and their friends and relatives hawked their tapes in the neighborhoods.

Despite the lack of radio play and the primitive marketing system, rap recordings slowly attracted public attention. Spread by word of mouth and the sale or exchange of cassettes, rap's popularity gained momentum in the early 1980s. Rap recordings were made in apartments and in houses in New York and the Bronx. A rap record company was any organization which had a room to record in and one of the latest inexpensive, "professional" tape recorders with equalization controls and a couple of microphone inputs.

What made rap so significant in the history of recorded sound was that technology had completely taken over the process of making the music instead of just recording and reproducing it. As the authentic folk music of the black masses, rap could not be the product of musical instruments in expensive high-tech recording studios. The techniques of recording had seeped down to the street corner and home studio via the ubiquitous tape cassette. Rappers made their music with the equipment at hand: the home stereo. They appropriated the technology of turntable, microphone, and cassette deck and used it in ways that the manufacturers had never intended.

The Soundabout revolution

The steady miniaturization of solid-state amplifiers and the recording heads of magnetic recorders made it possible to reduce cassette tape recorders even smaller than the paperback book sizes achieved in the 1960s. But why would anyone want to own a tape player that was just slightly larger than the cassette tape it played? Masuru Ibuka of Sony was interested in a very personal stereo, and the company's

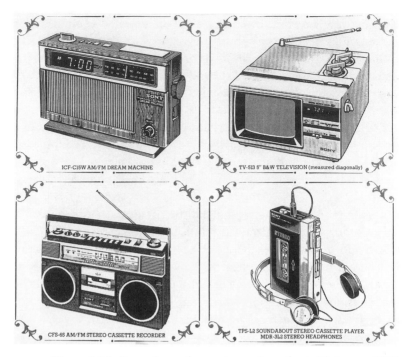

Figure 15.1. Some Sony electronic products from Christmas 1979, including the new Soundabout tape player. (Courtesy of Sony Corporation)

engineers made a model for him. The company he co-founded had made a profitable practice of reducing the size of electronic consumer goods and finding a market for them. Ibuka and his partner Akio Morita were the leading proponents of the miniature tape player within Sony, where there was considerable resistance to the idea. Ignoring the advice of their marketing department, Sony took a chance with a product that the experts said would never sell.

In 1979 Sony introduced their Soundabout cassette player, which was later called the *Walkman*. The innovative elements of the Walkman system were the tiny headphones, which produced good quality sound with only the smallest signal from the amplifier, and the increased output of the batteries, which powered the machine.[17] The Soundabout was initially treated as something of a novelty in the audio industry. It was priced at $200 and could not be considered as a product for the mass market. Although it sold very well in Japan, where people were used to listening to music on headphones, sales in the United States were not encouraging. Sony's engineers reduced the size and cost of the machine. In 1981 the Walkman II was introduced. It was 25 percent smaller than the original version and had 50 percent fewer moving parts. Its price dropped considerably.

The Walkman opened up a huge market for tape players that nobody knew existed. It took about 2 years for Sony's Japanese competitors, including Matsushita, Toshiba, and Aiwa, to bring out portable personal stereos. Sony kept ahead of the competition by constant innovation: Dolby noise-reduction circuits were added in 1982, and a rechargeable battery feature was introduced in 1985. The machine grew smaller and smaller until it was hardly bigger than the audio cassette it played.

The Walkman became one of the most successful audio products of the postwar period; as with the Victrola before it, any personal portable cassette player was called a Walkman, irrespective of manufacturer. Sony's hunch was right; Americans did buy them in the millions, and the Walkman became one of those products that everybody owned, like a television, radio, or VCR. In the 10 years after the introduction of the Walkman, Sony sold 50 million units, including 25 million in the United States. Its competitors sold millions more. They were manufactured all over the Far East and came in a broad range of sizes and prices, with the cheapest model selling for around $20. By the 1990s the market for personal stereos in the United States was around 20 million to 30 million units a year.[18]

Those doubters who had asked what possible use there was for a personal tape recorder were silenced by the variety of uses that only a Walkman could provide. Waterproofed Walkmen were marketed to customers who wanted musical accompaniment to water sports. There were special models for tennis players and runners. Whether sitting in a crowded subway car or jogging through a park, one could still enjoy high-fidelity recorded sound in stereo.

Although a tribute to the semiconductor and the ingenuity of Japanese engineering, the Walkman is significant not in the way it works but in what it represents. It is the final step in the process that began about a hundred years before its introduction when the pioneers of recorded sound began to reduce the size and cost of their machines.

It is the ultimate expression of portability. It is the symbol of the ubiquitous nature of recorded sound; Americans are now able to go anywhere or do anything with the accompaniment of music from the cassette tape. It established a closer association with the listener, a one-on-one relationship between people and their machines that changed the way that we hear recorded sound.

The Walkman has even had a noticeable effect on the way that people listen to music. The sound from the headphones of a portable player is more intimate and immediate than the sound coming from the loudspeaker of the home stereo; the listener can hear a wider range of frequencies and more of the lower amplitudes of music, while the reverberation caused by sound bouncing off walls is reduced. Personal stereos also enable the listener to experience more of the volume of recorded sound because it is injected directly into the ear. The listening public has become accustomed to the Walkman sound and expect it to be duplicated on commercial recordings. Recording studios that once mixed the balance of their master recordings to suit the reproduction characteristics of car or transistor radios now mix them for Walkman headphones.

The Walkman is not only the symbol for the modern blessing of recorded sound; it also constitutes the antidote for its curse: one very important function of the portable personal stereo is that it acts to drown out the oppression of noise in our society. Putting on the soft plastic earphones and playing a tape instantly cuts out the background noise of modern life – a necessity in a world full of amplified noise.

The universal popularity of the Walkman ensured that the tape cassette would become the dominant form of sound recording in the last quarter of the twentieth century. The compact cassette changed the way that people used their talking machines, and this is its significance in the history of recorded sound. The 78-rpm shellac disc was the product which best represented the power of the empires of sound. It was a play-only technology, a consumer product which brought entertainment and prestige to its purchasers but gave them no power to alter it in any way. Microgroove discs were a technological step forward but still remained play-only. The compact cassette gave control back to consumers by allowing them to record their own music on it.

The ease of recording on cassettes caused a giant headache for the empires of sound because home taping became part of the experience of enjoying recorded sound. Recording onto a cassette involved learning a new set of skills – timing the recording, editing it, and adjusting the recording level – which soon supplanted the old craft of playing a revolving disc. Combined radio/phonograph/cassette units made it possible to record customized tapes from radio programming or prerecorded music on disc. Every collection of records and tapes soon contained personalized recordings on cassettes. Although sales of prerecorded discs and tapes continued to rise, the industry saw home taping as a threat greater than any competing technology. By the 1980s the RIAA and its members claimed that piracy of its products was costing them billions of dollars of revenue each year.[19]

The cassette tape also had a dramatic effect in other countries, where it changed listening habits and brought out new forms of music. In underdeveloped countries like India, the ease of recording and duplicating cassettes allowed small companies to enter the industry and break up the hegemony of popular music on disc. The compact cassette enriched the regional music of India by destroying the monopoly of the large record companies, the subsidiaries of the empires of sound, and enabling new voices to be heard. Mass duplication of cassettes and widespread piracy of recorded-sound products restructured the Indian entertainment industry and brought significant changes to popular music.

In his book on this transformation, Peter Manuel coined the phrase "cassette culture" to describe the economic and social consequences of the new form of tape recording, and to show how it helped create new musical forms in India.[20] The cassette culture is a very real part of life in the United States, especially for urban youth, and it has brought forth one of the most important new musical styles of the twentieth century. Rap is now on record and compact disc, but it could have begun only on cassette tape. Its vitality and aggression was left intact because of the accessibility of the recording system. The convenient cassette tape that spread the rap sound from city to city in the United States has now made it a global music, heard in Europe, Africa, the Far East, and South America.

PART THREE
THE DIGITAL ERA

16. The media conglomerates

The company that developed the tape cassette was a multinational electrical manufacturer. The Philips corporation of Holland began by manufacturing Edison's incandescent bulbs and became one of the largest electronics concerns in Europe. It made a variety of electrical equipment including televisions, radios, tape recorders, and home stereos. It developed elements of the cassette technology with the Theo Staar engineering concern of Belgium and worked closely with large Japanese electrical manufacturers such as Sony and Matsushita in designing cassette players. Philips also owned the PolyGram record group, which provided software for its players.

Philips was a large, diversified group of companies, a *conglomerate*, with interests in both the machines and the music they played. With their varied interests in numerous lines of business, and their strong commitment to research and development, the media conglomerates were ideally positioned to exploit new trends in entertainment and technology.

The merger movement which created media conglomerates began in the 1960s and in many ways reflected the consolidations of the 1930s, when large corporations bought out smaller companies. Instead of depression, profit was the cause of the takeover trend of the 1960s. The total record sales of $6 million in 1960 doubled to $1.2 billion by the end of the decade, making the record business a highly profitable undertaking.[1]

This dramatic increase in sales was basically the result of a change in format for popular records. The 45-rpm single had always been the format for rock'n'roll, but the Beatles changed this with LPs such as "Sgt. Pepper." This was a landmark recording not only because it made rock more acceptable to adults; it moved rock from the 45- to 33-rpm format. The baby boomers were growing up, and the concept album or "rock opera" replaced the 45-rpm single in their record collections. At $4.98 a unit, compared with the 98¢ single, the popular-music LP was the foundation of the huge volume of sales in the late 1960s and 1970s – the maturing baby boom audience was purchasing LPs instead of singles. Album rock also provided the programming for FM radio stations which sought out the important 25–35 age group.

The major companies took the lion's share of the popular music market of the 1960s; by 1967 Columbia (renamed CBS Records), RCA, and Capitol dominated the U.S. record business with a market share of 12 to 13 percent each.[2] Yet the independent companies were again the leaders in introducing new music. Many were formed by the artists themselves, such as A&M records (Herb Alpert) and Reprise (Frank Sinatra), or by song writers like Jerry Lieber and Mike Stoller, who formed Red Bird Records in 1964. Labels which had begun as independent companies with a narrow audience, such as Atlantic or Elektra, moved into the mainstream of popular music. Elektra began as a folk label but successfully became a force in recording progressive rock.

The most successful independent record company of the 1960s was Tamla/Motown Records, a black-owned company which profited from a growing white audience for African American *soul* music. It was founded by the entrepreneur Berry Gordy in Detroit, and the "Detroit sound" was an appropriate name because Gordy successfully devised a system to mass-produce hit singles. He carefully aimed his records at the youth audience and mixed his singles to suit the limited sound of car radios – where he knew the kids would hear it first. Berry decided to promote female singers first because they were less threatening to his white customers. He groomed several very successful groups – the Supremes, the Temptations, and the Miracles – and had the highest hit-to-release ratio of any American record company.[3]

In addition to hundreds of independent record companies, there were also hundreds of independent studios. The Beatles and other powerful rock groups had helped move recording away from corporate control by creating their own studios. Only the manufacture and distribution of their records was carried out by the record company. George Martin began another trend by leaving EMI and setting himself up as a free-lance record producer. He built his own recording studio and rented it to performers. The old studio system that had dominated popular music from the 1930s to the 1950s was now truly over; sound recording became a technical service that was hired out by the hour.

The elements that made a successful recording could be assembled from many different pieces in several different places. A performer could record parts of his or her song in independent recording studios all over the country. He or she could hire independent record producers to manage the sessions and mix the tracks. Separate mastering laboratories put the final tracks onto duplicating matrices or tapes. Although there were some technological considerations, such as the quality of the equipment and editing capabilities, the main factor in choosing a studio or a producer was the sound that they achieved.

The big studios in New York might have the most advanced equipment and the most experienced producers, but that does not guarantee a hit record. In the 1960s the record producer Jerry Wexler left New York and found gold in Memphis and Muscle Shoals. A partner in Atlantic Records, Wexler got bored with recording in New York and tried his luck first in the Stax recording studio in Memphis and then at the Fame and Muscle Shoals Sound Studios in Alabama. Here he made recordings of Wilson Pickett, Otis Redding, and Aretha Franklin, which helped define the sound of soul music. What gave these regional studios a distinctive sound was not the technology but the special skills of the session men and the unique ambience of the place where the recording was done.[4]

Wexler produced a series of hits for Atlantic and made recording in the Deep South fashionable. He also made Atlantic more profitable and a more desirable asset for a larger corporation. The leading independent companies, with a track record of identifying new talent, were prime targets for takeovers. Warner Records took over Reprise in 1963, Atlantic in 1967, and Elektra in 1968. Warner followed the strategy of acquiring promising young record labels and was soon to challenge CBS records as the largest record company in the United States. Although the record business in the 1960s appeared to be a profusion of many independent companies, this was only an illusion. Behind the mass of labels and exotic company names were a small number of integrated entertainment corporations.

The huge American market attracted several foreign companies in the 1960s in a reprise of the European encroachment of the 1920s. EMI enlarged its American operation by taking full control of Capitol. Its leading competitor in Europe was the giant PolyGram concern, which was formed in 1962 by two European electrical manufacturers. Together the recording subsidiaries of Philips and the great German company Siemens had an impressive presence in classical music (with the Deutsche Grammophon label) but made only small inroads in popular music with the Polydor label. They purchased Mercury Records to get a footing in the United States and then formed the Spring label to market new music there. In the 1970s the renamed PolyGram group bought out several American labels, including MGM and Verve, and took over the United Artists record-distribution system.

Not all the predators stalking independent labels were other record companies. The well-publicized profits of the entertainment business with its blockbuster hits in records, films, and television attracted several buyers at a time when merger and acquisition was seen as an easy way to increase assets. Conglomerates took over any profitable business which might enhance the value of their stock. By virtue of their products, film and recording studios were high-profile, glamorous businesses, which made them attractive takeover targets.

Conglomerates began their acquisitions in the 1960s when a small film producer, Seven Arts, took control of Warner Bros. films and records in 1966. Transamerica Corporation bought United Artists in 1967, and Gulf and Western (an energy company with interests in publishing) acquired Paramount pictures. GRT, a manufacturer of magnetic tape, took over Chess in 1968. By 1967 the old Warner Bros. logo was adorning the offices of a new corporate owner; it was now part of the Kinney corporation, which was involved in property development, funeral parlors, and car rentals. The entertainment part of this conglomerate was renamed Warner Communications. Its four record companies (Warner Bros., Atlantic, Elektra, and Nonesuch) coexisted with film and television companies, publishing divisions, toy manufacturers, cosmetic companies, and a soccer team.

A typical media conglomerate was MCA. Formed as a booking agency for dance bands in the 1920s, it built a strong base in television in the 1950s. It then acquired Decca records, Universal Pictures, and a publishing house. In the 1960s it distributed records, films, television programs, and print media. MCA's link with Universal Pictures was used to get its recording stars onto popular television shows such as "Miami Vice," which was filmed at Universal Studios.[5]

The power of these large organizations was in the promotion and distribution of the product, which was especially important in the record business. Although several independent distribution networks had been created in the 1950s and 1960s, the national systems were still in the hands of the majors, who had the resources to promote their records all over the world. At the end of the 1960s, CBS, Warner Bros., RCA, Capitol-EMI, PolyGram, and MCA dominated the industry of recorded sound. Each had a group of subsidiary labels under its control and usually a music publishing arm. These organizations had the same resources and reach as the empires of sound, but operated within a much larger context of business interests.

They coopted the music, the recording techniques, and even the rebellious stance of the independent companies. In the 1960s the revival of folk music and the wave of protest songs which accompanied the civil strife over the war in Vietnam made popular music the bastion of the counterculture. An advertisement in *Rolling Stone* magazine reminded its audience in 1967: "You know rock and roll is more than just music; it is the energy center of the new culture and youth revolution." Behind the earnest and undoubtedly sincere young folk singers (who relied more on the justness of their cause than showmanship to get their message across) stood the media conglomerates. The leading poet of the counterculture, Bob Dylan, recorded for CBS records, the giant company that claimed in 1967: "The Man can't bust our music. . . . Know who your friends are. And look and see and touch and be together."[6]

The Man had no interest in suppressing rebellious music when it could be so easily annexed and exploited for profit. Every type of new music was sooner or later wrested from the control of the independent companies who had first recorded it. It was then integrated into the entertainment products of larger business organizations in a cycle that had changed little from the early years of the twentieth century.

The punk movement marked a resurgence of the independent record company, which had always fostered new styles in music. Small companies were founded in clothes stores or dormitory rooms in London and New York. There was a profusion of new labels, such as Bell, Chiswick, and Rough Trade. Studios were created in rooms in pubs or over record shops. Records were made hurriedly in only a few hours and cost from $50 to $100 dollars to record. They were distributed to local record stores from the trunks of automobiles. The essence of punk was a revolt against both the sound and the system of popular music. The punk record companies thought of themselves as subversives. Their abrupt ascent returned the music business to the halcyon days of the postwar independents and duplicated the prehistory of rock'n'roll in the 1970s.

Punk, like rock before it, was sooner or later coopted by the major labels, and its rebellion curbed as the sound was assimilated into popular music. With the example of rock'n'roll before them, record companies were desperate not to be left behind in any new music. They struggled to acquire punk acts, often with disastrous results. Malcolm McLaren, the creator of the Sex Pistols, convinced EMI that punk music was an invigorating stimulus to the music business and predicted that the Sex Pistols would "inspire a whole new wave of new bands." Once signed to EMI, McLaren's protégés indulged in offensive behavior which enhanced their image but horrified large segments of the population. Thoroughly embarrassed by the antics of the Sex Pistols, EMI effectively bought out their contract – the price of entering the punk scene was too much for them.[7]

Yet McLaren had been right. The Sex Pistols were followed by less outrageous imitators who did sell records as punk gave way to new wave or underground rock. When the smoke lifted after the punk assault, the music business had been injected with a new set of values which might have outraged many listeners but increased interest in recorded music. As the first major stylistic change in popular music after rock'n'roll, punk can be interpreted as a postmodern movement not only in music, which constituted only one part of its appeal, but also in its call to action. As a self-conscious attempt to produce violent change in all things, punk easily assumed the mantle of the counterculture of the 1970s.

This mantle was taken up by rap in the 1980s; once it had demonstrated an appeal to large groups of American youth, its takeover by the industry of recorded sound was inevitable. Rap record labels such as Def Jam were the smallest and most underfinanced independent companies in the history of the industry. Yet they cornered the market for the new sound and made millions of dollars. Rappers found themselves stars as the proud boasts of their rhymes came true. There were soon rap films and rap videos on MTV. Yet as rap and hip-hop recordings began to sell, the major companies started to sign up promising young stars and buy out independent rap labels. Def Jam, which had been established in a dormitory room at New York

University, joined with CBS records in distributing rap songs. The music of urban angst and black rebellion was soon on the record labels of the media conglomerates.

Predictably, rap stars became less threatening to the white audience as rap crossed over into popular music. They also became more photogenic as the music acquired a visual image. M.C. Hammer was a typical product; he had an impressive dance step to accompany his million-selling hit "U Can't Touch This" and several commercial sponsorships to advance his career and promote his image. "U Can't Touch This" was the kind of song which cried out for radio play and which could easily be incorporated into an advertising jingle.

It was also predictable that white artists would appropriate the newest form of black music and make it more palatable for the mass audience of white teenagers. An album produced by the Beastie Boys, the first white rappers, sold 4 million copies in 1987. Vanilla Ice, a pale imitation of the authentic rapper, achieved the first Number 1 with a rap single, and his LP vied with Hammer's "Please Hammer Don't Hurt 'Em" for the top spot in the *Billboard* album chart in 1990.

Much the same process of commercialization had occurred in punk music. After the Sex Pistols' highly publicized and unavoidable self-destruction, punk teetered on the edge of popular music before crossing over in the 1980s. Soon punk (in the guise of new wave or grunge music) had its MTV videos, its superstars, and its commercial sponsors. The post-punk world of the 1990s was a confusing diversity of different sounds and business strategies which encompassed various declensions of new wave, industrial, and house (dance) music. Punk had entered the world of entertainment but in doing so had lost its reason to exist.

The media conglomerates and technological change

In the 1970s and 1980s, the media conglomerates grew even bigger. They brought the channels of record distribution under their control and made independent distribution a thing of the past. The shortage of vinyl caused by the oil crisis of the mid-1970s gave them the excuse to cease custom pressing of the masters of independent companies. Instead of physically taking over an independent, they made arrangements to invest in its operations and handle the distribution of its records. The same process occurred in the film industry. The postwar years marked the rebirth of the independent film-producing company, but the major film studios still controlled promotion and distribution of their films.

After investing in an independent and managing the distribution of its records, it was a not a big step to take over all its assets. This was the route that MCA took in its gradual takeover of Motown. MCA finally bought out the company in 1988. Warner Communications made a deal with the record producer Neil Bogart to establish Casablanca records in 1973, a so-called independent company which relied heavily on Warner for capital, promotion, and distribution.

This was a wise investment for Warner because Bogart played a leading part in fomenting the disco craze. Although it is remembered primarily as dance music, disco was also a visual phenomenon. The two top-selling disco albums, each selling about 30 million copies, both came from the wildly successful film musicals "Saturday Night Fever" and "Grease." Bogart was astute enough to link his recording stars with film producers and merged Casablanca records with a film company in 1976 to form Casablanca Record and FilmWorks. His goal was to use records and films to promote his leading lady Donna Summer.[8]

Disco was a profitable venture. In 1977 Casablanca enjoyed gross revenues of $55 million. Warner had become alarmed at Bogart's financial irresponsibility and had broken its ties with Casablanca, but other media conglomerates were more than ready to move in. In 1977 PolyGram secured half of Casablanca records with a large investment. The year before, it had acquired half-ownership of RSO, which issued the sound track albums of "Saturday Night Fever" and "Grease." In 1978 it was the first record company to reach $1 billion in sales.[9] By the end of the decade, Polygram had exploited the disco craze to join CBS, Capitol-EMI, Warner Communications, and MCA in dominating the record business in the United States.

In 1977 Warner Communications proudly announced that its business "reflects a marriage of culture and technology unprecedented in history."[10] The next 10 years were to prove this statement true, at least in the arena of recorded sound. The Warner organization had a record of exploiting opportunities created by new technology. In 1980 it branched out into the new field of computer games. Its Atari game division became one of the most profitable parts of its entertainment empire, more than making up for the losses in record sales as the disco craze declined.

The important entertainment technologies of the 1980s were both linked to television: video cassette recording and cable communications. The idea of using magnetic tape recording to save television images was an old one – the first commercially successful video tape recorder was introduced by the Ampex company in 1956. Unlike audio recording, video recording remained in television studios and did not break into the home market. When it did, it was in the form of the cassette. The video tape cassette had all the advantages of its audio brother, including the creation of an inviolate standard. The VHS video cassette recorder proved to be the most popular consumer durable since the television set.

At this time most Americans watched television broadcast by the networks via a local station, but by the end of the 1980s, cable had completely outstripped broadcast television, and the networks had seen their share of the audience drop from 85 percent in 1979 to 65 percent in 1988. Warner quickly moved into cable and satellite television, joining with American Express to acquire half-ownership in the country's second largest cable television operation.[11]

While broadcast television was restricted to a small number of choices, cable could bring twenty or thirty channels into the home. Now television programs could be profitably directed at a much more narrowly defined audience. Cable enabled television to seek out special markets in the same way that the breakup of the networks freed radio to cater to the tastes of new audiences in the 1950s. Although this technology provided many options for new types of television programs, little was done to create appropriate visual entertainment.

The Music Television cable channel (MTV) was introduced in 1981 with the intention of bringing rock music to viewers from 12 to 34 – the latter, baby boomers who were now in adulthood and at the peak of their consumer spending. A result of the collaboration of two mighty corporations, Time-Warner Inc. and American Express, MTV was one of the first attempts to provide innovative programming for cable television.

Television in the 1980s proved to be a much more potent promoter of popular music than either radio or motion pictures. By the end of the 1980s, MTV's audience of over 40 million affluent young adults had become the most sought after group of record buyers in the country. A rock music video had become essential for the national promotion of a recording, providing an alternative to FM and AM radio. A video placed on "heavy rotation" on MTV ensured its exposure 3 to 5 times a day, 7 days a week for up to 2 months. By 1990 the MTV music video could reach up to 56 million homes – a number exceeding the audience for the Ed Sullivan show or "American Bandstand" in the golden age of television. Although it could not be said that cable television could make any record a best-seller, it showed time and time again that it did have the power to make the right song an overnight hit.

MTV spawned a new group of image-conscious performers – Michael Jackson, Madonna, and Paula Abdul – whose outfits and choreography were at least equal in importance to their music. Instead of a mimed performance on network television, the rock video presented a complete performance constructed and edited on video tape. Pop stars no longer had to imitate their performance by miming to their songs on network television. The rock music video was produced with all the craft and artistic care of a full-length motion picture. Audiences at concerts, who had once expected a live rendition of a recording, now wanted to see a performance which mirrored the TV video.

Where once the image augmented the music, the music now served the image. Rock'n'roll stars in the 1960s benefitted from the promotion of their images in films and on television, but they usually required a modicum of performing talent to get to the top. On the other hand the 1980s were understandably full of scandals in which popular (and highly photogenic) performers were forced to admit that they did not play on their recordings. Even the live performance had to be accompanied by familiar visual images, and large television screens became standard equipment at the great arena concerts, providing fans with a simultaneous television version of the show.

The music video began as a promotional tool but soon became an entertainment product in its own right. As the video tape recorder became a popular consumer product, viewers purchased more prerecorded tapes because they wanted their own copies of the music videos they watched on television. The media conglomerates soon added video music cassettes to their line of businesses.

The importance of the music video in promoting a record brought more attention to its creation. Some of the major record companies expended as much money and energy on the video as they did on making the recording. The expenses of making a music video reached epic proportions: first tens of thousands of dollars and then hundreds of thousands of dollars. Some of Michael Jackson's elaborate videos cost half a million dollars to make.

The costs of succeeding in the popular music field might have been high in the 1980s, but the rewards were even higher. Michael Jackson's "Thriller" album, released by the Columbia subsidiary Epic records in 1982, ultimately sold close to 40 million copies worldwide and became the most successful product in the history of recorded sound. Propelled by dramatic, high-gloss music videos, the album produced seven best-selling singles. "Thriller" dominated the *Billboard* charts in 1983 and 1984, earning $60 million in profits for CBS records.

Only the media conglomerates had the resources to market their products internationally in both sight and sound; they created megastars, megagroups, megatours, and megaprofits. The great star of popular music in the 1980s was more a corporate spokesperson with a global audience than a rebellious youth with dangerous attitudes.

The supremacy of the music video was not welcomed by the smaller independent companies, because they did not have the resources to make them. In the 1980s the rich got richer, and the poor got poorer – this was especially true in the record industry. The decade of the 1980s was also a period of mergers and acquisitions, which were fueled by easy money and lax regulation. There were attempts to produce even larger conglomerates, such as the plans to merge EMI and Paramount in 1979 and Warner and PolyGram in 1983. The use of high-yield "junk bonds" to finance leveraged buyouts of companies encouraged ambitious empire building. The cable television magnate Ted Turner tried to use this financial device to take over CBS but failed. In 1985 General Electric bought out RCA Corporation, the parent company of RCA records and the NBC television network. In order to finance the purchase, it sold RCA records and its subsidiaries to the Bertelsmann Music Group (BMG) of West Germany, an international entertainment conglomerate with a base in publishing and television.

The amalgamation of RCA and Bertelsmann meant that three of the six major record organizations in the United States were part of international media conglomerates based in Europe. ABC, Warner, CBS, RCA, EMI, and PolyGram dominated the record business. In 1974 they accounted for 81 percent of the year's 100 best-selling LPs. London-based EMI owned Capitol Records, Columbia and Colgems Music, and United Artists Records in the United States. It also ran record, music publishing, television, and musical-equipment companies worldwide. The Dutch-owned PolyGram group included the Polydor, Mercury, Smash, MGM, and Verve labels. It also owned Chappel Music, one of the largest music publishers in the United States. EMI and PolyGram were the first to exceed $1 billion per year in record and entertainment sales.[12]

The pattern of creation of new companies and their consolidation into larger concerns remained the same from the 1920s to the 1980s. The independents came and went as each new wave of popular music at first sustained them and then ebbed and left them prey to the major companies. Technological innovation had largely worked against them, because it was normally initiated by the majors, with their links to the manufacturing side of the business, and it raised the stakes of doing business in the world of recorded sound. This was especially true of the union of sound and image achieved by video tape and cable television in the 1980s. This created a new environment for promoting recordings which initially favored the large companies, especially those with interests in film and television. In the 1980s the media conglomerates dominated what had become a global entertainment industry.

The Big Three revisited

The Big Three companies, which dominated the industry of recorded sound during the first 30 years of the twentieth century, had all begun as equipment manufacturers who had moved into recording music. The empires of sound and the media conglomerates were highly diversified organizations with interests in many different types of manufacturing and entertainment services. The introduction of new sound recording technology in the 1980s once again made the manufacturing companies a force in the industry, with European and Japanese companies taking the lead.

Digital recording gave Japanese electrical manufacturers a powerful position in the international entertainment business. Companies like

Sony, Matsushita, Aiwa, and Denon had exploited opportunities provided by the new audio technologies, such as transistors and magnetic tape recording, to establish themselves in the industry of recorded sound. Their factories produced the majority of the audio equipment sold in the United States. They were a mighty force in manufacturing: their stereo equipment and magnetic tape dominated both the high and low ends of the market.

Several of the largest companies had become true multinational operations by setting up manufacturing facilities in overseas markets. Sony, for example, built a factory in San Diego to make electronic equipment and one in Alabama to produce audio tape. Japanese manufacturers bought out their American competitors and took over their factories. They acquired companies that made audio equipment for the mass market, such as Emerson, and smaller concerns that served the high-fidelity market, including the prestigious Fisher company. In most cases the Japanese increased the productivity of the American plants by reorganizing them and instituting Japanese management practices.[13]

The Japanese kept out of the artistic side of the business and concentrated on manufacture. Yet the advantages of moving into the production of music and films to be recorded and played back on their equipment was clear. Sony realized the importance of producing the programming after its failure to stay in the video tape market. Although it was the pioneer in video cassette recorders, Sony was beaten by its great rival Matsushita in establishing the video recording standard. The Sony Betamax was a superior technology but lost out to the more widely accepted VHS video cassette. By the end of the 1970s, the Betamax format was dying out because few commercial tapes were made in it. Sony got few returns on the great investment it had made in video tape recording and learned an important lesson – things might have been different if the company had access to films to put onto its tape. As part of its strategy of pioneering audio technology, Sony began tentative steps to acquaint itself with the creative process. It made an agreement with CBS records to co-produce recordings for the Japanese market in 1967. CBS had the expertise in record production and marketing which Sony coveted.

Some of the leading electronic manufacturers joined with record and film companies in introducing new technologies. Philips already had its own record labels, but it wisely made an agreement with

MCA, who had film and television studios, to jointly introduce its laservision system of video discs.[14] The English electrical manufacturer Thorn acquired EMI in 1979 and went from an engineering concern to an international entertainment conglomerate.

In 1988 the Sony Corporation took the plunge and purchased CBS Records for $2 billion, the largest Japanese acquisition of an American company up to that time. As a leading producer of compact discs, Sony now had the manufacturing and artistic resources to provide the music for its digital recordings. Sony also had a large stake in video technology; it was working on a high-definition television system and several video cassette projects and had ambitions to apply its wealth of visual technology to the big screen of the movies. After swallowing up Columbia Records, it began looking for a film studio. At first it courted the MCA entertainment conglomerate, but rebuffed by MCA's chairman Lew R. Wasserman, Sony turned to Columbia Pictures.

The purchase of Columbia Pictures Entertainment (CPE) in September 1989 was one part of a business strategy to make Sony Corporation of Japan a multi-media entertainment empire. The Sony Software Corporation was created in 1991 to oversee the record business (now renamed Sony Music Entertainment), CPE, Digital Audio Disc Corporation (the manufacturer of compact discs), Sony Electronic Publishing, and the SVS video distribution operation. The other branch of Sony USA was the Sony Corporation of America, which produced electronic equipment, video and audio tape, semiconductors, and in-flight entertainment.

The American public did not interpret the event as a logical business strategy but as a glaring reminder of the power and ambition of Japanese companies. A survey by *Newsweek* magazine that was published in October 1989 found that 43 percent of those surveyed felt the acquisition was "a bad thing" for the United States.[15] In fact, this was not the first Japanese incursion into American business: Sony and numerous other Japanese companies had been purchasing American companies for decades. Several had set up their own plants in the United States in the 1970s and 1980s, yet none of these moves generated the criticism that followed Sony's purchase of Columbia.

The furor over the sale of Columbia had hardly settled down before Sony's greatest rival made its move. Matsushita paid $6.6 billion for MCA in 1990. This was a much bigger takeover than Sony's buyout of Columbia Pictures. Matsushita acquired Universal Pictures, Universal Television, MCA Home Video, MCA Records, a large number of film theaters, and numerous other holdings. Matsushita was now the largest entertainment conglomerate in the world. Its Panasonic brand is very popular in the United States, as are the high-quality video and audio products made by its subsidiary JVC.

Sony, Matsushita, and Philips are the modern equivalent of the Big Three: their base is in the mass production of hardware, their business superiority is a result of their commitment to research and development, and their operations are international. Their acquisition of film studios, talent agencies, music publishers, and record companies in the 1980s and 1990s parallels the artistic domination of the Big Three who signed up all the leading classical and vaudeville talent in the early years of the twentieth century. The modern Big Three have considerable technical expertise and business interests outside the audio field, and it is unlikely that any new, competing technology will catch them off guard in the way that radio destroyed the dominance of the talking machine in the 1920s. These companies played an important part in the development of digital technology, and they owe much of their current economic power to its successful commercial introduction.

17. Into the digital era

In 1977, when the audio industry was celebrating the 100th anniversary of Edison's invention of the phonograph, a research project in Japan had already established the technology of the next hundred years of recorded sound. While the mature technology of analogue recording was being honored, an entirely new system of saving sound had been successfully developed in the laboratory. Digital recording brought improvements in reproduction which surpassed the advances of electric over acoustic technology. Digital recording brought about a whole new era in the history of recorded sound.

Digital transformation of sound was first attempted in the laboratories of the telephone companies in their never-ending quest to get more messages on their wires. Like the acoustic and electrical eras that preceded it, the digital era of sound recording was an application of technology devised to send telephone messages of electric speech. Turning the sounds of speech into numbers meant that more words could be crammed into a single cable and that the problem of crosstalk between messages was minimized. The binary codes of digital speech could also be easily transmitted.

The first method of electrical communication was in fact digital: Samuel Morse's method of opening and closing electrical circuits sent numbers (dots or dashes) rather than measurable physical quantities. It was Bell's invention of the telephone that established analogue communication and saving of sound; his device turned the varying pressure of sound waves on a diaphragm into currents of electricity which varied in direct relationship to the changes in pressure.

Analogue technology served the communications and recorded-sound industry well, but in the 1930s researchers in telephone laboratories began to examine digital methods of transmitting sound. Their experiments were based on pulse-coded modulation (PCM) of a continuous signal. This technique was based on the concept that a continuous signal could be reconstructed from isolated samples and

346

that these samples could be approximated by discreet numbers. PCM was first outlined in a patent obtained by P. M. Raincy of Western Electric in 1926 and elaborated by A. H. Jeeves, another telephone engineer, in 1937. During World War II research laboratories examined PCM as a way to send signals in code. After the war Bell Labs constructed an experimental multichannel communication system. In 1962 the first PCM transmission system went into operation on the Bell system.[1]

Pulse-coded modulation of audio signals into digital code achieved standards of reproduction which exceeded even the best analogue system: an enormous dynamic range of sounds with no distortion or background noise. The PCM processor turns audio signals into a series of pulses which correspond to the voltages produced by a transducer like a microphone. The processor does not continuously transform sound but samples it by analysing thousands of minute slices of it per second.

Experimenters at Sony, Matsushita, and Mitsubishi in Japan produced experimental PCM processors which could be used in digital recording systems. The three Japanese companies had developed their own processors, which sampled at different rates, and each company had different methods for manipulating the output of their PCM processors. One common approach was to store the information on a plastic disc and use a laser reader to play it back.[2]

PCM technology was essentially a product of the astounding advance of semiconductors after the introduction of the transistor. The first transistors were based on one piece of semiconducting material and could carry out only one function. In 1959 the integrated circuit was invented in which hundreds of transistors were embedded in the semiconductor. The bulky vacuum tube amplifier, which was the heart of the home stereo, was replaced by a thin piece of semiconductor inlayed with numerous circuits. The integrated circuit was the beginning of solid-state technology, in which more and more transistors, capacitors, and resistors were crowded onto a slice of semiconductor. One chip could contain thousands of microscopic transistors.

The quantum leap forward in the power and efficiency of electronic switching, control, and amplification was the bedrock on which several important new technologies were built, including the home computer. Without integrated circuits the millions of electronic transactions required in computing would have overloaded transistorized electronic processors, but the microchip could perform these tasks with ease. As the capabilities of these microprocessors increased, their size and price decreased, which brought their astounding electronic powers within the reach of the average consumer. In the 1980s the first home computers appeared, and microchips began their takeover of a thousand and one applications in everyday life, from running an automobile engine to controlling a coffee maker.

The microprocessor also opened up many new possibilities in saving and reproducing data, including data which represented sound. The PCM required integrated circuits to change audio signals into digital code. Sony's PCM-F1, one of the first analogue-to-digital conversion processors, was the brain of the new system of digital recording.

Edison's phonograph mechanically copied the wave form of sound into the soft wax groove of the cylinder. The Western Electric electrical recorder converted sound into varying voltages of electric current. This signal could be converted back into a wave form in a record groove, or it could be stored on magnetic tape in which varying areas of magnetism represented the varying electric current. Digital recording turned the sound wave into a pulsating electric current that is measured and expressed as a binary code of digits.

Binary codes are basically groups of on–off electric pulses usually represented by 1s or 0s. Complex numbers can be represented by groups of 1s and 0s: a 3-bit code has three 1s or 0s, a 5-bit code has 5 of them, and so on. These codes are used by computers to handle information. The development of more complex and longer binary codes was a consequence of the rapid growth of the computer business in the 1960s and 1970s. The 16-bit binary code now used in digital recording can measure up to 65,000 levels of voltage and consequently can make up extremely accurate samples of the varying current. The electric current coming from the microphone is sampled more than 40,000 times a second to make up the binary code.

Once the complexity of sound has been reduced to a stream of numbers, there remains the problem of storing them. The laboratories of the computer companies had solved this problem with devices which saved binary code magnetically. The computer takes the 1s and 0s and stores them as areas of high or low magnetism on floppy discs or on hard discs in basically the same way that sound is stored on magnetic tape. Any kind of information can be reduced to binary code and stored magnetically, from the letters of the alphabet to the images and sounds of a musical event.

Several companies in Europe, Japan, and the United States began experimenting with digital sound in the 1970s. Using PCM techniques to turn sound into digital code, they recorded this information on tape – not magnetic audio tape but the more advanced video tape which could handle much more information. Experiments with digital recording occurred simultaneously with the accelerated development of video recording technology and owed a lot to the enhanced capabilities of video recorders. At this time video cassette recorders were being developed in several corporate laboratories in Japan and Europe. In 1972 the Nippon Columbia Company began to make its master recordings digitally on an Ampex video recording machine. Sony was one of the companies developing video recorders at this time, and its U-matic machines were successfully used to record digitally.[3]

There were powerful links between the new sound recording systems and the emerging technologies of storing and retrieving video images. Television had proved to be the most widely used and profitable electronic product of the 1950s, but the market for color television was saturated by the end of the 1960s, and manufacturers had to look for a replacement. A machine to save and replay television images was seen as the ideal companion to the family TV set. The great consumer electronics companies – GE and RCA in the United States, Philips and Telefunken in Europe, and Sony and Matsushita in Japan – began experimental programs to find a way to save video images.[4]

Japanese domination of the cassette tape format was established in the 1970s. Their manufacturing experience led them to concentrate on magnetic tape as the basis of the video recorder. The introduction of the microgroove record in 1948 had shown that the revolving disc still had great potential as a means of storing information, even the great amount of information required to save television images. So, in the United States, RCA and GE mounted large experimental projects based on the disc.

Recording at even higher densities of information promised to take the stylus and disc format to its highest level of technical development, because the former was made more sensitive and the latter was crowded with even more analogue signals.[5] The vinyl recording medium of the disc was replaced with more sensitive thermoplastics, in which sound was etched upon them in patterns of varying density or electrical capacitance. The recording stylus was replaced by an electron beam, which encoded information on the plastic. The playback stylus was a laser beam which bounced light off the surface of the disc.

RCA's experimental teams developed an optical videodisc system called Selectavision, which used an electronic stylus to read changes in capacitance on the disc. The greatest challenge to them came from Philips, whose optical videodisc used a laser beam to read information from a revolving disc in which a layer of reflective metal contained coded information. With the aid of the engineering department of Deutsche Grammophon, Philips had an experimental laser disc in hand by 1964.[6]

The laser was another important innovation which came out of the research efforts of World War II, emerging as a product of research on radar and associated electromagnetic waves. Radar made a vital contribution to the allied victory in this conflict. The forced development of this technology had started scientists along the path of exploring the extremes of the electromagnetic spectrum to find new sources of radar beams. Laser beams were highly concentrated streams of light. Once they were focused they provided a powerful and surgically precise beam of energy, which could be used in many different tasks – the first of which was highly accurate range finding.[7] As the beam travelled in a perfectly straight line, it could "read" differences in the distance it travelled. Here was a substitute for the clumsy sapphire stylus which scratched and scraped as it ran down the groove of the vinyl disc.

The Philips "Laservision" videodisc was not initially a commercial success, but it carried forward a very important idea. The research and engineering work carried out in the laboratories at Eindhoven proved that the laser reader could do the job. More importantly, Philips engineers had found that this very fragile device could be mass-produced as a cheap and reliable component of a commercial product.

The laser optical decoder was applied to reading the binary codes of digital sound, and by the end of the 1970s, Philips engineers had produced a working system. The binary code was represented as minute pits on the underside of a revolving disc, in which 0s were the pits and 1s were the unpitted surfaces of the disc. The laser beam moved across the disc from the center to the edge, and each pit reflected back the light in a different way. The microgroove record had magically saved sound in a few thousandths of an inch of vinyl groove, but the laser operated at distances measured in billionths of a meter – the nanoscale. The laser beam reflected back from the disc was turned into an electric current by a light-sensitive photodiode.

It can be seen that many elements in the history of recorded-sound technology were appropriated in the development of digital recording. Sound on film provided the foundation for the conversion of light into electricity. Magnetic recording was the basis of saving the binary code of digital sound. The disc format remained at the heart of several methods of encoding sound and image information and then retrieving it for playback.

Ten years of experimental work on the Laservision system proved to be a valuable investment for the Philips corporation. Around 1979 it started to work on a digital audio disc (DAD) playback system. This involved more than the basic idea of converting information about the varying electric current of the sound wave onto a disc. The spiral line of pits on the compact disc carries a great deal of information: the left- and right-hand tracks of the stereo system are identified, and a sequence of pits also controls the motor speed and corrects errors in the laser reading of the binary codes.

This research was carried out jointly with the Sony Corporation of Japan, which had produced a superior method of encoding digital sound. The binary codes which carried the information were manipulated in Sony's 16-bit system. Their PCM chip for analogue to digital conversion was also employed. Together Philips and Sony produced a commercial digital playback record, which they named the *compact disc* (CD). The name is significant: it does more than describe the size of the disc; it indicates its family ties with the widely used compact cassette. Philips and Sony had already worked to establish this standard in the magnetic tape format and were aiming to make their compact disc the standard for digital-sound reproduction.

Philips began to demonstrate their compact disc system to representatives of the audio industry in 1981. As in stereo sound there was more than one way to achieve the goal and more than one system available. The Japanese Victor Company, a subsidiary of Matsushita, had developed its version of digital recording from their VHD videodisc design. It was called the audio high density disc (AHD). Instead of the small CD, the AHD system used a 10-inch vinyl disc.[8] Each digital recording system used a different PCM chip, which had a different rate of sampling the audio signal.

The problem of standardization was again of vital importance in commercial introduction of the new method of sound recording. The total failure of quadraphonic sound in the 1970s had provided a harsh lesson to those in the industry who had forgotten the problems with the "battle of the speeds" in the introduction of microgroove discs.

Quadraphonic sound was a successful technology only as far as it could reproduce four channels of sound and provide double the effect of stereo. Many thought it was the next step in the inexorable advance of audio technology, but there were several versions of quadraphonic systems available. CBS in the United States produced one, and there were two Japanese versions – one from Sansui and one from JVC. Politics proved more powerful than technology in deciding which system was going to be adopted.[9] It proved impossible to decide on a quadraphonic standard. Although the technology itself worked, there were too many competing systems of four-track sound, and none of them were compatible – the listener had to stick with one system for both the playing machine and its records. The prospective buyer was faced with a difficult choice in choosing a quadrophonic system.

Once the machine was acquired, the choice of suitable recordings was limited. Only a small number of dedicated audiophiles bought quadraphonic machines and records, and the much heralded technology died a slow, public death. Suitably chastened, stereo manufacturers and record companies were unwilling to repeat this fiasco with digital sound.

Standardization of the Philips/Sony CD system was therefore a major victory for these companies and an important event in the digital era of sound recording. Sony was to discover that the technical performance of an innovation is irrelevant when compared with the politics of turning it into an industry-wide standard. Its failure to make its Betamax cassette the standard for video tape recording was more political than technological.[10]

Recorded sound in the digital era

The commercial introduction of the compact disc in 1982 heralded the beginning of a new sound technology. Instead of the stylus travelling along the groove, a laser beam reads off binary code from a mirror-like surface. The only element surviving from the electrical era was that the recording was still on a disc, and it still rotated. The compact disc was standardized at 12 cm (about 4¾ inches) in diameter, and it revolves at 200 to 500 rpm. But in all other respects, it was a completely new technology.

The compact disc represented the apex of recorded-sound technology. Simply put, here at last was a system of recording in which there was no extraneous noise: no surface noise of scratches and pops, no tape hiss, and no background hum. The compact disc has a signal-to-noise ratio of 96 db, which in effect makes it noiseless recording. Audiophiles might have been aghast that music was now sampled rather than being recorded, but the results of the digital system were so astounding that it was difficult to find fault with it.

The almost clinical reproduction of the CD took some getting used to. Its range of frequency response matched that of the human ear, and it reproduced both highs and lows so exactly that it brought new meaning to many old recordings. It was uncommonly clean sound, so pure that it initially battered eardrums used to the comforting hiss of tape and the blurred, partly obscured highs of vinyl discs.

In addition to perfect reproduction of sound, the compact disc could also play much longer than the microgroove record or long-playing cassette tape. Up to 75 minutes of sound can be stored on a compact disc, far exceeding the length of playing time of any other system. The innovation of the microgroove long-player record paled in comparison. The CD player gave the user the ability to choose selections at random, and the rapid introduction of infrared remote-control devices made it possible to operate a talking machine without leaving the comfort of the armchair. Digital technology had reached the pinnacle of user friendliness.

But the most important, and the most desirable, achievement of digital recording was that it finally realized the dream of a nondestructive system of reproduction. Unlike the vinyl record and magnetic tape, a CD plays without deterioration. Each time the user plays a disc or tape, a slight amount of damage is done to the recording

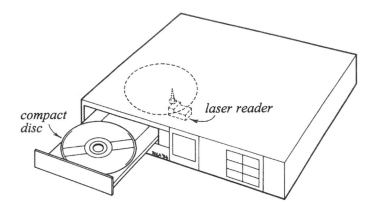

compact disc

laser reader

A compact disc player

medium. In contrast digital recording will not suffer degradation over time. In principle it will last forever, and each playback will sound as pure as the first. The compact disc represented the culmination of a long search to find a system of sound reproduction in which the recording medium was not in some way altered, scratched, or stretched as it played and replayed.

Digital technology, for all its wonders, did not immediately produce any new sounds or any new music. It did nothing to change the direction of popular music, which still reflected the megalomania of the 1970s. The Japanese and European incursions into American show business reinforced the status of the musical superstar. Although these multinationals proved to be innovative in devising electronic hardware, they were conservative in developing new talent, preferring to make long-term contracts with high-profile stars such as Michael Jackson and Madonna despite the great expense and their fading reputations.

Digital equipment simply did a better job of recording, although this was hotly contested by some record producers and music lovers. Digital sound, it was said, was cold and impersonal. It was inhuman. It carried the same mechanical-music stigma that many rock enthusiasts applied to the use of synthesizers. Some claimed that they could hear a warmer, rounder, and more pleasing sound from the old vinyl

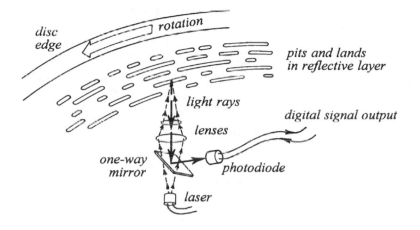

disc edge

rotation

pits and lands in reflective layer

light rays

digital signal output

lenses

one-way mirror

photodiode

laser

Digital reproduction

discs and continued to buy them, despite the fact that album shelves in record stores shrank as more and more space was taken up by compact discs.[11]

When the first CDs were introduced in 1982, the microgroove record was still the leading form of recorded sound, with 273 million LPs sold compared with 125 million pre-recorded cassette tapes. The ratio of LP to cassette sales was shifting in favor of the latter; in 1981 the sales had been 308 million LPs to 100 million cassettes. The compact disc sold slowly, achieving sales of 50 million units in 1986. By that time the cassette tape had taken the lead with just under 350 million units sold, and the LP was in decline with only around 110 million units sold. Compact discs first outsold vinyl records in 1988. In the 10 years from 1978 to 1988, the sales of vinyl records dropped nearly 80 percent. In 1989 CDs accounted for over 200 million sales, but cassettes still led the field with total sales of 450 million.[12]

The LP began to disappear from record stores at the end of the 1980s, but it did not die out. In 1991 there were still about 60 million phonograph turntables in American homes, and 4.5 million new ones were sold in 1990. At that time there were about 90 million turntables in use compared with 20 million CD players. Worried manufacturers pleaded with record retailers to ask themselves the question: "Do I really believe consumers will stop playing records . . . and throw their turntables away?"[13] The turntables were not being thrown away, but a more relevant question would have asked if they were still being used very much.

Digital recorders for studio use were introduced by the 3M corporation in the United States and by Sony in Japan. They were capable of recording up to 32 tracks. Editing with digital tape cannot be done with scissors; consequently special digital editors had to be devised. Sony acquired the MCI Company of the United States, a leading manufacturer of multitrack mixing consoles, as part of its efforts to devise a digital sound mixer. Several digital consoles are now on the market. They have the advantage of manipulating the signal while it is in digital form, and there is no conversion to analogue (except for studio monitoring functions) until the sound gets to the consumer's CD player.[14]

Turning sound into a string of numbers provides an opportunity to manipulate the data just like a computer can manipulate the binary code of a document typed into its memory. Instead of cutting and gluing tape together, the digital editor changes the binary codes. It is possible to make hundreds of edits in a few seconds of digital sound. This capability makes it possible to cover up defects in a recording. A gap in the sound caused by a faulty microphone cable, for example, can be reconstructed by a computer. Scratches can be edited out and the gap filled in.

An American company called Sonic Solutions is the leader in re-processing old analog recordings by digitally editing out scratches and pops. It uses a system that provides a graphic representation of the sound in which the scratch stands out. The scratch is removed, and the program restores the gap by synthesizing the missing sound. Using techniques like this, many jazz classics of the 1930s have been digitally re-recorded to higher standards than those possible with the old 78-rpm master records.[15]

The digital system was not immediately adopted in recording studios, because the improvement in sound quality did not justify its great expense. Many recording managers were prepared to forgo the slightly better signal-to-noise ratio and stay with Ampex 1/2-inch, multi-track tape, which was considered by many to be almost as good as digital recording.[16] Although digital recording became standard in studios in the early 1990s, most popular recordings were still made on multi-track tape recorders. The reels of master recordings were changed into digital sound in the digital mastering studio.

Digital technology made an impact in the area of synthesizing sounds. The first Kurzweil digital synthesizer was commercially available in 1983. Ray Kurzweil was an inventive genius who started by designing computers which could read for the blind and moved into re-creating sound electronically. He acquired the services of Robert Moog, and together they produced synthesizers that could mimic any sound so perfectly that it was hard to distinguish between the original and the electronic substitute. Kurzweil successfully staged the same kind of sound comparison tests which had proved the superiority of the Edison Diamond Disc years before.

The Kurzweil was a unique machine, a device so complex and expensive that only a few musicians could afford it. Yet the Japanese manufacturers took the basic idea and developed simpler and more economical models, as they had done for radios, record and tape players, televisions, and video cassette recorders. The Yamaha DX7 digital synthesizer was introduced in 1983. Although it cost $2,000, it could do everything that a much larger and elaborate Bell Labs experimental synthesizer could do, and it did not need a mainframe computer to do it. The price of the digital synthesizer dropped sharply during the 1980s; by the end of the decade, a Yamaha synthesizer sold for $200.[17] Digital synthesizers and drum machines were soon cheap enough for the smallest home studio.

The agreement which led to standardization of digital signals, the musical instrument digital interface (MIDI), made it possible to use a wide range of different equipment to produce digital sounds because they all communicated in the same way. With this standard interface it was possible to fill the recording studio with synthesizers and do away with musical instruments altogether. The computer was the critical interface between the recording engineer and the banks of synthesizers. The MIDI sequencer became a word processor for music.

The transfer from analogue-to-digital technology in the studio established the computer as a vital part of recording. It managed the complex manipulation of mixing tracks. The physical activity of cutting a groove into a master recording was replaced by the electronic manipulation of digital signals. The complex arrangement of faders and dials on the mixing console could be remembered and re-created

Figure 17.1. The modern digital recording studio, with 72 inputs and a computerized mixing board. (Courtesy Joanne Nathan, Unique Recording Studios, New York)

by a computer, and each version of a mix could be recalled. With computers doing all the work, mixing became automated and foolproof – at least when it came to saving the mix. The latest digital mixing consoles come complete with their own computers and the "total recall" of the computer's magnetic memory.

Sampling recorded sound

Digital recording technology was based on sampling, and the commercial introduction of digital samplers made this technique more accessible to musicians. Samplers take pre-recorded inputs (in analogue or digital format) and edit and reconstitute them. Sampling as a creative act had been formalized by punk and rap performers who had drawn heavily on older musical styles for their inspiration, not the insipid sounds of the 1970s but rock'n'roll of the 1950s and soul of the 1960s. Much of the punk repertoire was based on new versions of old rock'n'roll standards, from the Clash's remake of Bobby Ful-

Figure 17.2. The new wave gets nostalgic for the music of the 1950s and 1960s. (Author)

ler's "I Fought the Law" (first recorded in 1966), to the Flying Lizards' homage to the Beatles' "Money," which in turn was a cover of a song written by Berry Gordy and released on his Tamla label in 1960.

This nostalgia for the good old days of rock'n'roll was part of punk's effort to identify with a truly original youth music which had not sold out to commercial interests. They embraced several musical styles outside the boundaries of pop, especially reggae from the West Indies. This was an indigenous interpretation of the rock music broadcast from the United States with several important additions, including an emphasis on the backbeat and the practice of talking, or "toasting," over the playing of records. The influx of West Indian immigrants into the United Kingdom brought reggae to the ears of many English musicians, and the process of learning from records achieved another fortuitous mixing of musical styles. Reggae was a communal music, the sound of the streets and the shantytowns, and punk groups wanted to make their music reflect their community in the same way.[18]

In the United States disc jockeys from the Caribbean had introduced the practice of manipulating the playback controls of sound systems to alter the sound of recordings and had played a very important part in the creation of rap. They called this practice *dubbing*, a term which meant something different to American sound engineers. These two concepts of dubbing were to come together in rap music as young rappers mastered the techniques of editing recordings and added sampling to their armoury of sounds. A *dub* was the name for both the sound and the piece of the recording which was edited into it.

Sampling was a technological solution to the time-consuming problem of assimulating new musical ideas. It made a world of music easily accessible. Young musicians scoured their record collections to find the raw material for their digital samplers. The hip-hop disc jockeys and the rappers had their own sacred texts on vinyl: James Brown and other soul pioneers of the 1960s, and several funk bands from the 1970s. Parliament Funkadelic, an influential assembly of funk musicians led by the mercurial George Clinton, provided material that was used in over 400 rap songs.[19]

But where the punks, and the rock singers who preceded them, had been inspired by old records and had tended to merely reinterpret them in their music, the rappers took the more direct expedient of taking a small part of a previously issued record and incorporating it into their songs. Sampling had been developed by disc jockeys who used snatches of recordings in their mixes. Rappers employed the editing capabilities of tape to make music out of the parts of other songs. A disc jockey who called himself Grandmaster Flash was one of the first to use sampling on a hip-hop record. "The Adventures of Grandmaster Flash on the Wheels of Steel," issued on Sugar Hill Records in 1981, acknowledged the inputs of Chic, Blondie, Queen, and the Sugar Hill Gang.[20]

Sampling made an aural collage of pre-recorded music. It paralleled the visual collages of the futurist movement of the early twentieth century, in which letters and images were cut out from many sources and brought together. Although the punks avoided such complicated assembling in the recording studio, they did use collage in their promotional material. There was no limit to the type of music which was integrated into rap. The musical resources of the rappers ranged from James Brown, whose 1965 "I Got You" was the basis of a rap song by Eric B. and Rakim's called "I Feel Soul," to white heavy-metal bands such as Aerosmith, whose "Walk This Way" was covered by Run-D.M.C. Rap drew heavily on previous recorded sound both for its inspiration and the texture of its music.

Sampling took advantage of digital technology to take apart and reassemble pre-recorded music to give it new meaning. Sampling was the musical equivalent of the postmodern movement in literature, which attempted to deconstruct the old texts and uncover new truths. Popular music in the twentieth century had always sought inspiration in previously recorded sounds, but in the 1980s "pop plundered its archives with a truly postmodern relish, in an orgy of pastiche."[21]

Sampling made its way into the pop mainstream with groups such as Frankie Goes to Hollywood and M/A/R/R/S, who used snatches, or bytes, of sound from many sources in their recordings. M/A/R/R/S's hit single "Pump Up the Volume" of 1989 used parts of about thirty other recordings. It was accompanied by a video which appropriated visual images from an equally large number of sources.

Sampling in the digital era was not confined to pre-recorded sound. Digital technology turned all sound and images into binary code and could be used to access an unlimited library of previously released entertainment. Several of the survivors of the punk movement adopted sampling, not just from old records but from film sound tracks and television commercials. Big Audio Dynamite, the successor to the Clash, used snatches of sound from records, films, and television in their songs. In a song entitled "Stalag 123," which dramatized work in the recording studio, they employed the theme music and parts of the sound track from "The Great Escape" (a World War II movie about an escape from a German prison camp) to emphasize the drudgery of making a record:

> I'm fixing on a jail break/but the door is open wide
> "cooler!" [shouts the German commandant from "The Great
>   Escape"]
> I've got the studio blues/and some other bad news (*chorus*)
> Day dreams of the great escape/of music on the run
> "There will be no escape from this camp!"
> Do an Albert R.N./and go straight to Number 1.

Television had provided a powerful precedent for sampling in its fast cutting from image to image and its ravenous appetite for different images which were constantly introduced into new assemblages. The generation reared on television had the visual acuity to tolerate extremely fast shifts from one visual idea to another and the short attention span which made this process both possible and necessary. The introduction of new technology, especially cable television with its myriad choices and the infrared remote control, encouraged a visual grazing of a multitude of television images. Although the glitter and pageantry of heavy metal and dance music was suited to the image-heavy rock of MTV, it was rap music which best reflected the technological environment created by television. The fast shifts in lyrics and rhythmic discontinuity of rap music are aural equivalents of browsing through cable television channels with the speed of a remote control.[22] Sampling was based on the technology of editing recordings. The techniques developed in the film studios of the 1930s to present seamless constructions of perfect sound had been taken in another direction to produce discontinuous juxtapositions of bits of recorded sound. It was a fresh new sound which truly represented the heritage of modern recording technology.

If the sound of the new wave of punk and rap came from the machine, its voice came from previously recorded information, a vast archive of sounds on disc and tape. The new composers envisaged by Glenn Gould did not have to be classical musicians working in a high-tech studio; they could just as easily be teenagers composing and recording in their dorm rooms. Inexpensive digital synthesizers, samplers, and recorders – combined with computer software that integrates all elements of the home studio – brought the most advanced sound recording techniques within the reach of the home user. The advance of digital technology and its union with the computer put even larger sound archives at the disposal of the modern musician.

Competing technologies

The evolution of digital recording from play-only disc to recordable tape occurred very quickly. Digital magnetic tape for the home consumer was not long in coming, because that technology was already available for commercial recording systems. Digital audio tape (DAT) was introduced by Sony in the United States in 1990. It employed the cassette format to record digitally with the differences of smaller-sized cassettes and almost perfect reproduction of sound.

Despite these advantages DAT did not make much of an impression on the market. The players were expensive, from $800 to $1,700, and the digital cassette was not compatible with any other tape player. The first pre-recorded DATs were limited in number and, like CDs, the music on them tended to be classical or jazz – the better to illustrate the amazing frequency response and quietness of the medium. The inexpensive compact cassette retained its dominant position as the format for popular music. At the end of the 1980s, many Americans had just made the transition from vinyl to digital compact disc and were wary of further change.[23]

A powerful opponent of the DAT format was the RIAA and the record companies which it represented. Piracy of copyrighted recordings had been a major issue in the industry since the widespread use of compact cassettes had made copying pre-recorded tapes and discs an easy matter. The record companies were fearful that DAT users would copy their CDs and therefore deny them millions of dollars of revenue. The matter was important enough to be brought before the United States Congress, where the industry of recorded sound argued its case and the Home Recording Rights Coalition countered with its appeal for freedom of taping. Congress finally agreed to a royalty on blank digital tapes to repay the companies, song writers, and performers for losses resulting from bootlegging their products. The DAT manufacturers also agreed to install a "copy lock" on the tapes to prevent them from being used as sources for more digital recordings: this prevents the home taper from using them to make copies of copies.

The major issue in DAT technology was not the problem of piracy or the matter of cost, which was expected to drop as more machines were made, but in the ever-present question of what digital tape format was to become the standard.

In the early 1990s Philips introduced a digital compact cassette (DCC), which had the great advantage of being compatible with their magnetic audio cassette. The DCC was the same size as the ubiquitous cassette, and the new players had the ability to play both formats. Philips worked with the Matsushita Company to develop a small playing unit (under the brand name Panasonic) which was put on the market at $500.[24] Philips also introduced a more expensive home model which could record digitally.

Sony had failed to reach agreement with Philips over the format of digital recording technology. They responded to the challenge of DCC by introducing the mini disc (MD), which combined the reproduction quality of a CD with the ease of recording of an audio cassette. The MD is 2½ inches in diameter and as thin as a computer floppy disc. Unlike the audio DAT and DCC, its tracks can be accessed very quickly. It has a special feature which prevents the reader from skipping tracks when it is bumped or moved around – a drawback of the digital Walkman machines – and which gives Sony the means to claim full portability. The MD player is smaller than the average Walkman, and an even smaller playback model can easily fit into a shirt pocket.[25]

With three competing digital formats on the market besides the CD, the prospective buyer is confronted with some difficult choices, because the DAT, DCC, and MD are not compatible. If the consumer makes the wrong choice, he or she is stuck with an obsolete technical system and a dwindling number of pre-recorded units to choose from.

Historically the decisive factor in winning the struggle of formats will not be technology. Commercial supremacy will hinge on the amount (and type) of pre-recorded music available in each format. DAT's commercial introduction had been hindered by the reluctance of record companies to release their product in this format for fear of piracy. Sony has energetically made arrangements for 500 albums to be released on MDs and has relentlessly promoted this product as a replacement for the audio cassette Walkman. Introducing digital technologies in both recorded sound and visual products requires the resources of both high-tech manufacturers and the producers of films and music. It took many years to achieve mass acceptance of tape cassettes and to persuade record companies to issue their product on them, and it is unlikely that we shall see a victor in the digital tape war during the last years of the twentieth century.

Any purveyors of digital equipment must be able to span a broad range of entertainment businesses, because digital transformation brings a better and closer union of sound and image than any other technology. The sound on film developed in the 1930s pales in comparison with the power and flexibility of the digital system, which turns both sound and image into the same binary codes and can play back the picture and the music from the same source.

The future of digital technology, and the talking machine, will be found in integrated entertainment systems which combine video, audio, text, animation, and an interactive component which will allow the user to take part. Philips began to sell its compact disc interactive (CD-I) technology in 1990 to industrial users and then marketed it as an entertainment system for all consumers. It is based on a CD-ROM (read only memory) technology, which reads and stores information in the same way as a compact disc. One of the advantages of CD-ROM technology is its enhanced storage capacity: an average floppy disc contains about 1.5 million characters of information, while CDs can hold over 650 million characters – well over 250,000 pages of text. This technology is also a boon to the samplers, because it can store thousands of pieces of sound. Philips CD-I systems can play audio discs and movies and show the viewer hundreds of software publications, from computer games to illustrated encyclopedias.

The new digital technologies also have the advantages of very compact size. Sony introduced the Data Discman in 1990. It is a palm-sized electronic book which can reproduce text and images on a tiny screen. It should not be too long before this kind of technology is available to the home user at a reasonable price.

Instead of the discrete and competing systems of television/VCR, stereo unit (with phonograph, tape player, and compact disc), and computer games, the home stereo of the twenty-first century will be one integrated unit that processes digital information. Instead of two or three infrared remote controls, there will be only one to cover all the images and sound of mechanical entertainment. The home computer will control the interfaces between the equipment and manage the saving and retrieval of information, both in its own memory and in the digital memories of individual machines.

Behind this equipment will be the fully integrated corporation. This organization will have the technical capability to develop digital technology in all its forms (including computers) while it will also control the artistic side of producing films, television shows, recorded-sound products, and computer software. It will be an international business most likely based in Europe or Japan, where most of the previous advances in digital technology have occurred. It will have to be a truly transnational organization, because it will serve the whole world with pre-recorded entertainment.

Abbreviations used in the notes

AHC   Eldridge R. Johnson Papers, American Heritage Center, Univ. of Wyoming, Laramie, WY

AT&T   AT&T Archives Center, Warren, NJ

CBS   Columbia Record Company archives, CBS/Sony Corporation, New York

ENHS   Edison Archives, Edison National Historic Site, West Orange, NJ

EMI   EMI Archives, Hayes, United Kingdom

ERJ   Eldridge Reeves Johnson

IJS   Institute of Jazz Studies, Newark, NJ

LOC   Recorded Sound Reference Center, Library of Congress, Washington, DC

NJSL   Special Collections, New Jersey State Library, Trenton, NJ

NSA   National Sound Archives, British Library, London, United Kingdom

TAE   Thomas Alva Edison

Notes

Introduction

1. Edward Bellamy, *Looking Backward 2000–1887* (Boston: Houghton Mifflin, 1966), p. 69.
2. *Billboard*, 6 Nov. 1982, p. wc3.
3. Barbara Elna Benson, *Music and Sound Systems in Industry* (New York: McGraw-Hill, 1945), pp. 22, 23, 32, 69; "Industrial Health Research Board," *The Voice* 24 (1940).
4. "Riveting to Rhythm," *New York Times*, 31 Aug. 1941, sec. 7, p. 17.
5. Steven Traiman, "The Record Industry in the United States," *Journal of the Audio Engineering Society* 24 (Oct. 1977): 787–788.
6. Michael Fermer in *Music Connection* (22 Aug. 1988), quoted in George Plasketes, "Romancing the Record: The Vinyl De-Evolution and the Subcultural Evolution," *Journal of Popular Culture* 26:1 (Summer 1992): 118. EMI was still pressing vinyl discs in 1993.
7. Daniel Boorstin, *The Americans: The Democratic Experience* (New York: Random House, 1973), p. 379; Thomas Edison, *North American Review* (June 1878) in ibid., p. 380.
8. Seymour M. Hersh, *The New Yorker*, 14 Dec. 1992, pp. 76–81.

1. The inventors

1. For an overview of telegraph technology, see Paul B. Israel, *From Machine Shop to Industrial Laboratory: Telegraphy and the Changing Context of American Invention* (Baltimore: Johns Hopkins University Press, 1992).
2. See Andre Millard, "Machine Shop Culture and Menlo Park," in William S. Pretzer, ed., *Working at Inventing: Thomas A. Edison and the Menlo Park Experience* (Dearborn, MI: Henry Ford Museum, 1989), pp. 48–64.
3. The background of this machine shop is given in Lillian Hoddeson, "The Emergence of Basic Research in the Bell Telephone System 1875–1915," *Technology and Culture* 22 (July 1981): 515–518.
4. Robert V. Bruce, *Bell: Alexander Graham Bell and the Conquest of Solitude* (Ithaca, NY: Cornell University Press, 1990), pp. 145–147; Catherine Mackenzie, *Alexander Graham Bell: The Man Who Contracted Space* (New York: Grosset & Dunlap, 1928), p. 94.
5. Bruce, *Bell*, p. 144.

6. This event supposedly occurred after Bell had spilled acid on his trousers (Mackenzie, *Bell*, p. 115); however, it might be myth rather than one of the great events in the history of American technology.

7. Robert Bruce, "Alexander Graham Bell," in Carroll W. Pursell, *Technology in America* (Cambridge: MIT Press, 1990), p. 108.

8. Batchelor Diary, Edison National Historic Site (ENHS), Cat. 1339, 1906, p. 59.

9. See Reese V. Jenkins et al., eds., *Thomas A. Edison Papers*, Vol. 3 (Baltimore: Johns Hopkins University Press, 1994), document numbers: 972, 973, 18–19 July 1877. See also nos.: 1004, 1013 (August); 1039–40, 1062 (September); 1099, 1101–2, 1109, 1119, 1133 (November); and 1134, 1137, 1140, 1144, 1147, 1150 (December). My thanks to Paul Israel of the Edison Papers for indicating the relevant phonograph documents in the Edison Papers.

10. Robert Conot, *A Streak of Luck* (New York: Seaview, 1979), p. 13; Batchelor Diary, 1339, p. 60.

11. Warren Rex Isom, "A Wonderful Invention But Not a Breakthrough . . . ," *Journal of the Audio Engineering Society* 24 (Oct. 1977): 657–658; Roland Gelatt, *The Fabulous Phonograph, 1877–1977* (New York: Macmillan, 1977), p. 23. In France, Charles Cros committed to paper a method of sound recording in April 1877 which was much like the one that Edison put into practice, but this was unknown to Edison in the United States.

12. Bruce, *Bell*, p. 252.

13. Edward Jay Pershey, "Drawing as a Means to Inventing: Edison and the Invention of the Phonograph," in Pretzer, *Working at Inventing*, p. 108.

14. Ibid., p. 112.

15. U.S. patent 200,521, filed 24 Dec. 1877, granted 19 Feb. 1878. Edison remembered that in the early days of the phonograph, tapes were used as the recording medium but they were "not as desirable as the cylinder," TAE annotation on L. Porter letter, 25 Feb. 1910, ENHS.

16. TAE to G. Notage, 25 March 1878, ENHS.

17. F. K. Harvey, "Mementos of Early Sound Recording," *Society of Motion Picture and Television Engineers Journal* (March 1982): 237–244. Hereafter this journal will be cited as *SMPTE Journal*.

18. Henry Edwards, "The Graphophone," *Journal of the Society of Arts* 36 (Dec. 1888): 41–45.

19. TAE to (E. H. Johnson), undated in 1888 Phonograph folder, ENHS.

20. *Scientific American* 57 (31 Dec. 1887): 422.

21. G. Gouraud, "The Phonograph," *Journal of the Society of the Arts* 36 (Nov. 1888): 23–33.

22. Allen Koenigsberg, *The Patent History of the Phonograph* (Brooklyn, NY: APM Press, 1990), xxix; Robert Brockway, "The Gramophone," *Audio* (June 1974): 28–32.

23. Mark Henry Clark, "The Magnetic Recording Industry, 1878–1960: An International Study in Business and Technological History," Phd Diss.

Delaware 1992, chap. 1, p. 3; Oberlin Smith, "Some Possible Forms of the Phonograph," *The Electrical World* 12 (8 Sept. 1888): 116.

24. Koenigsberg, *Patent History*, xxiv.

25. Poulsen demonstrated the first working magnetic recorder in 1898; his telegraphone patent was filled in 1899 and granted in 1900. Carmen F. Wilson, "Magnetic Recording, 1888–1952," *IRE Transactions on Audio* (May–June 1956): 53.

2. A phonograph in every home

1. TAE, "The Perfected Phonograph," *North American Review* 146 (June 1888): 641–650.

2. TAE to G. S. Notage, 23 Mar. 1878, ENHS.

3. O. Read and W. Welch, *From Tin Foil to Stereo: Evolution of the Phonograph* (Indianapolis: Howard Sams, 1977); "The Gramophone Company Limited Corporate History," EMI; Koenigsberg, *Patent History*, xxix.

4. Agreements in 1888 Phonograph folder, ENHS; Gelatt, *Fabulous Phonograph*, pp. 41–42.

5. *New York Journal*, 13 May 1888, ENHS; *Scientific American* 57 (29 Oct. 1887): 273.

6. A. O. Tate, *Edison's Open Door* (New York: E. P. Dutton, 1938), pp. 161–162.

7. T. C. Hepworth, "The Phonograph," *The Technical Educator* (1890): 154–156.

8. Read and Welch, *Tin Foil to Stereo*, p. 50.

9. Koenigsberg, *Patent History*, xxix.

10. TAE to S. E. Eaton, 11 Dec. 1890, ENHS.

11. Allen Koenigsberg, *Edison Cylinder Records, 1884–1912* (New York: Stellar, 1969), xxii.

12. Byron Vanderbilt, *Thomas Edison, Chemist* (Washington, DC: American Chemical Society, 1971), pp. 119–125.

13. Emile Berliner, *Three Addresses* (1914?), pamphlet of speech given to Franklin Institute 21 May 1913 in LOC.

14. Eldridge Johnson's personal recollections, as dictated to D. E. Wolff, 25 Oct. 1910, Box 11, AHC. The first motor delivered to the company was too expensive to manufacture, and it was followed by an altered model which went into production in August 1896. The reproducer was developed with Alfred Clark, and a joint patent was issued.

15. E. R. Johnson, "History of the Victor Talking Machine Company," Feb. 1913 AHC; "Sworn Statement by E. R. Johnson," June 1928, Box 8, AHC.

16. Batchelor Diary, cat. 1338, p. 51, quoting Aylsworth, 1 Sept. 1903, ENHS.

17. TAE note to Edison United Phonograph Co., 16 June 1893, ENHS.

18. Numbers from accounts sheet in 1912 phonograph folder, ENHS; Victor numbers from B. L. Aldridge, "The Victor Talking Machine Company,"

reproduced in Ted Fagan and William R. Moran, *The Encyclopedic Discography of Victor Recordings* (Westport, CT: Greenwood, 1983); Edgar Hutto, "Emile Berliner, Eldridge Johnson, and the Victor Talking Machine Company," *Journal of the Audio Engineering Society* 25 (Oct. 1977): 670; Koenigsberg, *Patent History*, xli.

19. *American Machinist* 12 (18 April 1889): 8; Tate to Lippincott, 17 Nov. 1888, LB 870621, p. 394 ENHS.

20. *American Machinist* 36 (23 May 1912): 827–828.

21. *American Machinist* 36 (7 March 1912): 361–366; (28 March): 486–491.

22. Annual Reports of the Victor Company, Box 32, AHC; Robert W. Baumbach, *Look for the Dog: An Illustrated Guide to Talking Machines* (Woodland Hills, CA: Stationary Press, 1981), pp. 59–67.

23. Alfred Chandler, "The Beginnings of Big Business in American Industry," in James P. Baughman, ed., *The History of American Management* (Englewood Cliffs, NJ: Prentice-Hall, 1969), p. 5.

24. *Edison Phonograph Monthly*, Feb. 1907, ENHS.

25. Susan Strasser, *Satisfaction Guaranteed: The Making of the American Mass Market* (New York: Pantheon, 1989), pp. 46–47, 110–113.

26. Victor Company, "De La Chappelle's Talk," 15 Jan. 1927 in ENHS. Victor spent about $4 million a year on advertising.

27. *Talking Machine World* 10 (15 Mar. 1914): 21.

28. McChesney to F. Dyer, 18 Apr. 1910, ENHS.

29. See Fred W. Gaisberg, *The Music Goes Round* (New York: Macmillan, 1942) p. 47, LOC; Caruso Artist File, EMI.

30. J. B. Steane, *The Grand Tradition: Seventy Years of Singing on Record* (New York: Scribners and Sons, 1974), pp. 41–43.

31. Enrico Caruso, Jr., *New York Times*, 13 May 1990, pp. 27–28. See also Enrico Caruso, Jr., *Enrico Caruso: My Father and My Family* (New York: Amadeus Press, 1990).

32. Joel Whitburn, *Pop Memories: The History of American Popular Music* (Menomonee Falls, WI: Record Research Inc., 1986), p. 78; Caruso Artist File, EMI.

33. A. Michaelis to W. B. Owen, 14 Nov. 1902, EMI.

34. Italian Company to Birnham, 12 May 1906, EMI; Edward Fowler, "Milestones of Recording," *Eminews* (June 1961), EMI.

35. TAE to T. Graaf, 20 Nov. 1911, LB 110628, p. 622, ENHS.

36. Craig H. Roell, *The Piano in America, 1890–1940* (Chapel Hill, University of North Carolina Press, 1989), pp. 31–32.

37. Edison Phonograph Advertisements, 1915 Document File, ENHS. Hereafter the Document File will be cited as DF.

3. The international industry of recorded sound

1. *Talking Machine World*, 17 (15 June 1921), p. 105.

2. Victor engineers' report on the Edison Diamond Disc noted its clumsy

construction but mentioned the ingenuity by which Edison had circumvented the Victrola patents. The discs themselves were "infinitely better than any other." The conclusion was that "in the hands of more progressive people" this machine could be a big threat, but under the present management of the Edison company, it was not. ERJ to Alfred Clark, 3 Feb. 1913, Box 4, Johnson Papers, AHC.

3. George L. Frow and Albert F. Self, *The Edison Cylinder Phonographs 1877–1929* (Sevenoaks, Kent: G. Frow, 1978), pp. 174–175.

4. "The Gramophone Company Corporate History," EMI; see also *The Story of Edison Bell* (London: City of London Phonograph and Gramophone Society, circa 1924), LOC.

5. Will Hayes, Personal Recollections, ENHS; W. B. Owen to ERJ Correspondence 1900–1907, Technical File, EMI.

6. Gaisberg, *Music Goes Round*, pp. 38–41; Fowler, *Milestones*, Gelatt, *Fabulous Phonograph*, p. 105.

7. Columbia Catalogue, 1915, CBS; W. Miller to Charles Edison, 22 March 1915, ENHS; Whitburn, *Pop Memories*, p. 647.

8. David Ewen, *All the Years of American Popular Music* (Englewood Cliffs, NJ: Prentice-Hall, 1977), p. 232; 1918 Annual Report of the Victor Company, Box 31, Johnson Papers, AHC.

9. *The Voice*, Sept. 1918, p. 12, EMI.

10. *Talking Machine World* 17 (15 June 1921): 105.

11. Brian Rust, *The American Record Label Book* (New York: Da Capo, 1984), pp. 117–118, 189, 220.

12. Samuel B. Charters, *The Country Blues* (New York: Rinehart, 1959), pp. 49–50.

13. *Talking Machine World* 10 (15 Oct. 1914): 20.

14. ERJ to Leon Douglas, 2 Sept. 1915, Box 7, Johnson Papers, AHC, Johnson called Aeolian "a high class act."

15. Edison archives; 1922 Victor Annual Report, Box 11, Johnson papers, AHC; C. King Woodbridge, *Dictaphone* (New York: Newcomen Society, 1952), p. 14.

16. *Talking Machine World* 20 (15 Jan. 1924): 10; W. Maxwell Report, 1911, Records of the Musical Phonograph Division, ENHS.

17. *Talking Machine World* 14 (15 Mar. 1918): 4.

18. Dane Yorke, "Rise and Fall of the Phonograph," *American Mercury* 27 (Sept. 1932): 1–12.

19. LeRoi Jones, *Blues People: Negro Music in White America* (New York: Morrow, 1988), p. 95; Giles Oakley, *The Devil's Music: A History of the Blues* (New York: Taplinger, 1977), p. 81.

20. Oakley, *Devil's Music*, p. 92; Paul Oliver, *Blues Fell This Morning: Meaning in the Blues* (London: Cambridge University Press, 1990), p. 1; August Wilson, *Ma Rainey's Black Bottom* (New York: Plume, 1985), p. 12.

21. Jones, *Blues People*, p. 129.

22. Chris Albertson, liner notes on Columbia reissue of *Bessie Smith: The*

Complete Recordings, II, p. 13, Richard Hadlock, *Jazz Masters of the 1920s* (New York: Da Capo, 1988), p. 223.

23. Calvin Child to ERJ, 13 June 1917, Box 4, Johnson Papers, AHC.
24. John Harvith and Susan Harvith, *Edison, Musicians and the Phonograph* (Westport, CT: Greenwood, 1987) pp. 13, 43–44.
25. Maxwell's Report, 1911, ENHS.

1. The music

1. Joe Batten, *Joe Batten's Book* (London: Rockliff, 1956), p. 33.
2. Edward Fowler, "Milestones in Recording," *Eminews* (May, 1961), EMI.
3. Steane, *Grand Tradition*, p. 14.
4. Fred W. Gaisberg, *Music on Record* (London: Robert Hale, 1946), p. 23.
5. Pauline Norton, "Nineteenth Century American March Music," in Jon Newsom, ed., *Perspectives on John Philip Sousa* (Washington, DC: Library of Congress, 1983), p. 49.
6. Ewen, *All the Years of American Music*, pp. 179–183.
7. Anonymous history of an Edison recording engineer, in 1895 Phonograph folder, ENHS.
8. Whitburn, *Pop Memories*, p. 232.
9. See Isaac Goldberg, *Tin Pan Alley: A Chronicle of the American Music Racket* (New York: John Day, 1930).
10. Bernt Ostendorf, "The Diluted Second Generation: German–Americans in Music," in Hartmut Keil, ed., *German Workers Culture in the United States* (Washington, DC: Smithsonian Institution Press, 1988), pp. 274–279.
11. Steane, *Grand Tradition*, p. 60: "You know well that music means ten times more to a foreigner in your town than to the American citizen," *Talking Machine World* 10 (15 July 1914): 14.
12. Strasser, *Satisfaction Guaranteed*, p. 140; Richard K. Spottswood, "Commercial Ethnic Recordings in the United States, in *Ethnic Recordings in America: A Neglected Heritage* (Washington, DC: Library of Congress, 1982), p. 55.
13. *Talking Machine World*, 9 (15 Nov. 1913), New York Talking Machine Co. catalogue. See also the six-volume, definitive study of ethnic recordings: Richard K. Spottswood, *Ethnic Music on Records: A Discography of Ethnic Records Produced in the United States, 1893–1942* (Champaign, IL: University of Illinois Press, 1990).
14. "The Ediphone," 1898, in promotional literature collection, CBS.
15. Steane, *Grand Tradition*, p. 125.
16. Maxwell's report, 1911, ENHS.
17. See Lawrence W. Levine, *Highbrow/Lowbrow: The Emergence of Cultural Hierarchy in America* (Cambridge, MA: Harvard University Press, 1991), pp. 130–144; Roell, *Piano in America*, p. 39.

18. Harvith and Harvith, *Edison, Musicians and the Phonograph*, p. 2: quote from *Talking Machine World* 10 (15 Feb. 1914): 10.
19. Dwight Blocker Bowers, *American Musical Theatre* (Washington, DC: Smithsonian Collection of Recordings, 1989), pp. 9–10.
20. Whitburn, *Pop Memories*, p. 327; *Talking Machine World* 13 (15 Jan. 1917): 47.

5. Recorded sound in the Jazz Age

1. Jones, *Blues People*, p. 100.
2. Russell Sanjek, *American Popular Music and Its Business* (New York: Oxford University Press, 1988), Vol. 2, *From 1790 to 1909*, p. 274; see Robert C. Toll, *Blacking Up: The Minstrel Show in Nineteenth Century America* (New York: Oxford University Press, 1974).
3. Columbia 1909 Catalogue, Columbia record #A745, CBS.
4. Charles Musser, *Before the Nickelodeon: Edward S. Porter and the Edison Manufacturing Company* (Berkeley: University of California Press, 1991), pp. 50, 101.
5. Peter Gammon, *Scott Joplin and the Ragtime Era* (New York: St. Martin's Press, 1975), p. 170.
6. Michael Rogin, "Blackface, White Noise: The Jewish Jazz Singer Finds His Voice," *Critical Enquiry* 17 (Spring 1992): 417–453.
7. See Thomas L. Riis, *Just Before Jazz: Black Musical Theatre in New York* (Washington, DC: Smithsonian Institution Press, 1989).
8. Mark C. Gridly, *Jazz Styles: History and Analysis* (Englewood Cliffs, NJ: Prentice-Hall, 1985), p. 57.
9. Arnold Shaw, *The Jazz Age: Popular Music in the 1920s* (New York: Oxford University Press, 1987), p. 35.
10. Alan Lomax reviews of London records "archives," *Melody Maker* 30 (Feb. 1954): 13.
11. Mezz Mezzrow in Neil Leonard, *Jazz and the White Americans* (Chicago: University of Chicago Press, 1962), pp. 61–64.
12. Richard Hadlock, *Jazz Masters of the 1920s* (New York: Da Capo, 1988), p. 223.
13. James Lincoln Collier, *Louis Armstrong, An American Genius* (New York: Oxford University Press, 1983), p. 169.
14. Wilson, *Ma Rainey*, p. 19.
15. See Leonard, *Jazz and the White Americans*, pp. 29–35; quote in Richard Maltby, *Passing Parade: A History of Popular Culture in the Twentieth Century* (New York: Oxford University Press, 1989), p. 72.
16. *Talking Machine World* 10 (15 Feb. 1914): 13.
17. F. Scott Fitzgerald, *This Side of Paradise* (New York: Scribners and Sons, 1920), p. 59.
18. Russell B. Nye, "A Word About Whiteman," in Timothy E. Scheurer,

ed., *American Popular Music: Readings from the Popular Press*, vol. 1, *The Nineteenth Century and Tin Pan Alley* (Bowling Green, OH: Bowling Green State University Popular Press, 1989), 143–149. Hereafter this press will be cited as Popular Press.

19. Shaw, *Jazz Age*, p. 47, quoting Isaac Goldberg, *Tin Pan Alley*, p. 265.
20. Gershwin quote in Leonard, *Jazz and the White Americans*, p. 86.
21. Bowers, *American Musical Theatre*, p. 109.
22. Roell, *Piano in America*, p. 33.
23. Oakley, *Devil's Music*, p. 21; Richard Waterhouse, "The Minstrel Show and Australian Culture," *Journal of Popular Culture* 24 (Winter 1990): 147–166.
24. Gaisberg, *Music on Record*, pp. 44–45; interview with Roger Thorne.
25. Orrin Layton Suthern, "Minstrelsy and Popular Culture," in Scheurer, *American Popular Music*, I, p. 81.
26. Gaisberg, *Music on Record*, p. 45.
27. *Talking Machine World* 14 (15 April 1918): 49; Paul Oliver, "Jazz Is Where You Find It: The European Experience of Jazz," in C.W.E. Bigsby, ed., *Superculture: American Popular Culture and Europe* (Bowling Green, OH: Popular Press, 1975), pp. 141–143.
28. Allen G. Debus, "Elsie Janis, The First World War and the Introduction of Jazz to England," *Popular Music and Society* 2 (Fall 1972): 334.
29. Leonard, *Jazz and the White Americans*, pp. 69–70.

6. The machines

1. F. Chrisman interview, *St. Louis Republican*, 3 July 1899, ENHS; Millard, *Business of Innovation*, p. 169.
2. *Scientific American* 57 (31 Dec. 1887): 415.
3. "The Gramophone" advertisement, circa 1900, CBS.
4. Koenigsberg, *Patent History*, xxxviii–xlii.
5. *The Official Price Guide to Music Collectables* (New York: Random House, 1986), p. 158.
6. "An Outline of Facts Pertaining to the Talking Machine Industry," typed document of the Victor Company used for advertising purposes, ENHS 1913 Phono folder.
7. Fred Gaisberg interview in B. E. G. Mittel, "Disc Recording Standards," *I. R. E. Proceedings* (Jan. 1950): 5, EMI; *Playback: The History of Recorded Sound* (London: EMI, 1977), p. 9.
8. E. C. Wente, "General Principles of Sound Recording," *Bell Laboratories Record* 7 (Nov. 1928): 82.
9. J. Aylsworth's notebook, N 880823, ENHS.
10. Eldridge Johnson's personal recollections, as dictated to D. E. Wolff, 23 Oct. 1910, Box 10, Johnson Papers, AHC.
11. "Apparently the average purchaser does not listen to the various makes

of phonographs and determines which has the superior playing qualities," W. Maxwell Report, 1911, Records of the Musical Phonograph Division, ENHS; "Discs are simpler to operate . . . no intelligence or care required in handling," Graf to F. Dyer, 14 Nov. 1910, phonograph DF ENHS.

12. Roell, *Piano in America*, pp. 40–42.
13. F. Dolbeer to Dyer, 23 Dec. 1910; J. Blackman to Dyer, 8 Dec. 1910, ENHS.
14. P. Cromlin to F. Dyer, 17 Aug. 1911, ENHS.
15. *Edison Amberola Monthly* 17 (Feb. 1919): 3, ENHS.
16. C. Edison to T. A. Edison, 1927 DF phonograph, ENHS. As early as 1911 the term *phonograph* was falling "into disrepute in some quarters," F. Dolbeer to C. H. Wilson, 1 Dec. 1911, DF phonograph, ENHS.

7. Competing technologies

1. Susan J. Douglas, *Inventing American Broadcasting, 1894–1922* (Baltimore: Johns Hopkins University Press, 1987), xv.
2. Eric Barnouw, *A Tower in Babel: A History of Broadcasting in the United States to 1935* (New York: Oxford University Press, 1966), p. 25; *New York Times*, 14 Jan. 1990, p. 30.
3. E. R. Fenimore Johnson, *His Master's Voice Was Eldridge R. Johnson* (Milford, DE: State Media, 1974), pp. 112–113.
4. C. J. Pusateri, *A History of American Business* (Arlington Heights, IL: Harlan Davidson, 1982), p. 243.
5. Gleason Archer, *A History of Radio* (New York: American Historical Society, 1938), pp. 112–113. Sarnoff thought that the ideal price for the radio would be around $75, about the same price as the first phonographs.
6. Fenimore Johnson, *His Master's Voice*, p. 112. Estimates produced by the radio industry put sales at $60 million in 1922. The figure for 1924 was $358 million (Barnouw, *A Tower in Babel*, p. 125); Hutto, "Berliner, Johnson, Victor," p. 672.
7. Sheldon Hochheiser, "AT&T and the Development of Sound Motion-Picture Technology," Mary Lea Bandy, ed., *The Dawn of Sound* (New York: Museum of Modern Art, 1989), pp. 24–25.
8. M. Fagen, ed., *A History of Engineering and Science in the Bell System* (Indianapolis: Bell Telephone Laboratories, 1975), pp. 928–933.
9. Edward C. Wente, "General Principles of Sound Recording," *Bell Laboratories Record* 7 (Nov. 1928): 83; Affidavit of Joseph P. Maxfield, Vitaphone Co. vs ERPI 1933, p. 348, AT&T; see J. P. Maxfield and H. C. Harrison, "Methods of High Quality Recording and Reproducing of Music and Speech Based on Telephone Research," *Bell Laboratories Record* 7 (Nov. 1928).
10. S. Watkins diary, (1920–1924), Box 96 06 686, AT&T.
11. Maxfield Affidavit, p. 352; Watkins diary (1923), AT&T.

12. Alfred Clark, "His Master's Voice," unpublished manuscript about his experiences working for Victor, p. 233, AHC; Gelatt, *Fabulous Phonograph*, pp. 221–222.

13. ERJ Financial folder, Box 11; Annual Reports of the Victor Company, Box 31, AHC.

14. Ivor D. Groves, *Acoustic Transducers: Benchmark Papers in Aoustics* (Stroudsburg, PA: Hutchinson Ross, 1981), p. 2.

15. *Talking Machine World* 13 (15 Jan. 1917): 30, 32.

16. *Talking Machine World* 23 (15 Jan. 1927): 29, 90.

17. *Business Week*, 11 Jan. 1930, p. 30.

18. Roell, *Piano in America*, p. 48.

19. Hugh M. Stoller affidavit, Vitaphone Co. vs ERPI, 1933, pp. 357–362, AT&T.

20. Stanley Watkins, "The First Sixty: A Sortabiography," unpublished manuscript, Box 84 10 03, p. 151, AT&T.

21. Frank Lovette and Stanley Watkins, "Twenty Years of Talking Pictures, An Anniversary," *Bell Telephone Magazine* 25 (1946): 95. See also Douglas Gomery, "The Coming of Sound: Technological Change in the American Film Industry," in Elizabeth Weis and John Belton, eds., *Film Sound: Theory and Practice* (New York: Columbia Unversity Press, 1985), pp. 5–24.

22. Sanjek, *American Music Business* 2: 47–51.

23. Jack L. Warner with Dean Jennings, *My First Hundred Years in Hollywood* (New York: Random House, 1964), pp. 168–169.

24. Hochheiser, "AT&T and the Development of Sound Motion Picture Technology," pp. 27–28.

25. John Izod, *Hollywood and the Box Office* (New York: Columbia University Press, 1988) p. 74.

26. Herbert Goldman, *Jolson: The Legend Comes to Life* (New York: Oxford University Press, 1988), pp. 80–83.

27. Warner, *First Hundred Years*, p. 177.

28. Gomery, *Coming of Sound*, p. 15.

29. John G. Frayne, "Motion Picture Sound Recording," *Journal of the Audio Engineering Society* 24 (July 1976): 512.

30. John Brooks, *The Telephone: The First Hundred Years* (New York: McGraw-Hill, 1975), pp. 180–183.

31. David Robinson, *Chaplin: His Life and Art* (New York: McGraw-Hill, 1985), p. 389.

32. Douglas Gomery, "Hollywood Converts to Sound," in Evan William Cameron, ed., *Sound and the Cinema: The Coming of Sound to American Film* (Pleasantville, NY: Readgrave, 1980), pp. 24–33.

8. Empires of sound

1. Gomery, *Hollywood Converts to Sound*, p. 27.

2. Gomery, *Coming of Sound*, pp. 22–23.

3. Rust, *Record Labels*, p. 50.
4. D. Shepard and R. Slatzer, *Bing Crosby: The Hollow Man* (New York: St. Martin's Press, 1981), p. 91.
5. Gomery, *Coming of Sound*, p. 12.
6. Shaw, *Jazz Age*, p. 215; Barnouw, *A Tower in Babel*, p. 232.
7. *Talking Machine World* 26 (15 Jan. 1920), advert.
8. *The Gramophone* 8 (June 1930): 93; 8 (Sept. 1930): 237, 245.
9. *Business Week*, 10 Aug. 1932, pp. 14–15; Gomery, *Coming of Sound*, p. 23.
10. Gelatt, *Fabulous Phonograph*, pp. 225–226.
11. TAE to M. Silverstone, 8 Apr. 1924, ENHS.
12. *Business Week*, 26 Oct. 1932, p. 13.
13. *Business Week*, 11 June 1930, p. 21; Douglas Gomery, *Movie History: A Survey* (Belmont, CA: Wadsworth, 1991), p. 168.
14. Thomas Schatz, *The Genius of the System: Hollywood Filmmaking in the Studio Era* (New York: Pantheon, 1988), p. 87.
15. Robert Sklar, *Movie Made America: A Cultural History of the Movies* (New York: Vintage, 1975), p. 162; see also Izod, *Hollywood and the Box Office*, p. 96.
16. Amy Henderson, *On the Air: Pioneers of Broadcasting* (Washington, DC: Smithsonian Institution Press, 1988), p. 274.
17. Gunther Schuller, *The Swing Era: The Development of Jazz, 1930–1945* (New York: Oxford University Press, 1989), p. 18; John Hammond and Irving Townsend, *John Hammond on Record* (New York: Summit, 1977), p. 120.
18. EMI Corporate History, EMI.
19. E. R. Lewis, *No C.I.C.* (London: Universal Royalties, 1956), pp. 12–16.
20. Welch and Read, *Tin Foil to Stereo*, p. 319.
21. Joseph Gustatis, "The Jukebox: America's Music Machine," *American History Illustrated* 24 (Nov. 1989): 44–46.
22. Sanjek, *American Music Business*, 2: 136; Bill Barol, "The Wurlitzer 1015," *American Heritage* (Sept. 1989): 28.
23. Henderson, *On the Air*, p. 22.
24. Warren J. Sussman, *Culture as History: The Transformation of American History in the Twentieth Century* (New York: Pantheon, 1984), p. 159.
25. Daniel J. Czitrom, *Media and the American Mind* (Chapel Hill: University of North Carolina Press, 1982), p. 77.
26. Lewis J. Paper, *Empire: William S. Paley and the Making of CBS* (New York: St. Martin's Press, 1987), pp. 28–29; Czitrom, *Media and the American Mind*, p. 80.
27. Barnouw, *A Tower in Babel*, p. 226.
28. Sanjek, *American Music Business* 2: 130–131.
29. *Business Week*, 18 Nov. 1939, p. 32.
30. Gelatt, *Fabulous Phonograph*, pp. 268, 274.

9. Swing and the mass audience

1. Hammond, *On Record*, pp. 165–167.
2. Shepard and Slatzer, *Bing Crosby*, pp. 165–177.
3. Whitburn, *Pop Memories*, p. 109.
4. Izod, *Hollywood and the Box Office*, p. 103.
5. Hammond, *On Record*, p. 151.
6. James Lincoln Collier, *Benny Goodman and the Swing Era* (New York: Oxford University Press, 1989), p. 166.
7. Ishmael Reed, *Mumbo Jumbo* (New York: Doubleday, 1972), introduction, p. 73.
8. Gunther Schuller, *The Swing Era*, p. 201.
9. See Michael Brooks, liner notes, *The Quintessential Billie Holiday*, Columbia; Holiday describes the recording sessions in Billie Holiday with William Duffy, *Lady Sings the Blues* (London: Penguin, 1984), pp. 59–60.
10. *Business Week*, 10 Aug. 1935, p. 24.
11. Frederick Lewis Allen, *Since Yesterday: The 1930s in America* (New York: Harper & Row, 1986), p. 270; Henderson, *On the Air*, p. 52.
12. Collier, *Goodman and the Swing Era*, p. 257.
13. *New York Times*, 8 Dec. 1940, sec. II, p. 5.
14. Schuller, *The Swing Era*, pp. 661–667, 783. A gold disc is awarded when a million dollars worth of records are sold.
15. Gelat, *Fabulous Phonograph*, p. 252; *Business Week*, 18 Nov. 1939, pp. 32, 34.
16. *New York Times*, 14 Mar. 1942, p. 10. There were a few all-female bands, such as The Sweethearts of Rhythm.
17. Christopher Sterling and John M. Kittross, *Stay Tuned: A Concise History of American Broadcasting* (Belmont, CA: Wadsworth, 1990), p. 214.
18. *New York Times*, 19 Mar. 1943, p. 5; Eric Barnouw, *The Golden Web 1933–1953* (New York: Oxford University Press, 1968), p. 160.
19. Collier, *Goodman and the Swing Era*, p. 5.

10. High fidelity at last

1. John Hilliard, "Movie Sound Reproduction," *Audio* (March 1977): 45–60.
2. Arthur Haddy, oral history, *Developments in Recorded Sound* C90/16/01, RSA.
3. Arthur C. Keller, *Reflections of a Stereo Pioneer* (San Francisco: San Francisco Press, 1986), p. 16.
4. James H. Kogen, "Record Changers, Turntables and Tone Arms – A Brief Technical History," *Journal of the Audio Engineering Society* 24 (Oct. 1977): 751.
5. Keller, *Stereo Pioneer*, p. 25; J. Frayne, A. Blaney, G. Groves, and H.

Olson, "A Short History of Motion-Picture Sound Recording in the United States," *SMPTE Journal* 85 (July 1976): 522.

6. Doreen Marshall, oral history interviews, C90/07/02, NSA.; Haddy interview, all in *Developments in Recorded Sound*, NSA.

7. Welch and Read point out that the move to all electric machines was slower in the United Kingdom (where I grew up), *Tin Foil to Stereo*, p. 353.

8. *Talking Machine World* 13 (15 Jan. 1927): 75; an estimated 200,000 portables a year were being sold; advert. in *Life*, 12 June 1939.

9. *Talking Machine World* 8 (15 April 1931): 525.

10. Keller, *Stereo Pioneer*, p. 10; George L. Frow, *The Edison Disc Phonographs and the Diamond Discs* (Tunbridge Wells, U.K.: G. L. Frow, 1982), p. 72.

11. Mark Clark, "The Magnetic Recording Industry, 1878-1960," Phd Diss., Chap. 6, pp. 91–114.

12. Thurston Clark, *Pearl Harbor Ghosts: A Journey to Hawaii* (New York: William Morrow, 1991), pp. 120–121.

13. Barnouw, *Golden Webb*, p. 199; thanks to Steven Ambrose for pointing this out.

14. *The History of Magnetic Recording*, reprinted from *Tape Recording*, (1958), p. 4.

15. Joel Toll, "The Art of Tape Recording," *Audio Engineering* (May 1950): 13.

16. John T. Mullin, "Magnetic Recording for Original Recordings," *Journal of the Audio Engineering Society* 25 (Oct 1977): 697; the patent for magnetically coated strips was obtained by Pfleumer in 1927.

17. Loren L. Ryder, "Magnetic Sound Recording in the Motion-Picture and Television Industries," *SMPTE Journal* 85 (July 1976): 528.

18. Arthur Haddy, Oral History, C90/16,01; Harvey Scwartz, Oral History, C90/08/01; Kenneth Wilkinson, Oral History, C90/21/01, all in *Developments in Recorded Sound*, NSA.

19. Ibid.: Affidavit of Joseph P. Maxfield, Vitaphone Corp. vs ERPI, Chancery Court Delaware, 1933, AT&T, p. 348.

20. Stuart Copeland, *Sound Recordings* (London: British Library, 1991), p. 26; Arthur Haddy, Oral History, C90/16,01; Harvey Scwartz, Oral History, C90/08/01, all in *Developments in Recorded Sound*, NSA.

21. Mark Clark, "The Magnetic Recording Industry, 1878–1960," Phd Diss., pp. 155–163.

22. Ibid., pp. 165–168; *Chronology of Tape Recording*, pp. 9–10; Shepard and Slatzer, *Bing Crosby*, p. 181.

23. C.A. Schicke, *Revolution in Sound: A Biography of the Recording Industry* (Boston: Little, Brown, 1974), pp. 114–115.

24. *New York Times*, 21 June 1948, p. 29.

25. Richard A. Peterson and David G. Berger, "Cycles in Symbol Production, The Case of Popular Music," in Simon Frith and Andrew Goodwin, eds.,

On Record: Rock, Pop, and the Written Word (New York: Panthcon, 1990), p. 144.

26. Philco advertisement, *Life*, 20 Dec. 1943.
27. Warren Rex Isom, "Evolution of the Disc Talking Machine," *Journal of the Audio Engineering Society* 24 (Oct. 1977): 720.
28. Fenimore Johnson, *His Master's Voice*, p. 78.
29. *Plastics Today* 41 (Dec. 1971): 2–13; Keller, *Stereo Pioneer*, p. 18–19.
30. Warren Rex Isom, "Evolution of the Disc Talking Machine," *Journal of the Audio Engineering Society* 24 (Oct. 1977): 720.
31. Peter C. Goldmark, *Maverick Inventor: My Turbulent Years at CBS* (New York: E. P. Dutton, 1973), p. 129.
32. "Philco attachment," press release, CBS; "Transcription Recordings for the Home," *Electronics* (Sept. 1948): 86–87.
33. Goldmark, *Maverick Inventor*, p. 130; Gelatt, *Fabulous Phonograph*, p. 292.
34. Goldmark obit., *New York Times*, 8 Dec. 1977; "High Fidelity on LP," Jan 1958, CBS; see also Goldmark, *Maverick Inventor*, pp. 129–147.
35. "The Design of L-P Records," *Electronics* (Dec. 1948): 110.
36. "What's All This about a 'Record War,'" Columbia flyer, "Report on Dealer & Public Reaction to Victor's 45 rpm System," report, CBS; Carl Belz, *The Story of Rock* (New York: Oxford University Press, 1969), p. 53.
37. John Tobler and Stuart Grundy, *The Record Producers* (New York: St. Martin's Press, 1982), p. 7, John Mosely, oral history, *Developments in Recorded Sound*, C90/62/01, NSA.
38. John Aldred, oral history, ibid., C90/64/01.
39. CBS Long Player Survey, Oct. 1948, CBS.
40. Welch and Read, *Tin Foil to Stereo*, p. 345.
41. *How to Make Good Recordings* (New York: Audio Devices, 1940), pp. 43–65.
42. Russell Sanjek, *American Popular Music and Its Business*, Vol. 3, *From 1900 to 1984* (New York: Oxford University Press, 1988), pp. 359–360.
43. H. Sherman, *Audio Engineering Society Journal* 1 (1953): 142–143; *Electronics* (1948): 88; "New Audio Trends," *Electronics* (Jan. 1950): 68.
44. 1953 Audio Fair in Review, *Audio Engineering* (Dec. 1953): 28; Emory Cook, "Binaural Disc Recording," *Audio Engineering Society Journal* 1 (1953): 1–3.
45. Gelatt, *Fabulous Phonograph*, p. 298.
46. Robert Long and Norman Eisenberg, "Tape Recording at Twenty-Five," *High Fidelity* (Aug. 1970): 41.
47. B. Mittel to G. E. Condlifee, 9 April 1954, EMI; "Notes on a Visit to DGG Hanover," 13–15 Aug. 1957, EMI.
48. Ralph W. Wright, "How the Westrex 45/45 System was adopted by Record Makers," *Audio* (March 1975): 24.

49. B. E. G. Mittel, "A Talk on Record Production," 9 Dec. 1947, EMI archives; Welch and Read, *Tin Foil to Stereo*, pp. 345, 381.

50. Sanjek, *American Music Business* 3: 243; William S. Bachman, "The Columbia Hot Stylus Recording Technique," *Audio Engineering* (June 1950): 11.

51. John Koss, "1969 New York High Fidelity Show," *Audio* (Oct. 1968): 26.

52. Akio Morita, E. Reingold, and M. Shimomura, *Made in Japan: Akio Morita and Sony* (New York: E. P. Dutton, 1980), pp. 14–16, 50–57.

53. R. Serge Denisoff and Richard A. Peterson, eds., *The Sounds of Social Change* (Chicago: Rand MacNally, 1972), p. 293, citing *Billboard* (1968): 13.

11. Rock'n'roll and the revolution in music

1. Richard Welch, "Rock'n'roll and Social Change," p. 32; Charlie Gillett, *Making Tracks: The Story of Atlantic Records* (London: Souvenir Press, 1988), p. 3.

2. Jan H. Rieger, "Crisis in the Youth Music Market," *Popular Music & Society* 5 (1975): 21; Hugh Mooney, "Just Before Rock, Pop Music 1950–1953 Reconsidered," *Popular Music & Society* 3 (1974): 93–94.

3. Gillett, *Making Tracks*, p. 132–133.

4. Tobler and Grundy, *Record Producers*, p. 11.

5. Peterson and Berger, "Cycles in Symbol Production," p. 143.

6. Nelson George, *The Death of Rhythm & Blues* (New York: Pantheon, 1988), pp. 26–34.

7. Charlie Gillett, *The Sound of the City: The Rise of Rock and Roll* (New York: Pantheon, 1983), p. 78; Tom McCourt, "Bright Lights, Big City: A Brief History of Rhythm and Blues, 1945–1957," in Tim Scheurer, ed., *American Popular Music*, Vol. 2, *The Age of Rock* (Bowling Green, OH: Popular Press, 1989), p. 53; Fredric Dannen, *Hit Men* (New York: Vintage, 1991), p. 40.

8. Willie Dixon with Don Snowden, *I Am the Blues: The Willie Dixon Story* (New York: Da Capo, 1989), pp. 78–80.

9. Nick Tosches, *Unsung Heroes of Rock'n'Roll* (New York: Scribner's Sons, 1984), pp. 38–41.

10. Gillett, *Making Tracks*, p. 98.

11. Donald J. Mabry, "The Rise and Fall of Ace Records: A Case Study in the Independent Record Business," *Business History Review* 64 (Autumn 1990), 419; Interview with Dick Cooper, May 1994.

12. R. Serge Denisoff, *Solid Gold: The Popular Record Industry* (New Brunswick, NJ: Transaction Books, 1975), p. 113.

13. Katherine Hamill, "The Record Business – 'Its Murder' " *Fortune* 94 (May 1961): 148–150.

14. Charlie Gillett, "The Black Market Roots of Rock," in Dennisoff and Peterson, eds., *Sounds of Social Change*, p. 279. At this time there were

no more than thirty black-owned stations. Thanks to Jenny Walker for this statistic.

15. Steve Chapple and Rebe Garofalo, *Rock'n'Roll Is Here to Pay* (Chicago: Nelson Hall, 1977), p. 8; Peter Guralnick, *Sweet Soul Music: Rhythm and Blues and the Southern Dream of Freedom* (London: Penguin, 1991), p. 26.

16. Interview with Shelley Stuart, 1990.

17. Sterling and Kittross, *Stay Tuned*, pp. 339–340.

18. Dixon, *I Am the Blues*, p. 89.

19. McCourt, "Bright Lights," p. 54.

20. Peterson and Berger, "Cycles in Symbol Production," in Simon Frith, *Sound Effects: Youth Leisure and the Politics of Rock'n'Roll* (New York: Pantheon, 1981), p. 146.

21. Chapple and Garofalo, *Rock'n'Roll Is Here to Pay*, p. 44; Hamill, "The Record Business – 'Its Murder,' " p. 151.

22. McCourt, "Bright Lights," p. 58.

23. Denisoff, *Solid Gold*, p. 117.

24. Belz, *The Story of Rock*, pp. 69–70, 101–103.

25. Dave Lang, *The Sound of Our Time* (London: Sheed and Ward, 1969), pp. 85–86.

26. Philip H. Ennis, *The Seventh Stream: The Emergence of Rocknroll in American Popular Music* (Middletown, CT: Wesleyan University Press, 1992), p. 173.

27. Graham Wood, *An A–Z of Rock and Roll* (London: Studio Vista, 1971), p. 121. See also Philip Jenkinson and Alan Warner, *Celluloid Rock: Twenty Years of Movie Rock* (New York: Warner, 1974).

28. Belz, *Story of Rock*, p. 48.

29. Gillett, *Sound of the City*, p. 168.

30. Sanjek, *American Music Business* 3: 246; Quentin J. Schultz and Roy M. Anker, *Dancing in the Dark: Youth, Popular Culture, and the Electronic Media* (Grand Rapids, MI: William Eerdmans, 1991), p. 90.

31. William J. Dowlding, *Beatlesongs* (New York: Simon & Schuster, 1989), p. 640.

32. Stuart Hall and Paddy Whannel, "The Young Audience," in Frith and Goodwin, *On Record*, pp. 34–35.

12. The record

1. Anthony Seeger and Louise S. Speer, eds., *Early Field Recordings* (Bloomington, IN: Indiana University Press, 1987), pp. 1–6.

2. Gronow, "Ethnic Recordings," p. 15; *Tampa Tribune* (Florida), 24 April 1926, ENHS.

3. John A. Lomax, *Adventures of a Ballad Hunter* (New York: Macmillan, 1947), p. 44.

4. Ibid., pp. 61–62.

5. Oakley, *Devil's Music*, p. 124; Charters, *Country Blues*, pp. 78–88.

6. Bill C. Malone, *Country Music USA* (Austin, TX: University of Texas Press, 1985), pp. 35–39, 80–84; Shaw, *Jazz Age*, pp. 135, 202. It was Peer who recorded Rodgers for Victor.

7. Gronow, "Ethnic Recordings," pp. 7–9.

8. Oliver, *Blues Fell*, p. 9.

9. Jones, *Blues People*, p. 144.

10. Evan Eisenberg, *Recording Angel: Music, Records and Culture from Aristotle to Zappa* (London: Picador, 1987), p. 116; Collier, *Goodman and the Swing Era*, pp. 18–19.

11. Hammond, *On Record*, pp. 29–30: Holiday, *Lady Sings the Blues*, pp. 10–11.

12. Leonard Feather, *From Satchmo to Miles* (New York: Stein & Day, 1972), p. 13.

13. Ira Gitler, *Swing to Bop: An Oral History of the Transition in Jazz in the 1940s* (New York: Oxford University Press, 1985), p. 33.

14. Eisenberg, *Recording Angel*, p. 121. The allusion here is to Ralph Ellison's *The Invisible Man*, in which the protagonist listens endlessly to Armstrong's recording of "(What Did I Do to Be So) Black and Blue."

15. Charters, *Country Blues*, p. 171.

16. Shepherd and Slatzer, *Bing Crosby*, p. 42.

17. Woody Herman, Smithsonian Jazz Oral History Program, p. 5, IJS; Gitler, *Swing to Bop*, p. 56; Dixon, *I Am the Blues*, p. 35.

18. Gitler, *Swing to Bop*, p. 35.

19. Gitler, *Swing to Bop*, pp. 146–147.

20. Stephen LaVere, liner notes, *Robert Johnson: The Complete Recordings* (Columbia), p. 46.

21. Dixon, *I Am the Blues*, p. 39.

22. Chapple and Garofalo, *Rock'n'Roll Is Here to Pay*, p. 41; Tosches, *Unsung Heroes*, p. 37. This is not to say that Elvis was only a copier; Simon Frith has pointed out that his genius was in his interpretation of the songs.

23. Feather, *Satchmo to Miles*, pp. 13–14; Hammond, *On Record*, pp. 88–108.

24. Ian Whitcomb, *After the Ball: Pop Music from Rag to Rock* (London: Limelight Editions, 1986), p. 166.

25. Leonard, *Jazz and the White Americans*, p. 135. Hugues Panassie, *Le Hot Jazz* (Paris, 1934 / U.S., 1936), was the book which set in motion the serious study of jazz.

26. *Melody Maker* 24 (10 Jan. 1948): 3; 24 (13 March 1948): 1; 24 (20 March 1948): 2.

27. Frith, *Sound Effects*, p. 46.

28. Dick Hebdige, *Subculture: The Meaning of Style* (London: Methuen, 1979), p. 50.

29. Tony Jasper, ed., *The Top Twenty Book: 1955–1990* (London: Blandford, 1991), p. 8; Peter Wicke, *Rock Music: Culture, Aesthetics and Sociology* (New York: Cambridge University Press, 1993), p. 57.

30. *Life* 28 June 1958, p. 85; *Melody Maker* 32 (15 Sept. 1956): 1.
31. Rev. David A. Nobel, *Rhythm, Riots and Revolution: An Analysis of the Communist Use of Music* (Tulsa, OK: Christian Crusade Publications, 1966), p. 115. The use of the disparaging term *jungle music* goes back to attacks on popular music in the first decade of the twentieth century (Walt Mason to W. McChesney, 3 Feb. 1911, ENHS).
32. *Melody Maker* 30 (2 Jan. 1954): 1.
33. Interview with Mark Lewisohn, Beatles Artist file, EMI; Wicke, *Rock Music*, p. 64.
34. Whitcomb, *After the Ball*, p. 192.
35. Dowlding, *Beatlesongs*, p. 40.
36. Hebdige, *Subculture*, p. 50.
37. Interview with Mark Lewisohn, Beatles Artist file, EMI.

13. The studio

1. Jerrold Northrop Moore, *A Voice in Time: The Gramophone of Fred Gaisberg* (London: Hamish Hamilton, 1976), pp. 23, 74; "The Reminiscences of John H. Bieling," *Talking Machine World* 10 (15 Mar. 1914): 38. Emerson ran the U.S. Phonograph Company studios.
2. Fred W. Gaisberg, *Music on Record* (London: Robert Hale, 1946), p. 12.
3. William Hayes recollections, ENHS.
4. *Talking Machine World* 9 (15 Oct. 1913): 13.
5. Rust, *Record Labels*, p. 307; Bob Gooch, oral history interview, *Developments in Recorded Sound*, C90/83/02, NSA.
6. *The Phonograph and How to Use It* (New York: National Phonograph Company, 1900), pp. 152–156, NJSL.
7. Emma Eames, 1939 broadcast, cited in J. B. Steane, *Grand Tradition*, p. 9.
8. Thomas Chalmers, *Talking Machine World* 10 (15 Mar. 1914): 51.
9. Isabella Wallich, oral history interview, *Developments in Recorded Sound*, C90/24/01, NSA; Gaisberg, *Music on Record*, p. 41.
10. George Baker recollections in *Gramophone* 8 (June 1934): 125; Frank Andrews, *Edison Phonographs: The British Connection* (London: City of London Phonograph and Gramophone Society, 1986), p. 18.
11. Roger Thorne interview, Oct. 1991; Reports of Edison Recording Committee, ENHS. This can only be a subjective, limited conclusion; many Edison Diamond Discs had very good mid- and low-end reproduction.
12. This was the view of Rachmaninoff, *The Gramophone* 9 (April 1931): 525.
13. Howard Barlow oral history, Columbia University Oral History Project, Radio Pioneers, p. 102.
14. Harry F. Olson, "A History of High-Quality Studio Microphones," *Journal of the Audio Engineering Society* 24 (Dec. 1976): 799–800.

15. Peter Copeland, *Sound Recordings* (London: British Library, 1991), p. 19.
16. *Talking Machine World* 14 (15 Mar. 1918): 29; (15 May 1918): 68.
17. Albertson, liner notes, *Bessie Smith: The Complete Recordings*, pp. 24–25.
18. Thomas Cowan oral history, Columbia University Oral History Project, Radio Pioneers, p. 22.
19. Barry Norman, *The Story of Hollywood* (New York: New American Library, 1987), p. 16.
20. Barlow, Columbia oral history, pp. 93, 102.
21. George Martin, oral history, *Developments in Recorded Sound*, C90/26/02, NSA. One famous visitor to the Abbey Road studios commented that the control room looked like part of a hospital!
22. Wilson, *Ma Rainey*, p. 18.
23. Lovette and Watkins, "Twenty Years of Talking Pictures," *Bell Telephone Magazine* 25 (1946): 94.
24. Christopher Sterling and John M. Kittross, *Stay Tuned: A Concise History of American Broadcasting*, 2nd ed. (Belmont, CA: Wadsworth, 1990), p. 107.
25. Harold Barlow, oral history, Columbia Oral History Project, Radio Pioneers, p. 80.
26. Cameron, *Sound and the Cinema*, p. 78.
27. Recollections of Nathan Levison, 11 Sept. 1937, in Box 96 03 686 04, AT&T.
28. The quote is from Louella Parsons, in Warner, *First Hundred Years*, p. 180; John Aldred, oral history, *Developments in Recorded Sound*, C90/64/01, NSA.
29. Ira Konigsberg, *The Complete Film Dictionary* (New York: New American Library, 1987), p. 213.
30. James G. Stewart, "The Evolution of Cinematic Sound: A Personal Report," in Cameron, *Sound and the Cinema*, p. 43.
31. Barry Salt, *Film Style and Technology: History and Analysis* (London: Starword, 1983), p. 280.
32. Harry F. Olson, "Microphones for Recording," *Journal of the Audio Engineering Society* 25 (Nov. 1977): 678–679.
33. Ralph Stephenson and J. R. Debrix, *The Cinema as Art* (London: Penguin, 1970), p. 180.
34. Anthony Slide, *The American Film Industry: A Historical Dictionary* (New York: Greenwood Press, 1986), p. 97.
35. Salt, *Film Sound and Technology*, p. 281.
36. Hochheiser, "AT&T and the Development of Sound Motion-Picture Technology," p. 53.
37. Ken Morgan recollections; Western Electric announcement, Jan. 1913, Box 84-10-03, folder 06, AT&T.
38. Frayne et al., "Short History of Motion Picture Sound Recording," p. 523.

39. Stewart, *Evolution of Cinematic Sound*, p. 48.
40. John K. Hilliard, "Movie Sound Reproduction," *Audio* (Mar. 1977): 52.
41. Paul S. Carpenter, *Music as an Art and a Business* (Norman: University of Oklahoma Press, 1950), pp. 45–46; Hilliard, "Movie Sound Reproduction," p. 54.
42. Hilliard, "Movie Sound Reproduction," p. 52.
43. Mary Ann Doane, "Ideology and the Practice of Sound Editing and Mixing," in Weis and Belton, *Film Sound*, pp. 54–61.
44. James G. Stewart, "The Evolution of Cinematic Sound: A Personal Report," in Cameron, *Sound and the Cinema*, p. 48.
45. Noel Carroll, "Lang and Pabst: Paradigms for Early Sound Practice," in Weis and Belton, *Film Sound*, p. 266.
46. Hilliard, "Movie Sound Reproduction," p. 54.
47. J. P. Maxfield, "Techniques for Recording Control for Sound Pictures" *Academy Technical Digest* (1929), in Box 84-10-03, AT&T.
48. Evan William Cameron, "Citizen Kane: The Influence of Radio Drama on Cinematic Design," in Cameron, *Sound and the Cinema*, pp. 206–213; Robert L. Carringer, *The Making of Citizen Kane* (Berkeley: University of California Press, 1985), pp. 101–105.
49. *New York Times*, 19 Mar. 1940, p. 30; 10 Apr. 1940, p. 27.
50. Frayne et al., "Short History of Motion Picture Sound Recording," p. 524.
51. John Culhane, *Walt Disney's Fantasia* (New York: Abradale Press, 1983), pp. 19, 38.

14. Perfecting studio recording

1. Frayne et al., "Short History of Motion-Picture Sound Recording," p. 517.
2. Copeland, *Sound Recordings*, p. 22.
3. John Culhane, *Walt Disney's Fantasia*, p. 20.
4. Brian Southall, *Abbey Road* (Wellingborough, U.K.: Patrick Stevens, 1982), p. 20.
5. Christopher Parker, oral history interviews, *Developments in Recorded Sound*, C90/28/01, NSA.
6. Eisenberg, *Recording Angel*, p. 124.
7. Martin Pulling, oral history interviews, *Developments in Recorded Sound*, C90/61/01, NSA.
8. Mary Alice Shaughnessy, *Les Paul: An American Original* (New York: William Morrow, 1993), pp. 140, 186. Paul was not alone in using re-recording techniques; it had been tried by Mitch Miller on discs when he was a record producer for Columbia. Miller had managed to reduce some of the surface noise with primitive compression techniques, but this was a long, and therefore expensive, job in the studio. Mitch Miller interview, in Ted Fox, *In the Groove: The People Behind the Music* (New York: St. Martin's Press, 1986), pp. 42–43.

9. Denisoff, *Solid Gold*, p. 113.

10. This version of the story, which appears in print and on a recording of Sinatra's career, has been denied by Mitch Miller, who claims (somewhat unconvincingly) that Sinatra had full control of the choice of recordings (Fox, *In the Groove*, p. 49).

11. Dixon wrote "Hoochie Coochie Man," "I'm Ready," and "I Just Want to Make Love to You." He taught Muddy Waters the words and music to "Hoochie Coochie Man" in a washroom in the Zanzibar Club in Chicago. Howlin' Wolf was illiterate, so Dixon would whisper the words to the songs into Wolf's ear as he recorded. See Dixon, *I Am the Blues*, pp. 80–85.

12. Jerry Wexler interveiw, in Fox, *In the Groove*, pp. 144–145.

13. Oscar Hijuelos, *The Mambo Kings Play Songs of Love* (New York: Harper, 1989), p. 16.

14. Colin E. Scott and Martin Hawkins, *Sun Records: A Brief History of the Legendary Record Label* (New York: Quick Fox, 1980), pp. 66–67.

15. Albert Goldman, *Elvis* (New York: Viking, 1989), p. 107.

16. John Goldrosen, *The Buddy Holly Story* (New York: Quick Fox, 1979), p. 68.

17. Chuck Berry, *The Autobiography* (New York: Harmony Books, 1987), pp. 103, 107.

18. Goldrosen, *Holly*, pp. 167–170.

19. Richard Williams, *Out of His Head: The Sound of Phil Spector* (New York: Outerbridge and Lazard, 1977), pp. 81–82.

20. Hank Marvin, quoted in Southall, *Abbey Road*, p. 65.

21. Southall, *Abbey Road*, p. 57.

22. John P. Davis, "A Multi-Purpose Studio Recording System," *Journal of the Audio Engineering Society* 11 (Oct. 1973), pp. 361–370; Milton P. Putnam, "Recording Studio and Control Room Facilities of Advanced Design," *Journal of the Audio Engineering Society* 8 (Apr. 1960), pp. 111–134.

23. Southall, *Abbey Road*, p. 83.

24. Philip Erhorn, "New Trends for Stereo Recording Consoles," *Journal of the Audio Engineering Society* 9 (Oct. 1961): 272.

25. George Martin, oral history interviews, *Developments in Recorded Sound*, C90/26/02, NSA.

26. Williams, *Phil Spector*, p. 120.

27. *High Fidelity*, Nov. 67, pp. 63–66.

28. *The New Yorker*, 26 Feb. 1966, p. 27–28.

29. For an exhaustive examination of the Beatles studio work, see Mark Lewisohn, *The Beatles Recording Session* (New York: Harmony Books, 1988), pp. 67–77, 94–102, 105, 114.

30. *Rolling Stone*, 18 June 1987, p. 87.

31. This viewpoint has been attributed to several record producers and performers, including George Harrison, Phil Spector, and Berry Gordy. Jerry Leiber and Mike Stoller said "We don't write songs, we write records."

Jon Pareles and Patricia Romanowski, eds., *The Rolling Stone Encyclopedia of Rock & Roll* (New York: Summit, 1983), p. 322.

32. Paul Griffiths, *A Guide to Electronic Music* (London: Thames & Hudson, 1979), pp. 18–19.

33. Rick Altman, "The Evolution of Sound Technology," in Weiss and Belton, *Film Sound*, p. 49.

34. Christopher Parker, oral history interviews, *Developments in Recorded Sound*, C90/286/012, NSA.

35. John Hammond interview, in Fox, *In the Groove*, p. 4; Hammond, *On Record*, pp. 378–379; see also Stanley Dance, liner notes to *The Essential Count Basie*, vol. 1, Columbia Records.

36. Edison's responses to a questionnaire, in 1926 Phonograph DF.

37. Gelatt, *Fabulous Phonograph*, p. 232.

38. For an account of Legge's thinking, see Eisenberg, *Recording Angel*, pp. 95–97.

39. Geoffrey Payzant, *Glenn Gould: Music and Mind* (New York: Van Nostrand, 1978), p. 36.

40. Ibid., pp. 26–28.

41. Jim Curtiss, *Rock Eras: Interpretations of Media and Society, 1954–1984* (Bowling Green, OH: Popular Press, 1987), p. 303.

42. Jon Savage, *England's Dreaming* (New York: St. Martin's, 1992), p. 130.

43. Tricia Henry, *Break All the Rules! Punk Rock and the Making of a Style* (Ann Arbor, MI: UMI Research Press, 1989), p. 6.

44. Greil Marcus, *Lipstick Traces: A Secret History of the Twentieth Century* (Cambridge: Harvard University Press, 1990), p. 11.

45. Savage, *England's Dreaming*, p. 215.

46. Hebdige, *Subcultures*, p. 112.

15. The cassette culture

1. *Business Week*, 10 Sept. 1979, p. 38.

2. Warren Rex Isom, "Evolution of the Disc Talking Machine," *Journal of the Audio Engineering Society* 24 (Oct. 1977): 722.

3. Ralph Cushino, "Making Records," *Audio* (June 1976): 38.

4. Lee Hulko, "How Disc-Masters Are Made Today," *Audio* (Nov. 1969): 26–29.

5. Cushino, "Making Records," p. 42; Joseph C. Ruda, "Record Manufacture: Making the Sound for Everyone," *Journal of the Audio Engineering Society* 24 (Oct. 1977): 702–711.

6. Unnamed engineers, "Report of US Visit," 19 Dec. 1955, EMI.

7. Oscar P. Kusisto, "Magnetic Tape Recording: Reels, Cassettes, or Cartridges?" *Journal of the Audio Engineering Society* 24 (Oct. 1977): 828–831.

8. S. Hyman, "A New Business Office Dictating Machine," *Journal of the Audio Engineering Society* 1 (Oct. 1953): 317–319.

9. *Billboard*, 6 Nov. 1982, p. wc3.

10. Ray Dolby, "An Audio Noise Reduction System," *Journal of the Audio Engineering Society* 15 (Oct. 1967): 383–388.
11. *Billboard*, 3 April 1982, p. 1.
12. *Boston Globe*, 19 July 1981, p. 10.
13. Havelock Ellis and Michael A. Gonzales, *Bring the Noise: A Guide to Rap Music and Hip Hop Culture* (New York: Harmony, 1991), p. 137.
14. Nelson and Gonzales, *Bring the Noise*, xvi.
15. Jefferson Morley, introduction in Lawrence A. Stanley, ed., *Rap: The Lyrics* (New York: Penguin, 1992), xvi.
16. Nelson and Gonzales, *Bring the Noise*, x.
17. Morita, *Made in Japan*, p. 79. A German inventor, Andreas Pavel, has a good claim to be the first to come up with the Walkman idea. See *Der Spiegel*, 31 May 1993, pp. 124–125. Thanks to Erich Pauer for bringing this to my attention.
18. *Newsweek*, 7 Aug. 1987, p. 68: *Radio Electronics* 60 (Oct. 1989): 72–73.
19. *Billboard*, 6 Nov. 1982, p. wc3.
20. Peter Manuel, *Cassette Culture: Popular Music and Technology in North India* (Chicago: University of Chicago Press, 1993), p. 89.

16. The media conglomerates

1. Jan H. Rieger, "The Coming Crisis in the Youth Music Market, *Popular Music and Society* 4 (1975): 20.
2. Dannen, *Hit Men*, p. 74.
3. Don Waller, *The Motown Story* (New York: Scribners, 1985), pp. 11–12; Gerald Early, "One Nation under a Groove," *New Republic*, 7 July 1991, p. 35.
4. Slide, *American Film Industry*, p. 207; Dannen, *Hit Men*, p. 137.
5. Interview with Dick Cooper, Alabama Music Hall of Fame, May 1994; Guralnick, *Sweet Soul Music*, pp. 339–349.
6. David Buxton, "Rock Music, the Star System, and the Rise of Consumerism," in Frith and Goodwin, *On Record*, p. 428.
7. Leslie Hill to Sir John Read, 23 Dec. 1976, Sex Pistols File, EMI.
8. Bernard F. Dick, ed., *Columbia Pictures: Portrait of a Studio* (Lexington: University Press of Kentucky, 1992), p. 54; Dannen, *Hit Men*, pp. 168, 174.
9. Dannen, *Hit Men*, pp. 170–174; Frith, *Sound Effects*, p. 141.
10. Marcus, *Lipstick Traces*, p. 44.
11. *Washington Post*, 13 Dec. 1989, p. A20; Izod, *Hollywood and the Box Office*, pp. 177–178.
12. Sanjek, *American Music Business* 3: 594–602, 607.
13. *The Wall Street Journal*, 27 Feb. 1975, p. 17; 6 June 1975, p. 14; 10 Oct. 1978, p. 1.
14. Margaret B. W. Graham, *RCA and the Videodisc* (New York: Cambridge University Press, 1986), p. 22.

15. Dick, *Columbia Pictures*, pp. 52–53, citing *Newsweek*, 9 Oct. 1989, p. 62.

17. Into the digital era

1. S. Millman, ed., *A History of Engineering and Science in the Bell System: Communications Sciences (1925–1980)* (Short Hills, NJ: AT&T Bell Laboratories: 1984), pp. 399–418.
2. "Audio World Gets the Word: Digital," *Electronics* (24 Nov. 1977): 78–79; *Electronics* (29 Sept. 1977): 42–43.
3. Copeland, *Sound Recordings*, pp. 30–31.
4. Graham, *RCA and the Videodisc*, p. 22.
5. Graham, *RCA and the Videodisc*, pp. 134–135.
6. Wolfgang Immelman, oral history interviews, *Developments in Recorded Sound*, C90/99/02, NSA.
7. Joan Blomberg, *The Laser in America 1950–1970* (Cambridge: MIT Press, 1991), pp. 234–239.
8. Lawhon report, 12 June 1981, EMI.
9. John Mosely, oral history interviews, *Developments in Recorded Sound*, C90/62/01, NSA.
10. Michael A. Cusumano and Richard Rosenblum, "Strategic Maneuvering and Mass Market Dynamics: The Triumph of VHS over Beta," Working paper #40-91, Sloan School of Management, M.I.T., 1991.
11. George Martin, oral history interviews, *Developments in Recorded Sound*, C90/26/02, NSA.
12. *Billboard*, 6 Nov. 1982, p. wc3; numbers derived from statistics issued by RIAA. See also George Plasketes, "Romancing the Record: Vinyl De-Evolution and Subcultural Evolution," *Journal of Popular Culture* 26 (Summer 1992): 110.
13. Plasketes, "Romancing the Record," p. 114; *Billboard* (12 Oct. 1991).
14. George Martin, ed., *Making Tracks* (New York: Morrow, 1983), pp. 254–255.
15. Frank Vizard, "Solid Gold," *Popular Mechanics* (April 1990): 126.
16. *Billboard*, 13 Feb. 1982, p. 1.
17. *Business Week*, 26 Oct. 1987, p. 117.
18. Frith, *Sound Effects*, p. 20. Juke boxes were often the vehicle to bring reggae music to English musicians, which was the case with the Clash, as cited in John Swenson, ed., *The Musician Year in Rock, 1981–1982* (New York: G. P. Putnam's Sons, 1981), p. 111.
19. Morely, *Rap: The Lyrics*, p. xxiii. Clinton has released a CD entirely made up of samples.
20. Dave Marsh, *The Heart of Rock and Soul* (New York: Plume, 1989), p. 123.
21. Andrew Goodwin, "Sample and Hold: Pop Music in the Digital Age of Reproduction," in Frith, *Sound Effects*, pp. 258–261.

22. Jon Pareles, "How Rap Moves to Television's Beat," *New York Times*, 14 Jan. 1990, sec. 2, pp. 1, 28.
23. *New York Times*, 2 Dec. 1990, p. 6.
24. Andrew Kupfer, "The Next Wave in Cassette Tapes," *Fortune*, 3 June 1991, pp. 153–158.
25. *Popular Science* 239 (Aug. 1991): 64–68.

Select discography

The purpose of this discography is to point the reader towards some of the important recordings mentioned in the book. It is not intended as a guide to the history of recorded sound.

It is difficult to find cylinder recordings on cassette tape or compact disc today. For those still in the vinyl format there are several excellent compilations out by Murray Hill:

> *The First Recorded Sounds* (M60157)
> *The First Commercially Successful Recordings* (M60092)

On compact disc there are:

> *The Edison CD Sampler of Original Recordings 1877–1929*, compiled by Sony Records for educational use only.
> *Nipper's Greatest Hits 1901–1926* (RCA 3031-2-R), which includes songs by Billy Murray.

The Smithsonian has done a marvelous job of reissuing old recordings in compilations. These are attractively packaged and come with very helpful notes:

> *The American Song Book Series* (RC-048-1) contains songs of Irving Berlin.
> *American Popular Song* (RC 031) runs from Sophie Tucker to Aretha Franklin.

Scott Joplin was not recorded, but there are albums of his music played as he intended it:

> Joshua Rifkin, *Scott Joplin Piano Rags* (Nonesuch, 9 79159)

> Al Jolson, *The Golden Years in Digital Stereo, Movie Musicals 1927–1936*, (ABC 836044-2)
> Al Jolson, *Brunswick Rarities* (MCA 1560)
> Bing Crosby, *His Legendary Years, 1931–1957* (MCA 10887)

> George Gershwin, *Gershwin Plays Rhapsody in Blue* (Klavier 3552)

The Birth of Rhapsody in Blue: Paul Whiteman's Historic Aeolian Hall Concert of 1924 (Musical Heritage Society 11238), a reconstruction of the original performance by Maurice Peress. It starts with Livery Stable Blues (ODJB) and ends with the original rendition of Gershwin's masterpeice.

Music from the Film "Manhattan," Zubin Mehta conducting the New York Philharmonic (CBS MK 36020). This film score of Gerschwin's music reveals some of the differences when music is transferred to the big screen.

The New Orleans Rhythmn Kings and Jelly Roll Morton (Milestone 47020-2), a reissue of the Gennet recordings.

Louis Armstrong, *The Hot Fives and Hot Sevens* (Columbia 44253, 44422)

Bessie Smith, *The Complete Recordings* (Columbia 47471)

Count Basie, *The Essential Count Basie, Vol. 1* (Columbia 40608). This digital reissue contains "Oh, Lady Be Good"

Count Basie, *One O'Clock Jump* (Decca 42394)

1930s Jazz: Big Bands (Columbia 40651)

1930s Jazz: Small Combos (Columbia 40833)

Billie Holiday, *The Quintessential Billie Holiday, Vol. 3* (Columbia 44048) Holiday and Lester Young together

Serge Rachmaninoff, *The Complete Recordings* (RCA 048-1)

Leopold Stokowski, *Fantasia Soundtrack* (Buena Vista 600072)

Glenn Gould, *J. S. Bach: The Goldberg Variations* (Columbia MK 37779)

Kirsten Flagstad, *Tristan und Isolde* (Angel C-47321)

Elisabeth Schwartzkopf, *Die Meistersinger* (Angel, H-63500)

Benny Goodman, *Let's Dance* (Pro Arte 3418)

Benny Goodman, *Live at Carnegie Hall* (Columbia 40244)

Glenn Miller, *The Unforgettable Glenn Miller* (RCA 1-5459)

Charlie Parker, *Original Bird* (Savoy 1208)

Charlie Parker, *The Original Recordings* (Verve 837 176-2)

Robert Johnson, *The Complete Recordings* (Columbia 46222)

Muddy Waters, *Muddy Waters on Chess, 1948–1951* (Vogue 600052)

Willie Dixon, *The Chess Box* (MCA 16500)

Howlin' Wolf, *Memphis Days* (Bear 15460), a reissue of the early Sun recordings carried out by Sam Phillips

The Sun Story (Rhino 75884) contains the first Elvis Presley singles for Sun.

Elvis Presley, *The Great Performances* (RCA 2227-2-R) has everything from his original demo for Sun to the final songs
Eddie Cochran, *Legendary Masters Series* (United Artists 60017/8)
Buddy Holly/The Crickets, *20 Golden Greats* (MCA 3040)

Frank Sinatra, *A Man and His Music* (Reprise 1016-2)
Frank Sinatra, *Come Fly With Me* (Capitol 7 48469 2)

Phil Spector, *The Best of the Ronettes* (Abkco 7212-2)
Tamla Motown, *The First 25 Years, Vol. 1: The 1960s* (Tamla 3746 353432)
The Rolling Stones (Abkco 73752), their first LP of mainly R&B songs.
The Beach Boys, *Pet Sounds* (Capitol 81294)
The Beatles, *Sgt. Pepper's Lonely Hearts Club Band* (Parlophone 7 46442 2)
The Beatles, *Abbey Road* (Parlophone 7 464462)
Van Morrison, *The Best of Van Morrison* (Mercury 841 970-2)

Donna Summer, *Anthology* (Chronicles 5181442)
Saturday Night Fever Soundtrack (Polydor 800068-2)
Devo, *New Traditionalists* (Capitol, C2 46722)
Depeche Mode, *101* (Sire 25853-2)

The Sex Pistols, *Never Mind the Bollocks, Here's the Sex Pistols* (Warner Bros. 3147.2)
The Clash, *The Story of the Clash* (Epic E2K 44035)
Big Audio Dynamite, *Megatop Phoenix* (Columbia 45212)

Parliament, *The Clones of Dr. Funkenstein* (Casablanca 7034)
George Clinton, *The Best of* (Capitol 7 48424-2)
Beastie Boys, *Licensed to Ill* (Def Jam 40238)
Grandmaster Flash/Sugarhill Gang, *Hip-Hop Greats: Classic Raps* (Rhino R2 70957)
Techno State (Cookie Jar, CD 2)

Select bibliography

Several general histories of the phonograph and recorded sound are available. All are now out of print but can be found in public libraries. Oliver Read and Walter L. Welch, *From Tin Foil to Stereo: The Evolution of the Phonograph* (Indianapolis: Howard Sams, 1977) provides a good technical history, although the authors are biased in favor of Edison. An updated edition of this work is currently being written. Roland Gelatt, *The Fabulous Phonograph, 1877–1977* (New York: Macmillan, 1977), is less technical and more readable and has more information on the music.

A concise history of recording is currently available. Peter Copeland, *Sound Recordings* (London: British Library, 1991) is an insightful and knowledgeable history written by a recording engineer. Eric L. Reis, *The Compleat Talking Machine* (New York: Vental, 1986), is about rebuilding and repairing old machines. It has a wealth of technical detail and some useful appendices. Christopher Proudfoot, *Collecting Phonographs and Gramophones* (London: Studio Vista, 1980), is a well-illustrated guide to collecting antique phonographs. Hans Fantel of the *New York Times* writes a very informative column on audio technology. His book on stereo explains all the complexities of the machines: Ivan Berger and Hans Fantel, *The New Sound of Stereo* (New York: New American Library, 1986).

Allen Koenigsberg, *The Patent History of the Phonograph* (Brooklyn, NY: APM Press, 1990) is an absorbing, well-researched book about the early talking machines drawn from patent applications. Koenigsberg also operates the APM Press, which reprints many valuable old publications about the phonograph, including little gems like *Phonographs and Phonograph-Graphophones*, first published in 1889 by the New York Phonograph Company.

George L. Frow and Albert F. Self, *The Edison Cylinder Phonographs 1877–1929* (Sevenoaks, Kent: G. Frow, 1978), and Allen Koenigsberg, *Edison Cylinder Records, 1884–1912* (New York: Stellar, 1969), are the definitive histories of Edison phonographs and records. George L. Frow, *The Edison Disc Phonographs and the Diamond Discs* (Tunbridge Wells, U.K.: G. L. Frow, 1982), is the main source of information about the Edison discs. Less has been published about Victor machines. Robert W. Baumbach, *Look for the Dog: An Illustrated Guide to Talking Machines* (Woodland Hills, CA: Stationary Press, 1981), is a useful reference guide.

Several biographies of Edison are in print, but none of them are fully satisfactory. Robert Conot, *A Streak of Luck* (New York: Seaview, 1979) is too sensational and suffers from numerous errors. Matthew Josephson's *Edison* (New York: McGraw-Hill, 1959) is a classic but somewhat dated. Readers should wait until the publication of Paul Israel's biography, which will incorporate all the latest scholarship. Robert V. Bruce, *Bell: Alexander Graham Bell and the Conquest of Solitude* (Ithaca, NY: Cornell University Press, 1990), is the definitve account of Bell and the Volta Laboratory.

The history and origins of mass production are exhaustively researched in David A. Hounshell's classic *From the American System to Mass Production, 1800–1932* (Baltimore: Johns Hopkins University Press, 1984). Readers interested in Edison's business career could do worse than read Andre Millard, *Edison and the Business of Innovation* (Baltimore: Johns Hopkins University Press, 1990). The best account of the experiments to develop new recording materials is Byron Vanderbilt, *Thomas Edison, Chemist* (Washington, DC: American Chemical Society, 1971), which deals with the work of several inventors. Thomas P. Hughes has provided lucid explanations of technological systems in *American Genesis* (New York: Penguin, 1989).

The best overall account of the profusion of record companies is Brian Rust, *The American Record Label Book* (New York: Da Capo, 1984), and the development of ethnic recordings is chronicled in the definitive Richard K. Spottswood, *Ethnic Music on Records: A Discography of Ethnic Records Produced in the United States, 1893–1942* (Champaign, IL: University of Illinois Press, 1990). There are few accounts of individual companies, except for discographies. Rick Kennedy, *Jelly Roll, Bix and Hoagy: Gennett Studios and the Birth of Jazz* (Bloomington, IN: Indiana University Press, 1994) is the exception: detailed and well-written, it really puts the reader back in the old recording studio.

An eclectic, profound and often amusing account of the relationship of records and culture is Evan Eisenberg, *Recording Angel: Music, Records and Culture from Aristotle to Zappa* (London: Picador, 1987). John Harvith and Susan Harvith, *Edison, Musicians and the Phonograph* (Westport, CT: Greenwood, 1987), is a unique look at the first performers who sang into the recording horn. It uses many personal recollections to tell this story. Russell Sanjek's three-volume masterwork, *American Popular Music and Its Business* (New York: Oxford University Press, 1988), is the best account of the music business. Joseph Lanza has produced an intriguing history of background music, *Elevator Music: A Surreal History of Muzak* (New York: St. Martin's Press, 1994).

The best general introduction to African American music is *The New Grove Gospel, Blues and Jazz* (New York: Norton, 1986), edited by Paul Oliver, Max Harrison, and William Bolcom. Anyone interested in the blues should first consult Paul Oliver, the master of relating and understanding the importance of this music. Among his many books are *Blues Fell This Morning: Meaning in the Blues* (London: Cambridge University Press, 1990), which analyses blues lyrics. He has edited a series on the blues for the Stein and Day publishers of New York, including R. M. W. Dixon and J. Godrich, *Recording the Blues* (1970), and Derrick Stewart-Baxter, *Ma Rainey and the Classic Blues Singers* (1970). Samuel B. Charters, *The Country Blues* (New York: Rinehart, 1959) is dated but essential reading. LeRoi Jones, *Blues People: Negro Music in White America* (New York: Morrow, 1988) is an insightful look at African American music and culture.

A profusely illustrated general history of American popular culture is Richard Maltby, *Passing Parade: A History of Popular Culture in the Twentieth Century* (New York: Oxford University Press, 1989). There are numerous books on the social life of the 1920s, including Arnold Shaw, *The Jazz Age: Popular Music in the 1920s* (New York: Oxford University Press, 1987). Still available in libraries and secondhand bookshops is Mezz Mezzrow and Bernard Wolfe, *Really the Blues* (New York: Random House, 1946), an insider's look at the world of jazz, which often reads like a work of fiction.

The Da Capo publishing concern has an excellent series on jazz music in the various decades of the twentieth century, including Richard Hadlock, *Jazz Masters of the 1920s* (New York: Da Capo, 1988). James Lincoln Collier has written biographies of many of the leading jazzmen. *Louis Armstrong, An American Genius* (New York: Oxford University Press, 1983) and *Benny Goodman and the Swing Era* (New York: Oxford University Press, 1989). Gunther Schuller is probably the most respected historian of jazz; his multi-volumed history includes *The Swing Era: The Development of Jazz, 1930–1945* (New York: Oxford University Press, 1989).

Many recording artists have written of their experiences, notably Billie Holiday with William Duffy, *Lady Sings the Blues* (London: Penguin, 1984) and Willie Dixon with Don Snowden, *I Am the Blues: The Willie Dixon Story* (New York: Da Capo, 1989). Ira Gitler, ed., *Swing to Bop: An Oral History of the Transition in Jazz in the 1940s* (New York: Oxford, 1985) is made up of firsthand accounts of musicians. Nat Shapiro and Nat Hentoff, two very knowledgeable experts on jazz, have edited *Hear Me Talkin' to Ya* (New York: Rinehart, 1955). John Hammond with Irving Townsend tells the very interesting story of his recording career in *John Hammond on Record* (New York: Summit, 1977).

Eric Barnouw has written the best account of the rise of radio in his multi-volumed *A History of Broadcasting in the United States to 1935* (New York: Oxford University Press, 1966–1970). Aptly named is the work of Christopher Sterling and John M. Kittross, *Stay Tuned: A Concise History of American Broadcasting* (Belmont, CA: Wadsworth, 1990).

The best short history of the film industry and its impact on American culture is Robert Sklar, *Movie Made America: A Cultural History of the Movies* (New York: Vintage, 1975). Douglas Gomery is the authority on the transition to sound. He has written many essays, articles, and books, among them *Movie History: A Survey* (Belmont, CA: Wadsworth, 1991) and *Shared Pleasures: A History of Movie Presentation in the United States* (Madison: University of Wisconsin Press, 1993). Elizabeth Weis and John Belton, eds., *Film Sound: Theory and Practice* (New York: Columbia Unversity Press, 1985), is a first-rate collection of essays on film sound. Robert L. Carringer, *The Making of Citizen Kane* (Berkeley: University of California Press, 1985), tells the story of this important film in detail. Mary Lea Bandy, ed., *The Dawn of Sound* (New York: Museum of Modern Art, 1989), is the catalogue to an exhibit about the transition to sound in the movie industry; it is full of important photographs, including stills of the first talkies, and knowledgeable essays by various experts in the field. An entertaining account of the films of the 1930s, including Hollywood musicals, is Andrew Bergman, *We're in the Money: Depression America and Its Films* (Chicago: Ivan Dee, 1992).

There are so many books on rock'n'roll that it is hard to recommend a few. Charlie Gillett, *The Sound of the City: The Rise of Rock and Roll* (New York: Pantheon, 1983), is still the best overall history, being detailed but very accessible. Several writers have focused on this topic, and each has produced a succession of good books. I list only one work per author: R. Serge Denisoff, *Solid Gold: The Popular Record Industry* (New Brunswick, NJ: Transaction Books, 1975); Simon Frith, *Sound Effects: Youth Leisure and the Politics of Rock'n'Roll* (New York: Pantheon, 1981); Ian Whitcomb, *After the Ball: Pop Music from Rag to Rock* (London: Limelight Editions, 1986); and Greil Marcus, *Mystery Train* (New York: Penguin, 1991). Although Peter Wicke is German and his *Rock Music: Culture, Aesthetics and Sociology* (New York: Cambridge University Press, 1993) is translated, it is easy to read and offers some important sociological insights.

Steve Chapple and Rebe Garofalo, *Rock'n'roll Is Here to Pay* (Chicago: Nelson Hall, 1977), is a very good analysis of the finances of the popular-music industry. Fredric Dannen, *Hit Men* (New York: Vintage, 1991), describes the less than honest business dealings of the 1980s.

The Popular Press of Bowling Green State University in Ohio has produced several very good collections of writing on popular music. A two-volume history of *American Popular Music* (1989) is edited by Tim Scheurer, and Jim Curtiss has edited *Rock Eras: Interpretations of Media and Society, 1954–1984* (1987).

Several independent record companies have been profiled: Charlie Gillett, *Making Tracks: The Story of Atlantic Records* (London: Souvenir Press, 1988); and Colin E. Scott and Martin Hawkins, *Sun Records: A Brief History of the Legendary Record Label* (New York: Quick Fox, 1980). Mary Alice Shaughnessy, *Les Paul: An American Original* (New York: William Morrow, 1993), is an entertaining biography of a very important figure.

The best single volume on country music is Bill C. Malone, *Country Music USA* (Austin, TX: University of Texas Press, 1985). George Lewis has edited a collection of essays on the significance of this music: *All that Glitters: Country Music in America* (Bowling Green, OH: State University Popular Press, 1993).

Peter Guralnick, *Sweet Soul Music: Rhythm and Blues and the Southern Dream of Freedom* (London: Penguin, 1991), is an engaging history of R&B in the 1960s and 1970s. Nelson George, *The Death of Rhythm & Blues* (New York: Pantheon, 1988), is an account of its decline in the 1980s. Robert Pruter, *Chicago Soul* (Champaign: University of Illinois Press, 1991), outlines the origins of soul music in Chicago.

Brian Southall, *Abbey Road* (Wellingborough, U.K.: Patrick Stevens, 1982) is a full account of the history of this important studio, while Mark Lewisohn is the expert on what went on inside, *The Beatles Recording Session* (New York: Harmony Books, 1988). Philip Norman's *Shout: The Beatles in Their Generation* (New York: Simon and Schuster, 1981) is a good general account of the Beatles and their times.

Ted Fox, *In the Groove: The People Behind the Music* (New York: St. Martin's Press, 1986), is a compilation of interviews with some of the leading record producers. John Tobler and Stuart Grundy, *The Record Producers* (New York: St. Martin's Press, 1982) provides an insightful history of the rise of the record producer. Jerry Wexler with David Ritz has published his autobiography, *Rhythm and the Blues: A Life in American Music* (New York: Knopf, 1993). George Martin, ed., *Making Tracks* (New York: Morrow, 1983) is a clearly written introduction to the technology and techniques of recording, with essays from some of the leading figures in the music business.

Punk now receives a great deal of scholarly attention. One of the first accounts of this movement, which placed it into context, was Greil Marcus, *Lipstick Traces: A Secret History of the Twentieth Century* (Cambridge: Harvard University Press, 1990), followed by Jon Savage, *England's Dreaming* (New York: St. Martin's, 1992). Tricia Henry did some very interesting field work in producing *Break All the Rules! Punk Rock and the Making of a Style* (Ann Arbor, MI: UMI Research Press, 1989). John Lydon (Johnny Rotten) has published his account with Keith and Kent Zimmerman of the Sex Pistols, *Rotten* (London: Hodder, 1994).

There is a profusion of books on rap, most of them written by middle-class white academics like me. Havelock Ellis and Michael A.

Gonzales, *Bring the Noise: A Guide to Rap Music and Hip Hop Culture* (New York: Harmony, 1991), is an excellent reference book. Lawrence A. Stanley, ed., *Rap: The Lyrics* (New York: Penguin, 1992), has all the lyrics conveniently printed out. Houston Baker, *Black Studies, Rap and the Academy* (Chicago: University of Chicago Press, 1993), is a spirited defense of rap music that argues for its interpretaton as poetry. See also Michael Eric Dyson, *Reflecting Black: African American Cultural Criticism* (St. Paul, MN: University of Minnesota Press, 1993).

The subject of sampling is covered in Jeremy J. Beadle, *Will Pop Eat Itself? Pop Music in the Soundbite Era* (London: Faber and Faber, 1993), a timely look at recent developments in popular music.

Subject index

Recordings index

411

Motion picture index

413